FINANCING CITIES IN INDIA

FINANCING CITIES IN INDIA
Municipal Reforms, Fiscal Accountability and Urban Infrastructure

PRASANNA K. MOHANTY

⑤SAGE www.sagepublishing.com
Los Angeles I London I New Delhi I Singapore I Washington DC I Melbourne

First published in 2016 by

 SAGE Publications India Pvt Ltd
B1/I-1 Mohan Cooperative Industrial Area
Mathura Road, New Delhi 110 044, India
www.sagepub.in

SAGE Publications Inc
2455 Teller Road
Thousand Oaks, California 91320, USA

SAGE Publications Ltd
1 Oliver's Yard, 55 City Road
London EC1Y 1SP, United Kingdom

SAGE Publications Asia-Pacific Pte Ltd
3 Church Street
#10-04 Samsung Hub
Singapore 049483

Published by Vivek Mehra for SAGE Publications India Pvt Ltd, typeset in Minion 10/12 pts by Zaza Eunice, Hosur, Tamil Nadu, India and printed at Saurabh Printers Pvt Ltd, Greater Noida

Library of Congress Cataloging-in-Publication Data Available

ISBN: 978-93-515-0875-5 (HB)

The SAGE Team: Unni N. Nair, Sanghamitra Patowary, Shobana Paul, and Ritu Chopra

To Smita, my wife

Contents

List of Tables

List of Boxes

List of Abbreviations

ACIR	Advisory Commission on Intergovernmental Relations
ALT	Alternative Land Tax
AMRUT	Atal Mission for Rejuvenation and Urban Transformation
ANPR	Automated Number Plate Recognition
ASCI	Administrative Staff College of India
ARV	Annual Rental Value
BCC	Beneficiary Capital Contribution
BCT	Banking Corporation Tax
BDA	Bengaluru Development Authority
BMRCL	Bengaluru Metropolitan Rail Corporation Ltd
BRT	Bus Rapid Transit
BRTS	Bus Rapid Transit System
BSUP	Basic Services to the Urban Poor
BVT	Business Value Tax
BWSSB	Bengaluru Water Supply and Sewerage Board
CAMA	Computer Aided Mass Appraisal
CAP	Climate Action Plan
CDBG	Community Development Block Grant
CDP	City Development Plan
CDLF	Community Development Loan Fund
CEPAC	*Certificados de Potencial Adicional de Construcao*
CFC	Central Finance Commission
CIL	Community Infrastructure Levy
CIP	Capital Improvement Plan
CoP	Certificate of Participation
CREHT	Comprehensive Real Estate Holding Tax
CUV	Current Use Value
C&AG	Comptroller and Auditor General
DBT	Decreasing Block Tariff
DDA	Delhi Development Authority

DGT	Development Gains Tax
DP	Development Plan
DPC	District Planning Committee
DPR	Detailed Project Report
DMRC	Delhi Metro Rail Corporation
DTH	Direct-to-Home
D&O	Dangerous & Offensive
EAV	Equalised Assessed Valuation
EDC	External Development Charges
ERP	Electronic Road Pricing
EWS	Economically Weaker Sections
FAR	Floor Area Ratio
FSI	Floor Space Index
GCT	General Corporation Tax
GDP	Gross Domestic Product
GHG	Greenhouse Gas
GHMC	Greater Hyderabad Municipal Corporation
GIS	Geographic Information System
GLA	Greater London Authority
GNP	Gross National Product
GoI	Government of India
GPS	Global Positioning System
GST	Goods and Services Tax
HDFC	Housing Development Finance Corporation
HPEC	High Powered Expert Committee
HTF	Highway Trust Fund
HUDA	Haryana Urban Development Authority
HUDCO	Housing and Urban Development Corporation
IBT	Increasing Block Tariff
ICICI	Industrial Credit and Investment Corporation of India
IHSDP	Integrated Housing and Slum Development Programme
ILT	Increasing Linear Tariff
IL&FS	Infrastructure Leasing and Financial Services
ISS	*Imposto Sobre Servicos*
JDM	Joint Development Management
JLE	Jubilee Line Extension
JNNURM	Jawaharlal Nehru National Urban Renewal Mission
JV	Joint Venture
KMC	Karnataka Municipal Corporations

KUIDFC	Karnataka Urban Infrastructure Development and Finance Corporation
KWH	Kilo Watt Hour
LBT	Local Body Tax
LES	Local Government Equitable Share
LGT	Land Gains Tax
LGU	Local Government Units
LIG	Low Income Group
LTA	Land Transportation Authority
LTT	Land Transfer Tax
LVC	Land Value Capture
LVIT	Land Value Increment Tax
LVT	Land Value Tax
MIS	Management Information System
MPAC	Municipal Property Assessment Corporation
MPC	Metropolitan Planning Committee
MLTT	Municipal Land Transfer Tax
MMRDA	Mumbai Metropolitan Region Development Authority
MPAC	Municipal Property Assessment Corporation
MRIT	Metropolitan Region Improvement Tax
MRTS	Mass Rapid Transit System
MRV	Monthly Rental Value
MTA	Mass Transit Account
MTRC	Mass Transit Railway Corporation
NEG	New Economic Geography
NFHS	National Family Health Survey
NGT	New Growth Theory
NLTT	National Land Transfer Tax
NSS	National Sample Survey
NSSO	National Sample Survey Organisation/Office
NSW	New South Wales
NUCA	New Urban Communities Authority
NULM	National Urban Livelihoods Mission
OD	Organisation Development
ODC	Orestad Development Corporation
ODV	Official Declared Value
OECD	Organisation for Economic Cooperation and Development
OODC	*Outorga Onerosa do Direito de Construir*
ORR	Outer Ring Road
O&M	Operation and Maintenance

PAYT	Pay as You Throw
PFI	Private Finance Initiative
PGS	Planning Gain Supplement
PMAY	Pradhan Mantri Awas Yojana
PMS	Performance Management System
PPP	Public–private Partnership
PTIN	Property Tax Identification Number
PV	Planning Value
PVT	Personal Vehicle Tax
RAY	Rajiv Awas Yojana
RCC	Reinforced Concrete Cement
RES	Representative Expenditure System
RPGT	Real Property Gains Tax
RRS	Representative Revenue System
RSG	Revenue Support Grant
RTI	Right to Information
RTS	Representative Tax System
R&D	Research and Development
SAS	Self-Assessment Scheme
SEBI	Security Exchange Board of India
SEWs	Socially and Economically Weaker Sections
SFC	State Finance Commission
SJSRY	Swarna Jayanti Shahri Rozgar Yojana
SLB	Service Level Benchmark
SPV	Special Purpose Vehicle
SRLF	State Revolving Loan Fund
SVR	Site Value Rating
SVT	Site Value Tax
TDR	Transferable Development Right
TIF	Tax Increment Financing
TNUDF	Tamil Nadu Urban Development Fund
TNUIFSL	Tamil Nadu Urban Infrastructure Financial Services Limited
TOD	Transit Oriented Development
TPS	Town Planning Scheme
UAM	Unit Area Method
UAV	Unit Area Value
UDIC	Urban Development Investment Company/Corporation
UIDSSMT	Urban Infrastructure Development Scheme for Small and Medium Towns

UIG	Urban Infrastructure and Governance
ULB	Urban Local Body
ULT	Urban Land Tax
UMTA	Urban Mass Transportation Authority
URA	Urban Redevelopment Authority
UVT	Uniform Volumetric Tariff
VAT	Value Added Tax
VCF	Value Capture Financing
VIF	Value Increment Financing
VLT	Vacant Land Tax
WSPF	Water and Sanitation Pool Fund

Preface

The 21st century will be the century of the 'city'. It will usher in an urban revolution in the developing world, presenting opportunities to millions in urban and rural areas to raise productivity and escape poverty. India will be at the forefront of this revolution. Cities, as engines of economic growth and generators of public finance for socio-economic development, will drive India's transformation to a developed nation. The country must leave no stone unturned to convert the urban challenges into opportunities.

Urban economic theory emphasises that cities form and grow to reap the advantages of agglomeration economies. These externalities are returns to density arising from the co-location of firms, households and institutions in cities. They lead to benefits of learning, sharing, matching and networking, and facilitate productive activities. They also capitalise into tax bases of central, state and local governments, creating opportunity for self-financing of planned urban development. Agglomeration externalities, in conjunction with knowledge externalities, establish the pivotal importance of cities in the structural transformation of nations. However, cities in India face a gross mismatch between their functions and finances. They will not be able to discharge their fundamental role as drivers of growth unless they address the huge backlog, current and growth needs of urbanisation. India must invest in cities. This calls for major reforms in the country's urban public finance. The subject has been neglected by policymakers and researchers for long. This book combines theory and practice to draw a reform agenda for financing city development and services in India.

The Jawaharlal Nehru National Urban Renewal Mission (JNNURM), launched in 2005, was the first major national initiative in India to provide reform-linked funding support from the central government to cities for infrastructure and basic services to the urban poor. It emphasised the implementation of 23 state and city-level reforms, including those to strengthen municipal finances. The reforms, however, have met with only partial success. With the experience of JNNURM in the background, the Government of India (GoI) has recently launched new initiatives aimed at transforming urban India. These include: Smart Cities Mission, Atal Mission for Rejuvenation and Urban Transformation, and Housing for All by 2022. The success of these missions will crucially depend on how the current strategies to finance cities in the country are revamped. In this regard, this book refers to principles of urban public finance and to practices of financing urban infrastructure and services in countries across the globe to draw lessons.

While writing this book, I have relied on my own experience as Commissioner of Municipal Corporations of Visakhapatnam and Hyderabad, Vice Chairman of Hyderabad Urban Development Authority and Chief Secretary in the Government of Andhra Pradesh and Mission Director of JNNURM in the GoI. These responsibilities gave me insight into many apparently intractable urban issues. My academic background also helped me in applying theory and practice to address the financing and management challenges of cities. I owe gratitude to my postdoctoral adviser, Prof Jeffrey Williamson at Harvard University and my doctorate advisers, Prof Jerry Rothenberg at Massachusetts Institute of Technology, and Prof John Harris and Prof Kevin Lang at Boston University. They taught me the importance of theory and empirical research in the design of coherent policies and programmes.

This book is a logical follow-up on my earlier books, *Municipal Finance in India: An Assessment* and *Cities and Public Policy: An Urban Agenda for India* (SAGE Publications). It moves from assessment and policy to action planning for designing instruments to finance city development and services. I hope this book will receive the same encouragement from policymakers, planners, city administrators, researchers and students of urban economics, planning, management and finance as did my earlier books.

This book would not have been possible without the guidance and contributions made by many eminent scholars, practitioners, colleagues and well-wishers. I am particularly grateful to Dr Isher Judge Ahluwalia, Prof Abhay Pethe, Prof O.P. Mathur, Prof Amitabh Kundu, Prof Chetan Vaidya, Prof J. V. M. Sarma, Prof B. Kamaiah and Dr Alok K. Mishra. I express my sincere thanks to Smita, my wife, for her candid comments on the drafts of several chapters in the book.

—P. K. Mohanty

1

Overview

Indian municipalities are amongst the weakest, globally, in terms of access to resources, revenue-raising capacity and fiscal autonomy. The ratio of municipal revenues to gross domestic product (GDP) at factor cost in India is estimated at 1.03 per cent for 2012–13, compared to South Africa (6.0 per cent) and Brazil (7.4 per cent). Not only is the country's municipal sector very small compared to the international benchmark, but municipalities in India have also been subjected to significant erosion in their fiscal autonomy over time. Key ratios: municipal 'own' revenues to total revenues and municipal taxes to central and state taxes have declined progressively. In 2012–13, the municipal tax-GDP ratio stood at 0.33 as against the combined (central plus state) tax-GDP ratio of 17 per cent.[1] India spends only 20 per cent of what is required for the efficient delivery of civic services (HPEC 2011). Further, the country needs to increase capital spending in cities by eight times—to 2 per cent of GDP annually (McKinsey 2010).

The precarious state of municipal finances is worrying as cities drive growth and productive employment. They also generate public finance for socioeconomic development, including rural development. In 2007, urban areas, with 30 per cent of population, contributed about 62–63 per cent of the country's GDP. This contribution would rise to about 75 per cent by 2021 (Planning Commission 2008). Over the next two decades, cities will create 70 per cent of all new jobs in India. They will account for 80–85 per cent of India's tax revenues. However, cities will not be able to perform their fundamental role as engines of economic growth and structural transformation, unless they are firmly in position to meet the 'backlog', 'current' and 'growth' needs of urbanisation.

Cities in India face a gross mismatch between their responsibilities and revenues. The lack of adequate revenues with municipalities has resulted in a vicious circle: insufficient investments in infrastructure, poor quality of services, lack of willingness of citizens to pay taxes and charges, poor state of municipal finances and so on. This vicious circle needs to be broken by addressing the factors responsible for fiscal gap in cities. These include: narrow resource base of municipalities, inadequate intergovernmental transfers, inefficient collection of taxes, user charges and benefit charges, lack of capacity to borrow and weak service delivery systems. Serious finance and governance issues plague India's cities, undermining their competitive strength in the globalising world economy. The haphazard growth of Indian cities is largely due to the haphazard way in which they have been financed. As India embarks on a programme of smart cities, urban public finance reforms stand out as a critical area for focused attention by policymakers, planners and researchers.

India is a peculiar country in the sense that in spite of increasing urbanisation and rising contribution of cities to GDP, the revenue-raising powers of municipalities have gone down. In the 1919 GoI Act, octroi, terminal tax and tax on trade, professions and callings were reserved for municipalities apart from land and property taxes, including land value tax (LVT). The Local Finance Enquiry Committee 1951 recommended some more local taxes, namely, tax on consumption or sale of electricity, tax on advertisements other than those published in newspapers, tax on vehicles, capitation tax and tax on entertainment for being assigned exclusively to municipalities. The Taxation Enquiry Commission (1953–54) added duty on transfer of property to the list of municipal taxes. However, with octroi abolished and states appropriating 'local taxes', such as profession tax, motor vehicles tax, entertainment tax and duty on transfer of property, municipalities have reached a state where they cannot even meet the cost of elementary civic functions on their own. The non-assignment of an alternative as buoyant and productive as octroi, after the tax was abolished, has given a severe blow to municipal finances in India. Compensations to cities from state governments for the loss of octroi and other local taxes have remained at abysmally low levels.

Not only do the urban local bodies (ULBs) in India have a narrow tax base, but they also do not have access to a formula-based sharing of major national and state taxes as in multi-tier countries, such as Brazil, China, South Africa, Nigeria and the Philippines. Internationally, country municipal finance regimes can be divided into two broad groups. Municipalities in a large number of federal and unitary countries have access to high-yielding and buoyant taxes, such as income tax and goods and services tax (GST). In a small number of unitary countries, where property tax is the dominant local tax, municipalities receive substantial formulae-based grants from the central government—often amounting to more than 70 per cent of their revenues. Unfortunately, municipalities in India have access neither to a broad-based basket of taxes nor to a sizable pool of predictable fiscal transfers from central and state governments.

The neglect of urban public finance in India for so long is intriguing. It is rooted in the inadequate understanding of the role of geography and externalities of cities in economic growth. If growth is the most funda-mental concern of the country, 'where' growth occurs ought to be a key area of attention. Urban economics, new growth theory (NGT) and new economic geography (NEG) suggest that growth does not occur every-where. It localises in city regions due to their agglomeration, knowledge and infrastructure externalities, leading to increasing returns at firm, industry, local, urban and regional scales. Economic activities that drive growth are heavily concentrated in urban areas. For these activities, both scale and location matter. Cities form and grow to reap external economies. City regions offer gains from clustering, sharing, learning, matching and networking. Metcalfe's law suggests that the value of a network increases with the square of the number of connected users in the system. Further, externalities in cities capitalise into the tax bases of central, state and local governments. Research in NEG suggests that 'agglomeration rents' accrue to both immobile and mobile factors of production. Thus, cities tend to be the reservoirs of public finance—so vital for addressing the challenges of development.

Empirical studies observe a strong positive correlation between economic growth and agglomeration. They find consistent evidence in favour of the hypothesis that agglomeration boosts GDP growth up to a level of economic development, roughly corresponding to some US$10,000 per capita in 2006 public–private partnership (PPP) prices. India is way below this threshold. Empirical research also observes that agglomerative effects become more prominent when an economy upgrades from manufacturing to knowledge-based sectors. Thus, at the present stage of India's evolution, the country has a historic oppor-tunity to accelerate economic growth and reduce poverty by devel-oping cities and harnessing the untapped power of their external economies. Agglomeration-augmenting, congestion-mitigating and resource-generating cities present not only a self-financing strategy for planned urban development, but also a huge opportunity to unlock growth and generate resources for rural development.

This book is concerned with reforms in urban public finance in India to enable cities to convert the urban challenges into opportunities. It identifies the lack of clarity, consistency, adequacy and predictability in municipal taxation, user charging, intergovernmental transfers, development financing and value capture and recycling as key factors plaguing city finances. It also recognises the need to align particular types of revenues to particular categories of expenditures so that local public services can be delivered in a responsive, transparent and accountable manner. Further, urban management, including financial management, needs to be strengthened; many factors responsible for the fiscal problem in municipalities relate to the constraints of their organisational structure and management system. We draw lessons from research and practice to suggest a roadmap for reforms in urban public finance in India. We propose to link benefit taxation to agglomeration economies in cities. This calls for broadening the definition of benefit to include externality-induced 'specific' as well as 'general' benefits. Thus, 'users pay', 'beneficiaries pay' and 'growth pays'. By corollary, those creating dis-benefits to the society pay for mitigation or amelioration. Accordingly, 'polluters pay', 'congesters pay' and 'exacerbaters pay'. We embrace these paradigms under the caption of the 'generalised benefit principle' and acknowledge it as the hallmark of urban public finance. This principle is fundamental to the exploration of intergovernmental and public–private partnerships for financing the colossal needs of urban and regional infrastructure in India.

This book is organised as follows. Chapter 2 presents the dimensions of India's urban fiscal problem and a logical framework to address the same. Chapter 3 discusses municipal taxation, including an alternative to octroi. It emphasises the need to empower cities with a broad-based portfolio of taxes that enables them to exploit agglomeration externalities. Chapter 4 is devoted to property tax reforms. Chapter 5 presents a case for taxation of urban land value. Chapter 6 examines issues of user charges, benefit charges and fees in the light of poor cost recovery record in municipalities and utilities. Chapter 7 focuses on the design of intergovernmental transfers to municipalities to correct for vertical and horizontal imbalances and address the huge demands of capital investment in cities. Chapter 8 deals with financing of land and infrastructure development. Chapter 9 discusses key instruments of value capture financing. Chapter 10 outlines a road map for reforms in India's urban public finance, taking into account principles and practices, as well as the context of India's fiscal federalism. We advocate value increment financing of cities with Build India municipal bonds and a cooperative fiscal federalism framework for tax increment financing.

Chapter 2 examines the factors behind the deplorable state of urban public finance in India. Cutting across expenditure assignment, revenue assignment, revenue-expenditure matching and urban management, these factors include: low level and poor quality of civic infrastructure and services, adversely affecting the willingness of citizens to pay taxes and charges; inadequate taxation powers of municipalities, not commensurating with the financing needs of their mandated functions; inappropriate user charges that are not corresponding to user costs; inadequate revenue mobilisation due to weaknesses in civic administration; complex procedures for assessment and collection of taxes, fees and charges and settlement of disputes; numerous tax exemptions and subsidies that are wrongly targeted; absence of formula-based and appropriate intergovernmental transfer systems; non-exploitation of borrowing as a versatile instrument to finance long-gestation infrastructure projects; lack of robust budgeting, accounting, expenditure management, performance tracking, public disclosure, fiscal responsibility and auditing in municipalities and so on. We present a framework for urban public finance reforms rooted in the generalised benefit principle, including golden rules of local public finance and principle of earmarked benefit taxes. This framework is aimed at guiding the levy of user charges, benefit charges, benefit taxes and general taxes, and the design of debt instruments to finance regional and urban infrastructure.

Chapter 3 deals with the narrow tax base of municipalities in India. It draws lessons from principles of tax assignment and global practices in municipal taxation to design tax reforms. Internationally local taxes include land and property taxes, motor vehicle and fuel taxes, 'piggyback' income tax, local payroll, sales, values added, goods and services, excise, business and financial taxes, etc. The generalised benefit principle presents a strong case for municipalities to 'piggyback' onto the relevant central and state taxes or to receive a statutory share in their collection. Local option taxes with income, business, value-added, and goods and services as base are regarded as general benefit taxes on living, working and shopping in a city. However, as 'piggybacking' may not be feasible within the contours of the present scheme of fiscal federalism in India, we suggest a city GST rate within state GST rate or a formula-based share in state GST for municipalities. Also, cities may be enabled to access the divisible pool of central taxes, including central GST through the Central Finance Commission route. It is only logical that cities, which create growth, are enabled to benefit from it to further augment growth. Moreover, following the 'local tax' and 'benefit tax' principles, city motor vehicles tax, entertainment tax, advertisement tax, business licensing tax, local utility user taxes and profession tax may be assigned to the third tier through a municipal finance list in the Constitution of India.

Chapter 4 presents a strong case for urban land value tax in India, citing theory and practice. The arguments for this tax run in terms of three major planks: intrinsic merits of land value tax as an instrument of urban public finance; returning unearned increments in land values due to planned urban development to the society; and role of land taxation to supplement land use planning to promote orderly urban development. We examine the practice of urban land value taxation adopted internationally, including two-rate tax, site value tax, unimproved land tax, land value tax, land value increment tax, comprehensive real estate holding tax (CREHT), land gains tax (LGT), city real estate transfer tax and vacant land tax (VLT). We advocate linking VLT to the capital value of land. Further, the tax on land may be levied at a rate higher than on built-up property to promote land development, including housing. The VLT may be imposed as a progressive tax, with tax rate increasing, depending on the time period land is held idle —as in Brazil. The land tax component of property tax and VLT may be escrowed to 'leverage' debt from the market to undertake infrastructure projects, leading to increased land values and making way for further resource mobilisation.

Chapter 5 addresses the issues of property tax reforms. Property tax–GDP ratio in India is very low compared to developed and most developing countries. Except in a few cities like Bengaluru, systematic property tax reforms have not been carried out in India. The untapped potential of property tax as a benefit tax suggests that the country has a significant opportunity to augment municipal revenues by rationalising property tax base, tax rate, administration, valuation, revaluation, inflation-indexing, billing, collection, enforcement and dispute resolution. Referring to property tax practices internationally and to the experiments of property tax reforms by Hyderabad, Bengaluru and Mumbai, we recommend a split-rate property tax: one rate for land and another for building. The land or general tax component of property tax may be in the form of a graduated land value tax, based on capital value of land. As the built-up area of property, taking into account the building and use characteristics, is a good proxy for consumption of collective civic services, specific benefit taxes for non-measurable services may be levied as a composite city services tax on the building component, adopting unit area method. Efforts may also be initiated to shift property tax base to capital value of land and buildings in large cities to benefit from the ongoing increases in real estate values due to urbanisation, agglomeration externalities and economic growth. The unit area value (UAV) method, followed by the municipal corporation of Bengaluru with mapping of properties using Geographic Information System (GIS) offers a promising approach to replicate. India may aim at a property tax–GDP ratio of one per cent in the next decade or so.

Chapter 6 reviews the state of municipal user charges, benefit charges and fees in India. It argues that the poor design of cost recovery instruments and inability of ULBs to demonstrate a close connection between charges and fees, and civic services are key factors as to why they are yet to become a major source of municipal finance in India. User charges include charges for water, sewerage, solid waste collection and public transport, entrance fees to parks and swimming pools, and tolls on roads. Benefit charges, which do not arise directly in the provision of public goods or services, are imposed on the value or physical characteristics of properties that are serviced or benefitted from local public expenditures. They include development charges and impact fees, paid upfront by developers while obtaining development permission. They also include special assessments and betterment levies, which are charges to recoup a part of the windfall gains in property values accruing to landowners after infrastructure investments materialise. Municipal fees are levied for regulatory and administrative functions. We argue that insufficient cost recovery in services hurt the urban poor with limited access to lifeline services the most. We suggest that charges for services should cover operation and maintenance (O&M), capital, environmental and resource opportunity costs, along with a component for cross-subsidising the poor. We advocate full cost recovery by combining instruments of 'users pay', 'beneficiaries pay', 'polluters pay', 'exacerbaters pay' and 'congesters pay'.

Chapter 7 deals with intergovernmental transfers. The system of fiscal transfers to municipalities in India is complex, with multiple channels and ad hoc mechanisms. These include: assigned revenues, compensations for loss of revenues, State Finance Commission (SFC) transfers, plan grants and non-plan grants from state government, Central Finance Commission (CFC) transfers, schemes of central Ministries and Planning Commission dispensations, etc. India is a unique country with two constitutional channels to review the devolution of resources to municipalities: SFC and CFC. However, fiscal transfers to ULBs in the country remain in a highly unsatisfactory state. Over the period of more than 20 years since the 74th Amendment was enacted, five CFCs and many SFCs have resorted to ad hoc recommendations on the ground that data are not available. The recommendations by CFCs and SFCs also bear no relation to the requirements of cities. Unlike many countries, intergovernmental transfers to ULBs in India are also not formula-based, incorporating weights to 'fiscal need', 'fiscal capacity' and 'fiscal effort' factors.

The Constitution (74th Amendment) Act stipulates that the SFCs recommend the 'principles' of devolution of state resources to municipalities. By logic, it is imperative for the CFC to review the 'principles' recommended by SFCs. However, there has been little attempt by SFCs and CFCs to suggest principles or architecture of a robust system of urban public finance, including intergovernmental transfers. While the 13th Finance Commission broke new ground by linking central transfers for municipalities to a formula-based share in the divisible pool (over and above the share of states), the 14th Finance Commission chose to depart from the same. The latter also did not consider the McKinsey and HPEC reports on capital and O&M requirements of cities. When vertical imbalance is built into the constitutional scheme, there is no way cities can meet the requirement of urban infrastructure and services to the tune of ₹5.92 million crore over the period 2012–31—projected by HPEC (2011)—without a substantial devolution forthcoming through central and state government channels. Apart from vertical imbalance, horizontal imbalance, inter-jurisdictional spillovers, adoption of national standards for service and exploitation of scale economies in tax administration, the financing of redistributive functions and core infrastructure facilities also warrant intergovernmental transfers. There is a significant national case for supporting cities to develop mass transit and wastewater management systems in a time-bound fashion.

Chapter 8 deals with key instruments of land development financing adopted internationally. They assume that a worthwhile project with benefits exceeding costs must be able to finance itself. Development financing tools require real estate developers to install infrastructure facilities needed by new growth or make one-time in-lieu payments to the local authority for the same. They include developer exactions, impact fees, development contributions, planning obligations, community infrastructure levy, and internal and external development charges. They also cover 'in-kind' mechanisms such as land readjustment, land consolidation, land pooling and town planning schemes. Development-financing instruments promote planned urban expansion and renewal, without burdening local, state and central government exchequers. Often they are used in concert with instruments such as zoning, development control, land taxation, debt financing, equity financing, general fund revenue, dedicated fund and land value capture. Debt financing, including municipal bonds, bond banks, pooled finance bonds, financial intermediation, lease purchase contracting and so on, offer considerable opportunities to undertake urban infrastructure development in India. However, the fact that only 23 municipal bonds could be issued by municipal corporations and water utilities in the country over a period of more than 15 years, mobilising a meagre sum of about ₹13,531 crore suggests that apart from debt market development, comprehensive reforms in municipal finance to enhance the credit-worthiness of municipalities would need to be pursued with a long-term programme.

Chapter 9 discusses key instruments of value capture financing, including land value capture (LVC). These tools enable public authorities to trade anticipated future revenues for a present infrastructure programme. They aim at appropriating and recycling the values generated by public sector actions and private sector investments in cities. In particular, spatial planning and infrastructure investments capitalise into increased land and property prices due to improved accessibility, better serviceability, and greater scope and intensity of development associated with re-zoning. These benefits could be captured indirectly through their conversion into public revenues in the form of taxes and charges, or directly through on-site and off-site infrastructure improvements benefitting the community. Land value capture instruments can be 'recurrent' or 'one-time', fiscal or non-fiscal. Recurrent methods include: leasing of space benefiting from infrastructure, betterment tax, special assessment and tax increment financing (TIF). One-time instruments include developer exactions, impact fees, betterment charges, sale of land and development rights, joint development mechanisms and town planning schemes. If an infrastructure project passes the cost-benefit test, the rise in land values in the project-served areas is likely to exceed its cost. Therefore, the project cost can be covered by reclaiming a part of the uplift in land values, leaving the rest to landowners as net windfall gains.

TIF, a key instrument of value capture, has a considerable potential for application in India to finance panned urban development and renewal. Subscribing to the 'growth pays' principle, TIF essentially allows an authority to ring-fence future tax increments within a designated development area or city to finance development which contributes to this increment. Most ULBs in India do not have a current revenue surplus. However, a well-designed programme for their development could be possible, with favourable changes in zoning and density norms, by earmarking a portion of the future collections from land-based and other taxes of various tiers of government for debt-servicing. A special purpose vehicle, representing the local body, private sector partners, and state and central governments could act as a TIF authority. It may raise resources upfront through tax-free municipal bonds or other forms of debt with a long maturity period of, say, 20–25 years to meet infrastructure costs. Long-tenor funds like provident funds, pension funds and insurance funds may subscribe to these bonds. As in other countries, the financing options for a TIF may also include debt-service coverage provided by higher levels of government for the first few years when TIF is most risky. Further, tax increments could be supplemented by special assessment, impact fee, betterment levy and dedicated funds as needed.

In a 'status quo' or 'no TIF' scenario, no authority stands to gain. On the contrary, when a TIF is implemented well, central, state and local governments reap substantial fiscal and non-fiscal benefits. In particular, the TIF manifests in higher income tax, GST, business tax, property transfer tax, motor vehicles tax and other revenue sources. However, due to the limitations of fiscal federalism, local and regional authorities engaged in value-creating ventures in an urban area may not be able to fully internalise the benefits generated by their efforts. This is because they may not have the necessary financial instruments authorised to them under the Constitution or law. Thus, inter-jurisdictional partnerships beyond the traditional inter-distribution of functions and finances between tiers of government are inevitable. When central, state and local governments cooperate in value-increment financing of cities, a win-win-win self-financed and spiralling process of planned urban development could be engineered through TIF. The TIF principle is robust and can also be applied to PPPs as well. But values need to be captured and recycled to finance investments that create such values.

Chapter 10, drawing lessons from theory and practice presents a road map for reforming urban public finance in India. It refers to the international benchmark to suggest that the ratio of municipal expenditures to GDP be progressively enhanced from the present abysmal level of one per cent to five per cent by the time India reaches the 50 per cent urban mark—two per cent for capital expenditure, and three per cent for O&M and debt-servicing. This goal may be translated to five-year targets, coinciding with the period of the CFC. The chapter presents an urban finance framework to guide the choice of revenue instruments to finance city development and services—from user charges to general taxes—based on the generalised benefit principle, golden rules of local public finance and principle of earmarked benefit taxes. This framework covers: expenditure assignment, revenue assignment, revenue-expenditure matching and design of revenue instruments, including a portfolio of municipal taxes and intergovernmental transfers. We suggest an amendment to the Constitution of India to include a 'municipal finance list' corresponding to the 12th Schedule. This list may include: property tax, land value tax, land use conversion tax, profession tax, payroll tax, business licensing tax, advertisement tax, entertainment tax, utility user taxes, carbon tax, a statutory share in motor vehicles tax, motor fuel tax, transfer of property tax/stamp duty and mining royalties, a city GST or statutory city share in state GST, user charges, benefit charges including Floor Space Index (FSI) charges, betterment charges, development charges and impact fees.

Empowering municipalities with a versatile alternative to octroi remains a critical unfinished task. It is appropriate that the revenue that could have accrued to ULBs had octroi not been abolished and 'local taxes' not been taken over, or appropriated by state governments in the past or subsumed under GST is considered as the baseline to arrive at a city GST rate within state GST or a city share in state GST. This calls for a consensus between the centre and states as their own tax rates will be affected. International practice in multi-tier countries like Brazil, China, Nigeria, the Philippines and South Africa suggest that a statutory city GST rate at 25 per cent of the state GST rate or 25 per cent share of municipalities in state GST could be appropriate. Further, the cities may be enabled to have a share in the divisible pool of central taxes, including central GST through the CFC route. India may aim at a transfers-GDP ratio of three per cent for municipalities by the time the country reaches 50 per cent urban mark—one per cent through central channel and two per cent through state channel, including statutory city GST or formula-based share in state GST. The goals may be broken into five-year targets, coinciding with the period of the CFC.

Cities create value through externalities, spatial planning, infrastructure, local economic development and growth. When external economies are vibrant, benefit taxation and value capture financing mechanisms offer unique opportunities for self-financing urban development. Externalities lead to many benefits for many actors in the urban economy in many ways; they create 'agglomeration rents' to both immobile and mobile factors of production that can be captured and recycled. These can be taxed without losing the tax base to finance city and regional infrastructure and contribute to further agglomerative effects. Similarly, land use planning, including zoning, conversion of rural land to urban, institution of land use, change in land use, assignment of development rights, including FSI, transferable development right (TDR), etc. confer windfall benefits on landowners. The development of trunk infrastructure facilities and transportation-land use integration lead to 'accessibility' and 'serviceability' premium to properties at vantage locations, resulting in unearned increments in values. A two-pronged approach to urban public finance reforms is thus called for: enabling growth to pay its way and making beneficiaries of windfall gains to pay for planned urban development, benefitting them and the society at large.

As India faces resource crunch to meet the challenges of development, there is compulsion to search for investments that cost less but bring more gains to the country through externality-linked multipliers. At this stage of India's evolution, cities present opportunities for such investments. They create growth and public finance by combining agglomeration, knowledge and infrastructure externalities, and setting in motion 'circular and cumulative causation' processes. However, these externalities spill over the constitutional boundaries of revenue assignment. Therefore, a cooperative federalism framework is warranted to promote cities as locomotives of growth and structural transformation. This can power India to effectively address the concerns of development, including rural development. Public policy needs to catalyse agglomeration-augmenting, congestion-mitigating, resource-generating, credit-worthy and bankable cities that subscribe to 'generalised benefit principle', embrace 'golden rules' of local public finance and adopt 'users pay', 'beneficiaries pay', 'polluter pay', 'exacerbaters pay', 'congesters pay' and 'growth pays' instruments. These cities and special purpose vehicles representing partnerships between tiers of government and private sector need to be enabled to issue Build India municipal bonds rooted in value increment financing. Good urban governance lies at the core of this paradigm.

Note

1. Figures are based on ASCI (2014), Indian Public Finance Statistics 2013–14 and 14th Finance Commission of India (2015), India; Buckley (2005), South Africa; and Afonso and Araujo (2006), Brazil.

2

India's Urban Fiscal Problem

State of Urbanisation in India

The urban population of India increased from 62 million in 1951 to 286 million in 2001 and 377 million in 2011. The level of urbanisation rose from 17 per cent in 1951 to 28 per cent in 2001 and 31 per cent in 2011. The number of urban agglomerations (UAs)/towns was 7,935 in 2011, compared to 5,161 in 2001. While the number of statutory towns increased from 3,799 to 4,041 between 2001 and 2011, the number of census towns went up from 1,362 to 3,894. These trends indicate that considerable urbanisation is occurring outside the statutory limits of municipalities. In 2011, cities with more than 1,00,000 people numbered 468. They contained 264.9 million people, representing 70 per cent of India's urban population. The number of million-plus cities was 53 in 2011. With 160.7 million people, they accounted for 43 per cent of urban residents. The five largest urban agglomerations in India recorded population at the 2011 census as follows: Greater Mumbai (18.4 million), Delhi (16.3 million), Kolkata (14.1 million), Chennai (8.7 million) and Bengaluru (8.5 million).[1]

India's urban population, estimated at 410 million in 2014, is projected to reach 814 million in 2050. With an estimated rural population of 857 million in 2014, the country would still have 806 million living in rural areas in 2050 (United Nations 2014, 22). Thus, India will confront the dual challenges of rural and urban development for several decades. Ironically, it is the cities that have to shoulder the responsibility of raising resources to address the country's urban as well as rural development concerns.

By international comparison, India's urbanisation process has been rather slow. As the United Nations data on 'percentage urban' for 2014 reveals, India, with about 32 per cent of its population in cities and towns, is less urbanised than many developing countries of Asia and Africa:

Malaysia (74), China (54), Indonesia (53), Thailand (49), Philippines (44), South Africa (64), Ghana (53), Nigeria (47), Egypt (43) and Zambia (40).[2] Globally, the share of urban population in total population was 54 per cent in 2014. The corresponding figure for Asia was 48 per cent, while that for Africa, Europe, Northern America, Latin America and the Caribbean was 40, 73, 81, 80 per cent respectively. In 1950, the level of urbanisation in China was 11.8 per cent as against 17 per cent for India. However, China caught up by 1990 and overtook India thereafter (United Nations 2012, 128; United Nations 2014, 20–25).

In addition to low level, the pace of urbanisation in India has also been slow. The simple average increase in the level of urbanisation over the 60-year period 1951–2011 is about two per cent per decade. While the level of urbanisation in the world increased by 23 per cent between 1950 and 2011, the level in India rose by only 14 per cent. According to UN projections, the country would lag behind many developing countries in reaching the 50 per cent urban threshold. It is likely to attain the 50 per cent urban mark in 2050 (United Nations 2014).

Not only the trends of urbanisation, but also the patterns of employment growth in India suggest that the desired structural transformation of the Indian economy is not occurring. Till two decades ago, agriculture contributed 70 per cent of the country's total employment. This figure has gone down to 53 per cent in 2009–10. Considering that agriculture accounts for about 15 per cent of GDP at present, the decline in the share of agriculture in total employment has undoubtedly been tardy. Employment in agriculture increased from 238 million in 1999–2000 to 259 million in 2004–05. It decreased to 245 million in 2009–10. There was a net increase in agricultural employment between 1999–2000 and 2009–10, a period which witnessed an unprecedented growth in production outside agriculture. Further, manufacturing employment experienced only a modest increase of 6.5 million between 1999–2000 and 2009–10. Services added 22 million during the same period. Between 2004–05 and 2009–10, employment in services went up by a mere 3.5 million, that in manufacturing declined by five million (Mehrotra et al. 2012, 67).

Economists consider the slow pace of urbanisation a disturbing phenomenon, reflecting the failure of cities to create jobs (Mohan 1996). They argue that insufficient investments in infrastructure in cities might have hampered secondary and tertiary growth, leading to too few jobs created in these sectors. Rise in capital intensity of urban production, lack of affordable housing and basic civic services to workers, especially those residing in low-income settlements, and absence of skills required for urban jobs might have discouraged rural–urban migration. Researchers also attribute the observed deceleration in adult male migration to cities to 'exclusionary urbanisation'. They contend that cities have been less accommodating and hospitable to migrants. The process of 'sanitisation and formalisation' in cities seems to be acting against the migration of the rural poor to cities (Kundu and Saraswati 2012). Slow urban growth might have contributed to misery in the countryside through adverse effects on employment, productivity and urban–rural remittances.

While both the level and pace of urbanisation in India have been low, there are strong reasons to believe that the country would witness an accelerating phase of urban growth in the coming decades. Demographic research points to three stages of urbanisation. The first stage is marked by traditional rural society, with agrarian predominance and dispersed settlements. The second stage is the acceleration stage when basic restructuring of the economy and investments in social overheads take place. The proportion of urban population increases gradually in the initial phase but accelerates after attaining a level of around 30 per cent. The third stage is the terminal stage where urban population share exceeds 70 per cent or more (Davis 1962 and 1965). With urbanisation reaching a level of 31 per cent in 2011, India has entered the take-off stage of urbanisation.

Apart from demographic factors, economic forces would also accelerate urbanisation in India. A targeted double digit growth would largely come from non-agricultural sectors, notably, services, manufacturing and construction. For these sectors, the scale, location and agglomeration matter. Economic activities subject to scale economies agglomerate. Structural and geographic transformation move together in economic development process. Secondary and tertiary activities cluster in cities to reap the benefits of agglomeration externalities. Thus, the contribution of agriculture to GDP and employment will decline further. In a high growth scenario, it may be possible to reach a level of urbanisation of 50 per cent in India well before 2050. This would mean an unprecedented increase in the pace of urbanisation. Some developed and developing countries have coped with such pace successfully during their urban transition by adopting appropriate policies and urban management strategies. There is no reason why India cannot do so.

Economic Significance of Cities

The economic significance of cities derives from their agglomeration externalities, leading to increasing returns—at firm, industry, local, urban and regional scales. Cities form and grow to reap the economies of agglomeration. These are returns to density and spatial contiguity due to the co-location of firms, households and institutions. They manifest in scale, scope, localisation and urbanisation economies, facilitating production, transaction and distribution activities. Cities promote specialisation, diversity and competition. They offer benefits of market size, backward and forward linkages, learning, matching, sharing and networking. They lead to productivity-enhancing networks—economic, social, political, technological, knowledge and infrastructure. Metcalfe's law suggests that the value of a network increases with the square of the number of connected users in the system.[3]

Research in urban economics and new economic geography reveals that agglomeration economies raise total factor productivity. They are instrumental in making cities the repositories of skill and capital, hubs of knowledge and innovation, and engines of economic growth (see Box 2.1).

Box 2.1

Cities and Economic Development

A strong positive relationship exists between urbanisation and per capita income across countries. A correlation coefficient of 0.85 is observed between the GDP per capita and the level of urbanisation in a cross-section of developing countries (Henderson 2000). Urban-based economic activities account for upto 55 per cent of GDP in low-income countries, 73 per cent in middle-income countries and 85 per cent in high-income countries (UN–HABITAT 2006, 48).

Large cities act as locomotives of growth. Some even outpace large nations in economic output. If the five largest cities of the United States, New York, Los Angeles, Chicago, Boston and Philadelphia, were treated as a single territory, it would rank as the fourth largest economy in the world. New York, with a gross metropolitan product of $950 billion in 2005, would rank seventeenth globally if it were a country (World Bank 2009).

The ten largest metropolitan areas of Mexico, containing one-third of the country's population, generate 62 per cent of its national value added (UN–HABITAT 2012). São Paulo accounts for just over 10 per cent of the total population of Brazil, but more than 40 per cent of its GDP; a similar picture is obtained for Bangkok in Thailand (UN–HABITAT 2008). In Vietnam, with urbanisation at about 30 per cent, the share of cities in national output is 70 per cent (Gill and Kharass 2007). In China, only 120 cities account for three quarters of the country's GDP (Au and Henderson 2006a, 2006b). In India, the contribution of urban areas to GDP increased from 29 per cent in 1950–51 to 47 per cent in 1981, 55 per cent in 1991 and 60 per cent in 2001.[4] In 2007, cities and towns, with an estimated three per cent of geographical area and 30 per cent of population, contributed about 62–63 per cent of the country's GDP. This contribution is expected to rise to about 75 per cent by 2021 (Planning Commission, 2008, 394).

Source: Mohanty (2014).

Agglomeration economies differ between habitations of different sizes. Market towns generate scale economies in marketing and distribution of agricultural inputs and outputs. Medium-sized cities present localisation economies linked to specialisation. Larger cities create urbanisation economies due to diversity, leading to innovation. Metropolitan city regions offer the benefits of localisation, urbanisation and networking. They represent a mass of interconnected economic activities, typically characterised by high productivity due to 'jointly-generated' and 'mutually-reinforcing' agglomeration economies. These regions act as innovators of products, processes and techniques. They drive regional and national economic growth. As gateways to national and international economies, they are exposed to powerful forces of globalisation, including transportation, communication and information technology revolutions. Metropolitan city regions around the globe engage in economic activities that are increasingly structured on national and international planes. Population densities in these regions are high. The population density in the 50 km vicinity of the seven largest metropolitan agglomerations in India (with populations above four million in 2001) was 2,450 in 2005. A third of India's new towns were 'born' within a 50 km radius area of existing metros (Work Bank 2013a).

Agglomeration economies are dynamic. Their nature changes as economic development progresses. When a country shifts away from agriculture to industry and services, it enters a new arena of agglomeration. Production moves away from diminishing or constant returns to increasing returns. Entrepreneurs and workers resort to non-farm activities wherein both scale and location matter. Production of manufacturing and services involves increasing returns. It is also more efficient when carried out in a denser constellation of firms and households. These activities use modest land and more skills as inputs in production. Manufacturing requires relatively more land compared to services. Most services need built-up space, efficiently provided by cities. Manufacturing and services cluster in city regions to gain from lower transport costs, intra- and inter-industry linkages, larger markets, shared inputs and facilities, specialised labour pooling, learning and networking.

Agglomeration economies are, however, not without limits. When the concentration of economic activity exceeds a threshold, diseconomies of agglomeration arise in the form of overcrowding, housing shortage, deterioration in civic services, traffic congestion, pollution, slums, poverty, crime, social unrest and the like. This threshold may be different for different cities depending on their spatio-economic contexts, determined by geography, history and economics. Unless effective measures are taken to augment agglomeration economies and mitigate congestion diseconomies, the positive benefits of clustering in cities may be offset by its negative effects. In particular, the issues of urban land market and spatial planning in making adequate serviced land and floor space available for the growing needs of urbanisation must be addressed.

Apart from agglomeration externalities, cities are homes to knowledge and human capital externalities. In a city setting, the production of new knowledge by one firm generates a positive externality to other firms as knowledge spills over and cannot be kept secret (Romer 1986). Acquisition of skill by a worker increases the productivity of other workers by enhancing the economy's pool of human capital. The effects of 'external human capital' are founded in the ways people interact, exchange and learn in cities (Lucas 1988). Shaped by market forces and public policies to promote economic growth, agglomeration and knowledge externalities reinforce each other through 'circular and cumulative causation'. Growth leads to agglomeration, which fosters growth by facilitating the transmission and diffusion of knowledge, and promoting specialisation, diversity and innovation. Agglomeration and knowledge externalities act as powerful drivers of growth. They establish the unique importance of cities in the structural transformation of nations.

A strong positive correlation is observed between growth and agglomeration. The industrial revolution in Europe and the United States led to the emergence of spectacular city regions that have thrived till date. Kuznets referred to the spatial concentration of economic activity as an ingredient of modern economic growth. A study based on panel data set, covering up to 70 countries over 1960–90, shows that urban primacy, measured by the share in population of a country's largest city, is advantageous to growth in low-income countries. Urbanisation, however, has no significant growth-promoting effect (Henderson 2003b). Another study examining the effects of spatial concentration of economic activity within European regions over 1980–2000 lends evidence to the growth-inducing effects of agglomeration (Crozet and Koenig 2007). A recent research covering cross-country data set for 105 countries for 1960–2000, finds 'consistent evidence' in favour of the hypothesis that agglomeration boosts GDP growth up to a level of economic development. The critical threshold is some US$10,000 per capita in 2006 PPP prices, corresponding roughly to the current level of development of Brazil (Brulhart and Sbergami 2009). The study also finds that in terms of foregone growth, the cost of policies inhibiting economic agglomeration is the highest in the poorest nations. Policies aimed at preventing spatial concentration of economic activity are most damaging in these countries.

The theoretical and empirical relationships between agglomeration and economic growth suggest that at the current stage of India's evolution, the country has a historic opportunity to accelerate economic growth and reduce poverty by developing cities and harnessing the power of their external economies. However, researchers, policymakers and planners in India in the past hardly recognised the role of geography and externalities of cities in growth. In the process, they did not address the fundamental issue of how economic development, including rural development, can be financed without vibrant and agglomerating cities. The issues of urban public finance remain grossly neglected in India—in both policy and academic circles.[5]

Importance of Urban Public Finance

The importance of urban public finance derives from the role of cities not only as places of living and working, but also as catalysts of economic growth. Starting with the pioneering work of Aschauer, econometric studies find a positive relationship between public infrastructure, especially transportation and aggregate output of the private sector (Ashauer 1989, Duranton and Turner 2012, Easterly and Rebelo 1993, Munnell 1990, Straub 2008, World Bank 1994). City and regional infrastructure enhance the working efficiency and productivity of households and firms. They produce 'wider economic benefits' through externalities. Urban public finance is critical for the installation of such infrastructure and the provision of public services. Moreover, local government finance forms an integral part of state government finance in India. The latter is firmly tied to central government finance in view of the fiscal federalism framework mandated by the Constitution of India. With rising contribution of cities to GDP, urban public finance will play an increasingly important role in the country's public finance system.

Cities generate public finance for economic development. In particular, externalities of cities create 'agglomeration rents' to both immobile and mobile factors of production. Agglomeration economies capitalise into tax bases of all levels of government. Cities are, thus, instrumental in the mobilisation of income tax, corporation tax, service tax, business tax, commercial tax, excise tax, stamp duty, motor vehicles tax, entertainment tax, land value tax, property tax, profession tax, entertainment tax, etc. (see Box 2.2). Jane Jacobs (1984), based on a study of many cities over the course of history, emphasised their role

Box 2.2

Cities and State Public Finance

Cities constitute the tax bases of governments. Data for Hyderabad and Ranga Reddy districts in the erstwhile state of Andhra Pradesh in India reveal that these two urban districts, containing the bulk of Hyderabad metropolitan area, accounted for less than 11 per cent of state population in 2011. Their share in state commercial taxes in 2011–12, however, was 71.5 per cent.[6] In the same year, these two districts generated 32 per cent of motor vehicles tax and other transport-related revenues, and 31 per cent of registration fees and stamp duty of the state.

Share of Hyderabad and Ranga Reddy Districts Combined in the Collection of Major Taxes in Andhra Pradesh 1997–2012 (Per Cent)

State Tax Collection	1997–98	2001–02	2011–12
Commercial Tax	58.37	72.85	71.5
Registration and Stamps	32.75	36.18	32.0
Transport and Motor Vehicles	27.00	27.80	31.0

Source: Government of Andhra Pradesh: Finance Department Data, 2014.

as 'the greatest yielders of revenues in a nation or empire'. She informs that when the United States' income tax was first adopted in 1913, a third of the nation's entire tax yield came from New York State alone, most of it from New York City. Jacobs cautions that until a nation has well-developed and productive cities, it cannot afford programmes for basic necessities or transfer payments, including those to the rural poor (see Jacobs 1984, 186).

Paradoxically, Indian cities suffer from a 'rich city–poor city government' syndrome. Municipalities in many states depend on state governments even for salaries and maintenance of elementary services. They face a gross mismatch between responsibilities and resources. This is a result of the long neglect of urban public finance by policymakers, administrators and researchers. The matter is of grave concern as the contribution of cities to GDP cannot be sustained without substantial investments in infrastructure needed by firms and households in cities and their regions. The livability and environmental sustainability of cities in the future also depend on what policies and programmes are undertaken now to address the 'backlog', 'current' and 'growth' needs of urbanisation. The haphazard growth of India's cities reflects the haphazard way they are financed.

State of Municipal Finance in India

Indian municipalities are amongst the weakest, globally, in terms of fiscal capacity and autonomy. Their revenue base is narrow, inflexible and non-buoyant. Ironically, the ratio of municipal revenues to combined central and state revenues has declined from 3.92 per cent in 2007–08 to 3.62 per cent in 2012–13. The ratio of municipal taxes to combined central and state taxes has gone down from 2.11 per cent to 1.79 per cent between the two years.[7] These trends are disturbing as urbanisation is increasing, and so also is the contribution of cities to GDP.

India is far behind developed and comparable developing countries in expenditure and revenue decentralisation to local bodies. Municipal expenditure–GDP ratio in India is estimated at 1.0 per cent in 2012–13.[8] In contrast, local expenditure–GDP ratios in select Organization for Economic Cooperation and Development (OECD) countries in 2010 were as follows: Belgium (7.0), Germany (7.9), Austria (8.2), France (11.8), United Kingdom (14.0), Italy (15.9), Finland (22.6), Sweden (25.1) and Denmark (37.3; OECD 2012). The ratio of municipal revenue to GDP in India is estimated at 1.03 per cent for 2012–13,[9] compared to Poland (4.5), South Africa (6.0), Germany (7.3), Brazil (7.4), Austria (7.8), United Kingdom (13.9), Norway (14.2), Italy (15.3), Finland (22.4) and Denmark (37.1).[10] Table 2.1 presents the ratios of local government revenues to GDP, taxes and user fees to local spending and local revenues by category to total local government revenues in OECD countries.

Table 2.2 presents data on revenues of municipalities by source in India in 2007–08 and 2012–13. In 2002–03, 'own revenues' accounted for 63 per cent of total municipal revenues in India. The share declined to 55.7 per cent in 2007–08 and 51.6 per cent in 2012–13. The share of tax revenues declined from 37.2 per cent to 32 per cent between 2007–08 and 2012–13. Non-tax revenues accounted for 18.5 per cent in 2007–08 and 19.7 per cent in 2012–13. The share of central transfers increased marginally from 9.1 per cent to 9.5 per cent. That from state government sources went up from 32.4 per cent to 34.5 per cent between the two years. All the key municipal fiscal autonomy ratios, own revenues-GDP, own taxes-GDP and property tax-GDP, had declined between 2007–08 and 2012–13.[11]

Table 2.3 presents the distribution of municipal revenues by category of ULBs in India. Between 2007–08 and 2012–13 the ratio of 'own revenues' to total revenues declined in all groups of ULBs, that is, municipal corporations (tier I), municipalities (tier II) and nagar panchayats (tier III), indicating an erosion in municipal fiscal autonomy across the

Table 2.1

Distribution of Local Government Revenues: Select OECD Countries, 2010

Country	Local Government Revenues as % of GDP	Taxes and User Fees as % Local Spending	As % of Total Local Government Revenues			
			Taxes	User Fees	Transfers	Other Revenues
Austria	7.8	68.7	62.0	10.2	18.7	9.1
Czech Republic	11.6	55.3	40.7	16.1	41.7	1.5
Denmark	37.1	39.1	34.3	4.9	57.5	3.2
Estonia	10.4	54.6	44.6	9.0	44.6	1.8
Finland	22.4	66.9	46.2	21.4	29.6	2.8
Germany	7.3	51.3	40.0	15.5	40.6	3.9
Hungary	11.5	28.6	21.2	10.2	67.1	1.5
Ireland	6.7	23.7	13.4	9.2	67.2	10.1
Italy	15.3	45.3	40.1	7.0	50.9	2.0
Luxembourg	5.2	49.2	31.2	18.1	49.2	1.5
Norway	14.2	50.1	41.1	12.7	42.2	4.0
Portugal	6.3	40.7	34.3	12.6	43.2	9.9
Slovenia	9.9	51.3	42.0	11.4	45.3	1.3
Spain	6.4	47.5	45.1	8.9	44.4	1.6
United Kingdom	13.9	25.4	12.7	12.9	71.8	2.6

Source: OECD (2012).

country. The smaller the size of ULB, the greater is the dependency on intergovernmental transfers to finance civic services and facilities.

Table 2.4 presents the distribution of municipal revenues by source in 18 states of India in 2012–13. Except Maharashtra and Punjab, the dependency of ULBs on intergovernmental transfers is very substantial, exceeding 70 per cent in the cases of Himachal Pradesh, Jammu and Kashmir, Kerala, Bihar, Madhya Pradesh, Uttarakhand, Odisha and Karnataka. The Maharashtra case is explained by the presence of octroi in Mumbai and local body tax (LBT) in other municipal bodies; in Punjab, the municipalities have access to excise revenues.

Table 2.2

Trends in Municipal Revenues in India by Source: 2007–08 to 2012–13

			2007–08		2012–13	
Sl. *No.*	*Sources of Revenue*		*Total* *(₹ Crore)*	*% of Total* *Municipal* *Revenue* *(%)*	*Total* *(₹ Crore)*	*% of Total* *Municipal* *Revenue* *(%)*
A. Own Sources						
1.	Total Taxes		18,366	37.20	30,912	32.00
	Property Tax		8,159	16.53	15,110	15.64
	Other Taxes		10,207	20.68	15,801	16.35
2.	Non-taxes		9,134	18.50	19,002	19.70
	Total Own Source Revenues		27,501	55.70	49,913	51.60
B. Other Sources						
1.	GoI Transfers		3,515	7.10	5,387	5.60
2.	Central Finance Commission Transfers		986	2.00	3,760	3.90
3.	State Assignment/Devolution		9,342	18.90	18,537	19.20
4.	State Grant-in-aid		6,653	13.50	14,809	15.30
5.	Others		1,355	2.70	4,234	4.40
	Total Other Source Revenues		21,851	44.30	46,727	48.40
C. Total Revenues			49,351	100.00	96,640	100.00
Gross Domestic Product at Factor Cost in Current Prices (GDP)			45,82,086		93,88,876	
Property Tax as % of GDP				0.18		0.16
Own Taxes as % of GDP				0.40		0.33
Own Revenues as % of GDP				0.60		0.53
GoI/Central Finance Commission Transfers as % of GDP				0.10		0.10
State Government/State Finance Commission Transfers as % of GDP				0.35		0.36
Municipal Revenue as a % of GDP				1.08		1.03

Source: ASCI (2014). Based on data furnished by state governments to the 14th Finance Commission of India, *Indian Public Finance Statistics 2013–14*.

Table 2.3

Distribution of Municipal Revenues by Category of Urban Local Body: 2007–08 and 2012–13 (Percentage)

Sl. No	Sources of Revenue	Municipal Corporations		Municipalities		Nagar Panchayats	
		2007–08	2012–13	2007–08	2012–13	2007–08	2012–13
A. Own Sources							
1.	Total Taxes	45.5	40.9	18.6	14.7	10.9	8.2
2.	Non-taxes	22.2	23.9	9.3	10.5	11.3	11.8
	Total Own Sources	67.6	64.8	27.9	25.2	22.1	20.1
B. Other Sources							
1.	GoI Transfers	7.0	4.6	8.4	7.3	3.0	2.2
2.	Central Finance Commission Transfers	0.8	2.1	5.3	8.8	2.8	8.8
3.	State Assignment/ Devolution	11.4	12.6	31.2	29.0	63.1	49.9
4.	State Grant-in-aid	10.4	12.2	24.2	23.8	6.9	14.0
5.	Others	2.7	3.8	3.0	5.8	2.1	5.2
	Total Other Sources	32.4	35.2	72.1	74.8	77.9	79.9
C. Total Revenue		100.0	100.0	100.0	100.0	100.0	100.0

Source: ASCI (2014). Based on data furnished by state governments to the 14th Finance Commission of India.

The per capita 'municipal revenues' and per capita 'own municipal revenues' in India in 2012–13 are estimated at ₹3,123 and ₹1,681 respectively. Per capita municipal expenditure in 2012–13 is estimated at ₹3,116, comprising the per capita revenue expenditure of ₹1,986 and the per capita capital expenditure of ₹1,130.[12] McKinsey (2010) informs that India's annual per capita spending on cities at $50, including capital and operational expenditures, is 14 per cent of China's $362, less than 10 per cent of South Africa's $508 and less than three per cent of the United Kingdom's $1,772. In terms of capital expenditure, India's per capita annual urban spending is $17 as against $116 in China, $127 in South Africa and $391 in the United Kingdom. The report argues that India needs to increase the figure eightfold, from $17 to $134, raising it from 0.5 per cent of GDP to two per cent of GDP a year.

McKinsey (2010) suggests that India would need to spend ₹9.74 million crore on its cities by 2030, with ₹5.31 million crore for capital

Table 2.4

Distribution of Municipal Revenues by Source in India (Percentage): 2012–13

Sl. No.	State	Taxes	Non-taxes	Central Transfers*	State Transfers**	Others
1.	Andhra Pradesh	33.5	24.3	7.5	34.7	–
2.	Assam	14.9	14.7	11.9	23.3	35.2
3.	Bihar	13.2	5.2	28.4	52.5	0.8
4.	Gujarat	18.8	12.1	5.4	57.1	6.5
5.	Haryana	18.5	24.3	14.9	37.6	4.9
6.	Himachal Pradesh	–	–	55.8	44.2	–
7.	Jammu & Kashmir	6.1	5.5	31.5	56.9	–
8.	Karnataka	20.2	8.8	17.8	53.2	–
9.	Kerala	9.8	5.9	39.1	45.1	–
10.	Madhya Pradesh	10.0	8.6	8.8	69.2	3.4
11.	Maharashtra	53.2	29.9	3.8	9.8	3.4
12.	Odisha	10.2	9.2	41.4	33.7	5.5
13.	Punjab	69.2	16.8	8.9	2.8	2.3
14	Rajasthan	7.0	32.1	12.0	47.7	1.3
15.	Tamil Nadu	21.6	12.0	6.6	56.6	3.2
16.	Uttar Pradesh	10.8	5.6	10.4	54.7	18.6
17.	Uttarakhand	5.9	3.4	7.6	69.3	13.8
18.	West Bengal	20.1	19.1	13.7	46.2	0.8
	All India	32.0	19.7	9.5	34.5	4.4

Source: ASCI (2014). Based on data furnished by state governments to the 14th Finance Commission of India.

Notes: * GoI transfer + Central Finance Commission transfer.
** Assigned revenues from state governments + devolution through State Finance Commission + state government grants-in-aid.

expenditure. The largest demand for capital funding would come from affordable housing, followed by mass transit. If we exclude affordable housing, the capital spending required till 2030 would be ₹3.54 million crore (McKinsey 2010). The High Powered Expert Committee (HPEC) for estimating the investment requirements for urban infrastructure services projects estimated that India would need ₹3.92 million crore for urban infrastructure investment over the period 2012–31. If operation and maintenance costs are added, the figure would swell to ₹5.92 million crore (HPEC 2011).

The operation and maintenance norms adopted by HPEC suggest that municipalities in India spend about 20 per cent of what is needed for the efficient delivery of civic services (Mathur 2013). A Reserve Bank of India study, using data of 35 metropolitan municipal corporations for the period 1999–2000 to 2003–04, also finds that these corporations are subject to massive under-spending relative to normative requirement— varying between 94.43 per cent for Patna to 30.78 per cent for Pune. The average under-spending was 76 per cent (Mohanty et al. 2007).

Anatomy of Urban Fiscal Problem

An anatomy of India's urban fiscal problem brings out certain key underlying factors as described below:

Improper Revenue Mix

India is one country where the power of ULBs to levy taxes has dwindled over the years, eroding their autonomy. Property tax is the only major municipal tax. Octroi, once a buoyant resource with ULBs, has been phased out in all states, excepting Maharashtra.[13] No state has, however, assigned a revenue source as buoyant as octroi to municipalities. User charges are yet to dominate the municipal scene. Borrowing is not exploited as an important source of municipal finance in India.

Vertical Imbalance

Vertical imbalance and fiscal dependency are built into India's fiscal federalism. They owe to the non-assignment of revenue sources to local bodies to suffice the financing needs of their mandatory functions. Municipalities suffer from inadequate 'own revenues', making them dependent on state governments for day-to-day civic administration. 'Ad hoc' intergovernmental transfers constitute the largest source of revenue for many of them.

Horizontal Imbalance

Public service responsibilities and resources available to finance them vary considerably between municipalities. Horizontal imbalances occur between cities of different sizes, with varying composition of economic activity and even within cities in the same population group. For example, the resource needs of cities with a large slum population may be substantially higher than those that are largely slum-free. The resource bases of some cities may be disproportionately smaller than those of comparable cities due to many reasons.

State Government Control

State governments control municipal authority to levy taxes and charges, and borrow. They post managers to municipalities, set municipal tax rates, grant exemptions, and determine fiscal transfers and conditions of access to market funds. Grants-in-aid are often discretionary. In some states, municipalities even need approval from state authorities to enter into public–private partnerships. Further, the presence of parastatals like urban development authorities and water boards undermine the role of elected municipalities in city planning and service delivery.

Systemic Inadequacies

Municipalities face acute systemic problems: lack of professional cadres, absence of robust human resource management, financial management and public accountability frameworks; mismatch between staff needed and available; high administration costs; large-scale corruption; and inadequate involvement of the community in service delivery. These factors lead to a vicious cycle: inability of municipalities to provide the services wanted by citizens, poor citizens' satisfaction, unwillingness of citizens to pay taxes and charges, poor revenue collection, lack of finance to deliver services and so on.

Bridging the Urban Fiscal Gap

An analytical framework to study the urban fiscal problem is to consider the following simplistic expressions for a representative municipality (Bahl and Linn 1992):

Required expenditures = Unit cost × Quantity of service to be provided per capita as per service norms × Population

Revenues = Own taxes + User charges and fees + Transfers (assigned revenues and grants) + Loans

Own taxes = Collection rate × Legal tax rate × Base-to-income ratio × Per capita income × Population

Legal tax rate = Legal liability of tax/Base of tax

User charges = Unit user charge for service × Quantity of service provided per capita × Population

Shared revenues = Rate of sharing × State/Central revenues

Grants = Per capita grant × Population

Fiscal gap = Required expenditure – Available revenues

Municipal budget deficit is the difference between budgeted expenditure and budgeted revenue. The ratio of actual revenue to potential revenue represents municipal collection efficiency. The ratio: (own taxes + user charges + other own revenues)/municipal expenditure reflects municipal autonomy, while (shared revenues + grants)/municipal expenditure ratio symbolises municipal dependency.

As the analytical framework suggests, the urban fiscal gap can be bridged by: (a) rationalising municipal responsibilities, (b) cutting down service costs, (c) enhancing municipal revenue base and authority to raise resources, (d) stepping up local revenue effort; (e) increasing transfers from higher levels of government, (f) resorting to larger borrowings by enhancing credit-worthiness and (g) partnering with the private sector to reduce demand on public resources for civic services and infrastructure. The strategy to address the urban fiscal problem thus needs to consider the following: (a) expenditure assignment, (b) revenue assignment, (c) function–finance matching and (d) urban management, aimed at providing services efficiently, raising resources needed and reducing unnecessary expenditures.

Expenditure Assignment

The starting point of a strategy to address the urban fiscal problem is 'expenditure assignment', namely, clarifying the functions of municipalities vis-à-vis other tiers of government. The 12th Schedule, inserted into the Constitution of India by the 74th Amendment Act provides an illustrative list of eighteen legitimate municipal functions (see Box 2.3).

A comparison of the 12th Schedule with the functions assigned by states to their municipalities following the 74th Amendment Act reveals that there are wide variations in the patterns of expenditure assignment between states. This is particularly so for planning-related and redistributive functions. The Act prescribes the entrustment of 'urban planning including town planning' and 'planning for economic and social development' to ULBs (Article 243W), 'district planning' to District Planning Committee (DPC; Article 243ZD) and 'metropolitan planning' to Metropolitan Planning Committee (MPC; Article 243ZE). However, the non-operationalisation of these committees and continued presence

Box 2.3

Functions of Urban Local Bodies in India: 12th Schedule (Article 243W)

1. Urban planning including town planning
2. Regulation of land use and construction of buildings
3. Planning for economic and social development
4. Roads and bridges
5. Water supply for domestic, industrial and commercial purposes
6. Public health, sanitation, conservancy and solid waste management
7. Fire services
8. Urban forestry, protection of the environment and promotion of ecological aspects
9. Safeguarding the interest of weaker sections of society, including the handicapped and mentally retarded
10. Slum improvement and upgrading
11. Urban poverty alleviation
12. Provision of urban amenities and facilities such as parks, gardens and playgrounds
13. Promotion of cultural, educational and aesthetic aspects
14. Burials and burial grounds; cremations, cremation grounds and electric crematoriums
15. Cattle pounds; prevention of cruelty to animals
16. Vital statistics, including registration of births and deaths
17. Public amenities, including street lighting, parking lots, bus stops and public conveniences
18. Regulation of slaughter houses and tanneries.

Source: The Constitution 74th (Amendment) Act 1992.

of urban development authorities keep the urban and regional planning functions fragmented. Functions such as protection of interests of weaker sections, urban poverty alleviation and slum upgradation have traditionally been funded by central and state governments. Due to this, the ULBs are hesitant to accept them as 'own functions'. Further, several states continue to maintain a distinction between 'obligatory' and 'discretionary' functions. A few states have also a peculiar provision in municipal law, providing for 'functions as may be assigned by the state government from time to time'. Thus, ambiguities persist in expenditure assignment to municipalities.

Some outstanding questions in expenditure assignment to ULBs, DPCs and MPCs in India are:

1. Which functions in the 12th Schedule can be regarded as 'exclusively municipal' and which ones need to be shared with state and central governments?
2. When some functions are shared by more than one tier of government, how should the component activities like planning, financing, implementing and regulating be divided and synchronised?
3. Who shoulders the responsibility of redistributive functions such as welfare of weaker sections, poverty alleviation, slum improvement and upgradation?
4. How should the urban planning function be shared between ULBs, DPC, MPC and state government?

There is no consensus on an answer to these questions. However, the rich research literature in public economics provides broad directions to address them. This research concerns with the question: '[W]ho should do what in a federation to ensure the most efficient allocation of resources consistent with peoples' preferences'. (See Bahl 2001; Bahl and Bird 2008; Bahl and Linn 1992; Bird and Smart 2010; Litvack et al. 1998; Musgrave 1959; Musgrave and Musgrave 1989; Oates 1972, 1996, 2006, 2008; Olson 1969 and Shah 1994.)

Musgrave (1959) identifies three functions of the public sector: (a) macroeconomic stabilisation, (b) income redistribution and (c) resource allocation. He suggests that while stabilisation and redistribution functions are best performed by national government, sub-national governments, including local governments, have an important role in resource allocation. Further, while national government has a dominant role in redistribution of income, local governments have a crucial stake in implementation of poverty alleviation and income redistribution programmes (Hirsch 1970 and Oates 1999).

The public choice theory emphasises equating local political jurisdiction with benefit area. In this regard, Olson (1969) advocates the 'fiscal equivalency principle'. He argues that if political jurisdiction and benefit area overlap, then the 'free-rider problem' can be overcome, thereby ensuring optimal provision of public services. Oates (1972) presents the theory of fiscal federalism in terms of the 'correspondence principle'. It argues that the jurisdiction that determines the level of provision of each public service should include precisely the set of individuals who consume the good. Oates (1972) formulates the Decentralization Theorem as follows:

> For a public good—the consumption of which is defined over geographical subsets of the total population, and for which the costs of providing each level of output of the good in each jurisdiction are the same for the central or for the respective local government—it will always be more efficient (or at least as efficient) for local governments to provide the Pareto-efficient levels of output for their respective jurisdictions than for the central government to provide any specified and uniform level of output across all jurisdictions.

The theorem suggests that a public good should be provided by the lowest geographical jurisdiction which can internalise its provision:

> [E]ach public service should be provided by the jurisdiction having control over the minimum geographic area that would internalise benefits and costs of such provision. (Oates 1972)

The theory of fiscal federalism rests on the foundation that efficient allocation of public resources matching peoples' preferences occurs when the public authority has access to local knowledge. This facilitates the alignment of resources to demand for services, cost-effective service delivery, local autonomy and accountability. Correspondence between benefits from public services and revenue-raising potential is important because it promotes accountability on the part of local government (Bird 2000 and Litvack et al 1998). The second generation theories of fiscal federalism also arrive at similar conclusions (Oates 2008 and Weingast 2006). A key principle of fiscal federalism, formally adopted by the European Union in the Maastricht Treaty of 1992, is 'subsidiarity'. It advocates that a central authority should perform only those functions which cannot be performed effectively at a level closer to the people. It is the opposite of 'residuality' principle, typically applied in unitary countries.

The principles of 'fiscal equivalency', 'correspondence' and 'subsidiarity' all suggest that municipalities should perform those functions whose benefits and costs can be internalised by them. Thus, functions with significant inter-jurisdictional spillovers need to be assigned to higher levels of government. Following these principles, we divide municipal functions into three groups: 'essentially municipal', 'agency' and 'shared'. 'Essentially municipal' functions are those whose benefits and costs can be internalised within a local jurisdiction. 'Agency' functions belong to higher levels of government, but their discharge by local bodies as 'agents' is warranted on the ground of efficient management of services. Planning, financing and regulating responsibilities for 'agency' functions rest primarily with higher levels of government, but implementation is assigned to local authorities. 'Shared' or 'concurrent' functions warrant a partnership between state/central and local governments on considerations such as benefit spillovers, scale economies, need for resource pooling and promotion of national interest.

'Urban planning including town planning' is 'essentially municipal'. Regional planning, including 'district planning' and 'metropolitan planning' is, however, a 'shared' function. As mandated by the 74th Amendment Act, district and metropolitan development plans must address integrated spatial planning covering multiple jurisdictions, regional infrastructure development, environmental conservation and sharing of natural and other resources. We suggest that state governments prepare 'state spatial plan' and draw 'structural plans' for metropolitan regions and districts subject to which urban and rural local bodies can prepare their local development plans.

The redistributive functions included in the 12th Schedule are 'agency' functions. Apart from national considerations, the access of the centre and states to more buoyant sources of revenue also places them in a better position to finance programmes like urban poverty alleviation and slum upgradation. In fact, urban poverty alleviation programmes in India have been implemented by cities under the centrally-sponsored Swarna Jayanti Shahari Rozgar Yojana (SJSRY) since 1997. This scheme was funded on a 75:25 sharing pattern between centre and state. It has given way to National Urban Livelihoods Mission (NULM) with a similar financing pattern in 2013. Similarly, slum improvement programmes in cities were funded under Basic Services to the Urban Poor (BSUP) and Integrated Housing and Slum Development Programme (IHSDP) of JNNURM launched in 2005. The central share for these schemes ranged from 50–90 per cent. The GoI also launched Rajiv Awas Yojana (RAY) in 2011, aimed at ushering in a slum-free India. Under RAY, central support at 50–90 per cent of project cost was extended to states. The scheme has been recently restructured and replaced by a new mission called Housing for All by 2022.

Table 2.5

Typology of 12th Schedule Municipal Functions

Function Group	Functions
'Essentially municipal' functions	Urban planning including town planning; public health, sanitation, conservancy and solid waste management; provision of urban amenities and facilities such as parks, gardens and playgrounds; public amenities including street lighting, parking lots, bus stops and public conveniences; regulation of land use and construction of buildings; burials and burial grounds, cremations, cremation ghats/grounds and electric crematoria; cattle pounds, prevention of cruelty to animals; vital statistics including registration of births and deaths; regulation of slaughter houses and tanneries.
'Agency' functions	Safeguarding the interests of weaker sections of society, including the handicapped and mentally retarded; slum improvement and upgradation; urban poverty alleviation.
'Shared' or 'concurrent' functions	Planning for economic and social development; roads and bridges; water supply for domestic, industrial and commercial purposes; fire services; promotion of cultural, educational and aesthetic aspects; urban forestry, protection of the environment and promotion of ecological aspects.

Source: Author.

Table 2.5 classifies the 12th Schedule functions into 'essentially municipal', 'agency' and 'shared' categories based on the framework presented above.

It is desirable to unbundle the 'shared' functions based on 'activity mapping'. Such an exercise was undertaken for rural local bodies in Karnataka. Every function involves a bundle of activities. Which activities need to be undertaken at what level must be clarified. For example, while roads are included in the 12th Schedule, national highways fall into the domain of central government; state highways and district roads belong to state domain. Within a district, major roads passing through multiple local jurisdictions can be regarded as 'shared' responsibilities. Similarly, water supply can be unbundled into production, transmission and distribution functions. While distribution of water is 'essentially municipal', production involving the construction of water reservoirs at faraway places and transmission through trunk mains passing through multiple jurisdictions can be regarded as 'shared' functions. The rules of division of responsibilities between authorities for 'shared' or 'concurrent' functions, especially those related to financing, need to be spelt out clearly to promote accountability in service delivery. The greater the inter-jurisdictional spillover, the larger is the need for sharing resources.

Revenue Assignment

Once 'expenditure assignment' is clarified, the next step is 'revenue assignment'. Finances follow functions; revenues follow responsibilities. As the European Charter of Local Self-Government (Article 9) states: 'Local authorities' financial resources shall be commensurate with the responsibilities provided for by the constitution and the law' (Council of Europe 2010). The revenues assigned to a tier of government should match, as far as possible, the expenditures required so as to induce 'fiscal responsibility' (Ter-Minassian 1997). However, the Constitution (74th Amendment) Act, 1992 does not provide a 'municipal finance list' corresponding to the Twelfth Schedule. Article 243X of the Constitution leaves the authorisation of taxes, tolls, charges and fees, assigned revenues, grants-in-aid and so on to states. While very few states have assigned additional sources to ULBs to match the additional responsibilities included in the 12th Schedule, some states have even curtailed the powers of municipalities to levy taxes after the enactment of the 74th Amendment.

Table 2.6 presents the revenue sources of ULBs in India based on a study of the budgets of select municipal corporations in India.

The current sources of revenues of municipalities in India are grossly inadequate for their mandated functions. Octroi, an obnoxious tax, is abolished in all cities excepting Mumbai. However, compensations from states to ULBs for the loss of octroi have remained at precariously low levels. Municipalities largely depend on property tax and intergovernmental transfers. Only a few states share stamp duty, profession tax, entertainment tax and motor vehicles tax with ULBs. User charges are not imposed on many services even where such levy is feasible. Borrowing through municipal bonds and other forms of debt has not been exploited due to poor creditworthiness of municipalities and restrictions imposed by state governments.

The Constitution (74th Amendment) Act provides for two safeguards to address the mismatch between municipal expenditures and revenues. First, Article 243Y of the Constitution mandates the SFC to review and recommend the 'principles' of devolution of state revenues to municipalities, determination of revenue sources to be assigned to or appropriated by municipalities, provision of grants-in-aid to municipalities and 'measures' needed to improve their finances. Second, amendment to Article 280 of the Constitution mandates the CFC to recommend, 'measures needed to augment the Consolidated Fund of a State to supplement the resources of its Municipalities on the basis of the recommendations made by the Finance Commission of the State.' The constitutional provisions to link municipal finances to state and central

Table 2.6

Revenue Sources of Municipal Corporations in India

Revenue Head/Category	Sources of Revenue
Tax revenue	Property tax; octroi (only Mumbai); advertisement tax; tax on animals; vacant land tax; taxes on carriages and carts; tax on consumption and sale of electricity; toll tax
Non-tax revenue	User charges; trade licensing fee; town planning charges; building permission fees; sale and hire charges; lease rentals
Other receipts	Law charges/costs recovered; lapsed deposits; fees, fines and forfeitures; rent on tools and plants; miscellaneous sales
Assigned (shared) revenue	Entertainment tax; surcharge on stamp duty; profession tax; motor vehicles tax
Grants-in-aid	(a) Plan grants from state and central governments under programmes, for example, JNNURM, National Urban Livelihoods Mission, etc. (b) Non-plan grants from state governments to compensate for loss of income; specific transfers
Debt	Loans borrowed for capital projects from HUDCO, LIC, state and central governments and banks; municipal bonds.

Source: Budgets of Municipal Corporations.

government finances are laudable. However, there is a general consensus that a review mechanism cannot substitute a fundamental requirement. A robust system of revenue assignment to ULBs corresponding to expenditure assignment is a must.

Revenue–Expenditure Matching

A fundamental principle of revenue assignment is that there should be broad clarity on how each assigned function is adequately, consistently and predictably financed. Efficient public service delivery calls for identifying revenue sources that match expenditure responsibilities. Research in local public finance provides the following 'golden rules' for identifying revenue sources appropriate for financing particular types of local public expenditures (Bahl and Linn 1992):

1. Where the benefits of public services are measurable and accrue to readily identified individuals in a jurisdiction, user charges are the most appropriate financing instruments;
2. Local public services such as administration, traffic control, street lighting and security, which are services to the general public in the sense that identification of beneficiaries and measurement of benefits and costs to individuals are difficult, are most appropriately financed by taxes on local residents;
3. The cost of services for which significant spillovers to neighbouring jurisdictions occur (for example, health, education and welfare), should be financed substantially by state or national intergovernmental transfers; and
4. Borrowing is an appropriate source to finance capital outlays on infrastructure projects, particularly public utilities and roads.

Economic theory suggests that user charges promote efficiency by providing information on demand to public service providers and ensuring that the services are valued (at the margin) by citizens. For achieving efficiency, user charges should be levied on the direct recipients of benefits. Where charging is impracticable due to difficulties in identifying beneficiaries or measuring benefits, 'benefit taxes' levied on local residents are desirable. Intergovernmental transfers are necessary to finance services when user charges and specific and general benefit taxes are not adequate. Importantly, municipalities should face a hard budget constraint; accountability must go hand-in-hand with autonomy. Thus, the design of intergovernmental transfers needs to incorporate incentives for the exploitation of revenue sources assigned to municipalities. They should not bail out the inefficient. Borrowing is appropriate for financing long gestation projects.

Benefit taxes occupy a pivotal place in local public finance. For many 'collective' local public services, benefits are not measurable and beneficiaries not identifiable. Thus, levying user charge is difficult. However, when a clear linkage between taxes and services is established, earmarked benefit taxes act as indirect user charges or 'surrogate prices'. Nobel laureate Buchanan (1963) regards 'earmarking' as a 'first best' operational way to address the fundamental normative problem of public economics: how to provide services that match peoples' preferences. Earmarking introduces market prices in the budgetary process and facilitates rational choice by tax-payers. The efficacy of earmarking, however, depends on the following conditions:

1. Expenditure specificity: Expenditures to be financed by earmarked revenues are well defined and specific in that taxpayers can identify their obvious benefits,
2. Tight earmarking: The linkage between earmarked revenues and expenditures is tight at the margin and
3. Strong benefit linkage: Revenues are in the form of direct user charges such as payments for use and indirect user charges such as specific benefit taxes.

Drawing from research in public economics, we suggest the following framework for matching municipal responsibilities and revenues: (a) the 'essentially municipal' functions be financed by user charges, fees and other 'own revenues', including benefit taxes, (b) the 'agency' functions by intergovernmental transfers, primarily based on centre–state partnerships, with a small contribution by the municipality to induce 'ownership', and (c) the 'shared' functions, through a mix of user charges, benefit taxes and 'revenue-shared' taxes. Earmarking of benefit taxes is desirable when clear linkages are established between services and taxes. Intergovernmental transfers are appropriate when municipal functions involve significant spillovers or vertical and horizontal imbalances are overwhelming. As the benefits from lumpy infrastructure investments spread over generations, borrowing is an efficient and equitable way to finance the same. Debt repayment needs to be linked to user charges, benefit charges and benefit taxes.

Professional Urban Management

The issues of urban management are central to any strategy to address the urban fiscal problem. Efficient and accountable delivery of services, prudent management of expenditures and cost-effective collection of revenues depend on the quality of urban managers. Perhaps, the single most important problem plaguing cities in India at present is the lack of professional management capacity in municipalities. The establishment of robust systems of expenditure assignment, revenue assignment and revenue–expenditure matching is necessary, but by no means sufficient for the efficient delivery of services to citizens. There is a need to ensure that right functionaries with right incentives are placed in the right position to plan, finance, manage and monitor civic infrastructure and services. They must be equipped with the skill, competency, technical know-how and managerial expertise required to perform the tasks assigned.

As a rule, the services delivered by functionaries must be commensurate with financial outlays. Managers must be responsible for performance, which needs to be measured and monitored. An accountability framework for service delivery must be established. Mechanisms for upward accountability to higher levels of government for funds provided and downward accountability to general public for services delivered should be specified by law. In this regard, the role of management information system (MIS) is crucial. It involves the collection, organisation, management, use and dissemination of information. A robust MIS is the key to the performance of individuals, organisations and institutions. It encompasses financial management, including budgeting, accounting, and internal control and auditing; human resource management, including appointing, promoting, transfering and performance tracking; service delivery management, including service level benchmarking; public works management, including procurement; grievances redressal and so on. New technology, including smart e-governance and m-governance tools, GIS, Global Positioning System (GPS), Computer Aided Mass Appraisal (CAMA), remote sensing and geo-informatics can lead to significant improvements in city planning and service delivery outcomes.

Urban Public Finance Reforms

The anatomy of India's urban fiscal problem suggests that multiple factors that are responsible for the abysmal state of urban public finance at present need to be addressed simultaneously. Cutting across expenditure assignment, revenue assignment, revenue-expenditure matching and urban management, these factors include:

1. Low level and poor quality of infrastructure and services provided by municipal authorities, adversely affecting the willingness of citizens to pay taxes, charges and fees;
2. Inadequate taxation powers with municipalities, not commensurate with the financing needs of the functions mandated to them by the Constitution (74th Amendment) Act;
3. Inappropriate user charges that do not relate to user costs, resulting in insufficient cost recovery to meet operation and maintenance expenditures of services and recoup capital costs;

4. Inadequate mobilisation of revenues due to weaknesses in public administration to identify revenue bases, rationalise rates, improve collection efficiency and exploit revenue potential;
5. Complex procedures for the assessment and collection of taxes, fees and charges, and settlement of disputes;
6. Numerous tax exemptions and subsidies that are wrongly designed or not well-targeted and which lead to corruption;
7. Absence of an appropriate intergovernmental transfer system to address vertical and horizontal imbalances, inter-jurisdictional spillovers and needs of urban poverty alleviation, slum upgradation and core infrastructure;
8. Non-exploitation of borrowing as a versatile instrument to finance long-gestation urban and regional infrastructure projects linked to user charges, benefit charges, benefit taxes, development financing tools and value capture mechanisms;
9. Lack of robust budgeting, accounting, expenditure control, performance tracking, auditing, fiscal responsibility and public disclosure frameworks in municipalities to convince citizens and lenders that the mobilised resources are properly used and accounted for.

As regards expenditure assignment, the list of 18 municipal functions in the 12th Schedule has gained wide acceptance with policymakers and administrators. Robust activity mapping based on the 'subsidiarity' principle could ensure further clarity in expenditure assignment. However, what is worrying is that revenue assignment and civic administration continue to remain deficient. The narrow resource base of municipalities, non-availability of fiscal instruments linked to agglomeration externalities and economic growth, and lack of capacity in municipalities to effectively manage finances and services are primarily responsible for the present state of affairs. If cities are to drive growth and structural transformation, lifting India to the status of a developed country, the factors underlying the precarious state of urban public finance will need to be addressed in earnest. This book draws lessons from theoretical and empirical research in public economics, urban economics, NGT, NEG and general management to suggest a roadmap for reforms in urban public finance in India.

This book identifies the lack of clarity, consistency, adequacy and predictability in municipal taxation, user charging, intergovernmental transfers, development financing and value creation-capture-recycling as key factors plaguing urban finances in India. It also recognises the need to align particular types of revenue sources to particular categories of expenditures so that services can be delivered in a responsive, transparent, accountable and 'as needed' manner. Further, urban management, including financial management, needs to be strengthened; many factors responsible for the current fiscal problem in municipalities relate to the constraints of their organisational structure and management systems.

Primarily centred on resource mobilisation to finance civic infrastructure and services, this book makes an attempt to address some fundamental questions of revenue assignment:

1. How can the tax structure be revamped to enable municipalities to mobilise an adequate share of the growing taxable capacity in the urban economy that accompanies spatial concentration of economic activity and growth?
2. What fiscal instruments need to be authorised to ULBs so that they can exploit external economies of agglomeration while mitigating congestion diseconomies, and in the process mobilise resources on 'users pay', 'beneficiaries pay', 'polluters pay', 'exacerbaters pay' and 'congesters pay' principles?
3. What is the potential of recovering the full costs of civic services and infrastructure by municipalities and other authorities from direct and indirect users? How can 'growth pays' principle be adopted in a big way?
4. How can central and state transfer systems be designed to correct for vertical and horizontal imbalances and inter-jurisdictional spillovers? In particular, how can municipalities be enabled to discharge redistributive functions such as urban poverty alleviation, slum upgradation and protection of the interests of weaker sections?
5. How should the required costs of critical urban and regional infrastructure facilities like public transit, which facilitate growth and whose benefits spillover multiple jurisdictions be met?[14]
6. Urban land being a largely untapped resource, how can urban land taxation, land development financing and value capture financing instruments be adopted to finance the capital improvement plans of cities and their regions?

In this book, we focus on municipal finances and do not directly deal with the finances of parastatals like urban development authorities and water supply and sewerage boards in view of the constraints of data. Some municipal governments in India do discharge urban planning and water supply and sewerage functions, and our discussions on municipal finances cover the instruments adopted by parastatal authorities. Thus, the broad conclusions from our analysis would not undergo change if parastatal finances are taken into account. Our primary attention is on principles and practices of urban public finance with a view to strengthening the third tier. The potential contribution of this tier to economic growth and productivity is yet to be harnessed. For a large federal country like India, the third tier deserves to have its own unique place in the scheme of national development.

Notes

1. Office of the Registrar General (2011); the Census defines an urban area as a statutory place with a municipality, corporation, cantonment board or notified town area committee and so on—called statutory town or a place satisfying the following three criteria simultaneously: (a) a minimum population of 5,000; (b) at least 75 per cent of male working population engaged in non-agricultural pursuits; and (c) a density of population of at least 400 per sq. km. (1,000/sq. mile) called census town.
2. It may be noted that there is no uniform definition of 'urban area' adopted by countries. However, the United Nations adopts the country definitions as they are.
3. Attributed to Robert Metcalfe, the co-inventor of Ethernet, the law states that the value of a network increases with the square of the number of members in the network. Though conceived in the context of computer networking technology, the law applies to transportation, communication and other networks as well.
4. Ministry of Urban Affairs, GoI.
5. Although the term 'urban' is broader than 'municipal', we use the terms 'urban' and 'municipal' interchangeably in this book with a primary focus on municipalities and their finances.
6. The data on commercial tax collection are based on tax returns filed; they do not provide a picture of collection by district of origin.
7. Figures are based on reports submitted by state governments to the 14th Finance Commission of India, ASCI (2014) and Indian Public Finance Statistics 2013–14.
8. Based on data submitted by state governments to the 14th Finance Commission of India, ASCI (2014) and Indian Public Finance Statistics 2013–14.
9. Based on data furnished by state governments to the 14th Finance Commission of India, ASCI (2014).
10. See Buckley (2005) for Poland and South Africa, Afonso and Araujo (2006) for Brazil and OECD (2012) for other countries.
11. The data submitted by state governments to the 14th Finance Commission contain certain gaps. However, these are the only up to date figures available to arrive at an all India picture on municipal finances. A comparison between the data for 2007–08 submitted by state governments to the 13th Finance Commission (mostly unaudited) and the data for 2007–08 submitted to the 14th Finance Commission (mostly audited) suggests that the figures for 2012–13 might reflect an under-estimation to the tune of 10 per cent.

The author's simulation exercises reveal that the broad conclusions regarding the size of the municipal sector presented in this chapter are robust and apply even when the figures are modified to take into account the likely gaps.

12. Per capita revenue and capital expenditures for municipal corporations, municipalities and nagar panchayats are estimated by ASCI (2014) as 2,869 and 1,491; 962 and 790; and 982 and 424 respectively.

13. The word 'octroi' is of French origin—derived from 'octroyer', which means 'confer, authorise, empower'. Octroi empowered local governments to tax goods entering their boundaries for use, sale or consumption therein. The 1919 GoI Act reserved octroi exclusively for local bodies. The tax has been the most important source of municipal revenues in states till its abolition. Currently, octroi is levied only in Mumbai—likely to be abolished in view of the new GST regime.

14. The 12th Schedule includes roads and public amenities under municipal functions, but not public transit specifically. However, as this book deals with the principles and practices of financing core city services and infrastructure, it will cover public transit facilities, whether provided by municipalities or regional authorities.

3

A Portfolio of Municipal Taxes

A Model of Municipal Taxation

The public finance literature presents the following simplistic model to analyse the key issues in municipal taxation (Bahl and Linn 1992):

$$T = t \times e \times (B - L) \qquad (3.1)$$

where T = total tax collection, t = tax rate, e = collection efficiency or collection rate, B = tax base and L = leakage, that is, part of the tax base not brought to the tax net.

Alternatively, Equation 3.1 can be presented with slight modification as follows:

$$T = t \times e \times c \times B \qquad (3.2)$$

where $c = (B - L)/B$ = coverage ratio, that is, ratio of the portion of tax base included in tax registry divided by tax base.

As Equation (3.2) shows, the tax revenues mobilised by a municipality depend on its tax base, coverage ratio or extent of access to tax base, tax rate and collection efficiency. Empirical research suggests that local taxes have high visibility and tax-payers vehemently resist high local tax rates. Thus, expanding tax base, plugging leakages and improving collection performance are preferred directions for enhancing municipal tax revenues.

This chapter deals with the issues of tax base of municipalities in India. Presenting an overview of municipal taxation in the country, we refer to international practices and public finance principles to draw lessons for reforming the municipal tax system in India. In particular, we emphasise the need to equip municipalities with a portfolio of taxes that relate to agglomeration of economic activity and economic growth. We propose to connect municipal taxation to agglomeration economies of cities following the 'beneficiaries pay' principle. The presence of externalities in cities calls for broadening the definition of benefits to include direct as well as externality-induced general benefits. Later chapters in this book discuss other financing principles and mechanisms such as 'users pay', 'polluters pay', 'exacerbaters pay', 'congesters pay' and 'growth pays'.

Municipal Taxes in India

While 'own' taxes accounted for 32 per cent of municipal revenues in India in 2012–13, the country's municipal tax–GDP ratio is very small. The figure, which was 0.39 per cent in 2002–03 and 0.40 per cent in 2007–08, has also declined to 0.33 per cent in 2012–13.[1] This is low compared to central tax–GDP ratio of 10.3 per cent and state tax–GDP ratio of 6.8 per cent in 2012–13 (see Finance Commission of India 2015, 56). In contrast, the local tax–GDP ratio was more than two per cent in 22 out of 34 OECD countries in 2010. Excepting for unitary countries, which have robust systems of central–local transfers, the ratio exceeded four per cent; it was 16.1 per cent in Sweden, 12.7 per cent in Denmark, 10.4 per cent in Finland, 7.2 per cent in Japan, 4.2 per cent in Korea and four per cent in the United States (OECD 2012). Unlike developed countries, municipalities in India do not have access to a portfolio of versatile non-property taxes such as income tax and GST. Out of 34 OECD countries, income tax is the dominant local tax in 14 and GST in six countries (see Table 3.1).

Municipal taxation in India suffers from two basic problems. First, municipalities do not have access to a broad basket of 'own' taxes, commensurate with their mandated responsibilities (see Table 3.2). Second, even the potential of assigned taxes, such as property tax, is not fully exploited by municipalities due to poor design of tax mobilisation instruments and inefficiency of tax administration.

Octroi, a 'distortionary' tax, is abolished in all cities of India excepting Mumbai. However, states that abolished octroi have not been able to assign to their municipalities an alternative source as high-yielding and buoyant as octroi. In fact, octroi accounted for upto 70 per cent of municipal revenues before abolition, compared to a 20 per cent share of property tax (Rao and Singh 2005). Ironically, compensations from state governments to municipalities for the loss of octroi have remained at abysmally low levels. In a few states, 'own' municipal taxes include profession tax, entertainment tax and advertisement tax. In a few others, profession tax, entertainment tax, motor vehicles tax and stamp duty are collected by state authorities and shared with municipalities. However, unlike developed countries, municipalities in India do not have access to taxes with income, business, sales, value added or goods and services as a base that keeps pace with economic growth.

VLT is a separate tax under municipal statute in states like Andhra Pradesh. Even without a separate legal provision, VLT can be levied as a variant of property tax. However, most municipalities in India, including those in Maharashtra and Gujarat, which benefited significantly from octroi for long, do not levy VLT. This is presumably due to the vested interests of landowning classes. It appears that local authorities have failed to impress upon landowners that the increase in the value of their land due to infrastructure investments financed by VLT could be many times more than the amounts paid by them.

International Perspectives

In the United States, municipalities have access to a broad range of taxes. They levy property tax, local option income and sales taxes, excise tax, payroll tax, motor vehicles tax, gasoline tax and a variety of special taxes (see Box 3.1). Larger cities rely more on income and sales taxes and less on property tax. Apart from taxes, US municipalities have recourse to special assessments, developer exactions, impact fees, tax-free and taxable bonds, bond banks, revolving loan funds, lease purchase contracting, tax increment financing, etc. The hallmark of US local finance is the absence of too many specifications. State governments assign taxes to municipalities and fix their maximum rates. Rules are clear as to whether a municipality needs to seek voter referenda on matters such as setting tax rates, undertaking new borrowing and so on. Municipalities can also formulate their own user charges. The result of openness in tax assignment rules in the United States has been a relatively flexible and smoothly-functioning municipal finance system.

The financing regimes of local authorities in the United Kingdom include: (a) a system of non-domestic rates, being property tax on industrial and commercial property—set and collected nationally and distributed among local jurisdictions based on adult population, (b) a system of

Table 3.1

Distribution of Local Taxes: OECD Countries, 2010

	Local Taxes			As % of Local Taxes			
	As % of Total Taxes	As % of Local Revenues	As % of GDP	Income*	Goods and Services	Property	Other**
Australia	3.5	n.a.	0.9	0.0	0.0	100.0	0.0
Austria	3.3	62.0	1.4	61.4	9.9	15.4	13.3
Belgium	5.1	n.a.	2.2	36.7	9.9	53.2	0.3
Canada	10.2	n.a.	3.2	0.0	2.0	91.2	6.8
Chile	6.2	n.a.	1.2	0.0	59.7	40.3	0.0
Czech Republic	1.3	n.a.	0.5	0.0	48.5	51.5	0.0
Denmark	26.7	36.1	12.7	89.0	0.1	10.8	0.1
Estonia	13.4	49.0	4.7	89.6	2.6	7.8	0.0
Finland	24.4	46.2	10.4	93.6	0.0	6.3	0.1
France	10.8	n.a.	4.6	8.4	25.3	53.8	12.5
Germany	7.0	40.0	2.9	78.1	6.0	15.8	0.1
Greece	1.1	n.a.	0.3	0.0	21.4	24.0	54.7
Hungary	6.4	21.2	2.4	0.2	80.0	14.2	5.6
Iceland	25.5	n.a.	9.0	77.4	2.0	20.6	0.0
Ireland	3.2	14.8	0.9	0.0	0.0	100.0	0.0
Israel	7.5	n.a.	2.4	0.0	4.8	95.2	0.0

Italy	15.4	40.1	6.6	25.0	32.9	9.4	32.7
Japan	25.9	n.a.	7.2	48.6	19.4	29.8	2.2
Korea	16.7	n.a.	4.2	16.8	26.7	16.3	40.1
Luxembourg	4.4	31.2	1.6	92.2	1.4	4.4	2.0
Mexico	1.2	n.a.	0.2	0.3	1.7	59.3	38.7
Netherlands	3.8	n.a.	1.5	0.0	50.0	47.6	2.3
New Zealand	7.2	n.a.	2.3	0.0	8.7	91.3	0.0
Norway	13.6	41.1	5.8	88.5	1.4	4.8	5.3
Poland	12.7	n.a.	4.0	58.2	8.3	29.1	4.4
Portugal	5.7	34.3	1.8	34.6	26.4	33.9	5.2
Slovak Republic	2.9	n.a.	0.8	0.0	49.2	50.8	0.0
Slovenia	10.9	42.0	4.2	78.5	6.5	11.9	3.2
Spain	9.5	45.1	3.1	20.6	39.2	29.6	10.6
Sweden	35.4	n.a.	16.1	97.4	0.0	2.6	0.0
Switzerland	15.6	n.a.	4.4	84.3	1.3	1.4	13.1
Turkey	9.5	n.a.	2.4	24.5	49.8	11.1	14.5
United Kingdom	5.1	12.7	1.8	0.0	0.0	100.0	0.0
United States	16.1	n.a.	4.0	5.2	21.4	73.4	0.1

Source: OECD (2012). Revenue Statistics, 1965–2011.

Notes: * Includes income and payroll taxes.

** Includes social security contributions, other property-related taxes and other taxes.

Table 3.2

Major Own Tax Revenue Sources of Municipal Corporations in India

Name of State	Name of Municipal Corporation	Major Taxes
Bihar	Patna	Property tax; 9rofession tax
Delhi	Delhi	Property tax: advertisement tax; tax on consumption and sale of electricity; toll tax
Gujarat	Ahmedabad	Property tax; vehicles tax
Karnataka	Bengaluru	Property tax; advertisement tax
Kerala	Kochi	Property tax; profession tax
Madhya Pradesh	Indore	Property tax; advertisement tax
Maharashtra	Mumbai	Octroi; property tax
Odisha	Bhubaneswar	Property tax; advertisement tax
Punjab	Ludhiana	Property tax
Rajasthan	Jaipur	Property tax
Tamil Nadu	Chennai	Property tax; profession tax
Telangana	Hyderabad	Property tax; profession tax; entertainment tax
Uttar Pradesh	Varanasi	Property Tax; advertisement tax
West Bengal	Kolkata	Property tax; profession Tax; advertisement tax.

Source: Budgets of Municipal Corporations.

exchequer grants, principally the revenue support grant (RSG) designed to compensate local authorities for differences in the cost of providing municipal services, (c) a capital finance system (grants and loans) within which local authorities are also able to partner with the private sector under the private finance initiative (PFI) and (d) a system of local domestic taxation, known as council tax. Grants from the central government, however, constitute 70–80 per cent of the expenditures of local bodies in the United Kingdom (McKinsey 2010, 21).

Municipalities in Brazil have access to urban land and property tax, real estate transfer tax, service tax on base other than that assigned to states, and a share in state and federal value added tax (VAT), federal income tax, federal financial transactions tax, state motor vehicles tax, etc. In 2005, Brazilian municipalities received the following shares: federal income tax, 22.5 per cent; federal VAT on manufactured goods, 22.5 per cent;

Box 3.1

Municipal Finance Regime in California, United States

The municipal finance regime in California state comprises the following:

General taxes: These include sales and use tax, property tax, transient occupancy tax, utility user taxes, business licensing taxes, vehicle licensing fees, property transfer tax, etc. The sales and use tax covers tax on sales as well as purchases for transactions in which sales tax is not collected. Property tax is an ad valorem tax limited to one per cent of the assessed value, excluding voter-approved rates to fund debt. Utility user taxes are imposed on utilities such as electricity, gas, telephone and cable television. The utility bills the customer collects tax as part of its normal operations and credits to local government. Transient occupancy tax is levied on the occupation of rooms in a hotel, motel, inn, tourism home or other lodge where the occupancy is 30 days or less. Tax rate ranges from 4 to 15 per cent. Business licensing taxes are linked to gross receipts or levied at a flat rate. Sometimes they are based on the quantity of goods produced, number employed, square footage of business premises, etc. Vehicle licensing fee is levied on ownership of registered vehicle. Property transfer tax is imposed when a transaction in property occurs. In 2005, the contributions of taxes to municipal 'general purpose' revenue of Californian cities were: sales and use tax, 30–45 per cent; property tax, 25–35 per cent; utility user taxes, 15–22 per cent; transient occupancy tax, 7–17 per cent, business licensing taxes, 3–6 per cent; vehicle licensing fee, one per cent; and property transfer tax, one per cent.

Special taxes: These are taxes imposed for special purposes which are placed into general fund of local government or kept in a separate account to meet the costs of specific facilities and services such as public libraries, fire safety, paramedic services, etc. Unlike property tax, they are not ad valorem and must be uniformly applied to all eligible properties on square footage basis. In 2005, special taxes accounted for three per cent of total municipal revenues in California.

Special assessments: These aim at particular and distinct benefits over and above general benefits conferred on real property located in the benefit area or on the public at large. Each parcel of property meets a reasonable cost of the proportionate special benefit conferred on it. Special assessments are applied to meet the cost of infrastructure improvements such as public transit, street paving, parking, drainage, water supply, sewerage, street lighting, fire protection, gas supply, tree plantation, landscaping, parks and playgrounds, etc. Sometimes bonds are issued to mobilise resources for these improvements subject to repayment tied to special assessments. In 2005, special assessments provided for one per cent of total municipal revenues in California.

Service charges, fees and permits: These include charges for services such as water, sewer, refuse, and so on, development impact fees aimed at addressing the consequences of new development, permit and application fees, regulation fees, and property-related fees and charges. In 2005, service charges accounted for 39 per cent of total municipal revenues in California; fees, licenses, permits and so on, accounted for another 10 per cent.

Source: League of California Cities (2005).

federal financial operations tax on gold, 70 per cent; federal rural land and property tax, 50 per cent; state tax on motor vehicles, 50 per cent; and state VAT on goods and interstate and intercity transportation and communication services, 25 per cent (Afonso and Araujo 2006).

China is one of world's most decentralised countries, with the central government accounting for just 20 per cent of the national budgetary expenditures in 2007. The rest was distributed subnationally: provincial, 18 per cent; municipal/prefecture, 20 per cent; and county and township, 40 per cent (Wong 2013). Municipal revenue sources in China include business taxes, real estate tax, resource taxes, urban land use tax, land appreciation tax, urban maintenance and construction tax, farm land occupation tax, deed tax, tax on vehicles, fixed assets capital gains tax, share in domestic VAT, income tax and stamp taxes, etc. In 2003, sub-provincial governments in China received the following shares from national and provincial taxes: VAT, 19 per cent; business taxes, 70 per cent; enterprise income tax, 21 per cent; individual income tax, 24 per cent; urban maintenance and construction tax, 90 per cent; and agriculture taxes, 96 per cent (Qiao and Shah 2006). Table 3.3 presents the composition of tax revenues by level and source in China in 2007.

As Table 3.3 shows, at municipal/prefecture level, business tax—levied on services—is the most important tax in China, followed by VAT and corporation income tax. The deed tax, an ad valorem levy on turnover of land and property, is the fourth most productive tax. This, along with property tax, land VAT and urban land use tax accounted for 17.4 per cent of municipal/prefecture revenues in 2007. The urban maintenance and construction tax, which is a surcharge on VAT, is also an important source of city revenues in China.

International practice in municipal taxation reveals that countries can be divided into two groups: a small number with local governments not important or depending heavily on central transfers (sometimes accounting for more than 70 per cent of their revenues) and the majority with municipalities relying on a broad range of taxes. The latter enable their municipalities to have access to productive and buoyant tax instruments linked to income, payroll, business, sales, value added, or goods and services base in addition to land and property taxes. International practice further reveals that there is an increasing search for local tax instruments that subscribe to the 'benefit principle', namely, those benefitting from local public facilities must pay towards their costs. This is because benefit taxes find less resistance from tax-payers compared to other types of taxes.

Table 3.3

Composition of Tax Revenues in China by Administrative Level and Source, 2007 (Percentage of Total)

Tax	National (2010)	Province	Municipality/ Prefecture	County
Business Tax	13.9	39.2	31.1	31.7
Value Added Tax*	39.2	17.4	19.2	21.1
Corporation Income Tax	15.9	24.3	15.4	12.5
Deed Tax	3.1	2.5	9.6	6.4
Urban Maintenance & Construction Tax	2.3	2.2	7.8	7.1
Personal Income Tax	6.0	10.1	5.8	5.3
Property Tax	-	0.8	3.6	4.0
Land Value-added Tax*	1.1	0.8	2.4	2.8
Urban Land Use Tax	1.6	0.6	1.8	2.7
Stamp Tax	1.2	1.1	1.8	1.9
Resource Tax	1.3	1.0	0.7	1.7
Farmland Occupation Tax	0.5	0.1	0.4	1.9
Vehicle Purchase Tax	1.1	0.0	0.4	0.5
Tobacco Tax	2.2	0.0	0.0	0.3

Source: China Ministry of Finance: Compendium of Local Fiscal Statistics (2007) and Wong (2013).

Note: * The national VAT includes VAT and excise on imports.

Principles of Tax Assignment

While countries differ in regard to tax assignment to municipalities, the theory of fiscal federalism presents certain principles of tax assignment, ranging from broad criteria to rationale for specific taxes. It addresses the question: '[W]ho should tax, where and what?' (Bahl 2001; Bird 1992, 2010a, 2010b; Musgrave 1983 and Oates 1972, 1999). The theory suggests that taxes dealing with redistribution or stabilisation, taxes on mobile factors, taxes requiring national level information and involving significant economies of scale in administration should be levied by federal government. Musgrave (1983) advocates the following principles of tax assignment in a federation:

1. Taxes suitable for economic stabilisation should be levied by central government;
2. Progressive redistributional taxes should be assigned to central government;
3. Personal taxes with progressive rates should be levied by the jurisdictions most capable of implementing tax on a global base;
4. Lower-level governments should tax revenue bases with low mobility between jurisdictions;
5. Tax bases distributed highly unequally between jurisdictions should be centralised; and
6. Benefit taxes and user charges may be appropriately used at all levels, especially in cities.

Researchers often club provincial and local governments under the head 'sub-national'. Bahl and Bird (2008) suggest the following principles of revenue assignment to sub-national governments:

1. Own-source revenues should ideally be sufficient to enable at least the richest sub-national government to finance from its own resources the services that primarily benefit residents;
2. To the extent possible, taxes levied by sub-national governments should burden their residents, preferably in relation to the benefits they receive from services;
3. Governments at all levels should bear clear public responsibility at the margin for financing expenditures for which they are politically responsible; and
4. Sub-national taxes should not unduly distort the allocation of resources.

Property tax, motor vehicles tax, surcharges on national personal income taxes, payroll taxes, well-designed regional VATs and business taxes are considered suitable for meeting the expenditure requirements of sub-national governments (Bahl and Bird 2008).

Some researchers also refer to the principles of 'local tax'. A local tax is one for which the local authority defines tax base, sets tax rate, collects tax and retains revenue for its own purposes (Bailey 1999). Bird (2006) presents the following attributes of a 'good local tax':

1. The tax base should be relatively immobile to allow the local authorities to vary tax rates without losing the base;
2. The tax should yield adequate revenues to meet local needs and also be sufficiently buoyant over time;

3. The tax should be stable and predictable over time;
4. It should not be possible to export the tax burden to non-residents except to the extent that such burden captures the benefits that non-residents obtain from local services;
5. The tax base should be visible to ensure accountability;
6. Taxpayers should perceive the tax to be reasonable fair; and
7. The tax should be relatively easy to administer.

A summary of the criteria identified by public finance literature for the choice of municipal taxes is presented below:

Efficiency:	Local taxes should promote allocative efficiency. Local voters should pay local taxes so that the use of service reflects their willingness to pay.
Equity:	The notions of vertical and horizontal equity should apply as far as possible.
Transparency:	Voters should know exactly how much they pay in taxes and receive in services.
Economy:	Local taxes should be collected with the least costs.
Local autonomy:	Local governments should be free to determine the rates at which local taxes are set.
Adequacy:	Local taxes should be adequate to finance the functions assigned, with an elastic tax base, expanding as fast as expenditures.
Revenue stability:	There should not be undue fluctuations in the flow of local revenues.
Immobility of tax base:	Local taxes may be linked to immobile tax bases such as land and building. This does not rule out the imposition of other taxes.

Unfortunately, research in public economics does not find many taxes satisfying the earlier-mentioned criteria. It regards taxes on immobile factors, especially urban land value tax and property tax as ideal taxes in terms of the criteria of local tax. However, research in urban economics and NEG provide useful hints for the prioritisation of taxes to be levied at local and regional levels. In particular, a recent body of research in NEG argues that agglomeration externalities in cities, apart from creating 'agglomeration rents' to immobile factors, create such rents to mobile factors which could be taxed without creating distortionary effects in the economy (See Anderson and Forslid 2003, Baldwin and Krugman 2004, Borck and Pfluger 2006, Ludema and Wooton 2000).

NEG refers to two key forces of agglomeration. The first is access to market. The closer firms are to a cluster of economic activity, the better their access to market for selling goods. Firms locate near workers, as the latter constitute their customers. Workers locate near firms as they get higher real wages and opportunities for learning in the vicinity of firms. The second force of agglomeration is access to producers. Final goods producers want to be close to their intermediate inputs suppliers and vice versa. A city with vibrant agglomeration economies can, thus, tax the mobile factors more without losing its mobile activities. If the tax on 'agglomeration rents' is used to provide the local public goods needed by firms and households, a further agglomerating force is set in motion. This could lead to 'circular and cumulative causation' and a self-financed process of planned urban development. Thus, the benefit principle, covering direct or specific and externality-induced or general benefits, ought to be a key criterion in the choice of municipal taxes. We call this the 'generalised benefit principle' and regard it as the hallmark of urban public finance.

Agglomeration externalities benefit many actors in the urban economy in many ways. The municipal tax system thus needs to be broad-based to apply the generalised benefit principle. For example, a local sales tax or transient occupancy tax can enable a municipality to capture some of the benefits it creates for visitors. Similarly, a 'piggyback' income tax, payroll tax, excise tax, business tax or GST can capture a part of the agglomeration rents accruing to businesses and residents. A broad portfolio of municipal taxes is also warranted on other considerations, such as revenue adequacy and moderate tax rates to minimise distortionary effects of local taxes. Externalities in cities call for design of municipal tax instruments to capture external benefits and promotion of investments to facilitate further agglomeration economies. They emphasise the need for establishing a close connection between local government revenues and expenditures.[2]

Land-based taxes are ideal benefit taxes. However, they are not as productive and buoyant as taxes with income, business or sales as a base. In fact, no developed country is able to raise more than 10 per cent of total tax revenues from property tax (OECD 2010, 181). Thus, in addition to assigning land and property taxes, countries enable ULBs to have access to motor vehicles tax, 'piggyback' income tax, payroll tax, VAT, GST, excise tax, business tax, financial tax and the like. These are general benefit taxes on the living, working and shopping in a city. As Bahl and Linn (2014, 16) observe:

Even flat-rate local income taxes can to a certain extent be justified on the grounds of the benefit principle, since high-quality local services will support the economic growth and income-generating capacity of a city.... Local business taxes, excises, and sales taxes may also be appropriate for metropolitan governments, to the extent that they reflect the costs and benefits of business services provided by the local government.

Land and Property Taxes

Land tax is levied on land only as base. Principal variants of land tax include VLT, LVT and land value increment tax (LVIT). Property tax is imposed on both land and improvements thereon. Immobility of tax base and capitalisation of local public expenditures on infrastructure and services into property values are factors that make land and property taxes, including real estate transfer tax attractive benefit taxes. These instruments make beneficiaries pay for collective benefits.

Property tax is levied on residential and non-residential properties. Non-residential property tax tends to get 'exported' when local jurisdictions are fragmented, causing distortion and blurring accountability of local government. Those paying taxes may not be the ones receiving benefits. However, administrative jurisdictions of Indian cities are fairly large. There is considerable evidence that agglomeration economies are vibrant in cities, generating externality-induced benefits for business. Thus, the bias of researchers against non-residential property tax on consideration of efficiency may not be called for in the Indian context. Such arguments are also not helpful while examining how the massive requirement of cities for capital investment, to the tune of ₹3.92 million crores over 2012–31, can be financed.[3] In fact, if non-residential property taxes are escrowed to finance critical infrastructure facilities in cities with vibrant agglomeration externalities, business enterprises may gain much more than what they pay by way of property tax.

Local Motor Vehicles Tax

Key variants of motor vehicles tax include: tax on value of vehicle and license fee to operate a vehicle. The latter is based on attributes such as age, engine capacity, axle weight and use. Apart from being benefit taxes, motor vehicles taxes are revenue-elastic and stable. They recoup the cost of investment in transportation infrastructure. Vehicle taxes are also called 'green' taxes in view of their beneficial impacts on the environment. They act against traffic congestion and air pollution. Ironically, cities account for 70 per cent of energy consumption and greenhouse gas emissions globally. Personalised motor vehicles play a key role in this. Economists thus make a strong case for taxing automobile ownership and use. However, only when city jurisdictions are not fragmented as in most Indian cities, do vehicles taxes satisfy the criteria of a good local tax.

Barcelona, Budapest, Istanbul and Madrid levy 'vehicles tax' on residents based on the value of the vehicle. Tokyo imposes 'automobile acquisition tax' on vehicle purchase. Seoul charges an 'automobile tax' to owners of cars linked to both vehicle capacity and use. Beijing, Shanghai and Guangzhou levy vehicle tax based on use. In Toronto, 'personal vehicle tax' (PVT) is levied since 2008; drivers pay PVT while renewing vehicle license plates (Martinez-Vazquez 2013). Singapore and Milan tax higher-polluting vehicles more heavily. Ahmedabad collects 'vehicle tax' at the rate of 1–2.5 per cent of a vehicle's value.

'Piggyback' Income Tax

The case for municipalities having access to income tax base rests on several arguments. First, a city income tax is a general benefit tax; quality infrastructure and services contribute to economic growth and personal and corporation incomes in cities by catalysing agglomeration economies and enhancing the productivity of workers and firms. Second, income tax is a buoyant tax that increases with growth; during booms it could finance critical infrastructure facilities that can be maintained with ease during recessions. Third, redistributive functions like urban poverty alleviation, slum upgradation and welfare of weaker sections are ideally financed by income tax, being closely related to the 'ability to pay'.

In 14 out of 34 OECD countries, income tax was the dominant local tax in 2010. These countries enable cities to 'piggyback' onto federal or state income tax. Piggyback income tax is also practiced in Moscow and Lagos. Rome and Milan charge an extra five per cent on national income tax. Tokyo, Geneva and Lisbon levy a surcharge on national corporation income tax (Martinez-Vazquez 2013, 202). In the United States, 18 states permit municipalities to levy local option income tax. New York City piggybacks onto state income tax. In 2009, personal income tax accounted for 11 per cent of the city's total revenues and 18 per cent of tax revenues. New York City also levies general corporation tax (GCT) at 8.85 per cent of income allocated to the city. In 2009,

GCT accounted for 3.8 per cent of the city's total revenue and 6.5 per cent of taxes mobilised (Rubin 2010, vii). Individual and corporation income taxes had a share of 66 per cent in Tokyo's tax revenues in 2008 (Martinez-Vazquez 2013, 202–04).

Local Payroll Tax

Payroll tax usually represents a percentage of wages that employers disburse to their employees. In several countries, federal and state governments levy some form of payroll tax. In the United States, municipalities are authorised to levy local option payroll tax. In Mexico, the national district in Mexico City metropolitan area imposes a payroll tax by place of work.

Payroll taxes subscribe to the benefit principle. They also yield sizable revenues even when tax rates are low. Further, they are not difficult to administer. Some critics argue that payroll taxes discourage employment in the formal sector and are distortionary. However, when agglomeration externalities are vibrant in cities and the rate of payroll tax is low, 'agglomeration rents' accruing to firms and workers may more than offset the payroll taxes paid. These taxes may be dedicated for public transportation, benefitting employees.

In France, establishments located in designated urban transport areas and employing more than nine persons pay a percentage of their wage bill as *versement transport* or transport tax. Initially applied to areas with more than 3,00,000 people, the tax was subsequently extended to communities with more than 10,000 residents. The tax rate varies from 1.4 per cent to 2.6 per cent in the Ile de France or metropolitan Paris region. It is limited to 0.9 per cent in areas with fewer than 1,00,000 inhabitants. The transport tax has provided a stable source of funding for the development or extension of 10 light rail transit systems in France since 1985 (Scheurer et al. 2000).

Local Sales Tax

Several countries authorise municipalities to levy general and selective sales taxes to enable them to have access to a buoyant tax base that keeps pace with economic growth. Some enable local bodies to levy a local surcharge on national or state sales tax. Bangkok, Seoul and Moscow 'piggyback' onto national VAT.

In six out of 34 OECD countries, sales tax was the dominant local tax in 2010. 38 out of 50 states in the United States authorise municipalities to levy local option sales tax. Three states levy mandatory, state-wide, local 'add-on' sales taxes: California (one per cent), Utah (1.25 per cent) and Virginia (one per cent). In Chicago and Los Angeles, sales taxes are typically levied at the local level; the local sales tax rates being 3.25 per cent and 1.5 per cent respectively. New York City has been levying 'sales and use tax' since 1934; in 2009 this tax was imposed at 4.875 per cent, accounting for eight per cent of the city's total revenues and 13 per cent of total tax revenues (Rubin 2010, vii). Sales tax accounted for 39 per cent of Beijing's tax revenues in 2009 and 54 per cent for Sao Paulo in 2010 (Martinez-Vazquez 2013).

The services tax (*imposto sobre servicos*, [ISS]) is the major municipal tax in Brazil. It is levied on all services except communications, and interstate and intercity public transportation, which are taxed by states. Generally the tax is imposed on retail sales at two to five per cent of gross receipts, depending on the type of service. The ISS is criticised as being distortionary, generating cascading effects and adverse incentives to producers. Economists advocate piggybacking onto central or state sales tax, or VAT with an additional city sales tax of one to two per cent to avoid such problems, including high administration and compliance costs (Bird and Gendron 2001, and Bird and Slack 2013).

Among specific local sales taxes, two prominent candidates are motor fuel taxes and parking fees. Some cities 'piggyback' onto state fuel taxes to avoid high enforcement costs. Others levy these taxes directly or receive a share of state and federal taxes. Istanbul levies a sales tax on gasoline as 'environmental sanitation tax'. Since 2009, metropolitan cities in South Africa have been granted access to fuel taxes levied by the national government. They have a 50 per cent share of the national fuel tax levy as of November 2010 (Steytler 2013). Parking fees, extensively enforced in developed countries, have a good potential in large cities of developing countries such as India. Research makes a strong case for enabling the private sector to deal with the business of providing parking facilities in cities and confining the local authority to enforcement of street parking regulations (Barter 2010).

Local Excise Tax

Local excise taxes include a percentage levy on the manufacture, consumption or use of locally produced goods, a percentage tax on a company's total receipts and a fixed tax on an activity. They have a good revenue potential. They are also easily administered, with wholesalers acting as withholding agents. Further, they are politically acceptable. Destination-based excise taxes on alcohol and tobacco satisfy the benefit principle as local authorities are responsible for public health. Berlin, Chicago, New York, Seoul, Tokyo, Bangkok, Beijing, Shanghai, Guangzhou and Jakarta levy general excise taxes. Frankfurt levies excise taxes on alcoholic beverages; Istanbul and Lima levy such taxes on gasoline. Seoul imposes tax on businesses 'exploiting natural resources'. Some cities levy taxes on polluting businesses (Martinez-Vazquez 2013). In Punjab, cities have access to a share of excise duty on liquor.

Excise taxes on public utilities such as electricity, telephone or cable TV fit the benefit principle well because their consumption tends to be a good proxy for the use of local public services by households and businesses. Utility user taxes tend to have high income elasticity and low price elasticity. They are revenue-buoyant and progressive; they are also less distortionary. These taxes yielded 15–22 per cent of general purpose revenues of cities imposing such taxes in California in 2005 (League of California Cities 2005). Chicago imposes utility user tax on telephone services. Cape Town, Jakarta and Delhi levy tax on electricity consumption. Utility user taxes accounted for 68 per cent of Cape Town's revenues in 2009 (Martinez-Vazquez 2013).

Local Business Tax

Key variants of local business tax include: corporate franchise tax, business licensing tax and gross receipts tax. Corporate franchise tax is imposed on enterprises for doing business in a city as a legal entity. *Patente, patente municipal or patente commercial,* is levied in Latin America as a local business licensing tax. It is meant to safeguard against the adverse impacts of increased business activities such as additional garbage, traffic congestion, noise pollution and so on. Gross receipts tax is a percentage levy on the total revenue of a company.

In Germany, the local business tax is called *trade tax,* levied by deducting a tax-exempt amount from trading profits and multiplying by a rate, usually five per cent. In Budapest, a tax is imposed on net sales revenue of goods sold and services provided. Seoul levies business tax based on the size of real estate. Tokyo imposes business tax by type of business. Colombian cities levy industry and commerce (*industria y commercio*) tax. It is in the nature of a classified gross receipts tax or general turnover sales tax. The tax is levied on the revenue from industrial, commercial and service activities carried out within a local jurisdiction. The tax rate varies between 0.2 to 0.7 per cent for industrial and commercial activities and between 0.2 to one per cent for service activities. It is the most revenue-elastic form of municipal tax in Colombia and often the biggest source of revenue in its largest cities: Bogota, Cali and Medellin (Bird 2012). The single business permit, a form of industry and commerce tax, is levied in Nairobi since 1999. Chennai Municipal Corporation levies a company tax based on the paid-up capital of a company. Seoul imposes surtax on national VAT. Gross receipts tax added on national VAT accounts for 70 per cent of revenues in the capital district of Buenos Aires. Local business tax on services, levied on gross turnover at rates of three to five per cent, accounts for one-third of the city and prefecture revenues in China (Wong 2013).

The case for local business taxes derives from these being general benefit taxes. They also grow with business and yield substantial revenues. However, gross receipts tax, and industry and commerce tax varieties are distortionary. Economists, thus, recommend a generalised business tax based on the benefit principle in lieu of them. Broad-based taxes that are neutral towards factor-mix in production, such as the origin-based business value tax (BVT), are appropriate local business taxes (Bird 2003). The base of BVT resembles that of VAT. But in contrast to destination-based VAT, the BVT is origin-based, therefore taxing exports and not imports. A tax similar to BVT was introduced in Italy in 1998, and later adopted in Japan in 2004 and in France in 2010 (Bird and Slack 2013, 147).

Local Financial Tax

Some large cities impose local taxes on banks and insurance companies. For example, New York City has been levying banking corporation tax (BCT) or bank tax since 1966. This is an extra business (profit) tax on banks operating within the city. In 2009, with a tax rate of nine per cent of the entire net income allocated to New York City, the bank tax accounted for about two per cent of the city's total revenue. New York also levies an additional two per cent profit tax on insurance companies operating in the city (Rubin 2010). Lagos implements a withholding tax on interests generated by savings accounts in banks (Martinez-Vazquez 2013). Local financial taxes are considered bad in theory, yet they are meant to capture a part of the agglomeration benefits accruing to banks and insurance companies.

Local Carbon Tax

Cities resort to a range of local environmental taxes, including resource taxes. An emerging form of environmental tax is the local carbon tax. While climate change and carbon levies are adopted at the national and provincial levels,[4] Boulder city, Colorado in the United States pioneered a local carbon tax in 2006 to finance its Climate Action Plan (CAP). The base of the tax is the residential and commercial consumption of electricity generated from fossil fuel. Electricity from renewable energy sources like solar and wind power is exempted from the carbon tax. Other cities in developed countries are embarking upon carbon taxes on sources of greenhouse gas (GHG) emission such as coal-based power and refrigerants. These levies, based on the 'polluters pay' principle, are meant to take into account factors such as damages caused to the environment and public health.

Municipal Tax Reforms in India

International comparisons reveal that municipalities in India do not have recourse either to substantial intergovernmental transfers or to broad-based 'own taxes' such as land value tax, transfer of property tax, motor vehicles tax, piggyback income tax, payroll tax, sales tax, excise tax, business tax, financial tax and carbon tax. Ironically, India is peculiar in the sense that the taxation powers of ULBs have progressively dwindled over the years instead of keeping pace with urbanisation and the rising contribution of cities to economic growth.

In the 1919 GoI Act, octroi, terminal tax, and tax on trade, professions and callings were reserved for municipalities apart from land and property taxes, including LVT. The Local Finance Enquiry Committee 1951 recommended some more local taxes, namely, tax on consumption or sale of electricity, tax on advertisements other than those published in newspapers, tax on vehicles, capitation tax and tax on entertainment exclusively for municipalities. The Taxation Enquiry Commission (1953–54) added duty on transfer of property to the list. However, with octroi abolished and taxes such as profession tax, motor vehicles tax, tax on sale of electricity, entertainment tax and tax on transfer of property appropriated by states, the ULBs in many states of India have reached a situation where they cannot even meet the maintenance cost of basic civic services. Obviously, the current regime of municipal taxation in India is unsuited to address the country's challenges of urbanisation and growth. It needs to be reformed urgently.

Experience with tax reforms internationally provides lessons for the choice of a portfolio of taxes to be assigned to or shared with municipalities in India. The best approach for tax reforms in a developing country like India, excellently summarised by Bird and Oldman (1990, 3) is as follows:

> The best approach to reforming tax in a developing country—indeed in any country—is one that takes into account taxation theory, empirical evidence, and political and administrative realities and blends them with a good dose of local knowledge and a sound appraisal of the current macroeconomic and international situation to produce a feasible set of proposals sufficiently attractive to be implemented and sufficiently robust to withstand changing times, with reasons, and still produce beneficial results.

The effective design of municipal tax reforms in India calls for blending the context, theory and practice. First, the reform must be grounded in the political economy of fiscal federalism of the country to be acceptable within the democratic milieu. In this regard, a study of the taxes that India's municipalities had earlier or have at present in some states and those recommended by expert committees can be useful. Second, the choice of municipal taxes must, as far as possible, subscribe to the 'generalised benefit principle', namely, beneficiaries of city infrastructure and services must pay for their costs. Urban development needs to be seen as a process of value creation, capture and recycling. Third, the basket of municipal taxes must be adequate to ensure both enough stability and enough elasticity. In particular, this must be in a position to leverage resources to meet the investment and O&M requirements of cities projected by McKinsey (2010) and HPEC (2011).

Theory and practice provide the following broad directions for designing municipal tax reforms in India:

1. Municipal tax laws and procedures should be simplified and tax administration professionalised to implement the 'generalised benefit principle' as the cornerstone of urban public finance. Modernisation of municipal and town planning laws in consonance with the changing realities is long overdue.
2. A close connection between local taxes collected, and infrastructure facilities and services provided by municipalities needs to be established to ensure cooperation from taxpayers and accountability on the part of service providers.
3. Property tax should be reformed and supplemented by other land-based taxes. As local public expenditures capitalise into land

values, leading to windfall benefits to landowners, a general rule is to assign all land-based taxes to municipalities. If not, these entities should be compensated by commensurate fiscal transfers. It may be noted that transfer of property tax, collected by state governments and capital gains tax on property, collected by central government, are land-based taxes.

4. Taxes authorised to municipalities in the past, including those under the GoI Act 1919 and those recommended by expert committees in the 1950s, which subscribe to the 'generalised benefit principle', should be restored back or assigned to them. Such taxes being levied in some states should be extended to others.

5. The municipal tax system should be diversified with a range of instruments that relate to the agglomeration forces of cities. Thus, municipalities need to be enabled to have access to income, business, sales, value-added and goods and services tax bases in principle; a versatile alternative to octroi is a must.

Alternative to Octroi

The absence of an alternative to octroi stands out as the most critical issue of revenue assignment to municipalities in India for decades. In spite of recommendations by expert committees, there has been no serious attempt to find a suitable alternative to octroi.

The Committee on Octroi (1985) had recommended the replacement of octroi with taxes, the incidence of which fell on the transport sector. The alternatives suggested include: surcharge on sales tax, entry tax, terminal tax, road tax and tax on motor vehicles. Further, if revenue from these taxes was insufficient, augmentation through property tax, entertainment tax, profession tax and so on was required. If revenue still remained inadequate, only then would special grants-in-aid need to be provided, but not without augmentation of tax base of local bodies, as this would take away their initiative and autonomy. Further, the alternative to octroi should not only yield revenue equivalent to the amount lost as a result of its abolition, but also be elastic enough to ensure future revenues. Due regard must be paid to the revenue potential of octroi while deciding compensation. These recommendations of the Committee on Octroi remain unimplemented.

Mumbai is the last city in India to have octroi.[5] The importance that octroi had in Maharashtra's cities can be gauged from the following statistics: it constituted 42 per cent of total municipal revenues for Greater Mumbai, 41 per cent for Pune, 57 per cent for Nagpur, 48 per cent for Navi Mumbai and 65 per cent for Ulhasnagar in 2008–09. The shares of property tax in total municipal revenue in the same year were: Greater Mumbai, 23 per cent; Pune, 15 per cent; Nagpur, 16 per cent; Navi Mumbai, 20 per cent; and Ulhasnagar, 13 per cent. The annual average growth rate in octroi collection between 1999–2000 and 2008–09 was 27 per cent for Greater Mumbai, 24 per cent for Pune, 23 per cent for Nagpur, 45 per cent for Navi Mumbai and 20 per cent for Ulhasnagar. The collection of octroi in Greater Mumbai Municipal Corporation during 2015–16 is targeted at ₹7,900 crore, accounting for 41 per cent of its income.

Octroi collected by 18 municipal corporations in Maharashtra amounted to about 25–30 per cent of the state's VAT in 2008–09. On the ground that hiking VAT to replace octroi would lead to its evasion and also penalise rural areas, the government of Maharashtra decided to replace octroi by a 'local body tax' (LBT) from 2010, in phases. The LBT was thus introduced and collected by municipal corporations in Maharashtra, excepting Greater Mumbai. This is a self-assessment tax based on books of accounts like VAT. Any goods brought into or imported to a local body area from outside for use, consumption or sale are liable for LBT. However, experience soon revealed that LBT did not match the buoyancy of octroi. Thus, a strong demand for the re-introduction of octroi was voiced by the mayors of cities that had octroi earlier. However, the Government of Maharashtra has, in its 2015–16 budget, announced the abolition of LBT with the levy of a state-wide VAT surcharge in lieu.

While any form of octroi is undesirable and LBT is not be a good replacement for octroi in theory, the legitimate concerns of cities across India to have one or more taxes that match the revenue potential and buoyancy of octroi is a key piece of municipal reform that needs to be addressed by central and state governments in earnest.

HPEC Recommendations

HPEC (2011) has examined the issues of revenue assignment to munici-palities, including a possible alternative to octroi. Among major recom-mendations, it has proposed the incorporation of a 'municipal finance list' into the Constitution of India with the following components:

Exclusive taxes:	Property tax, including vacant land tax, profession tax, entertainment tax, advertisement tax.
Revenue-shared taxes:	All taxes on goods and services levied by the state government.
Non-tax revenues:	User charges, trade licensing fee, floor space index (FSI) charge, betterment charge, impact fee, development charge.

The exclusive taxes proposed by the HPEC are justified in terms of criteria of 'good local tax'. Property tax is a benefit tax. Vacant land tax is a variant of property tax. Profession tax, entertainment tax and advertisement tax, already levied by some states, satisfy the criteria of local tax. The case of revenue-shared taxes is justified on the ground that no state has been able to assign a suitable alternative in the place of octroi to municipalities. FSI charge, betterment charge, impact fee and development charge are justified on the benefit principle.

A Portfolio of Municipal Taxes

Keeping in view the context of India's fiscal federalism, the theory and practice of municipal taxation, lessons from tax reforms and recommendations by expert committees, we suggest that apart from property and other land-based taxes, a range of non-property taxes that satisfy the criteria of 'local taxes' should be assigned to municipalities. Additional justification stems from the fact that they were municipal taxes in the past, and even at present, they are assigned to or shared with municipalities in a few states. The 'generalised benefit principle' also makes a strong case for the sharing of benefit taxes collected by central and state governments with municipalities. The tax base of municipalities in India at present is so narrow that in the absence of access to buoyant taxes levied by the centre and the state they cannot be expected to meet even a fraction of the urban infrastructure and services needed by economic growth in cities. The assignment of local taxes and sharing of central and state taxes with municipalities should be incorporated into the Constitution of India through a 'municipal finance list'. This is necessary in the interest of supporting growth and creating a vibrant third tier to meet the aspirations of citizens. Our suggestions for a portfolio of municipal taxes along with justifications for the same are as follows:

City Motor Vehicles Tax

Vehicles tax was exclusively reserved for municipalities under the GoI Act 1919. The same was emphasised by the Local Finance Enquiry Committee of 1951. However, presently motor vehicles taxes in India are levied by state governments and only a few states are sharing them with municipalities. This is puzzling as cities have to maintain an extensive network of roads and invest for public transport, which makes or mars a city. HPEC (2011) also estimates that the largest requirement of capital expenditure in India's urban areas will be for roads—at ₹1.7 million crore for 2012–31. A strong case thus exists for states to permit a surcharge on motor vehicles taxes in cities, especially metropolitan cities and dedicate the same to urban and regional transportation, including mass transit. Alternatively, they may share such taxes with municipalities based on a pre-determined formula.

India is witnessing the emergence of a large urban middle class, increasingly owning personalised automobiles. Thus, motor vehicles taxes can provide a stable and buoyant tax base to municipalities to finance transportation investments based on the benefit principle. They can also contribute towards mitigating the problems of pollution, congestion, GHG emission and climate change.

Entertainment Tax

The Local Finance Enquiry Committee 1951 had recommended that entertainment tax be exclusively reserved for local bodies. However, it is presently levied by state governments. The tax can be imposed on multiplexes, cinema halls, movie tickets, major commercial shows, big private festivals, cable/pay television, direct-to-home (DTH) television and broadcasting services, amusement and recreation parlours, cyber cafes, casinos, disco pubs, clubs, arcades, exhibitions, performances or pageants, games and sports, horse racing, etc. Generally states share entertainment tax with municipalities. In Andhra Pradesh and Telangana, entertainment tax is collected by state commercial tax department; 90 per cent of collection is assigned to municipalities.

In the past, some states have adopted very high rates of entertainment tax, for example, Jharkhand (110 per cent), Uttar Pradesh (60 per cent), Bihar (50 per cent) and Maharashtra (45 per cent). While a strong case exists for rationalising the entertainment tax rates to moderate levels to ensure better compliance, there is a long-felt need for the assignment of this tax exclusively to municipalities as a 'local tax', adopting the benefit principle. However, entertainment tax is proposed to be subsumed under the new GST regime. When the same occurs, the municipalities may be fully compensated for the loss of entertainment tax.

Advertisement Tax

The Local Finance Enquiry Committee 1951 had recommended the reservation of tax on advertisements other than those published in news papers for local bodies. Generally, states permit municipalities to levy a tax on advertisements under their municipal laws, including that on cable television. However, the tax remains grossly neglected in most states. Municipalities have thus not been able to exploit its potential in spite of growing commercial activities in cities.

Advertisement tax has a considerable potential to raise resources in large cities. Municipalities need to build an inventory of advertisements and a tracking mechanism. They need to be permitted to levy taxes on hoardings as well as advertisements thereon, separately, in terms of the existing municipal law provisions. A concerted attempt is also needed to tax the growing number of cable television advertisements based on accounts-keeping and filing of periodic returns by advertisers with ULBs.

Business Licensing Tax

Municipal laws in India authorise municipalities to levy trade licensing fee for regulating dangerous and offensive (D&O) trades. Over the years, the definition of D&O trade has extended to many categories of business on considerations such as traffic congestion, pollution and public safety. These include hotels, restaurants, other eating establishments, industries, factories, workshops, godowns, premises using machineries or power equipments of certain specification, shops selling offensive materials such as chemicals and explosives, and establishments causing traffic congestion. Municipalities issue notifications requiring that no place within their limits be used for any or more of the purposes specified under law without a valid municipal license. This is based on the 'legal nuisance doctrine' aimed at safeguarding health and convenience of the community.

Given the fact that municipalities in India have little access to the business tax base, it is desirable that they be enabled to levy business licensing tax as in Latin American countries, covering all businesses and adopting the 'nuisance' as well as 'benefit' doctrines.

Local Utility User Taxes

The Local Finance Enquiry Committee 1951 had recommended that tax on consumption and sale of electricity be exclusively reserved for municipalities. The Municipal Corporation of Delhi levied such tax; in 2005 the rate was five per cent of the billed amount. In case electricity consumers had captive power plants, the rate payable was 10 paise per kilowatt hour (KWH) and tax on electricity suppliers was also 10 paise per KWH. We suggest that utility user taxes on consumption and sale of electricity, telephone, cable television and so on at moderate rates be levied as 'local taxes' in the form of a surcharge on relevant state taxes on the ground of these being general benefit taxes. In Rajasthan, a cess is imposed on electricity charges paid by urban consumers to enable municipalities meet the increasing costs of street lighting. A similar cess may also be considered by other states based on the benefit principle.

Profession Tax

Tax on trade, profession and calling was reserved for local bodies in the GoI Act 1919. Profession tax is the only tax mentioned in the Constitution of India under Article 276 in connection with local body affairs. The tax is broad-based and can be levied on salaried employees, professionals and self-employed persons. It is paid by employers on behalf of employees and deducted from salaries at source. Profession tax is allowed as a deduction from gross salary under the Income Tax Act, with no monetary limit on such deduction. In Andhra Pradesh and Telangana, profession tax is collected by the state commercial tax department and 95 per cent of the collection in metropolitan cities is assigned to the concerned municipal corporations. Municipalities of other cities do not receive a share in profession tax as their staff salaries have been taken over by the state government.

Profession tax is the only tax available to municipalities in India with income as base. However, not all states imposing profession tax share it with local bodies. Also, the revenue potential of the tax is limited by the ceiling of ₹2,500 per person per year prescribed under the Constitution. The 14th Finance Commission has advocated raising the ceiling to ₹12,000. As cities contribute significantly to economic growth, a strong case exists for the reservation of profession tax for municipalities in India as a 'local tax'. Also, the ceiling on the same may be set as a percentage of salary or payroll by category of establishment rather than a fixed amount. A constitutional amendment is necessary.

Revenue-shared Taxes

Local taxes with income, business, excise, sales, value-added and goods and services as base are general benefit taxes on living, working and shopping in the city. But, municipalities in India do not have access to these productive and buoyant revenue sources that keep pace with city economic growth. As cities constitute the tax bases of all levels of government, the generalised benefit principle makes a strong case for municipalities to 'piggyback' onto the relevant central and state taxes. However, the same is not possible within the present contours of India's fiscal federalism without amending the Constitution. Thus, municipalities may be enabled to have a formula-based share in these taxes through a statutory mechanism. This may be based on a consensus between the centre and the states.

Income Tax and Payroll Tax

Civic services and infrastructure facilities to firms and households enhance their productivity and income. This is particularly so when vibrant externalities are catalysed, leading to 'wider economic benefits'. Thus, economic theory presents a strong case for granting municipalities an access to income and payroll tax bases. These taxes are also ideal instruments to enable ULBs undertake long-gestation infrastructure projects that contribute to growth and also discharge redistributive functions. However, as payroll tax is not levied in India, profession tax needs to be fully reserved for local bodies. Payroll tax may perhaps be included in the 'municipal finance list' when the same is incorporated into the Constitution. The CFC may also be required to consider the sharing of the divisible pool of central taxes, including income tax with municipalities.

Goods and Services Tax

GST is a harmonised tax on the manufacture, sale and consumption of goods and services. A dual GST, comprising a central GST and a state GST is slated for implementation in India. The case for GST is, in a way, similar to that advanced by the central government while calling upon states to abolish octroi for removing impediments to interstate trade and commerce and moving towards a unified market. GST aims at replacing the indirect taxes on goods and services levied by central and state governments. The central GST is likely to subsume central excise duty, additional excise duties, service tax, additional custom duty, special additional duty on customs, central cesses and surcharges and so on. The state GST may subsume value added tax, sales tax, entertainment tax, luxury tax, octroi, entry tax in lieu of octroi, taxes on lotteries, betting and gambling, state cesses and surcharges, purchase tax, luxury tax, etc. The GST may also cover sale of newspapers and advertisements therein.

The GST provides an opportunity to resolve the long-pending issues of non-assignment of a versatile alterative to octroi and other 'local taxes' to ULBs commensurate with their mandated functions. HPEC (2011) has already suggested the sharing of taxes on goods and services levied by the state government with local bodies. To enable ULBs to have access to the buoyant goods and services tax base that cities create, the GST regime needs to compensate municipalities fully for the loss of octroi, entertainment tax, entry tax, etc. The principle of 'subsidiarity' also suggests that tax reforms must first cater to the financing requirement of the mandatory functions of local bodies. Further, the criteria of 'local tax' and 'benefit tax' suggest that if it is not possible to assign a tax alternative to ULBs in place of octroi and other local taxes, then a 'piggyback' mechanism would be most appropriate. However, the same will not be feasible within the limits of the Constitution of India at present. Thus, a city GST rate within state GST rate, or a statutory, formula-based sharing of state GST with cities, pending the incorporation of a 'municipal finance list' in the Constitution is desirable. The rate of city GST or sharing may be to the tune of a minimum of 25 per cent.[6] The ULBs may also be enabled to have access to central GST through the CFC route.

Whatever be the strategies India adopts—a portfolio of 'local taxes' assigned to municipalities, a city GST rate within the state GST rate or a statutory share for municipalities in state GST and the access of ULBs to divisible pool of central taxes, including income tax and central GST—a robust system of municipal taxation in the country is long over-due. There is a need for an understanding between the centre and the states that municipalities ought to be strengthened with a broad range of local benefit taxes, such as land and property tax, motor vehicles tax, entertainment tax, advertisement tax, business licensing tax, utility user taxes and profession tax, and a statutory access to income and good and services tax bases. This is necessary to meet the colossal revenue and capital investment requirements of cities and unleash the power of their agglomeration economies to accelerate economic growth and generate public finance for development. Missing the opportunities offered by the 'urban revolution' and 'agglomerating cities' would be too costly for India.

Notes

1. Based on data furnished by state governments to the 14th Finance Commission of India–ASCI (2014). Per capita municipal tax revenues in India in 2012–13 amounted to ₹1,131 as against per capita municipal revenues of ₹3,449.
2. A genuine link between revenue and expenditure decisions, called the Wicksellian connection, can lead to the efficient provision of local public goods and services. See Breton (1996, 3).
3. Figure based on HPEC (2011).
4. Denmark, Finland, Ireland, Netherlands, Norway, Sweden, Switzerland and United Kingdom levy carbon tax at the national level. British Columbia in Canada levies carbon tax at the provincial level.
5. Octroi is likely to be abolished in Mumbai after the new GST regime comes into operation.
6. Octroi collected by 18 municipal corporations in Maharashtra amounted to about 25–30 per cent of the state's VAT in 2008–09. In Brazil, where local authorities receive 22.5 per cent share in federal income tax, are provided with an equal share in federal value added tax on manufactured goods. In Nigeria, 35 per cent revenues from VAT is assigned to local governments.

4

Taxation of Urban Land Value

Land Tax in Perspective

A land tax is a levy on a land-related base—often the value of land, expressed in capital value or rental value. The relationship between the two values is expressed as follows:

Rental value = Annualised capital value = Capital value × Prevailing discount rate (for example, cost of capital or the return expected from investment of capital)

Land taxation constitutes a part of the wider system of property taxation in both developed and developing nations.

Land taxes are levied on a number of bases. The most important ones are property, land value and increment in land value. Property tax includes a tax on both land and improvements. LVT is a variant of property tax in which only land value is taxed or a higher tax rate is imposed on land, compared to buildings. LVIT is based on the increase in land value over and above a base value. Other forms of land-based taxes include: VLT, landholding tax, real estate transfer tax, planning gain tax, development land tax, LGT, windfall tax, betterment levy, etc.

In the Roman period, land tax yielded considerable revenues for the provinces and its dominance continued into medieval times. Throughout the 18th century, land tax was the principal source of government revenues in the United Kingdom. Introduced in 1693 to pay for the French wars of William III's reign, it sufficed until 1799 when the cost of the wars forced Pitt the Younger, the then British Prime Minister, to introduce a graduated income tax. At that time, England was 33 per cent urban. Local property taxes, based on capital value of land and buildings, dominated US public finance from the 1840s to 1933 when its urbanisation level reached 56 per cent. By the Great Depression of the 1930s, local governments in the United States accounted for over half of the total tax revenues collected by all levels of government. It was only thereafter that income and sales taxes became the principal contributors to US public finance (Wallis 2000).

Land taxes played a key role in financing urban infrastructure in developed countries during their urban transition. They were key instruments that local governments relied upon to undertake planned urban development. However, land-based tools have not been exploited by Indian cities in spite of the GoI Act 1919 reserving land value tax for municipalities. This chapter draws lessons from theory and international practice of land taxation to argue the case for urban land value tax in India.

Theory of Land Taxation

Academic interest in land tax dates back to centuries. Some political scientists and economists proclaimed that the private ownership of land was a historical mistake. They contended that land in its unimproved state was a gift of nature. Others argued that land values resulted from 'community efforts' and 'progress of society'. They owed to public expenditure on infrastructure and services. Thus, private appropriation of land values was scandalous. Some radical thinkers even advocated for the nationalisation of land. They held that the public right to appropriate land value depended on the public right to land itself. Most scholars, however, favoured a differential tax on land—a tax different from that on other factors of production. According to them, the unique attributes of land makes it an ideal object of taxation. The arguments for differential taxation of land rely on the special characteristics of land—permanent nature, geographical fixity, inelastic supply, location externalities, return to land being a surplus and difficulty in evading land taxes.

Adam Smith argued that if the exigencies of the state require new taxes after all the 'proper' subjects of taxation are exhausted, only then improper sources be explored. He regarded land rents as a 'proper' subject of taxation:

> Both ground-rents and the ordinary rent of land are a species of revenue which the owner, in many cases, enjoys without any care or attention of his own.... Ground-rents and the ordinary rent of land, are therefore, perhaps, the species of revenue which can best bear to have a peculiar tax imposed upon them.

Nothing can be more reasonable than that a fund which owes its existence to the good government of the state should be taxed peculiarly, or should contribute something more than the greater part of other funds, towards the support of that government. (Smith 1976, 843–844)

Smith's arguments for taxation of land can be divided into the following principles:

1. *Efficiency*: Taxes on land rents are neutral in terms of effects on resource allocation;
2. *Equity*: It is fair to tax away surpluses that are more due to extraneous factors than to individual efforts; and
3. *Benefit*: People should pay for government actions and services that benefit them.

Ricardo presented a case for taxing land rent as it represented a private expropriation of the natural productivity of land that did not owe to human effort (1817). He differentiated between 'intensive' and 'extensive' margins of cultivation in rural land. However, he did not extend this distinction to urban land. Ricardo's theory of rent accordingly made no reference to land at the 'intensive' margin (constructing vertically) and at the 'extensive' margin (extending horizontally, that is, city limits).

The first fully-developed arguments for differential taxation of urban land originated from John Stuart Mill, who declared that land rents were 'created by circumstance'. His oft-cited observation regarding landlords is:

They grow richer, as it were in their sleep, without working, risking or economising. What claim have they on the general principle of social justice, to this accession of riches? (Mill 1909, 818)

Mill argued that the unique features of land made it an appropriate object for special taxation. He, however, identified two major hurdles in taxing land rents at a high rate as follows:

1. It is difficult to distinguish between the components of current land values due to private efforts and 'circumstances' or factors connected to progress of society.
2. Present landowners may not be the recipients of rents accumulated from history; they may have recently bought land at market price, expecting future rents.

Mill was in favour of taxation of unexpected windfalls in land value. He, however, recognised that the estimation of the same depended on the present value of land so that all future increments, not attributable to individual efforts, could be taxed at a higher rate.

Henry George proclaimed that the value of unimproved land was unearned; it did not arise from any sacrifice or opportunity cost shouldered by the landowner. Rather, it owed to the demand for a fixed extent of land. Thus, if land were taxed more heavily, it would not affect productive behaviour. The quantity of land would not reduce, as with other goods; nor would demand decline because of land's productive uses. George further argued that landlords had no moral right to land values and to existing rents or land value increments resulting from future expansion of the economy. He advocated 'the single tax movement', justifying that there was no need to confiscate land. A 100 per cent tax on land's annual rental value or confiscatory rent was adequate to meet public expenditures ([1879] 1979, 1897).

Marshall argued that Ricardo's concept of 'intensive' and 'extensive' margins of cultivation was equally applicable to urban land as it was to agricultural land. According to him, the taxation of 'site value' (or 'public value', as he called it) was in essence the taxation of monopoly profits. Marshall also recognised that additional local public expenditures owing to the taxation of public value of land might benefit the landowners in a way that they were not worse off than before (Marshall [1898] 1920).

Pigou distinguished between taxes on public value of land and taxes on windfalls or unearned increments. He favoured both. His main argument in favour of land value taxation was its neutrality in terms of resource allocation. Regarding a tax on windfall gains in land values, Pigou held that if windfalls were not foreseen or were not due to any enterprise on part of the recipient, they were ideal objects for taxation in terms of efficiency. From the equity or distributional angle too, such taxation was desirable (1927).

Debate on Unearned Increments

The case for taxation of unearned increments in value of urban and peri-urban land came into sharp focus in the historic debate on the 1909 People's Budget in British Parliament. The then Chancellor of the

Exchequer, David Lloyd George, proposed a tax on the capital value of underdeveloped land and a 20 per cent tax on future capital gains on land when realised by disposal, death or gift. Winston Churchill, the then President of the Board of Trade, vehemently argued in support of the government's proposals as follows:

> (T)he landlord who happens to own a plot of land on the outskirts or at the centre of one of our great cities...watches the busy population around him making the city larger, richer, more convenient, more famous every day, and all the while sits still and does nothing. Roads are made, streets are made, railway services are improved, electric light turns night into day ... water is brought from reservoirs a hundred miles off in the mountains—and all the while the landlord sits still. Every one of those improvements is effected by the labour and at the cost of other people. Many of the most important are effected at the cost of the municipality and of the ratepayers. To not one of those improvements does the land monopolist as a land monopolist contribute, and yet by every one of them the value of his land is sensibly enhanced. He renders no service to the community, he contributes nothing to the general welfare; he contributes nothing even to the process from which his own enrichment is derived.

> At last the land becomes ripe for sale—that means that the price is too tempting to be resisted any longer—and then, not till then, it is sold by the yard or by the inch at ten times, or twenty times, or even fifty times, its agricultural value.

> In fact, you may say that...the unearned increment on the land is reaped by the land monopolist in exact proportion, not to the service, but to the disservice done.[1]

Lloyd George's proposals in the People's Budget were rejected by the House of Lords, leading to a constitutional crisis and general elections in 1910. Since then, attempts to tax windfall gains in urban land have continued in the United Kingdom. Other countries have also pursued such action. Ironically, there are remarkably similar views on the taxation of unearned increments in urban land values internationally (see Box 4.1).

The Vancouver Action Plan of the United Nations Conference on Human Settlements 2006 observes:

> The unearned increment resulting from the rise in land values resulting from change in use of land, from public investment decision, or due to the general growth of the community must be subject to appropriate recapture by public bodies (the community). (United Nations 2006)

Box 4.1

Views on Unearned Increments in Urban Land Value: United States and India

Report of the National Commission on Urban Problems (1969), United States:

The owners of the land can go to Hawaii and rest languidly on the beaches or make prolonged safaris into the inmost regions of Africa. They may study Shakespearean literature at Stratford-upon-Avon or Zen Buddhism in Japan or ponder urban problems in Washington. They can go up in space capsules or down a hole in the ground. They will become richer and richer without trial or sweat. For as Dr. Johnson once remarked in another connection, here are 'riches beyond the dreams of avarice'. (396)

Report of the Committee on Urban Land Policy (1965), India:

While discussing the various measures for tackling the problems in the developed and undeveloped urban land we had stated that unearned increases in urban land and property values, being in the nature of 'social surpluses' must be mopped up for the benefit of the society as a whole. After all, development in and around a town takes place as a result of Government and municipal development activities and there is no reason why the huge profits should be allowed to be digested by speculators and profiteers.... The Third Five Year Plan also recommends the mopping up of unearned increases in urban land and property values as a measure to combat speculation and also as a measure to achieve social and economic equity. We also unreservedly endorse this idea. (Ministry of Health, GoI 1965)

Sources: Report of the National Commission on Urban Problems (1969) and Report of the Committee on Urban Land Policy (1965).

Case for Land Value Tax

LVT, also called site value tax (SVT) or site value rating (SVR) is a tax on unimproved value of land. It takes into account zoning or planning permission, but not improvements.

LVT has engaged the attention of prominent economists and political thinkers since long. They include: Tom Paine, David Ricardo, Henry George, John Maynard Keynes, Milton Friedman, Friedrich von Hayek, William Vickrey and Joseph Stiglitz. Friedman, winner of 1976 Nobel Prize in Economics stated:

In my opinion, the least bad tax is the property tax on the unimproved value of land, the Henry George argument of many, many years ago. (Cited in Mankiw 2004)

William Vickrey, winner of 1996 Nobel Prize in Economics observed:

> The property tax is, economically speaking, a combination of one of the worst taxes—the part that is assessed on real estate improvements ... and one of the best taxes—the tax on land or site value. (1999)

Economists make case for LVT on efficiency, equity and benefit principles. They argue that LVT scores over taxes that impact hard work (income), investment (capital gains) and consumption (from post-tax income).

Most taxes reduce returns on taxed activities, rendering otherwise viable enterprises and transactions unviable. The cost to the economy of these lost opportunities is called 'deadweight loss' or 'excess burden' of taxation. Arguably, LVT does not lead to such a loss. It does not affect the incentive to buy, develop or use land. On the contrary, LVT promotes the allocation of resources to create wealth. Land being immobile and in fixed supply, the incidence of LVT falls on land, not development. LVT is, therefore, neutral with respect to the density of development, its timing and the amount of investment in development. A tax on land mobilises resources without distorting the incentive to invest in its productive uses. Further, it penalises those who speculate or leave land idle. By contrast, a tax on improvements discourages investment in new structures and maintenance of existing buildings by reducing the return on such expenditure. It incentivises low density sprawl and discourages high rise construction. The value of land is determined by market forces depending on the land's worth and the willingness of buyers to pay does not depend on the land tax to be paid.

The equity argument for LVT rests on the premise that much of the return to land is unearned. It owes to external developments such as better transport links. LVT aims at recouping a part of the windfall benefits to landowners from public investments made out of taxpayers' money or private investments made by others. Georgists contend that LVT prevents the owners of land from monopolising benefits they did nothing to create and the market worth of which is social, not individual. Further, LVT is progressive as only households owning land pay any tax at all. Lower and middle class homeowners are not burdened by LVT as they own only modest parcels of inexpensive land under their houses.

Apart from efficiency and equity considerations, LVT is advocated on the benefit principle of taxation. Spatial planning and public investments in city infrastructure facilities benefit landowners by more than what they contribute. Even a mere announcement by government that certain areas in the periphery of a city would be included in the city master plan leads to substantial increases in land values in those locations. Similar is the case with development of trunk infrastructure such as highway, railway, public transit, water supply and sewerage.

LVT imposes a cost on land hoarding. It acts against speculation in urban land and moderates land price by removing the speculative element in land value. Land gets bid up to balance economic forces. Lower land values exert downward pressure on housing costs and rents. They make homes and business premises cheaper. Lower rents also lead to increased net wages. Higher net wages stimulate savings and consumption. LVT thus facilitates investments in production and jobs. It prevents a disproportionate amount of capital, often linked to a large debt, being tied up with idle property. Some economists also argue that LVT acts as a market stabiliser, reducing the chances of erratic property booms and busts. They contend that income and sales tax regimes suppress economic activity and encourage bubbles.

LVT promotes sustainable use of land and protection of the environment. By bringing brownfield sites to appropriate uses, it eases the pressure on green belts and conservation areas. LVT facilitates a more efficient use of infrastructure through intensive development. It acts against uneconomic extension of infrastructure facilities to the urban fringe. LVT promotes compact development, mixed land use and energy-efficient urban design. Economic activity is directed to areas with high development potential and gains. Owners of neglected properties are required to pay no less tax than those who manage properties more efficiently. LVT thus incentivises the revitalisation of blight areas and derelict neighbourhoods. Further, LVT stimulates infill development and density, leading to agglomeration economies and economic growth. It leads to better record-keeping of land value changes and, therefore, better spatial planning.

A land tax is difficult to evade, because land cannot be hidden. It is not amenable to transfer to an off-shore tax haven. The rich, who can avoid paying income tax, cannot avoid LVT on a palatial house. The cost of collecting LVT may also not be high, unlike a tax with mobile base. Local authorities need to have only the registers of landowners and the valuation of their land. Difficulty in arriving at land value is cited as a key factor against LVT. However, with GIS and CAMA techniques, the valuation of land no longer presents a major technical challenge. Land values are estimated for the registration of property. They are periodically published by valuation offices of state governments. Houses, including land, are also valued for insurance purpose. Further, professional standards in income taxation require tax assessors to report separate values on land and buildings.

The primary argument against LVT centres on how economic rent due to social enterprise can be isolated from that due to individual effort. Critics consider LVT regressive, in that it bears no relation to cash-flow from land; the 'asset-rich but cash-poor' might suffer. Further, there is the problem of whom to tax in the case of leasehold properties. However, the excess of tax over income is a common problem with any kind of taxation of assets, not simply land. A tax-credit feature may be included in LVT to reduce the burden on land-rich but income-poor citizens. Regarding leasehold interests, a suggestion for abolishing owner's liability in such cases and shifting the onus of tax payment to occupier instead has been mooted.

In summary, who gains and who loses from LVT? Business, retail and industry gain from LVT due to lower land prices and reduced risks of booms and busts associated with property markets. Poor and low income groups benefit from a more progressive tax system led by LVT. Higher tax on land compared to improvement facilitates housing, employment and income generation. Thus, the problems with an ill-functioning property market that rewards the rich with high value land assets at the cost of the poor needing shelter are alleviated. By extracting benefits accruing to landowners, LVT underwrites the investment by public authorities. An increase in land values that a worthwhile project generates automatically leads to an increase in tax resources to fund it. This encourages better public investment decisions.

In spite of merits, LVT remains politically challenging. This is because of its link to sensitive issues such as right to land and interest of landowners. The history of taxation of urban land in developed countries, particularly the United Kingdom, suggests that improper tax design, high tax rate, vested interests and politics are key factors because of which measures of land-based taxation were supported or opposed in legislative debates.

Taxation of Urban Land Value

Early arguments for taxation of urban land can be found in the report of the Royal Commission on Housing for the Working Class in Britain of 1885.[2] The Commission distinguished between the land and capital elements in a development. It argued that the land element, being a natural resource, resulted from community action including public expenditure on city improvements. The capital element, such as building erected on land, was the effort of landowner or developer. The Commission recommended a tax on the value of the land element to enable the community to recoup a part of it and also to prevent speculation in land. It observed that land monopolists could afford to withhold their land out of the market to raise price beyond the 'natural monopoly price'.

Modern arguments for urban land tax are founded on three planks: (a) intrinsic merits of LVT as an instrument of urban public finance, (b) returning unearned increments in land values due to urban development to the society, and (c) role of land taxation in planning for orderly urban growth. The first plank relies on the virtues of LVT in terms of efficiency, equity and benefit criteria. The second argument rests on the premise that spatial planning and infrastructure development lead to a substantial transfer of wealth from a large number of tax-payers to a small number of property-owners. The third plank is that a higher tax rate on land compared to buildings facilitates the conversion of unproductive land to productive uses such as housing and attainment of zoning objectives. Further, a general principle is that whenever a public authority grants a right to some and not to others, those benefiting from such right must pay annually to the authority for public expenditures. The payment must correspond to the value of the rights, measured by what the non-beneficiaries would be willing to pay to secure them.

A robust case for taxing urban land owes to the 'town planning movement' that originated in the United Kingdom. Spatial planning and infrastructure development by public authorities lead to increased land values which must be captured to finance planned urban development. In this regard, the design of tax instruments is of critical importance. As the current urban planning paradigm in India draws from the town planning laws in the United Kingdom, it is important to understand how the UK legal system has fared in adopting land-based financing tools.

The concept of taxation of land value increment due to spatial planning can be traced to the UK Housing and Town Planning Act of 1909. Section 58 of the Act stipulated a 50 per cent levy as 'betterment charges for property increased in value by town planning scheme'. Section 21 of the Town and Country Planning Act of 1932 increased this rate up to 75 per cent. The Town and Country Planning Act of 1947 stipulated a tax of 100 per cent on the 'development value' of land, defined as the difference between the value of land with permission for development and its current use value. The Act further provided that any land would be purchased by a developer at its 'existing use value'. After planning permission to develop the land was accorded, the developer would be assessed under Section 61 of the Act a 'development charge' equal to 'development value'.

As regards the expropriation of betterment envisaged in the 1909, 1932 and 1947 Acts in the United Kingdom, the same could not be achieved due to many reasons. Difficulties in establishing the cause of betterment and the levy not being due till the realisation of increment in land value were obvious bottlenecks. Landowners chose to wait to sell their land rather than pay heavy betterment charges. All these led to the repeal of the betterment levy in 1953. Since then there have been many attempts in the United Kingdom to tap the gains in land from spatial planning and development to meet public expenditures.

In 1964, a general capital gains tax was introduced in the United Kingdom. The maximum rate of tax on long-term gains by individuals was 30 per cent. Short-term gains were taxed as income. The Land Commission Act of 1967, however, considered the capital gains tax insufficient to capture land value gains due to planning permission for two reasons. First, it applied to realisations rather than accruals. Second, the rate of taxation was too small compared to the unearned increments. Accordingly, the 1967 Act fixed betterment levy at 40 per cent of land's increased development value initially, but with stated intention of increasing it to 50 per cent later. The base of the levy was 'net development value', calculated by deducting from the market value of land with grant of planning permission a 'basic value'. The occasion for betterment levy under the 1967 Act was not restricted to the grant of planning permission but included any transaction leading to realisation of development value. The levy was warranted on chargeable events, including sale or lease or development of land.

The 1974 Finance Act in the United Kingdom introduced the development gains tax (DGT), treating development gains as income rather than capital. It sought to tax income gains from disposal of land with development potential, at rates up to 82 per cent for individuals and 52 per cent for companies. DGT was chargeable whenever there was a 'disposal' or 'notional disposal' of land or building with development value. However, the Act could not be implemented due to various reasons. In 1976, the Development Land Tax Act was enacted, 'to restore to the community the increase in value of land arising from its efforts.' This Act provided for a tax of 80 per cent on the development value of land with the intention of increasing it to 100 per cent eventually. The DLT was to be levied on the landowner at the time of material development or realisation of development value. The rate of DLT was subsequently reduced to 60 per cent. The tax was abolished in 1985.

Following the abolition of DLT, a policy vacuum arose in the United Kingdom. Some smart local planning authorities viewed this as an opportunity to exact contributions from developers toward specific public facilities as a condition of planning permission. They argued that such contributions could easily be paid by the landowner or developer out of the huge, but largely untaxed, increase in land value conferred by planning permission. Known as 'planning gain', this increase represented the difference between land value with full planning permission or planning value (PV) and current use value (CUV). The Town and Country Planning Act, 1990, permitted negotiations between a developer and the local authority. Section 106 (1) of the Act stipulated that any person with an interest in land may, by agreement or otherwise, enter into a planning obligation, enforceable by the local planning authority, restricting development or use of the land, specifying development for which land can be used, or requiring payment of money to the authority. The Section 106 agreements are known as 'planning obligations', legalised and regularised under various planning Acts and government circulars.

The planning obligations under Section 106 were criticised as ad hoc, inconsistent, unfair, discretionary and non-transparent. Sometimes obligations were created that the developers considered arbitrary. Section 106 agreements were often used to secure affordable housing. Typically, a new housing development was required to provide a pre-determined proportion as affordable homes. This created friction between developers and local authorities. Criticisms of Section 106 agreements led to a report for the government in 2006 by economist Kate Barker (2006).[3] This report proposed a tax on planning gain, called 'planning gain supplement' (PGS) for implementation along with a simplified planning obligations system. However, the PGS was not put to practice.

After a long debate on the PGS, the UK Government announced a community infrastructure levy (CIL) in 2007. This levy was legislated in the 2008 Planning Act. Under CIL regulations issued in April 2010, the CIL is a hypothecated levy which local authorities could choose to fund new infrastructure in their areas, such as roads, public transport, parks or health centres, in addition to infrastructure schemes supported by mainstream public funding. Local authorities have the freedom to choose the CIL rate. The levy depends upon the size and type of development and is payable at the commencement of development. CIL regulations also provide for reform in planning obligations so that the two regimes operate effectively alongside each other. The regulations state that a planning obligation may only constitute a reason for granting planning permission for a development if the obligation is directly related to the development, is necessary to make the development acceptable in planning terms, and is fairly and reasonably related in scale and kind to the development. Recently, an annual tax on value of housing, imposed on the most expensive homes, for example, those costing more than £2 million—called 'mansions tax'—has been the subject of debate in the United Kingdom.

Table 4.1 presents a summary of legislative attempts in the United Kingdom over the course of more than a century to tax planning and development gains accruing to land.

More than a century of parliamentary debate in the United Kingdom on taxation of urban land presents many intellectual arguments, but no

Table 4.1

United Kingdom: Evolution of Taxation of Planning and Development Gains

Measure(s) Adopted to Extract Planning/Development Gains	Description of Levy	Years
Betterment Charges (Housing and Town Planning Act of 1909)	50 per cent levy on increase in land value due to town planning scheme.	1909–32
Betterment Charges (Housing and Town Planning Act of 1932)	Not exceeding 75 per cent levy on increase in land value due to town planning scheme.	1932–47
Development Charge (Housing and Town Planning Act of 1947)	100 per cent tax on increase in land value arising due to planning permission or a levy equal to development value of land.	1947–53
Capital Gains Tax (Finance Act 1965 and Capital Gains Tax Regulations 1967)	Capital gains tax at 30 per cent on gains arising on the disposal of capital assets, including land.	1967
Betterment Levy (Land Commission Act 1967)	40 per cent of net development value realised through land transaction or development.	1967–71
Development Gains Tax (Finance Act 1974)	Tax on disposal or notional disposal of land or building with development value.	1974
Development Land Tax (Development Land Tax Act 1976)	Tax of 80 per cent on development value of land with intention to increase it to 100 per cent; rate reduced to 60 per cent in 1979.	1976–85
Planning Obligation (Town and Country Planning Act 1990: Section 106)	Contribution from developers negotiated by local authority toward the cost of specific public facilities as condition of planning permission.	1990– till date
Community Infrastructure Levy (Planning Act 2008)	Hypothecated local levy to fund new infrastructure in addition to developer contribution under 'planning gain'.	2010– till date

Source: Mohanty (2014) and Prest (1981).

agreements on measures to mop up land value increments due to spatial planning and development. Attempts by Labour governments to tax unearned increments in land value due to planning permission witnessed their prompt rescindment by Conservative governments. However, even the Conservative government conceded to the principle of a differential tax on land in 1973.

Urban Land Value Tax in Practice

More than 30 countries across the world have implemented urban land value taxation. They include: the United States, Canada, Mexico, Jamaica, Argentina, Australia, New Zealand, Denmark, France, Finland, South Africa, Kenya, Tanzania, Zambia, South Korea, Taiwan and Japan.[4] These countries used land-based financing of urban infrastructure and services during their urban transition, especially when land values in cities soared. The key instruments adopted by countries are described as follows.

United States: Two-rate Taxation

Land value taxation spread in the United States after the publication of Henry George's *Progress and Poverty* (1879). George dealt with the question of why poverty persisted in spite of rapid industrialisation, technological progress and economic development. His conclusion was that the phenomena of social inequality and economic downturns owed their roots to speculations in the land market. George advocated the financing of public services by the values they create—the economic rent of land. Influenced by Georgist thinking, Hyattsville, Maryland was the first US city to enact LVT in 1898. In 1913, the Pennsylvania legislature permitted Pittsburgh and Scranton to adopt the 'split-rate' property tax, providing for a tax rate on value of land higher than on value of buildings thereon. A 1951 statute authorised smaller Pennsylvania municipalities the same option. Nineteen cities in Pennsylvania adopted a 'graded tax plan' under which land was taxed at a higher rate than improvements.

Pittsburgh implemented LVT from 1913 to 2001. It taxed land at a rate twice that on structures thereon till the end of 1970s. Subsequently the tax on land was raised to about 5.77 times that on improvements (Epple et al. 2010). The city has, however, rescinded its two-part property tax after nine decades of implementation. This is not due to the lack of intrinsic merit of LVT, but owing to factors such as 'infrequent and inaccurate assessments and clumsy rate-setting procedures' (Bourassa 2009).

Other states in the United States have also experimented with LVT. Virginia and Connecticut authorised their municipalities to levy two-rate property tax. Hawaii levied such tax from 1963 to 1977. Every state in the United States today has some form of property tax based on capital value and hence, in part, a tax on land value. Thus, if land values increased due to spatial planning or public infrastructure investment, the landowners are made to contribute towards such investment.

Australia: Site Value Tax

Australia provides the leading example of a country that relied heavily on LVT to meet federal, state and local public expenditures. The states of South Australia, Tasmania and New South Wales resorted to SVT years before the Australian federation was formed in 1901. The federal government enacted the Land Tax Assessment Act in 1910, introducing a levy on land value only. This was repealed in 1952 to accord additional tax base to states and local bodies. Currently, every state in Australia levies a tax on land value. This is imposed in Queensland under the Land Tax Act 1915, in South Australia under the Land Tax Act of 1936, in New South Wales under the Land Tax Management Act 1956 and in Victoria under the Land Tax Act of 1958. LVT is universal in Queensland and New South Wales. Sydney has the distinction of being the largest city in the world deriving the bulk of its revenues from LVT.

Perth metropolitan region levies a metropolitan region improvement tax (MRIT) in addition to land tax. MRIT is based on the aggregated taxable value of land owned (excluding exempt land) at midnight on the 30th of June. It is used to finance the cost of acquiring land for roads, open spaces, parks and similar public facilities. The tax rate is 0.14 cents for every Australian dollar of taxable value of land in excess of 3,00,000.[5]

New Zealand: Unimproved Land Tax

New Zealand provides an example of the successful long-term use of LVT to finance local government needs. Taxation of land values there began in 1849. The present system of LVT in New Zealand has its origins in the

Valuation of Land Act 1896. This Act defined the concepts of improved and unimproved values of land. Local governments have the option to choose from three alternative systems of property tax—(a) capital improved value: total value of land, buildings and other improvements; (b) unimproved value or land value only; and (c) annual rental value. The proportion of local authorities using unimproved value tax base in New Zealand increased from 64.2 per cent in 1956 to 76.1 per cent in 1966. The figure peaked in the 1980s at about 80 per cent. However, since 1985, there has been a noticeable swing back toward using capital improved value to arrive at property tax (Dye and England 2010).

Europe: LVT and LVIT

In Europe, Imperial Germany started LVIT in 1911, first at a local level and then at the central level. European countries that have experimented with land tax include Denmark, Finland, France and Estonia. Denmark introduced LVT in 1926 with the rate of tax on land higher than that on buildings. County and municipal authorities collect the tax based on a per thousandth share of the value of land. The tax rate for counties has been decided by the Danish Parliament since 1979—at one per cent of the market value of land. In municipalities, the councils set the land tax for their jurisdiction, varying per thousandth share depending on type of land use. This is subject to a minimum of six and a maximum of 24 thousandths of the value of land. The effective municipal land tax rate is thus 0.6–2.4 per cent. Thus, local authorities in Demark, including counties and municipalities, levy land tax at 1.6 to 3.4 per cent of the market value of land. There are ceilings for the annual increase in the land tax paid (seven per cent in the 2000s). There is option of deferred payment for those over 65 years. Since 2003, land valuations have been carried out in Denmark by the national government every two years, with indexation adopted for intervening years.

Apart from LVT, Danish municipalities levy service tax applicable to buildings used for commerce, administration and manufacturing. The rate cannot exceed one per cent of the value of building. Municipalities also impose property value tax on owner-occupied buildings and summer homes. The basic tax rate is one per cent of market value of property up to a certain threshold. For value above this, the basic rate is three per cent (see Muller 2000).

A special land development gain tax is collected in Denmark when agricultural land is brought into urban zone (*frigorelsesafgift*); the rate is about 50 per cent of the increase in land value due to changes in land use zoning. In Poland a tax is levied at 30 per cent on the increase in land value if the land is sold within five years of change in zoning (UN–HABITAT 2011).

South Africa: Three-rate System

Property tax, including tax on land value, has been a major source of municipal revenue in South Africa since 1836. For nearly a century, cities have resorted to urban land tax to finance city infrastructure, including land acquisition for public facilities. Municipalities were authorised by provinces to choose among three bases of property tax. These include site rating (unimproved land value or site value), flat rating (capital improved value) and composite rating (value of land and improvements rated differently). In early 20th century, several provinces adopted LVT through legislation. For example, SVT was introduced in the Transvaal in 1916. The three-rate system in South Africa has, however, been abolished by the Local Government: Municipal Property Rates Act 6 of 2004 for administrative reasons. Through this Act, the South African government has mandated the levy of a traditional property tax throughout the country (Dye and England 2010). The reasons for this shift in tax policy include: (a) political desire to tax the wealth in improvements, (b) motivation to reduce local options and enforce national uniformity and (c) belief that credible data on land values in highly developed urban areas were becoming increasingly difficult to gather (Franzsen and McCluskey 2008, 279).

South Korea: Aggregative Land Tax

South Korea undertook land policy reforms in 1990 and introduced Toji-Gong-Kae-Nyum or 'public concept in land', emphasising landowners' responsibility to put their private land into socially desirable uses. As part of these reforms, an aggregative land tax (ALT) was introduced. This expanded the scope of the erstwhile land tax base by aggregating the value of all lands owned by each taxpayer on a national basis. In order to discourage speculation, the reforms envisaged a heavy tax on land with a progressive structure. To deal with tax evasion, a single national computerised property registration and valuation system was launched by enacting the Compulsory Land Registration Act 1990; failure to register was made a criminal offence. Following this legislation, the Ministry of Construction and Transportation in South Korea developed the CAMA system.

Prior to ALT, the basic rate for both land and buildings in South Korea was a flat 0.3 per cent. Residential buildings were subjected to tax rates of 0.3 to seven per cent (Younghoon Ro 2001). With ALT, the country embraced a policy shift toward heavier land taxation, culminating in the CREHT. The objects of CREHT are land and residential houses, including land on which a house is located. In 2013, in the case of a residential house, the rates of CREHT varied from 0.5 per cent to two per cent, depending on tax base. The tax rates on vacant land ranged from 0.75 per cent to two per cent. The tax rates on land attached to store, office, buildings and so on varied from 0.5 per cent to 0.7 per cent (Ministry of Strategy and Finance 2013). In 2000, CREHT contributed as much as 30–80 per cent of the annual revenues of local authorities (Lee 2000).

Taiwan: LVT and LVIT

Taiwan presents an outstanding example of LVT and LVIT, leading to surplus local budgets. Influenced by the Georgist ideology, Taiwan enacted the Statute of Equalisation of Urban Land Rights in 1954. This was based on four principles: (a) fair assessment of land value; (b) taxation according to declared value; (c) optional public purchase of land at declared value and (d) public enjoyment of land value increments in the future. LVT and LVIT aim at curbing speculation in land and preventing the concentration of land ownership, apart from raising revenues to finance public services. They are levied in addition to house tax, deed tax, estate and gift tax, and agricultural land tax. House tax is levied at rates of 1.38 per cent of current value in case of owner-occupied house, 1.38 to three per cent for other residential property, 1.5 to 2.5 per cent for non-profit use, and three to five per cent for commercial use.

In Taiwan, LVT is based on official declared value (ODV) assessed by local authority every three years—with assistance from the Land Value Assessment Commission. It is a highly progressive tax with rates ranging from one to 5.5 per cent, depending on the percentage difference between ODV and a starting accumulative value assigned by the government.

LVIT, also a steeply progressive tax, is based on realised gains from land transaction. It is levied at rates varying from 40 to 60 per cent, depending on the percentage increase in land value from 1977. Taiwan also levies 'vacant land tax' at a rate two to five times the basic rate of LVT. This is aimed at curbing speculation and promoting development. Vacant land is defined as private urban land designated for building use in a town planning scheme, but not developed within the time period stipulated by local authority. For the purpose of tax, the improved site on which the value of buildings constructed is less than 10 per cent of land value is considered as vacant.

LVT constituted 8.21 per cent and LVIT, 23.03 per cent of local taxes collected in Taiwan in 1982. The figures increased to 20.58 per cent and 31.79 per cent respectively in 2004 (Tsui 2006).

USA and Canada: Land Gains Tax

The state of Vermont in the United States introduced (LGT) in 1973 to discourage speculation in land. Sellers of land are liable to pay LGT, in addition to capital gains income tax. The tax is imposed on the gain from sale or exchange of land if held by the seller for less than six years. It is highly progressive, with the tax rate going from a high of 80 per cent for gains over 200 per cent on land held less than four months to a low of five per cent for gains of less than 100 per cent on land held between five and six years. Property held longer than six years is exempted from LGT. The state of Ontario in Canada initiated LGT in 1974 with tax rate of 20 per cent on realised gains on all real estate.

Ireland: Windfall Tax

Ireland introduced windfall tax in 2009, with a special rate of 80 per cent on profits and gains accruing to individuals and companies on the disposal of 'development land' with re-zoning.[6] Development land is defined as land (including buildings) disposed of for a price higher than its 'current use value', that is, the value it would have fetched had no developments been carried out in relation to land. Windfall is defined as the increase in market value of land as a result of a relevant planning decision. The windfall tax is applicable to re-zoning of land made on or after 30 October 2009 and to cases where the gains are from the grant of planning permission on or after 4 February 2010 for undertaking development that materially contravenes the development plan for the area. Rezoning could be from non-development (for example, agricultural) to development (for example, residential, commercial or mixed) use. There is an exemption from the special 80 per cent rate of tax on the disposal of sites of less than one acre, provided the market value at the time of disposal does not exceed €2,50,000.

Malaysia: Real Property Gains Tax

Capital gains are generally not subject to income tax in Malaysia. Based on a 1976 law, the country levies real property gains tax (RPGT) on chargeable gains arising from disposal of real property or of interest, options or other rights in or over such land as well as disposal of shares in real property companies.[7] RPGT is levied on the difference between disposal price and acquisition price of real property. The disposal price is the money or value of consideration from disposing any asset minus the cost or expenditure incurred in upgrading, maintaining or selling the same. The acquisition price is the amount or value of consideration paid minus the sums received by way of compensation or insurance for damage to or loss of asset, and deposit forfeited in connection with intended transfer of asset. When there is a written agreement, the date of such agreement is taken as the date of disposal; otherwise it is the date when the asset is disposed.

Effective from 1 January 2010, gains from the disposal of real property in Malaysia were taxed at five per cent and collected through a withholding mechanism, whereby the purchaser withheld two per cent of the purchase value and paid to the Inland Revenue Board. From 1 January 2014, the Malaysian government has substantially increased the RPGT rate. Citizens and permanent residents are required to pay tax at 30 per cent in respect of properties disposed within three years of purchase. Disposals in the fourth and fifth years attract a tax rate of 20 per cent and 15 per cent respectively. The tax rates for companies are similar to those for citizens and permanent residents with the exception that disposals in the sixth and subsequent years would be subject to a tax rate of five per cent, unlike zero per cent for individuals. Non-citizens pay a tax rate of 30 per cent on the disposal of property within five years of acquisition.

Real Estate Transfer Tax

Real estate transfer tax is an ad valorem tax on the value of property or interest therein transferred. In Australia, Japan, Sweden, the United Kingdom and India the tax is called stamp duty. Ontario province in Canada levies land transfer tax (LTT) at 0.5 to 2 per cent of property value. The practice of who pays the real estate transfer tax varies between countries. In New York State the tax is paid by the seller. If the seller does not pay it or is exempted, it falls on the buyer. In Pennsylvania, the tax is equally divided between the buyer and the seller. In India, stamp duty is borne by the buyer. Andhra Pradesh levies a surcharge on stamp duty at two per cent of the property value and shares the same with municipalities.

In the United States, real estate transfer tax can be levied by cities. For example, in Pennsylvania, both the state and cities adopt a tax rate of one per cent each. From 2008, Toronto has introduced an additional municipal land transfer tax (MLTT) applied to the purchase price of land, adopting rates similar to those of Ontario province. In Indonesia, land and buildings transfer tax has become a local tax since 2011, with Jakarta being able to levy its own tax up to a maximum of five per cent (McCluskey and Franzsen 2013, 177).

Vacant Land Tax

Internationally, several cities such as Bogota, Buenos Aires, Mexico City, Rio de Janeiro, Cape Town, Durban, Johannesburg and Manila tax vacant land at a significantly higher rate compared to built-up property. The Constitution of Brazil, under Article 182, empowers municipalities to demand owners of un-built, under-used, or unused urban land to provide for adequate use thereof as per master plan, subject to the imposition of graduated vacant land tax—at rates that are progressive in time.

In metro Manila, cities have the authority to levy 'idle land tax' with a maximum surcharge up to five per cent. In Quezon City, the tax rate on idle land located adjacent to national highway is three per cent over and above the property tax. The prevailing tax rates for 2009–10 were: 1.5 per cent of the assessed value for residential property and two per cent for commercial, industrial and special properties. For other locations the surcharge is one per cent (McCluskey and Franzsen 2013, 176). In Andhra Pradesh, vacant land tax is levied at a rate of 0.50 per cent of the capital value of land in municipal corporations and 0.20 per cent in municipalities.

Table 4.2

Tamil Nadu: Urban Land Tax Scheme

S. No.	Chennai and other Urban Agglomerations (Sq. feet)	Tax (% of Market Value)	Urban Lands in Chennai City Belt Area (Sq. feet)	Tax (% of Market Value)
1.	Less than 4,800	Nil	Less than 7,200	Nil
2.	4,801–12,000	0.7%	7,201–16,800	0.7%
3.	12,001–24,000	1.0%	16,801–24,000	1.0%
4.	24,001–48,000	1.5%	24,001–48,000	1.5%
5.	More than 48,000	2.0%	More than 48,000	2.0%

Source: Government of Tamil Nadu: Revenue Department Policy Note 2011–12.

Tamil Nadu: Urban Land Tax

Tamil Nadu implements an urban land tax (ULT) scheme based on the market value of land as on 1 July 1981. Tax rates range from 0.7 per cent to two per cent (see Table 4.2).

Lessons from Theory and Practice

LVT is theoretically elegant—principled, coherent and fair. Apart from economic arguments, Henry George had cited moral reasons in favour of LVT, terming it as 'the taking by the community, for the use of the community, of that value which is the creation of the community' (George 1879). Most economists regard LVT an ideal source of financing local government, a stabiliser of land and housing markets, and a catalyst of planned urban development. LVT encourages capital, which would otherwise be invested in land and property for speculation, to move to more productive activities. It promotes land use in accordance with zoning by discouraging land-hoarding, preventing urban sprawl and supporting investments in core infrastructure. The economic merit of LVT is undeniable.

Property values in urban areas are heavily dependent on location. The market value of property comprises value of site and improvement values. Site values symbolise the phrase 'location, location and location'. They explain why some parcels of land are in great demand and others are not. The locational value of land reflects the wider efforts of society, including spatial planning and infrastructure development. Owners with land located at vantage locations reap windfall benefits due to public policies and programmes. It is thus reasonable that LVT finances city development, ushering in a win-win situation for both government and landowners. It is intriguing that such a powerful instrument to finance planned urban development is so comprehensively ignored by policymakers and researchers in India for so long.

A land value tax is not utopian. Several countries not levying LVT in a pure form also subscribe to its principles by including capital value of land and buildings in the base of property tax. Moreover, recent reviews of international evidence on land taxation suggest that the successful design and implementation of LVT is feasible. Problems of tax administration associated with the collection of data on land-ownership, use and valuation are not insurmountable. However, as history clarifies, it is the politics of land tax that overshadows the economic arguments in its favour. As Case observes:

> It may well be that the potential gain to holding leveraged assets during boom periods are so great that even high rates of taxation do not discourage many people from jumping in. The problem may simply be that the political will to raise land taxes to levels high enough to really retard boom cycles does not exist. How high is high enough? No one knows, but it is probably closer to Henry George's 100% than to the current laws around the world. (1992, 237)

Theory and practice provide the following lessons for designing an urban land value tax in India as a key instrument of financing planned urban development:

1. Land should be differentiated from other factors of production in tax base. This is because landowners or developers can fortuitously reap huge windfall benefits simply due to the decisions or actions of public authorities.
2. The paradigm that 'development value' vests in the government is well-accepted. There is no legal case for compensating landowners suffering from 'development loss' due to zoning. However, equity in the planning system remains a contentious issue which cannot be brushed aside.
3. While both planning permission and infrastructure create substantial increases in land values, it is often the former that constitutes the bigger source of unearned increments in cities.

4. High rates and complex formulations of taxes lead to their non-adoption. Political resistance to LVT can be tackled by adopting low tax rates with simple formulae and visibly linking the tax proceeds to developments that lead to further increases in land values, benefitting landowners by more than what they pay.

5. LVT is a local revenue-generation tool and also an instrument of planned urban development. Developed countries exploited LVT and other land-related taxes during their urban transition to fund planned urban development. Developing countries like India should do the same.

6. It is incorrect to say that landowners gain without risking or economising. Imperfections in urban land markets, poor state of land records and periodic property market booms and busts suggest that landowners and developers do face considerable risks and uncertainties. It is thus desirable that they are taken into confidence in LVT as partners with the government in the process of planned urban development.

Urban Land Value Tax in India

While municipal laws of some states in India specifically provide for the levy of VLT based on capital value of land, the definition of property in all states includes land. Thus, VLT can be imposed as an LVT under the existing legal provisions for property tax in all states. Further, while the components of property tax such as water tax, drainage tax, conservancy tax, lighting tax, street tax and fire tax need to be linked to the consumption of the relevant services based on 'golden rules' of local public finance, it is appropriate to link the general tax component of property tax to the capital value of land. However, as property tax in India is generally levied on annual rental value or unit area basis, urban land remains a grossly under-exploited resource. By not harnessing LVT, cities in India must have lost significant opportunities for developing infrastructure, particularly when they went through remarkable periods of land market booms.

What makes LVT special in the urban context is that it promotes urban development in accordance with spatial planning objectives, apart from subscribing to the benefit principle of taxation. A city development plan calls for the judicious allocation of urban land for various uses in accordance with zoning regulations and for development of 'leading' infrastructure. LVT acts as an instrument to not only prevent speculation in land, but also promote housing and other productive activities that generate economic growth and employment. It can also be a powerful instrument to promote the sustainable use of land with beneficial impacts on the urban design and form. However, a strong political will is needed for its levy.

In the light of discussions in this chapter, we suggest the following agenda for the implementation of urban land value tax in India:

1. A split rate property tax—one rate for land and another related to the consumption of 'collective' civic services—may be adopted on the ground that unearned benefits to land due to public investments may significantly exceed those to buildings. The general tax component of property tax may be in the form of a progressive land value tax, based on capital value of land. For the calculation of tax, the ready reckoner value of land determined for the purpose of stamp duty may be followed till a more robust method is put in place.

2. VLT, based on capital value of land, may be implemented in all states. International experience suggests that a VLT at 0.5 to two per cent of the capital value of land could generate a significant amount of municipal revenue to finance trunk infrastructure facilities. To start with, a VLT at 0.5 per cent of capital value of land in larger cities and 0.2 per cent in smaller towns, as practiced in Andhra Pradesh and Telangana may be adopted. The rates are very small compared to the international benchmark, but can yield substantial revenues considering the large extents of land that cities occupy and the extensions of boundaries that take place.

3. A time period of five years may be provided for the completion of construction on a vacant plot following the approval of layout or provision of connectivity infrastructure after which a steeply graduated VLT may be applied. The tax rate may go up to three per cent of land value depending on the period land is held idle.

4. The tax rate on vacant land should be set higher than that on built-up property to discourage speculation in land and promote investment in housing and other productive activities.

5. Properties with more than a certain percentage of land area utilised for building, say 50 per cent, may be exempted from VLT.

6. If the VLT levied on a property is not paid, the same may be recovered with penalty under law without limitation when a transaction or development in the property takes place.

7. The general tax component of property tax and VLT may be escrowed to 'leverage' market borrowing to undertake infrastructure development projects that lead to increased land values to owners and make way for further resource mobilisation.

8. Efforts may be made to shift to property taxation based on capital value of land and buildings in large cities to benefit from the ongoing increases in real estate values due to urbanisation, agglomeration externalities and economic growth.

9. A city real estate transfer tax may be considered for being levied on the seller subject to appropriate deduction under the capital gains component of income tax. This tax may be earmarked for city and regional infrastructure, including mass rapid transit.

Land value taxation is only one of the land-based instruments, though a critical one, available to ULBs to finance urban development. There is a need to combine it with other land-based local revenue sources, including property tax, benefit charge, development financing and value capture financing instruments. In Chapter 4 we dwell upon reforms in property tax. Chapter 5 discusses tools such as betterment levies and special assessments under the caption of 'benefit charges'. Chapter 7 throws light on land development financing tools, including non-fiscal mechanisms such as land pooling and land readjustment. Chapter 8 presents a range of value capture instruments, aimed at recouping and recycling the unearned increments in land values in cities to usher in a self-financed process of planned urban development.

Notes

1. Winston S. Churchill: Speech made to the British House of Commons on 4 May 1909. See www.wealthandwant.com/themes/Ripening.html (accessed on 30 October 2015).
2. See Prest (1981) for an excellent exposition of the history of urban land taxation in the United Kingdom.
3. Barker Review on Land Use Planning: Final Report, 2006
4. See Andelson (2000), Anderson (2009), Bird and Slack (2004), Dye and England (2010) and UN–HABITAT (2011) for review on theory and international practice on land value taxation.
5. Government of Western Australia, Department of Finance: http://www.finance.wa.gov.au/cms/ (accessed on 9 December 2015).
6. National Asset Management Agency Act 2009: http://www.irishstatutebook.ie/2009 (accessed on 9 December 2015).
7. Real Property Gains Tax Act 1976 (Act 169), Ministry of Finance, Malaysia.

5

Reforming the Property Tax

Importance of Property Tax

Property tax is the single-most important 'own' tax of ULBs in India, except Mumbai. On an average, property tax constituted 16 per cent of total municipal revenues and 30 per cent of 'own' municipal revenues in India in 2012–13.[1] Per capita property tax collected in the country in 2012–13 stood at ₹517, ranging from ₹70 for nagar panchayats to ₹206 for municipalities and ₹813 for municipal corporations.[2] The figure varied from ₹42 to ₹1,677 in 478 sampled municipal bodies across states (Finance Commission of India 2015, 116). At the current stage of India's urban evolution, property tax, with its components and variants such as holding tax, general tax, city services tax and vacant land tax, presents one of the most appropriate instruments to meet the costs of civic services and 'leverage' resources for planned urban development.

Property tax-GDP ratio ranged between 0.16 and 0.24 per cent in 36 largest municipal corporations in India in 2006–07 (Finance Commission of India 2009). The ratio for the country, as a whole, is estimated at 0.18 per cent in 2007–08 and 0.16 per cent in 2012–13. The figure is very low compared to state tax-GDP ratio of 6.8 per cent and central tax-GDP ratio of 10.3 per cent in 2012–13. Corporation tax-GDP, income tax-GDP and service tax-GDP ratios in the same year were 3.52 per cent, 1.94 per cent and 1.31 per cent respectively (Finance Commission of India 2015, 28 and 56).

International comparisons reveal that property tax is grossly under-exploited in India. For the 2000s, property tax-GDP ratio was 2.12 per cent for developed countries, 0.68 per cent for transitional countries and 0.60 per cent for developing countries (see Table 5.1).

Table 5.1

Property Tax Revenue as Percentage of GDP

	1970s	*1980s*	*1990s*	*2000s*
OECD Countries	1.24	1.31	1.44	2.12
	(9.7)	(9.9)	(13.65)	(12.40)
Developing Countries	0.42	0.36	0.42	0.60
	(18.7)	(15.97)	(13.49)	(18.37)
Transitional Countries	0.34	0.59	0.54	0.68
	(3.67)	(4.92)	(7.75)	(9.43)
All	0.77	0.73	0.75	1.04
	(14.49)	(12.89)	(11.63)	(3.40)

Source: Bahl and Martinez-Vazquez (2008).

Note: Figures in parenthesis show property tax as a percentage of total revenues of municipalities.

Assessed values of properties were estimated at 8–10 per cent of prevailing market values and on an average at 30 per cent in 36 largest municipal corporations of India in 2006–07. Only 63 per cent of the assessed properties and 56 per cent of the universe of properties were paying property tax. Further, as against the house properties actually assessed, collection efficiency was as low as 37 per cent (Finance Commission of India 2009). Except in the case of a few cities, such as Bengaluru, systematic property tax reforms have not been carried out in India. The large untapped potential of property tax suggests that the country has a significant opportunity to augment municipal revenues by improving the design, assessment and collection of property tax. This chapter deals with property tax reform in India in the light of the principles and international practices of property taxation.

Property Tax: Theory and Practice

In theory, property tax is a 'benefit tax', satisfying many characteristics of a good 'local tax'. Since the value that property-owners attach to civic services and infrastructure facilities reflects in property price and rent, property tax is regarded as an ideal instrument of financing local government expenditures. Research in local public finance presents the following theoretical arguments in favour of property taxes:

1. Property taxes are levied on an immobile tax base. They tax accumulated wealth, not productive behaviour. Therefore, they are efficient in terms of effects on resource allocation —supplying labour, accumulating, investing, producing, innovating and so on. In OECD countries, they are found to be the 'least distortionary' of taxes, followed by consumption taxes, personal income taxes and corporation income taxes (OECD 2010).

2. Property taxes, particularly those levied on local residents, act as 'quasi-benefit charges' for collective city services. When close linkages between taxes collected and services delivered are established, property taxes promote responsiveness by service providers and willingness to pay taxes by citizens.

3. Property-owners reap windfall gains from investments made out of land and property tax revenues. Fiscal differentials at local level capitalise into property values (Bahl and Martinez-Vazquez 2008). Thus, property taxes subscribe to the 'ability to pay' principle.

4. The high correlation between property ownership and income makes property tax a progressive tax. Land and capital are predominantly owned by the more affluent sections of society. The burden of property tax thus falls on upper and middle income households.

5. Property taxes have high visibility. This exerts pressure on municipalities to be responsible to their taxpayers for the provision of services, commensurate with the taxes paid. Transparency is likely to promote administrative and political accountability.

6. Property taxes incentivise property owners for more efficient use of land and buildings. When tax rate on vacant land is higher than that on built-up property, property taxes stimulate housing, commercial and industrial activities, enhancing economic growth and employment.

7. If properly designed, property taxes can mobilise a reasonably large sum of revenue, subscribing to the criteria of revenue productivity, elasticity, buoyancy, stability and predictability.

8. Property taxes are relatively straightforward. It is easy to identify tax base at local level and compile information for tax assessment, levy and collection. Mapping tools based on GIS, CAMA and area-based property tax regimes can increase the efficiency in property tax collection.

Despite theoretical merits, in practice, property taxes suffer from many difficulties. They are often levied on a subjective or judgemental basis. Benefits from property taxes are hard to observe. Assessment and enforcement costs tend to be high. Often exemptions granted and preferential treatments accorded to property owners are large. Free-riding on local public services creates difficulties in enforcing property taxes on urban elites owning large extents of land and buildings. VLT is not exploited. The visibility of property taxes also makes it difficult to undertake hard tax reforms due to opposition from local politicians. Further, property taxes are not productive or buoyant like income, business, sales and value added taxes. As Table 5.2 shows, property tax had a share of less than 25 per cent in total revenues of seven out of nine metropolitan cities in the world in 2010. Further, as Table 5.3 portrays, in six out of nine metropolitan cities, real property tax per capita registered a decline between 2006 and 2009 (McCluskey and Franzsen 2013, and Bahl and Linn 2014).

Property taxes are unpopular with taxpayers for several reasons. First, they are levied on potential income from property asset, not current income. People may be property-rich, but cash-poor. If land or property is not sold or rented out, this potential does not translate into liquid funds to pay tax bills. Second, if a property has not been sold recently, it does not have a determined value, agreed upon between property owner and local authority. Third, often the benefits received by the taxpayers do not correspond to the taxes paid. Fourth, property taxes are more

Table 5.2

Importance of Property Tax in Select Metropolitan Cities

Metro/City	Percentage of Total City Revenue		Percentage of Local Tax Revenue	
	2005	*2010*	*2005*	*2010*
Cape Town	22.6	20.5	33.1	41.1
Hong Kong	6.9	3.8	8.8	5.1
Johannesburg	19.9	16.3	30.0	43.8
Kuala Lumpur	68.4	44.9	92.0	93.0
Metro Manila	27.0	28.0*	43.0	54.0*
Pretoria	20.4	19.4	28.4	42.8
Rio de Janeiro	21.8	17.5	34.5	25.0
Sao Paulo	27.2	24.8	35.0	31.0
Singapore	6.1	5.8	6.9	6.3

Source: McCluskey and Franzsen (2013).

Note: * Figure for 2009.

Table 5.3

Trends in Real Per-capita Property Tax Revenues in Select Metropolitan Cities (US$)

Metro/City	2006		2009	
	Property Tax (millions)	Property Tax per Capita	Property Tax (millions)	Property Tax per Capita
Bengaluru	56.95	8.38	137.31	17.16
Cape Town	285.76	89.30	319.94	94.10
Johannesburg	364.13	98.41	321.52	80.38
Kuala Lumpur	174.74	25.32	178.38	25.12
Metro Manila	317.60	21.46	288.71	17.71
Porto Alegre	61.82	22.08	71.83	19.41
Pretoria	202.62	92.10	222.62	92.76
Rio de Janeiro	430.66	39.88	395.42	32.95
Sao Paulo	1087.81	61.46	997.64	53.07

Source: McCluskey and Franzsen (2013).

conspicuous compared to income or sales taxes. Income taxes are paid through deduction by employers at source; sales taxes are paid in small quantities hidden in commodity prices. In contrast, property taxes are raised in one or two large tranches in a year.

Problems with property taxation in India relate to tax base, tax rate, tax coverage, exemptions, valuation, assessment, billing, collection, enforcement, dispute resolution and record-keeping. In many cities property taxes are adversely affected by the lack of legal title to property, absence of land and fiscal cadastres, large scale unauthorised construction, and informal markets in transaction and leasing of properties. However, cities like Bogota, Bengaluru and Hyderabad have shown that substantial revenues can be mobilised through reforms in property tax. Initiating reforms in 2008, Bogota updated physical records and taxation values of 2.1 million properties, leading to an increase in property tax by US$171 million and the share of property tax in municipal own revenues reaching 40 per cent by 2010 (See Freire and Garzon 2014, 161). Due to a self-assessment scheme launched in 2008, property tax collection in Greater Bengaluru Municipal Corporation went up by 39 per cent between 2009–10 and 2010–11. With an enforcement-led drive, Greater Hyderabad Municipal Corporation was able to increase property tax collection by 32 per cent between 2012–13 and 2013–14.

An Analytical Framework

An analytical framework to examine the key issues in property taxation is provided by the following simplified equation (Bahl and Linn 1992):

$$R = t \times c \times v \times e \times B$$

where R = Revenue mobilised from property tax in a jurisdiction, t = average property tax rate, c = coverage ratio, that is, the ratio of taxable properties captured in the tax registry relative to all properties in tax base, v = valuation ratio or ratio of assessed to actual value of properties, e = enforcement rate or collection efficiency measured by actual tax collection as a percentage of total tax liabilities or invoices and B = legally defined property tax base.

The above equation reveals that property tax collection by a municipality depends on two policy variables: tax base (B) and tax rate (t); and three tax administration variables: coverage ratio (c), valuation ratio (v) and collection efficiency (e).

Property Tax Base

The property tax base depends on: (a) identification of properties to be included in the tax registry, (b) determination as to which properties should receive exemptions and concessions and whether tax liability will fall on the owner or the tenant, (c) collection of information on ownership and tenancy, (d) choice of valuation method, (e) preparation of valuation rolls and (f) mechanism for updating such rolls. Three approaches are used to 'assign' value to property tax base: rental value, capital value and area-based method (see Box 5.1). These methods are applied to components of property and their uses. Components of property include land only, improvements only, and land and improvements together. Property uses cover residential and non-residential; the latter divided into sub-categories such as commercial, industrial, institutional and recreational. In a sample of 121 countries around the world, the largest number are found to opt for capital value method, followed by area-based method, rental value method and flat rate tax system (Bell 2011).[3]

In rental and capital value-based systems, property-owners are primarily responsible for tax payment; in area-based regimes the occupiers of property are sometimes required to bear the property tax liability. In Bengaluru, if the owner does not pay property tax, the tenant is required to pay the same.

Box 5.1

Property Tax Base: Alternative Valuation Systems

Rental value method: Adopted in Hong Kong, Malaysia, Singapore, India, Ghana, Uganda, Niger and Trinidad, this method is based on the concept of rent being reasonably expected to a property in a fair market. Administrators using this method resort to rent surveys validated by expert judgement, or impute rent based on estimated capital value of property or net profit from property.

The merit of rental value method is that it links property tax to rental income of property owner. The difficulties with it are: (a) data on current rents may not be available, (b) some properties such as 'self-occupied' and 'industrial' rarely come to the market, (c) large tracts of vacant lands in cities have no rental value, (d) for properties subject to 'fair rent' under rent control law, tax rates become exorbitantly high, for example, exceeding 200 per cent of annual rental value in Mumbai and (e) rents represent the current use value and not value in the 'highest and best use' of property.

Capital value method: Used in most OECD countries, Latin America and South Africa, this method relies on the value of property in open market transactions. Sydney, Brisbane, Christchurch, Kingston and Nairobi implement site value or unimproved land value tax. South Africa resorts to valuation of land and buildings together.[4] Brazil and Philippines adopt separate valuation of land and buildings. Assessment of land in metro Manila is based on market transactions whereas that of buildings is based on depreciated replacement cost. This approach is followed by most Latin American countries. In Jakarta, land is classified into approximately 100 value zones according to use and location; buildings are categorised into 40 classes, with each class having a determined price per square metre.

The merits of capital value method are: (a) linkage to market value results in revenue buoyancy and productivity of property tax, (b) valuation of vacant land is possible unlike rental value method and (c) tax assessment is equitable as property values reflect benefits, those receiving more benefits paying more taxes. The difficulties with the method are: (a) adequate data on market sales may not be available, (b) in dense central areas of cities, the determination of value of properties with no comparable sales data is difficult, (c) registered property values may be underestimates as buyers underreport value to avoid stamp duty, while sellers underreport value to avoid capital gains tax, (d) property markets in cities of developing countries like India are not well-developed and a large number of transactions in property occur in informal property markets and (e) this method requires professional valuers who may be in short supply.

Area-based method: This method, under implementation in Eastern and Central Europe, India, Vietnam, Nigeria, Tanzania and so on, determines the 'unit area' value for property groups. It adopts simple area or 'calibrated' area that takes into account the characteristics of property such as location, type of construction and nature of use. Bengaluru has adopted a hybrid between an area-based and a value-based method.

The merits of area-based method are: (a) it is simple, transparent, fair and easy to implement, (b) rigorous valuation techniques or expert valuer services are not necessary and (c) it can be implemented when property markets are at a nascent stage or are informal. The demerits of this method are: (a) lack of linkage to market value deprives the tax of buoyancy and (b) arbitrariness and subjectivity creep in the classification of properties and fixation of unit values, leading to varying successes. The experiment with area-based tax has been successful in Bengaluru, but not in Delhi.

Sources: Author, Norregaard (2013) and McCluskey and Franzsen (2013).

Municipal laws provide for preferential treatments to certain categories of properties. Constitutions of countries like India exempt sovereign properties from paying property tax and subject them to 'in-lieu' payments. In South Africa and Uganda, however, government properties are mandated to pay property taxes. Cape Town and Johannesburg provide property tax rebate based on age or income. In Ahmedabad, Chennai, Delhi, Mumbai and Bengaluru, owner-occupied properties receive 50 per cent rebate. In Bengaluru, central government properties are presently taxed at 25 per cent of the private commercial property tax rates.

In Andhra Pradesh, deductions are allowed from annual rental value (ARV) toward repairs of aged buildings: 10 per cent if age is 25 years and below, 20 per cent when age is between 25 to 40 years and 30 per cent if age exceeds 40 years. A rebate of 40 per cent of ARV is allowed for owner-occupied residential buildings, inclusive of deduction permissible towards age of building. Owner-occupied residential buildings can also be exempted from property tax by a municipal council resolution, if the ARV does not exceed ₹900 in municipal corporations, ₹450 in major and ₹300 in minor municipalities. The state exempts the following categories of buildings and lands from property tax: places of public worship, choultries, recognised educational institutions including hostels, libraries and playgrounds, ancient monuments not used as residential quarters or public offices, charitable hospitals and dispensaries, hospitals and dispensaries maintained by railway institutions, burial and burning grounds, buildings and lands owned by municipality and irrigation works vested in government. In the case of houses constructed by government for weaker sections, the property tax is fixed at only one rupee per half-year.

Property Tax Rates

The rate structure of property tax: whether there should be a single tax rate for all properties or different tax rates for different classes and who sets the tax rate vary between cities. In most cities, different rates are adopted for residential and non-residential properties and classes within them. In Cairo and Jakarta, the central government fixes the tax rate. In metro Manila, Kuala Lumpur, Kampala and Lagos, cities have discretions to fix the tax rate, but such discretions are rarely used. In India, municipal regulations prescribe for ceiling on property tax rates, subject to which municipal councils can fix their own tax rates. In practice, however, property tax rates tend to be sticky. In Lagos, tax rates have not changed since 2003. In Hong Kong, property tax rates are not revised for many years, but buoyancy to the tax has resulted from annual revaluation. In Hyderabad, after the self-assessment scheme was introduced in 1999–2000, property tax rates have not been revised till date.

Property Tax Administration

Property tax coverage, valuation, assessment and collection depend on the quality of municipal tax administration. The latter is critical for identification of property parcels with boundaries and dimensions, inventorisation of land and improvements, verification of titles, assignment of unique numbers to properties, recording of owners and tenants, valuation of property, preparation of physical and fiscal cadastres, tax assessment, internal and external validation, appeal against assessment, billing, collection, dispute resolution, enforcement and updating of records. The tasks require qualified and trained professionals, including valuers/assessors to prepare, maintain and update tax rolls. International experience suggests that in a highly computerised environment such as that in Hong Kong or Kuala Lumpur, an assessor/valuer can handle 17,000–21,000 property records. In a manual, paper-based system as in metro Manila, the number may be 5,000–7,000. Competency in staff is critical for efficient tax assessment and effective tax collection. Thus, the issues of recruitment and training of municipal tax officials assume critical importance.

Efficient record-keeping calls for the integration of multiple databases. If a city has one million properties and each property has 20 pieces of information, then 20 million entries have to figure in the property tax roll. Information on many parameters in the roll change over time, including those obtained from the databases of entities functioning outside the municipal revenue department. These entities include town planning department within the municipality dealing with physical planning, land use changes, layout, sub-division and building approvals; land administration and registration departments outside the purview of municipalities; and agencies entrusted with the preparation of land and fiscal cadastres. The databases of several agencies need to be linked seamlessly to update property records and values. This calls for enterprise-based management information systems and robust e-governance applications, leading to intelligent decision-support systems.

Cadastral mapping using satellite imagery, remote sensing, aerial photography and GIS, and automation of valuation rolls have led to significant property tax revenue improvements in Latin American and South African cities, Hong Kong and Kuala Lumpur. In Bengaluru,

GIS mapping has been undertaken from 2008, leading to assignment of unique identification numbers to 1.7 million properties and linking them to location, size, use, ownership, tax liability, tax payment and other parameters. This, accompanied by self-assessment and mandatory filing of property tax returns, has led to impressive performance in the collection of property tax in the city.

Property Valuation Methods

Three methods are used internationally to value property: comparative sales, costs (often depreciated replacement costs) and income (or expenditures and receipts). The comparative sales approach arrives at objective estimates of property values based on market evidence. A subject property is compared to recently-sold similar properties in the market. However, the absence of dependable titles and reliable sales data creates difficulties in applying this method. Further, as no two properties are exactly similar, sales prices of comparable properties need to be adjusted for observed differences. The costs approach assesses what the land with no structures would cost, adds the cost of actually built structures and then subtracts depreciation. The income approach values property by the potential amount it can generate.

The emergence of an automated valuation system through CAMA from the 1980s has revolutionised property valuation using market evidence in many countries. The system is widely adopted by assessors/valuers in the United States, Canada and Western Europe. CAMA estimates a hedonic price index for a class of properties, for example, residential, based on a representative sample of sold properties. The index relates sales prices to physical and locational parameters of sold properties such as size, zone of location, access to amenities, use of property, etc. through a regression model. The coefficients of the estimated regression are then used as weights to value the unsold properties.

Revaluation of Property

Property values and rents change over time depending on geographic and property-related factors, thus, keeping the taxable values current calls for adjustments in valuation using updated data such as guidance value, registration value, building cost and letting information. Accordingly, municipal laws provide for comprehensive revaluation or general revision for wholesale updating of both property records and values once in every three to five years. However, in practice, these do not take place as stipulated. While revaluations are hampered by capacity constraints in municipalities, interferences from politicians are also responsible for the lack of regular revisions in property values and assessments. Examples include property tax rolls of Nairobi (1992), Kuala Lumpur (1992), Metro Manila (1993), Rio de Janeiro (1999), Sao Paulo (2000) and McCluskey and Franzsen (2013, 164).

As revaluation processes are expensive and time-consuming, cities such as Hong Kong, Kuala Lumpur, Bengaluru, Hyderabad, Ahmedabad, Chennai and Delhi have resorted to self-declaration by property owners through returns filed under self-assessment schemes. Sao Paulo and Bogota resort to value-indexing to revise the values of properties by category between comprehensive revaluations. In Hong Kong, Kuala Lumpur and Bogota, the legislation empowers municipalities to ask owners to furnish complete information on property, including rent and lease particulars. In Manila, when a property is sold, the owner must complete a tax declaration, a copy of which is to be lodged with the property tax assessor. Some cities resort to segmental reassessment, covering one-third of properties every year so that all properties are reassessed within three years.

Billing, Collection and Enforcement

Cities generally resort to property tax billing half-yearly or annually. In South African municipalities, property tax can be paid in the municipal office, post offices, large retail stores, online or by direct debit from a bank account. In Andhra Pradesh and Telangana, property taxes can be paid anywhere in computerised kiosks, operated by private operators selected by the government. In Bengaluru, these can be paid online, through banks and computerised kiosks or by credit card. Most cities provide for discounts for early payment and charge penal interest for arrears.

Municipal laws provide for appeal to a designated appellate authority or court against an assessment. As the appeal process takes a long time, to safeguard against the loss of revenue, municipal laws in countries require the appellant to deposit a certain percentage of the disputed tax amount before the appeal is heard. In Lagos, at least 50 per cent of tax assessed must be paid before appeal. In Andhra Pradesh, 100 per cent of the revised tax must be paid before the appeal is admitted. Laws also provide for attachment, sealing or seizure of properties for not paying taxes and for their sale in an open auction, subject to conditions. However, such drastic options are seldom exercised due to the lack of political will. In some countries, laws provide for disconnection of electricity or water supply in the case of persistent default in property tax payment. However, in states like Andhra Pradesh, the courts have held that such disconnection of essential services should not be resorted to as municipalities have other means to enforce tax payment. In South Africa and Nairobi, a 'no property tax due' certificate is asked for before a property registration can take place.

In many cities, properties with title disputes or unauthorised constructions are kept out of tax rolls. However, as these properties avail civic services, the occupiers must pay towards their costs. Some states in India subject such properties to property tax or service charge with a rider that tax payment does not tantamount to a conferment of title on the tax-payer, a subject which is to be decided by civil courts.

International experiences in property taxation suggest that simplification of tax laws, rationalisation of tax base and valuation procedures, preparation of land and fiscal cadastres using satellite and remote sensing data, field surveys for validation, adoption of GIS, GPS and geo-informatics, indexation of property tax to market value between revisions, upgradation of human resource, use of e-tools to track valuation, assessment, billing, collection and enforcement, and close involvement of political leaders as well as taxpayers associations are important measures to enhance efficiency in the property tax system. Some researchers advocate a 'collection-led' strategy in developing countries as against a 'valuation-pushed' strategy (Kelly 1995). However, experiences of Indian cites that have achieved impressive results due to reforms suggest that property taxation should be viewed with a systems approach, rather as a combination of disjointed activities. Systemic reforms must go hand-in-hand with efforts to improve collection efficiency.

India: Property Tax Reform Initiatives

Property tax is a neglected municipal revenue source in India. Article 243Y of the Constitution of India mandates the SFC to review and recommend 'measures' to improve municipal finances. However, no SFC in the past has provided a road map for property tax reforms. Article 280 of the Constitution also mandates the CFC to suggest 'measures' to supplement the resources of municipalities. However, while the 10th, 11th and 12th Finance Commissions did not go into property tax reforms, the 13th Finance Commission has gone into the issues in some detail. The 14th Finance Commission has suggested the levy of property tax on plinth area basis, minimising exemptions and introducing self-assessment.

The plinth area or unit area method (UAM) was launched in the country in the nineties. Under this, property tax is fixed based on a UAV, classifying properties by zone of location, type of building and type of use, and determining a unit value per square metre of plinth area or carpet area for a class of properties.

Unit Area Method: Patna Model

Prior to 1990, property tax had lost much of its buoyancy in most states of India due to archaic rent control laws linking property tax to 'fair rent'. Moreover, there was too much discretion with tax assessors and collectors, leading to under-coverage, under-assessment and under-collection. In this background, the first experiment with the UAM in India was made by Patna Municipal Corporation. In 1993, the corporation shifted to a presumptive area-based valuation system that took into account the location, usage, built-up area and type of construction to determine tax rates. Three norms of location (principal main road, main road and others), three types of construction (pucca with reinforced concrete roof, pucca with asbestos or corrugated sheet and others) and three categories of usage (commercial/industrial, residential and others) were adopted, thus providing for 27 combinations of properties. Tax base was determined by fixing annual rental value per square feet for each of these categories. The corporation effectively reduced the tax rate from 43.75 per cent to nine per cent.

The Supreme Court of India has upheld Patna's model of property tax on the ground that it reduced arbitrariness and discretion on the part of officials and scope for corruption.

Unit Area Method: Andhra Pradesh

Andhra Pradesh is the first state in India to adopt UAM-based property tax system state-wide, introducing it in 1993. It amended municipal law prescribing for the assessment of property tax with ARV of buildings and lands determined based on unit area rates. Municipalities in Andhra Pradesh fix the ARV of buildings with reference to location, type of construction, plinth area, age of building and the nature of use. Each municipality is divided into territorial zones with reference to expected rental value based on certain factors: availability of civic amenities like water supply, street lighting, roads and drains, proximity to markets and shopping centres, educational and medical institutions, banks, post services, public offices, factories and industrial areas. Buildings situated in each zone are divided into six categories based on nature of construction: (a) reinforced concrete cement (RCC) posh buildings, (b) RCC ordinary buildings, (c) Madras-terraced or jack arch-roofed or stone slab or slate-roofed buildings, (d) Mangalore tile-roofed or asbestos-roofed or galvanised iron-roofed buildings, (e) country-tiled buildings and (f) huts. Further, buildings are classified according to use: (a) residential; (b) shops/shopping complexes; (c) public use; (d) office complexes; (e) public and private offices and banks; (f) hospitals and nursing homes; (g) educational institutions; (h) commercial purposes; (i) hotels, lodges and restaurants; (j) godowns and other business establishments; (k) industrial purposes, that is, factories, mills, workshops and other industries; and (l) cinema theatres or places of public entertainment.

All buildings located in a zone in a municipality in Andhra Pradesh are classified into 36 categories based on type of construction and use. The Municipal Commissioner conducts sample survey and gathers information on average monthly rent per square meter of plinth area fixable for each category of building. He then issues a notification proposing monthly rental values (MRV) for various categories of buildings in each zone, calling for objections and suggestions from the public. After consideration of the same, the commissioner issues a final notification fixing MRV per square metre of plinth area.

Government of India Guidelines

The GoI issued guidelines on property tax reforms to states in 1998, taking into account the Patna and Andhra Pradesh experiments. These guidelines which prescribe tax levy based on the unit area method are presented in Box 5.2.

Hyderabad Self-assessment Scheme

The municipal corporation of Hyderabad introduced UAM-based property tax with a self-assessment scheme in 1999–2000. Response from the tax-payers led to a 123 per cent increase in property tax between 1999–00 and 2001–02 in spite of the effective tax rate being reduced by two-thirds (see Box 5.3).[5]

Box 5.2

Government of India: Salient Guidelines for Property Tax Reforms

1. A good property tax structure should be based on the following principles:
   - Set low rate of property tax so as to make it acceptable to the public at large;
   - Minimise the discretion on the part of assessors in tax levy;
   - Make the process of assessment, levy and collection transparent and simple;
   - Ensure equity between classes of tax payers/property owners; and
   - Facilitate self-assessment of the tax by property owners/occupiers.
2. Area-based methods to levy property tax should be adopted. Tax on built-up (both residential and non-residential) property may be linked to factors like location of building, type of construction, use of property and carpet area of building.
3. Water tax component of property tax may be gradually replaced by water charges based on metering. Drainage and sewerage charges may be levied as percentage of water charges. The charges may be such that they reflect at least the operation and maintenance costs of water supply, drainage and sewerage as well as depreciation and loan-servicing costs. They may also contain an element of cross-subsidisation for the poor.
4. Buildings may be considered as symbolising occupancy and service use. Therefore, building tax should be such that at least the direct (major) services like local roads, conservancy, lighting and fire services, whose costs and benefits are well-understood and which are amenable to the principles of benefit taxes on residents, may broadly correspond to the costs of those services.
5. Costs of other services listed in the 12th Schedule, cross-subsidisation needs for the urban poor and funds required for lumpy capital projects of city-wise significance/loan servicing may be broadly linked to the general tax or land component of the property tax.
6. Property tax exemptions should be minimised; even for tax-exempted properties, only the general tax and not the building tax may be exempted. When exemptions are granted by the state government, full compensation may be provided to the municipalities.
7. Property tax rate should be linked to the inflation index, preferably related to the cost of municipal services for capital works.
8. The task of verification and measurement of properties and detailed costing of services may be undertaken in a comprehensive manner once every five years.
9. Municipal Tax Appellate Authorities be constituted for hearing property tax appeals.
10. Properties under dispute or unauthorised construction shall pay property tax as per law.

Source: GoI (1998).

Box 5.3

Municipal Corporation of Hyderabad: Property Tax Self-assessment Scheme,
1999–2000

The municipal corporation of Hyderabad launched a property tax self-assessment scheme in 1999–2000, assigning a unique property tax identification number (PTIN) to all taxable properties. The objectives were to ensure accountability and transparency in property taxation, correct inequities and enable citizens to calculate their property taxes by themselves.

The scheme required property-owners to file a self-assessment return in pursuance of a notification issued by the commissioner of the corporation calling for mandatory property-related information under the provisions of the Hyderabad Municipal Corporation Act. A minimum of one month of market rent was fixed as the benchmark for verification and likely acceptance of tax return, although the municipal law refers to three months rent as the annual property tax payable, when determined by the municipality. Three simple benchmark rates were floated for three broad classes of properties; property owners were induced to undertake self-assessment and gravitate toward these rates.

The self-assessment scheme in Hyderabad was a resounding success. About 1,30,000 tax-payers filed self-assessment returns within four months of the launching of the scheme. Property tax collection registered a growth rate of 70 per cent in 1999–2000 and impressive rise thereafter. The sources of the increase have been the correction of inequities in the tax system, better coverage and record-keeping, and a computer-based decision-support system.

The self-assessment principle was extended by the municipal corporation to advertisement tax and trade licensing fee. The period 1998–2000 witnessed a rise in advertisement tax by more than 230 per cent. Trade licensing fee went up by 63 per cent during 1999–2000.

The self-assessment of property tax scheme introduced in Hyderabad in 1999–2000 is continuing. However, property tax rates have not changed over the last fifteen years. During 2012–13 to 2013–14, the corporation had achieved a remarkable success in property tax collection with a growth of 32 per cent by a sheer strengthening of enforcement.

Source: Municipal Corporation of Hyderabad: Budget Documents.

Bengaluru Self-assessment Scheme

The municipal corporation of Bengaluru provides a good example of property tax reforms adopting the UAV method. It launched the optional Self-assessment of Property Tax Scheme (SAS) in 2000. The city was divided into six zones: A, B, C, D, E and F, based on the guidance values notified by the Stamps and Registration department of Karnataka government. For each zone, rental rates per square foot were determined linking buildings to location, type of construction, built-up area, use and age.

Tax rates for rented buildings in Bengaluru were fixed at levels much lower than prevailing rates under the SAS. Owner-occupied buildings were given a concession of 50 per cent. Two months deduction in the ARV was provided for repairs, etc. Further, concession was given in accordance with the age of the building. Tax was levied at 20 per cent of ARV for residential use and 25 per cent for non-residential use. A cess of 34 per cent was levied, covering education cess (10 per cent), health cess (15 per cent), beggary cess (3 per cent) and library cess (6 per cent). To facilitate political acceptability, a cap on the property tax increase was set at 2.5 times the existing liability. The process was transparent and backed by political leaders. More than 60 per cent of taxpayers filed their declarations within the prescribed 45-days period. Due to the SAS, property tax collection in Bengaluru increased by 33 per cent during 2000–01.

Learning from the optional SAS-2000, Bengaluru has shifted to a mandatory scheme by amending the Karnataka Municipal Corporations (KMC) Act 1976 to provide for self-assessment based on UAV. Section 108A of the Act defines UAV as:

[A]n average rate of expected returns from the property per sq. ft. per month determined by the Commissioner, Bruhath Bangalore Mahanagar Palike on the basis of the average market rate determined through mass appraisal method or real estate market information or any other reliable source or combination of these sources that he may consider it as sufficient and reasonable having regard to the location, type of construction of the building, nature of use to which the vacant land or building is put, area of the vacant land, built-up area of the building, age of the building, parking area of vehicles in non-residential building where it is charged and such other criteria as may be prescribed. Different rates may be determined for different area or street by classifying into zones, different nature of use to which the vacant land or building is put and for different class of buildings and vacant lands.

Provided further that the land appurtenant to a building to the extent not exceeding thrice the area occupied by such building shall be exempted from the property tax.

SAS-2008 has shifted to the concept of UAV from ARV in SAS-2000 (see Box 5.4). Filing of annual property tax returns in Bengaluru is now mandatory. Up to 10 per cent of the returns filed are required to be verified randomly. The municipal corporation has supplied a handbook to tax-payers at nominal cost, explaining how self-assessment property tax can be calculated. An online tax calculator is also made available. Three hundred and sixty help centres were organised to propagate the features of SAS to citizens and clarify their doubts. Now property tax can be paid

Box 5.4

Bengaluru Municipal Corporation: Salient Features of Self-asessment of Property Tax Scheme, 2008

In 2008, the municipal corporation of Bengaluru introduced the (UAV) system of self-assessment of property tax with the following features:

1. The city is divided into six zones: A, B, C, D, E and F, based on published guidance value of land as was in the case of SAS-2000.

2. Residential use properties are classified into five categories: (a) RCC or Madras terrace buildings, (b) RCC or Madras terrace and where the flooring of the entire house is either cement or red oxide, (c) tiled/sheet of all kinds, (d) all hutments, houses built/allotted for the poor by government and all houses in declared slums with built-up area less than 300 square feet and self-occupied, and (e) special category—falling in 100 villages newly added to the corporation.

3. Non-residential use properties are classified into: (a) buildings not-equipped with central air-conditioning facility and which do not fall under other categories, (b) those equipped with central air-conditioning, (c) star hotels, classified so by central and state governments, (d) hotels/ restaurants other than star hotels having both boarding and lodging facilities, including service apartments, guest houses and so on—classified into three sub-categories based on average room tariff, (e) entertainment houses such as cinema theatres and multiplexes—classified into four sub-categories, (f) private hospitals and nursing homes—classified into four sub-categories depending on the year of commencement, (g) marriage halls, community halls, convention centres, function halls and the like—other than hotels/restaurants, (h) industrial buildings and (i) properties other than those falling into the categories of (b) to (h). Other categories include: (a) excess vacant lands and vacant land not built upon, (b) buildings exempted from property tax and which are required to pay service charges, (c) properties on which telecommunication towers are erected and (d) hoardings/billboards, including digital or electronic.

4. For each zone and category of property, a UAV per square feet is determined as per the method prescribed under Section 108A of the Karnataka Municipal Corporation Act.

5. For residential use building, the rate of tax is 20 per cent of the taxable annual value; for non-residential use buildings it is 25 per cent. The tax rate for owner-occupied properties is half of that for tenanted.

6. Vacant land exceeding three times the built-up area is assessed at 30 per cent of the rate fixed for built-up area.

7. Over a three-year-cycle, the value increase must be at least 15 per cent, resulting in steadily increasing property tax collection.

Due to SAS-2008, property tax collection in Greater Bengaluru Municipal Corporation increased by 39 per cent between 2009–10 and 2010–11. The tempo of property tax growth is continuing.

Source: Bruhath Bangalore Mahanagar Palike. See bbmp.gov.in (accessed on 10 December 2015).

online, at computerised kiosks in Bangalore One centres, municipal offices or banks. Credit card payments facilities are also available with no user charges to citizens. Property-owners who make payments in full before April 30 can avail a rebate of five per cent. Penalty at two per cent per month is levied on defaulters after 60 days from the date property tax is due—April for first half-year and October for second half-year. It is mandatory for all properties, including unlawful properties and those in unauthorised layouts, to pay property tax without any assurance for regularisation.

Bengaluru is the first city in India to adopt a GIS-enabled database for property tax on a city scale, identifying 1.7 million properties and assigning them unique property identification numbers.

Mumbai Capital Value-based Property Tax

The municipal corporation of Greater Mumbai shifted from rateable value or ARV-based property tax to a capital value-based system in 2010. The corporation issued rules for the fixation of capital value of land and buildings in 2012. Under the new scheme, the market value of property is determined based on the stamp duty ready reckoner, revised by the Government of Maharashtra every year. The market value is then multiplied with the carpet area of property (land area in the case of open land) and weight factors notified by the corporation for the nature and type of construction, age of building, floor characteristics and use of property. This gives the property's capital value, which multiplied with the property tax rate notified the city council, determines the property tax payable (see Box 5.5). Recently, in a batch of cases filed against the new property tax system, the Bombay High Court had ruled that the property-owners can pay under the old un-amended rates with 50 per cent differential between the old and new rates, pending the outcomes of the cases.

Directions for Property Tax Reforms

Property tax is identified with the versatility of local self-government and the strength of the third tier. It lies at the core of benefit taxation. However, India lost an opportunity to reform property tax under the JNNURM, which linked the release of central government grants to progress of reforms by states and cities.

Box 5.5

Municipal Corporation of Greater Mumbai: Capital Value-based Property Assessment and Tax Calculation System

In 2012, the municipal corporation of Greater Mumbai notified rules for fixing capital value of land and buildings, following the introduction of capital value-based property taxation scheme in 2010. Property tax is calculated based on capital value determined as follows:

Capital value of open land: $BV \times UC \times FSI \times AL$, where BV = base value of open land according to the ready reckoner, UC = user category factor, FSI = permissible or approved floor space index and AL = area of land.

Capital value of building: $BV \times UC \times NTB \times AF \times FF \times BA$, where BV = base value of building according to the ready reckoner, UC = user category factor, NTB = nature and type of building factor, AF = age of building factor, FF = floor factor and BA = built-up area.

Weight factors for various categories:

User category:
Open land: open land, commercial (1.25); open land, industrial (1.10); open land, residential (1.00), etc.

Residential buildings: bungalow (1.25); room, or flat, or apartment, or tenement and the like (1.00); car parking in stilt, or basement, or podium, or enclosed garage (0.25), etc.

Shops/commercial buildings: hotels, five stars and above (1.25); mall (1.25); multiplex (1.25); shop (1.00); hospital (1.00); educational institution (0.70); etc.

Industrial buildings: industrial estate (1.25), factory, including refinery/workshop (1.25), service industrial estate (1.25), etc.

Nature and type of construction:
Luxurious RCC (1.20), RCC building other than luxurious RCC building (1.00), pucca building, excluding chawl (0.70) and semi-permanent/kachha building, including chawl (0.50)

Age of building:
Buildings with age zero to five years (1.00); more than 5 to 10 years (0.97); more than 10 to 15 years (0.94); more than 50 years (0.70)

Floor factor for a RCC building with a lift:
Above 100 floor (1.35); from 76th to 100th floor (1.30); from 51st to 75th floor (1.25)....; from 5th to 10th floor (1.05); ground to 4th floor (1.00); basement used for car parking (0.70), etc.

Property tax rates:
Property tax rates are notified by the municipal corporation of Greater Mumbai from time to time under various components: general tax (including fire tax), street tax, municipal education cess, water tax, water benefit tax, sewerage tax, sewerage benefit tax and tree cess. The combined tax rates for various user categories ranged from 0.316 per cent to 2.296 per cent in 2013.

Source: Municipal Corporation of Greater Mumbai. See http://cvs.mcgm.gov.in (accessed on 05 October 2015).

The JNNURM agenda included a mandatory reform in property tax with GIS application and a targeted collection efficiency of more than 85 per cent by 2012. However, this reform has not met with the desired success due to lack of clarity on property tax base, absence of political will and relaxation of reform conditionalities by the GoI from time to time. Little attempt was made to scientifically define the denominator of the property tax collection ratio, leaving the same for loose interpretation by cities and states. Ironically, property tax-GDP ratio in India had declined between 2007–08 and 2012–13. At less than 0.2 per cent at present, the figure is far below the potential of two per cent estimated for developing countries (UN–HABITAT 2011). The country may aim at a ratio of one per cent in the next decade or so. This could be possible through the correction of inequities in the present system, expanding coverage and adopting benchmarking.

Considering the principles of urban public finance, good international practices and lessons from experiments with unit area-based property tax in cities such as Hyderabad and Bengaluru, we suggest the following directions for reforming the property tax in India:

Clarifying Role of State Government

Entry 49 of the State List under the 7th Schedule of the Constitution of India includes 'taxes on land and buildings'. However, while assigning these taxes to municipalities, most states have kept with them overarching powers of control in matters such as determination of tax base, tax rate, exemptions and concessions, valuation procedure, etc. Often states grant concessions to classes of property owners without compensating the municipalities. They also do not permit general revision of property tax for years. These and other arbitrary actions have adversely impacted the yield from property tax in the past. For example, Rajasthan did away with property tax in municipalities in 2006 and Haryana abolished tax on self-occupied property in 2008. These taxes were re-imposed only after persuasion and threat from the GoI that central grants under JNNURM would be stopped due to non-compliance with reforms. The government of Punjab agreed to withdraw certain exemptions from property tax by December 2008 to fulfil the JNNURM conditionalities, but did not do so subsequently (Rao 2013).

Municipal autonomy requires that the areas of state control over municipalities are clearly defined under law, without a scope for arbitrary action. We suggest that the role of the state government be limited to prescribing under statute, floor and ceiling rates of property tax and procedures for its levy, including automatic indexation of tax to inflation annually, assisting municipalities in professionalising tax administration, building capacity and incentivising tax performance.

Expanding Tax Base Coverage

The poor yield from property tax in many cities is largely owed to under-coverage and leakages in tax base, apart from inefficiency in collection. A 2009 study reports that against the total number of 25.3 lakh properties in Delhi, only 9.6 lakh were in the municipal tax register (Mathur 2009). Bringing all properties, especially vacant and under-used lands and unauthorised constructions, to the tax net ought to be a top priority. To address the failure to update tax base, duly accounting for construction of new buildings, and additions and alterations to existing buildings, a mechanism to seamlessly link the databases of the revenue and town planning departments in municipalities needs to be instituted. Similarly, the property databases of municipalities ought to be connected in real time with those of the registration department. The problems of ambiguity in property ownership and tenurial rights should be addressed by establishing a land titling system. Pending this, self-declaration and mandatory filing of returns through self-assessment mechanisms may be encouraged. Further, property tax exemptions and concessions, not backed by compensatory transfers from the state government, must be eliminated. The 14th Finance Commission has recommended:

> [T]he State Government should not provide exemptions to any entity from the tax and non-tax levies that are in the jurisdiction of local bodies. In cases where the grant of such an exemption becomes necessary, the local bodies should be compensated for the loss. (Finance Commission of India 2015, 120)

The lack of a cadastre that uniquely identifies properties and their owners calls for municipalities engaging professionals to take up GIS mapping, prepare and maintain physical and fiscal cadastres. The recent experience of Bengaluru city in bringing 1.7 million properties to tax roll, using satellite imagery, remote sensing, field surveys and mapping, assigning unique identification numbers to properties and making annual filing of property tax returns mandatory suggests that the use of technology, mass appraisal system, UAV method, self-assessment procedure and indexing property tax to inflation are key directions to ensure a signifi-cant improvement in property tax collection in India in the near future.

Taxation of Government Properties

Article 285 (1) of the Constitution of India stipulates that, 'the properties of the Union shall, save in so far as Parliament by law otherwise provide, be exempt from all taxes imposed by a State or by any authority within a State'. The GoI had clarified through circulars issued in 1954, 1967, 1976 and 1985 that properties of the Union which avail all services pro-vided by municipalities would pay them service charges at 75 per cent of the taxes applicable to similar private properties. When services are availed partially, the rate applicable would be 50 per cent. If no services are availed, service charges payable will be at the rate of 33.3 per cent. With the expansion of city boundaries over the years, it may not be possible to locate a central government property that does not avail any municipal facilities, including approach roads to airports and railway sta-tions, access to city parks, storm water drainage and sewerage systems, etc. Thus, the minimum service charges payable by central government properties may be fixed at 50 per cent in terms of the existing central government instructions.

A Supreme Court judgement in 2009 in the Rajkot Municipal Cor-poration Case upheld the principle of service charges payable by central government properties. However, in most cities, the non-payment of service charges by central government departments, especially railways, continues. Interestingly, the Supreme Court has ruled that wherever properties of the state government are exempted, such exemptions shall also apply to properties of the central government.[6] Keeping this position in view, there is a need for state governments to ensure timely payment of property tax in respect of their properties to the respective munici-palities without any budgetary restriction. In fact, the Constitution of India does not provide for any exemption to state government depart-ments or their undertakings from the payment of property tax. While the central government needs to instruct its offices to pay service charges due to municipalities, a law may be enacted by the Parliament giving teeth to the GoI instructions of 1954, 1967, 1976 and 1985. As regards central government undertakings, the Supreme Court had ruled in Dum Dum Municipality Case that they cannot invoke the 'immunity' created by Article 285 (1) and that 'the levy of property taxes by the relevant municipal bodies is unexceptionable'.[7]

Improving Property Valuation

No doubt, plinth area-based systems, recommended by SFCs and endorsed by the 14th Finance Commission, meet the criteria of objectivity, transparency, fairness and low compliance costs. However, they do not keep pace with the ongoing increases in land and property values arising due to urbanisation, agglomeration externalities and economic growth. An area-based property taxation system can thus be considered a transitional measure and an eventual shift to capital value-based property tax is warranted. However, at the present stage of India's urban evolution, with property markets characterised by significant informality, the switch-over to a full-fledged capital value system may not be feasible. Moreover, property sellers under-report to avoid capital gains tax and property buyers under-report to avoid stamp duty. Thus, without reforms in these taxes, property tax based on a capital value method may not be able to achieve the desired collection efficiency.

In view of the above factors, we suggest that ULBs in India shift to capital value-based property taxation in a phased manner. Nagar panchayats and municipalities may switch over from ARV-based taxation to simple UAM as practiced in states like Andhra Pradesh. Municipal corporations, especially those of metropolitan cities, may shift to the UAV method adopted by the municipal corporation of Bengaluru. The Bengaluru model is elegant in that it combines area-based and value-based approaches to property tax. While incorporating the key elements of a capital value method, it uses readily available land and property value data from the state registration department, obviating the necessity for cumbersome and costly property-by-property valuation. While the municipal corporation of Greater Mumbai has also shifted to capital value-based property tax, the system is yet to be firmly established. The UAV system in Bengaluru has, however, gained wide acceptance with taxpayers and worth replication widely.

A key problem with the new property tax systems in Bengaluru and Mumbai is that the tax rate chosen for vacant or underused land is much lower than that for built-up property. Theory and international best practice, however, suggest that a tax on idle land exceeding that on buildings acts against speculation in the urban land market and promotes housing. Thus, a higher rate of tax on land than on built-up property may be considered as part of the design of property tax reforms.

Automatic indexation of value between comprehensive revisions is a must. Hyderabad has not been able to take advantage of its rising property values and rents since 1999–2000, when it launched the self-assessment scheme. This is due to the lack of a legal provision for the indexation of property tax to inflation annually or in pre-determined time intervals. Ahmedabad followed a calibrated area-based property tax scheme under which each property is taxed based on location, building size, age, use and occupancy parameters. However, the scheme did not incorporate a clear provision as to how these factors can be calibrated or amended over time to bring buoyancy in the system. Thus, property tax growth in the city has not been impressive (See McCluskey and Franzsen 2013, 162). Bengaluru, however, has an in-built provision for 15 per cent hike in property tax every three years. Similar indexing may be adopted by other cities.

Two-part Property Taxation

We suggest that property tax be unbundled into two taxes: land tax in the form of a LVT and building tax in the nature of a composite city services tax. This is necessary to access the growing urban land tax base, while linking civic services to taxes to promote accountability. The land tax component of property tax, and also vacant land tax, may be based on the capital value of land. This may replace the general tax component of property tax. The rate of city services tax may be determined by taking into account the cost of collective services for which user charges cannot be levied. The unit area method may be used to calculate the city services tax as the area of a property is a good proxy for the use of civic services by the property owner or tenant. This method is particularly suitable for residential properties, which can be easily divided into homogeneous groups. For highly heterogeneous non-residential properties, the principle of 'averaging' inherent in the UAM makes the tax regressive, apart from resulting in a loss of tax legitimately due from high value properties. In Delhi, this was a key reason why property tax collection stagnated after the UAM was introduced. Thus, utmost care needs to be taken to classify non-residential properties.

Strengthening Institutional Framework

Strengthening municipal tax administration with professional manpower and technical support from expert bodies is necessary to address the problems plaguing property tax in India. In this regard, the 13th Finance Commission recommended the establishment of a central valuation board in each state with a view to standardising property valuation and setting guidance values from time to time (See Finance Commission of India 2009, 163–64). It has referred to the Municipal Property Assessment Corporation (MPAC) of Ontario province in Canada. MPAC is a non-profit corporation funded by Ontario's 445 Municipalities and has a Board of Directors appointed by the Ontario Ministry of Finance. The MPAC assists municipalities in assessing properties on a comprehensive, consistent and predictable basis. It collects property-related data and also prepares property tax notices for municipalities. The MPAC adopts a differentiated approach to value property and uses a CAMA system. In India, West Bengal has established a valuation board under law to enumerate and assess the value of properties in municipalities, excluding Kolkata Municipal Corporation. It has adopted a transparent approach to value property and made the valuation procedure publicly known.

While the establishment of a property tax board at the state-level is a desirable step, the institution will not be in a position to deliver desired results unless it has expertise and there is a political will to accord it independence and to accept its recommendations.

Revamping Tax Administration

The entire municipal administration in India, including tax administration, needs to be modernised. Application of satellite imagery, remote sensing and GIS techniques for mapping properties; seamless integration of multiple databases, linked to each other with a unique property identification number; and enhancement of capacity can lead to a powerful decision-support system for augmenting property tax collection. Structured interfaces between databases covering assessees of property tax and value added tax, consumers of water and electricity, holders of trade licenses, shops and establishments enumerated under labour law and hospitals, nursing homes and eating establishments registered under public health law, etc. can improve record-keeping and reduce property tax evasion. A strong property market information system linked to e-collection of property tax: online and through computerised kiosks or service centres as in Hyderabad and Bengaluru is a basic requirement for a well-functioning property tax system.

Promoting Ownership of Reforms

Ownership of property tax reforms by all stakeholders, especially taxpayers, is the key to their success and sustainability. In this connection, engaging political elites for their buy-in, institutionalising participation of residents' welfare bodies and taxpayers' associations in civic affairs, establishing close linkages between taxes paid and services delivered, instituting tax guidance facilities and conducting informed education campaigns are of critical importance. Tax reforms have succeeded when tax systems are simplified, made easily understood by taxpayers, owned by key stakeholders and driven by a capable, trained, well-motivated and taxpayer-friendly administration.

Both system improvement and collection-led approaches to revamp property tax need to go hand-in-hand. In fact, the experiences Hyderabad and Bengaluru Municipal Corporations with self-assessment schemes suggest that systemic innovations are largely responsible for improvement in collection performance. They have, in a way, marginalised the role of revenue collection machinery. Such systemic reforms require a robust regulatory framework for property taxation covering all aspects such as tax base, tax rate, tax liability, exemptions and concessions, valuation, revaluation, indexation, billing, collection, enforcement and dispute resolution. In particular, the archaic rent control laws still persisting in some states must be repealed. Such laws are outdated and have outlived their utility. They serve no purpose, except perpetuating vested interests.

Reforms in property tax are long overdue in India. Systemic reforms along with professionalisation of municipal administration will go a long way in making property tax a revenue-productive and buoyant tax to finance India's urban transformation.

Notes

1. Based on municipal finance data submitted by state governments to the 14th Finance Commission of India, ASCI (2014).
2. Based on municipal finance data submitted by state governments to the 14th Finance Commission of India, ASCI (2014).
3. The number of cities using various methods are: capital value of land and buildings together (52), capital value of land only (16), capital value of land and buildings separately (8), capital value of buildings only (4), area-based approach (42), rental value method (37) and flat rate tax (6).
4. South African metropolitan cities have set tax rates ranging from 0.5 per cent to 0.9 per cent of market values for residential properties and 1.0 to 2.5 per cent for commercial properties.
5. The author, who worked as Commissioner of Hyderabad Municipal Corporation during the period 1998–2002, designed and launched the Hyderabad self-assessment of property tax scheme.
6. See Supreme Court Order dated 19.11.2009 in Civil Appeal No.9458-63/2003: *Rajkot Municipal Corporation and Others vs. Union of India and Others.*
7. See Supreme Court Oder in *Municipal Commissioner of Dum Dum Municipality and Others Vs. India Tourism Development Corporation and Others (1995) 5 SCC 251.*

6

User Charges, Benefit Charges and Fees

Municipal Services and Cost Recovery

Municipalities levy charges and fees for the goods and services they provide.[1] These non-tax sources are broadly divided into user charges, benefit charges and fees. User charges are collected in the direct sale of local public goods and services that are in the nature of private goods. Benefit charges are imposed when the direct levy of user charges is not feasible or adequate, but investment in public facilities results in conspicuous benefits to identifiable individuals or groups. Fees are levied in connection with municipalities delivering regulatory and administrative services. Municipal user charges, benefit charges and fees subscribe to the benefit principle of local public finance.

User charges are prices of local public goods and services. They include charges for water, sewerage, solid waste collection and public transport, entrance fees to parks and swimming pools and tolls on roads. User charges differ from taxes in that they are voluntarily payable in the process of exchange for a benefit conferred on the payer. Taxes are compulsory payments that do not necessarily bear any direct or specific relation to the services that taxpayers receive. From a legal point of view, taxation is an exercise of a fundamental, necessary and sovereign power of the state. Its primary role is to raise revenues required by public authorities. Courts have ruled that user charges must be uniform within classes of customers and service. Further, they cannot exceed the allocable share of costs to the payer.

Benefit charges do not arise directly in the provision of public goods or services. They relate in some ways to the benefits received by individuals or groups as a result of public investments. They are often imposed on the value or physical characteristics of properties (for example, plot size, road width, road frontage, building height, etc.) that are serviced or benefitted from local public expenditures. Benefit charges such as on-site and off-site development charges, impact fees, betterment levies and special assessments have been used extensively by countries around the globe in the financing of urban infrastructure and even slum-upgrading projects (Bahl and Linn 1992, Bahl, Linn and Wetzel et al. 2013 Freire 2013 and Ingram et al. 2013). Development charges, impact fees and betterment levies are paid upfront by developers while obtaining development permission. Special assessments are charges to recoup a part of the windfall gains in property values accruing to landowners after specific infrastructure investments occur.

Fees are levied by municipalities in the discharge of regulatory and administrative functions. In general, fees are imposed when either the local government has monopoly in providing a service (for example, birth or death certificate) or use of a service is mandatory (for example, trade licence to do business or building permit to take up construction). In contrast, user charges involve the voluntary consumption of a service for which there may be competitive suppliers. Municipalities also collect fees in connection with processing applications for licences, conducting inspections and enforcing regulations.

Apart from user charges, benefit charges and service fees, local authorities also resort to 'polluters pay', 'exacerbaters pay' and 'congesters pay' charges. These are corollaries to the benefit principle of public finance, founded on the premise that those who are responsible for creating dis-benefits or adverse consequences to the community must pay for their mitigation. They are imposed under the police powers of the state on persons, activities or properties that create negative externalities.

User charges and fees, in addition to mobilising resources for financing civic services and infrastructure facilities, serve a vital purpose. They promote the efficient allocation of public resources and socially desirable outcomes. They provide a signal to local governments on how much to produce, and to service-users on how much to consume. User charges make local governments provide services what citizens want and are willing to pay for. They guide decision-making regarding investment in the expansion of infrastructure facilities that generate services. Correct pricing of environmentally-sensitive services also assists local authorities in addressing the problems of environmental degradation. Bird and Tsiopoulos (1997, 28) observes:

> User charges are potentially too important an instrument in improving public sector outcomes to be left to the vagaries of officials and politicians looking for money from any source, special-interest groups defending their particular subsidies on public-interest grounds, journalists looking for sensational headlines, or, for that matter, economists trying to sell efficiency as a panacea for all of society's ills.

In spite of the importance of user fees, not much has been done by municipalities in India to recover the 'full' costs of services—O&M, capital, environmental, social and, most importantly, opportunity costs. Ironically, a recent study of 360 water utilities around the globe indicates that average public utility water rates in India, instead of keeping pace with inflation, have declined between 2006 and 2012—from $0.154 to $0.152 per cubic metre. In contrast, water rates have increased at an average rate of nine per cent per year in Chinese cities over the same period—from $0.29 per cubic metre in 2006 to $0.47 per cubic metre in 2012. The price of water in Hong Kong and Tianjin is reportedly $0.65 per cubic metre (Becken et al. 2014).

Insufficient cost recovery in services subjects cities to a vicious circle. It leads to poor O&M of public facilities and resistance by citizens to pay charges and taxes. The inability of local authorities to provide services of a desired quantity, quality and reliability adversely affects the willingness of city residents to pay. This in turn leads to inadequate outlays on infrastructure and human resource, further deterioration in services and inability of authorities to raise tariffs to improve them. In the process the urban poor, with limited access to lifeline services such as safe drinking water and sanitation suffer the most. The vicious circle needs to be broken by adopting 'users pay', 'beneficiaries pay', 'polluters pay', 'exacerbaters pay' and 'congesters pay' principles.

This chapter reviews the state of municipal user charges, benefit charges and fees in India. It argues that the poor design of cost recovery instruments and inability of local authorities to demonstrate a close connection between charges/fees and services are key factors as to why they are yet to become a major source of municipal finance in India.[2] It refers to the principles and practices of urban economics and public finance to suggest a tool box of instruments for municipalities in India to raise resources based on the 'generalised benefit principle'. This principle states that those who receive benefits from public policies and programmes, 'specific' or 'general', including those from agglomeration externalities in cities pay for civic services and planned urban development. This can lead to a win-win situation for all stakeholders and a self-financed process of urbanisation and economic growth.

State of Municipal Services in India

Box 6.1 portrays the state of civic services in India. The picture for the urban poor, including slum-dwellers, is much worse than what the box portrays. For example, the percentage of slum households having access to closed drainage and to latrines with water closet in 2011 is 36.9 per cent and 57.7 per cent respectively. The corresponding figures for 'urban' stand at 44.5 and 72.6 per cent. Compared to 18.6 per cent for urban area as a whole, 34 per cent of slum households have no latrine facility within premises (Office of the Registrar General 2011). In Chennai, only 19 per cent of slum-dwellers have access to improved individual toilets; the figure is 21 per cent for Mumbai and 24 per cent for Kolkata and Delhi (MoHFW 2009 and UNICEF 2013).

The High Powered Expert Committee (HPEC 2011) projects that India would, in addition to capital investment requirement of ₹3.92 million crore, need ₹2 million crore for O&M expenditures in major urban infrastructure sectors over the period 2012–31. The committee finds that Indian municipalities spend about 20 per cent of what is required for efficient delivery of civic services (HPEC 2011). This state of affairs is primarily due to the lack of cost recovery in services: directly through user charges and fees and indirectly through benefit charges such as development charges, impact fees, betterment levies and special assessments. The problem is rooted in the politics of pricing and the deficient quality of local public services delivered by municipalities and public utilities.

Municipal Charges and Fees in India

Table 6.1 presents the major sources of user charges and fees in municipal corporations of India. They constituted less than 20 per cent of aggregate municipal revenue expenditure in 17 out of 26 metropolitan municipal corporations in 2007. The figure was less than 10 per cent in 11 such corporations, the ratio being the lowest in Patna at 0.82 per cent (Mohanty et al. 2007). Recent data reveals that in 2012–13, own revenues from non-taxes, the bulk of which comprises user charges and fees, was 19.7 per cent of municipal revenues in India. This amounts to 0.20 per cent of GDP as against 2.3 per cent in OECD countries. In Greece, Ireland and Netherlands, fee revenue even exceeds the mobilisation from local taxes (OECD 2010, 181).

Box 6.1

State of Urban Public Service Delivery in India

Water Supply

- Only 71 per cent of urban population is covered with an individual water connection in India compared to more than 91 per cent in China, 86 per cent in South Africa and 80 per cent in Brazil.
- The duration of water supply in Indian cities range from one hour to six hours—as against 24 hours in China and Brazil, and 22 hours in Vietnam.
- Per capita water supply in Indian cities ranges from 37 lpcpd to 298 lpcpd for a limited duration, while Paris supplies 150 lpcpd continuously and Mexico 171 lpcpd for 21 hours a day.
- Most Indian cities do not have metering for residential water connections. 70 per cent of water leakages occur from consumer connections and due to malfunctioning of water meters.
- Non-revenue water accounts for 50 per cent of water production, compared to five per cent in Singapore. System losses through unaccounted for water in four large cities of Madhya Pradesh ranged from 33 per cent to 66 per cent (UN–HABITAT 2006).
- The average cost recovery in water supply is 67.2 per cent and collection efficiency is 78.8 per cent.

Sewerage

- 94 per cent of cities and towns do not even have a partial sewerage network. Almost 50 per cent of households in cities like Bengaluru and Hyderabad do not have a sewerage connection.
- 13 per cent of urban households do not have access to any form of latrine facility; they defecate in the open.
- Only 21 per cent of wastewater generated is treated. Sewage treatment capacity is less than 40 per cent in cities with more than 1,00,000 population in nine out of 11 states; it is less than 20 per cent in five states—Rajasthan (four per cent), Odisha (eight per cent), Uttarakhand (10 per cent), Bihar (13 per cent) and Madhya Pradesh (15 per cent; CPCB 2009).
- Of the 79 sewage treatment plants under state ownership reviewed in 2007, 46 were operating under very poor conditions.

Drainage

- 44.5 per cent of urban households have access to closed drainage; 37.3 per cent face open drainage and 18.2 per cent have no drainage at all.
- Less than 20 per cent of the road network in the country is covered by storm water drains.

Solid Waste Management

- Solid waste collection coverage ranges from 70 per cent to 90 per cent in major metropolitan cities, and is less than 50 per cent in smaller cities and towns as against the benchmark of 100 per cent.
- Less than 30 per cent of solid waste generated is segregated; scientific disposal of waste is almost never practiced.

Urban Roads and Transport

- While urban areas accounted for only seven per cent of the total road length of India in 2002, the number of motor vehicles in the 23 largest cities was 30 per cent of the total number registered in the country (Agrawal 2006).
- Public transport accounts for only 27 per cent of urban transport in India compared with 49 per cent in Philippines, Venezuela and Egypt and 40 per cent in South Africa, South Korea and Brazil.
- The share of public transport fleet has decreased from 11 per cent of total registered vehicles in 1951 to 1.1 per cent in 2001. In 2009, only 20 out of 85 Indian cities with a population of 0.5 million had bus service.

Affordable Housing

- The shortage of dwelling units in urban areas in 2012 is estimated at 18.78 million. Out of this, 17.96 million or 95.7 per cent pertains to Economically Weaker Sections (EWS) and Low Income Group (LIG) segments (Ministry of Housing & Urban Poverty Alleviation, Government of India 2012).
- The projected slum population in India in 2012 is 94.98 million. As against this, the number of dwelling units sanctioned under JNNURM during the seven-year mission period 2005–12 is 1.6 million.

Sources: Office of the Registrar General (2011), HPEC (2011), Planning Commission (2013) and UNICEF (2013).

In 2010, user fees constituted more than 10 per cent of total revenues of local bodies in 10 out of 15 OECD countries. The figure was 12.9 per cent (1.8 per cent of GDP) in the United Kingdom, 15.5 per cent (1.1 per cent of GDP) in Germany and 21.4 per cent (4.8 per cent of GDP) in Finland (OECD 2012). In the United States, user charges and fees constitute about 25 per cent of own-source revenues of municipalities—35 per cent, if local public utilities are included. Similarly, local governments in Canada mobilise 25 per cent of their own-source revenues through user charges and fees (Bahl 2011 and Fox and Slack 2010). In Cape Town, South Africa more than one-third of the city's revenues is derived from user charges and fees (Martinez-Vazquez 2013, 193).

Table 6.1

Major User Charges, Benefit Charges and Fees in Select Municipal Corporations in India

Name of State	Name of Municipal Corporation	Charges and Fees
Gujarat	Ahmedabad	Water charges, development permit fee, betterment charges, impact fee
Karnataka	Bengaluru	Betterment levy, building licence fee, compounding fee, road cutting and restoration charges, duct service charge
Maharashtra	Greater Mumbai	Water charges, sewerage charges, building licence fee
Odisha	Bhubaneswar	Trade licensing fee, market fee, parking fee
Punjab	Ludhiana	Water and sewerage charges, building fee, development charges, trade licensing fee
Tamil Nadu	Chennai	Trade licensing fee, private scavenging fee, market fee, road damage restoration charges, registration fee, building licence fee, parking fee
Telangana	Hyderabad	City-level infrastructure development fee, building permit fee, development charges, betterment charges, advertisement fee, trade licensing fee, open space contribution
Uttar Pradesh	Kanpur	Building licence fee, market fee
West Bengal	Kolkata	Building plan sanction fee, water supply charges, sewerage and drainage charges, trade license fee, advertisement fee, market fee

Source: Budgets of Municipal Corporations.

Economic Case for User Charges

In economic theory, user charges for services levied directly on beneficiaries lead to optimal consumption when the price equals marginal cost. The first golden principle of local public finance states that when benefits are measurable and beneficiaries identifiable, user charges are the 'first best' instruments of financing local public services. A large range of local services such as water supply, sewerage, solid waste management, parking, transport, parks and sports are amenable to financing through user charges. The second golden principle of local public finance suggests that where the measurement of benefits or identification of beneficiaries is difficult, benefit charges and earmarked benefit taxes are appropriate. They act as 'surrogate prices' for public services. By similar logic, the costs administrative and regulatory services rendered by municipalities are ideally financed by service fees imposed on beneficiaries. They promote responsibility on the part of service users and accountability on the part of service providers.

If a service is charged below what users are willing to pay for, people will generally want more of it. But this does not mean that a city can afford to give it to them at below-cost. Municipal functions cost money, which needs to be mobilised from local residents as the first resort. Further, under-pricing results in over-consumption and ill-advised decisions to invest in augmentation of facilities. This situation is called the 'black hole' problem in local public finance; more and more public resources are pumped into the production of services even when commensurate values do not accrue to the society. Correct user charges provide information to consumers on the scarcity value of service and to service-providers on the intensity of consumer demand. They ration the use of public facilities and thus guide decision-making by authorities regarding when and how much to invest in capacity expansion. They also reduce pressure on urban public finance by avoiding over-investment in under-priced infrastructure (Bird and Slack 2013, 141).

Spatial planners argue that if users are required to pay the full costs of services, urban land is used more efficiently. When price equals marginal cost, consumers far away from an existing networks of services such as water supply, sewerage and public transportation, and thus more costly to serve, are required to pay more than those located nearby. Thus, user charges discourage urban sprawl and promote compact development. They act against the uneconomic extension of city boundaries which demands the installation of costly new infrastructure facilities. Thus, the conversion of fertile agricultural land or land preserved for conservation to urban use is avoided.

Political Economy of User Charges

In practice, the designing of tariff for civic services is a political process rife with controversy. The primary reason why user charges fall short of service costs in Indian cities lies in the political economy of user charges.

Many politicians regard local public services like water supply a 'social good' rather than an 'economic good'. They consider the same 'necessities' and user charges as 'regressive'. However, the perception that user charges burden low-income families is not supported by empirical evidence. In fact, the resistance to increasing the prices of civic services comes from consumers at higher echelons of the urban society, who use them most intensively and have enjoyed subsidies for long (Bahl and Linn 1992, and Bird and Slack 2013).

Many studies show that the poor loose in a regime of city-wide, below-cost tariffs for services. When authorities fail to provide regular services in slums and low-income settlements, the poor are compelled to adopt coping mechanisms such as installation of booster pumps to draw water from distribution lines or purchase of water from private vendors at exorbitant prices. They are also subjected to loss of income due to wastage of considerable time in procuring water from alternative vendors. A study of coping costs to slum-dwellers in Delhi to deal with reduced supply of water reveals that the monthly cost to a household was ₹262 as against the monthly water bill of ₹141 (UNICEF 2013, 13).

Studies further show that the urban poor, especially slum-dwellers disproportionately suffer from adverse health consequences due to the lack of basic services. Data from the 61st Round NSS survey (2004–05) reveals that urban poverty increases by 2.9 per cent when out-of-pocket health expenditures are considered. The prevalence rates of water-borne diseases such as diahorrea and dysentry are much higher amongst the urban poor compared to the non-poor. National Family Health Survey III (2005–06) data also show that the urban poor fare worse than the rural poor in several key health indicators. They are worse-off without reliable lifeline services compared to when these are provided at some cost. A relatively simple pricing strategy with a low initial tariff for the first band of service use can adequately address the so-called 'regressivity' issue in user charges.

An oft-cited reason why water user charges are opposed politically is that the costs of measuring water consumption through universal metering and of gathering information on costs of O&M, capacity augmentation, facility replacement and so on are high. These costs enter into the formula for fixing price for water services based on marginal cost. It is also argued that municipalities do not have technical expertise in cost accounting needed to determine an appropriate tariff structure for the sustained provision of services. Again the arguments are fallacious. Even a simple pricing mechanism such as that based on average cost can make municipalities and utilities better off by discouraging over-consumption of service and generating resource to suffice costs.

Economic theory advocates that the price for a public service should cover full costs: O&M, capital, environmental, social, regulatory and administrative, and resource opportunity cost. The opportunity cost is the value of the benefits that could have arisen from some alternative use of resources had the same not been deployed to produce the service. However, municipal user charges in India do not even cover O&M costs, thereby making services deteriorate and investments in capacity augmentation unsustainable. This hurts the poor most. Thus, it is necessary that user charges reflect the true cost of services. In case local authorities are required to subsidise the poor, the same should be through limited cross-subsidisation and direct subsidies rather than distorting the entire market for services and, in the process, making everyone, including the poor, lose.

Pricing of Municipal Services

Several approaches are discussed in research to compute user charges for public services. The prominent ones are: marginal cost pricing, average cost pricing, average incremental cost pricing and multi-part tariff.

Marginal cost pricing equates user charge for a service with the cost of providing an additional unit of it, taking into account all costs: internal and external, accounting and economic, fixed and variable, environmental and social. Marginal cost pricing signals the value that consumers attach to capacity expansion, as marginal costs rise when capacity bottlenecks become acute. The method is, however, difficult to implement as it requires complete information on the current cost of service and future augmentation of supply beyond present capacity. Further, the conditions that make marginal cost pricing efficient may not obtain in practice. Free-ridership, economies of scale, sunk costs, non-priced externalities and compulsion of subsidising the poor go against such pricing. Further, when investment in infrastructure is subjected to increasing returns or decreasing average cost, marginal cost pricing leads to revenues falling short of costs.

Average cost pricing makes user charge equal to average cost of service, aiming at full cost recovery. Unlike marginal cost pricing, it usually applies to the financial cost of a service. Average cost pricing estimates the financial cost of a service and divides it by the quantity provided. A key problem with this method is that it is not efficient. When average cost declines as output increases, the price will be too high and the quantity supplied will be less than what is wanted by the society. If average cost increases as output expands, the price will be too low leading to excess demand and misallocation of resources. A second problem is that the method warrants estimation of the responsiveness of demand to price changes. It requires not only information on how the average cost changes when the number of users changes, but also on how the number of users change when the price changes. In practice, it is difficult for local authorities and utilities to gather such kind of information.

The average incremental cost pricing method arrives at the additional cost to serve an additional user like marginal cost pricing, but designs the user charge to recover full costs while making it computationally feasible. It identifies all the elements of costs and assigns the incremental costs of provision of service to each additional user, on an average basis.

Multi-part tariff unbundles the service into components and determines a separate price for each component according to its price elasticity. It sets a fixed charge for basic consumption, with progressively higher charge for upper slabs. The fixed charge is meant to recover administrative and capital costs. A multi-part tariff incorporates built-in subsidies for low-income consumers into the tariff structure. It also provides for separate fees when new connections are added to the existing network. The fees are meant to cover the capital cost of investment in the infrastructure that generates the service. These characteristics make multi-part tariff economically efficient, socially attractive and politically acceptable. In a two-part tariff, a fixed access charge is combined with a variable charge that relates directly to the consumption of service. The latter charge approximates the price determined on the marginal cost principle.

Water and Wastewater Tariffs

Water and wastewater tariff structures vary widely between countries. Wastewater tariffs are usually levied as a percentage of water tariff based on a formula that links sewerage generation to water consumption.

The importance of setting water tariffs to recover full costs has been amply emphasised by global and national policy statements. For example, the 1992 Dublin statement on water and sustainable development declares:

> [W]ater has an economic value in all its competing uses and should be recognised as an economic good. (WMO 1992)

India's National Water Policy Statement 2002 also advocates:

[W]ater charges for various uses should be fixed in such a way that they cover at least maintenance and operation charges of providing the services initially and a part of the capital costs subsequently. These rates should be linked directly to the quality of service provided. The subsidy of water rates to the disadvantaged and poorer sections of the society should be well-targeted and transparent.

Efficient water pricing requires that the tariff covers costs of water storage, transmission, treatment and delivery, and also appropriate amounts toward capital, environmental, social and resource opportunity costs. In practice, municipalities and water utilities adopt a mix of criteria in fixing water tariff: (a) financial sustainability; (b) economic efficiency; (c) social equity; (d) affordability; (e) environmental sustainability; and (f) administrative simplicity. Financial sustainability requires meeting O&M costs and recouping capital costs. Economic efficiency demands that resources are allocated to maximise the net benefit to the society. It requires that the value that consumers place on water equals the cost of the resources used in its production and distribution. Prices should signal to the consumers all the costs that their decision to use water imposes on the rest of the system and the economy. Social equity encompasses both horizontal and vertical equity. Horizontal equity requires treating people placed in similar situations similarly. It prescribes that those benefitting from public service or necessitating government regulation pay for the associated costs. Vertical equity demands those with greater ability to pay to contribute more than those with lesser means. Affordability requires that poor households are able to secure adequate supplies of clean water at affordable price. Environmental sustainability calls for incentivising water conservation for future generations and avoiding wastage. Administrative simplicity demands that the tariff is well understood by users and that the collection process is simple.

While it is difficult to have a water tariff meeting all the desirable criteria, two methods are commonly used by countries: single-part tariff and two-part tariff. A single-part tariff has two variants: (a) fixed charge or flat rate and (b) volumetric charge. Under the fixed charge system, the monthly water bill is independent of water consumption. No metering is required. In the case of volumetric charge, monthly water bill varies directly with the quantity consumed, measured by meter. Volumetric charge fall into three categories: (a) uniform volumetric tariff (UVT), (b) block tariff: increasing block tariff (IBT) or decreasing block tariff

(DBT) and (c) increasing linear tariff (ILT). Under UVT, all units of water are priced at the same rate. In the case of ILT, the price that a consumer pays increases continuously with increasing consumption of water. Under IBT, the unit charge remains constant over a specified range of water use and then increases in steps as consumption increases. For DBT, the water rate per unit decreases as the volume of consumption increases. In a two-part tariff, a combination of fixed charge and volumetric charge is adopted. The latter may be uniform, IBT or DBT.

The following formula is used to arrive at water tariff when an IBT structure is adopted.

Let Q^* = amount of water sold to a specific consumer
Q_1 = maximum amount of water that can be sold in the first or lifeline block at price P_1
Q_2 = maximum amount of water that can be sold in the second block at price P_2
Q_3 = maximum amount of water that can be sold in the third block at price P_3

If $Q^* < Q_1$, then the consumer's water bill = $P_1 Q^*$
If $Q_1 < Q^* < Q_2$, the consumer's water bill = $P_1 Q_1 + (Q^* - Q_1) P_2$
If $Q_1 + Q_2 < Q_3$ the consumer's water bill = $P_1 Q_1 + P_2 Q_2 + [Q^* - (Q_1 + Q_2)] P_3$

The merit of a fixed charge method is that it is simple and does not require metering. Its demerits are that it does not provide incentive to conserve water and often fails to recover the full costs. The principal merits of UVT are that it is simple and provides clear signals about the short-run marginal cost of using water. Its main demerit is that it does not provide for cross-subsidisation to the poor. DBT and ILT are rarely used. IBT, which is widely practiced, promotes economic efficiency by making the high block consumers face the marginal cost of water. By providing for a lifeline or subsistence block, it also achieves the objective of affordability. Further, the method has a potential to raise sufficient revenues to meet costs. A key demerit of IBT is that as many poor people share water connections, it may subject them to above-lifeline charges.

Fixed charges for water are common in Canada, Norway and United Kingdom; New York City also adopted fixed charges till recently. Some cities adopt different fixed charges for different classes of customers. UVT is pervasive in the United States, Australia and many European countries. It is commonly applied to industrial and commercial water users around the world. IBT is used in half of the water utilities in OECD countries, arid regions of Spain, part of the Middle-East and many developing countries of Africa and Asia. A recent study of 94 utilities in developing countries indicates that one-third use IBT and the remainder use flat rates. The size of a first block varies from 5 to 15 cubic meters per household per month. In South Africa, the first block of six cubic meters per household per month is provided free. Many utilities charge tariffs for commercial and industrial customers higher than for residential users to subsidise residential customers (See Farvacque-Vitkovicand Kopanyi 2014, 176).

There is no consensus on the tariff structure for water supply to be adopted by a developing country like India. Most practitioners, however, favour a two-part tariff, that is, a minimum fixed charge plus a volumetric tariff with uniform or IBT structure. The fixed charge is meant to cover administration, metering and billing costs, while contributing to the recovery of the capital cost. The volumetric tariff is set equal to short-run marginal cost, including O&M, environmental, social and resource opportunity costs. Practitioners argue that a two-part tariff structure signals the scarcity value of water while simultaneously taking care of the financial needs of capital investment. The importance of a fixed charge is obvious when the capital cost is large but due to no constraints on raw water supply the short-run marginal cost, and hence the volumetric charge, is required to be set low.

Some researchers advance economic arguments against IBT. However, it is popular in developing countries, being politically acceptable. Policymakers and administrators prefer IBT for the second part of the two-part tariff. This is on the ground that full marginal cost pricing is not practical and that IBT makes cross-subsidisation of low-income households possible, promotes water conservation and incorporates a marginal cost pricing regime for high end users. Advocates of IBT suggest that the tariff for the first block, the 'lifeline' or 'subsistence' block, say up to five cubic metres, be set low to protect the interests of poor households. For a second or normal block, say 5 to 12 cubic metres, the price may be fixed to cover O&M costs, while for a third or high block, say more than 12 cubic metres, the price may cover the full cost of service.

In India, the following mechanisms are in vogue in cities to recover water supply costs: (a) connection fee linked to plot area, size of connection or ferrule, (b) volumetric charge linked to consumption, (c) one-time development charge and/or betterment charge while according permission for layout, sub-division or construction of building, (d) water tax and water benefit tax components of property tax, (e) water cess on property and other taxes and (f) beneficiary capital contribution. In most cities, a mix of user charges, taxes and contributions are adopted. The Municipal Corporation of Greater Mumbai levies water tax, water benefit tax, sewer tax and sewer benefit tax as components of property tax. The Bengaluru Municipal Corporation levied Cauvery Water Cess on property tax to mobilise resources for getting water from Cauvery river to Bengaluru city. Recently, a beneficiary capital contribution (BCC) has been levied in newly extended areas of Bengaluru to part-finance the Greater Bengaluru Water and Sanitation Project.

We suggest that the golden principles of local public finance may be followed while fixing water tariff in cities. As water is measurable and beneficiaries of water are identifiable, user charges are appropriate instruments to recover O&M costs, subject to cross-subsidising the poor and recouping a proportionate amount toward capital and environmental costs. A two-part tariff could thus be appropriate. Again, in terms of the principles, the capital cost of water supply may be funded by borrowing, supplemented by beneficiary capital contribution, current revenue surplus of local body or utility, development charges, impact fees and capital grants from higher levels of government. Debt repayment may be linked to the fixed charge component of water charge, water tax and water benefit tax components of property tax, vacant land tax and betterment levy which may be escrowed. Further, the sewerage and drainage charges may be hooked on to water charges and capital financing of these services may follow the pattern suggested for water supply. In Singapore, a water conservation tax, water user charge and a statutory charge to offset the cost of treating used water and for the maintenance and extension of public sewerage systems are combined to meet the costs of water and wastewater services.

In some countries, water tariff is determined by a formula embodied in national legislation (for example, Ukraine). In Colombia, it is regulated by a national regulatory body. In India, water tariffs by municipalities and utilities are regulated by state governments. This has resulted in anomalous situations, where due to political reasons tariffs have not been hiked for years, even to adjust for inflation. In reality, this has adversely affected the poor. There is thus a strong case for establishing a municipal services regulator at the state-level to facilitate the fixation of tariff for services, including water supply, sewerage and drainage on scientific lines, while safeguarding the interests of poor consumers and minimising adverse consequences on the environment.

Solid Waste Management Charges

The conservancy tax component of the property tax levied by municipalities in India is supposed to meet the costs of collection and disposal of solid wastes, including hazardous wastes. However, in practice, this covers only a fraction of the total costs due to free-ridership, improper disposal, inaccurate costing and other problems. In fact, conservancy tax is often levied by municipalities based on refuse collection and transport costs, ignoring the huge amounts needed for sanitary disposal. On the contrary, cities in developed countries collect 'tipping fees' to recover the cost of maintaining and capping sanitary landfill sites. In the United States, cities are moving toward volume-based Pay as You Throw (PAYT) charges and other innovative instruments. The cities of Dallas, Los Angeles, Phoenix and San Diego collected more than 100 per cent of their solid waste management costs in 2012. San Diego levies a refuse collector business tax at $8 per metric tonne and a recycling fee at $10 per metric tonne (see Citizens Budget Commission 2015).

The poor cost recovery in solid and hazardous waste management in India is a major concern as courts are laying down stringent standards for handling and disposing these wastes. There is thus a need to revisit the way waste management is handled and financed in Indian cities. Apart from adopting 'segregation at source' and 'reduce-reuse-recycle' paradigms, the 'polluters pay' principle should be implemented. A general rule is that trash collection, recycling and disposal charges and conservancy tax must meet the full costs of waste management operations. In particular, the bulk garbage generators must be made to pay for the quantity they generate. As part of municipal reforms, the municipal corporation of Hyderabad, in addition to door-to-door collection charges mobilised locally, introduced 'bulk garbage collection charges' on generators of large quantities of garbage such as hotels, restaurants, function halls, markets and so on. Similarly, hospitals and nursing homes generating hazardous wastes are required to undertake the sanitary disposal of wastes themselves under municipal supervision, without solid wastes and hazardous wastes being mixed, or pay for the full cost of safe disposal to the municipal corporation.

Benefit Charges and Service Fees

Apart from user charges for measurable services, municipal authorities resort to benefit charges to recoup the costs of collective services and installation of infrastructure facilities. They also levy service fees in connection with discharging administrative and regulatory functions, making beneficiaries pay for specific and general services. Key benefit charges and fees levied by municipalities include special assessments, betterment charges, town planning levies, surcharges on utilities, polluters pay charges, congestion charges, parking fees, trade licensing fees, advertisement fees, etc.

Special Assessments

Special assessments, extensively used in the United States from the 19th century, are charges or taxes levied on real property to help pay for specific local improvements that benefit the property. New developments, funded through the issue of municipal bonds, are made directly responsible for the infrastructure funding needs they generate. Special assessments are levied as a benefit charge or a value capture instrument.

Special assessments in the United States cover a wide range of public works. For example, the Improvement Act of 1911 in California enables the levy of special assessment by local authorities to develop transportation system, street paving and roads, sidewalks, parks, parkways, recreation areas, sanitary sewers, drainage systems, street lighting, fire protection system, flood protection, geologic hazard abatement or prevention, water supply system, gas supply system, retaining walls, ornamental vegetation, navigational facilities, land stabilisation and other 'necessary improvements' to the local agency's streets, property and easements. The Municipal Improvement Act of 1913 added works and appliances for providing water service, electricity power, gas service and lighting, and public transit facilities serving an area smaller than three square miles (including stations, structures, rolling stock and land acquisition related thereto).

Court rulings on the imposition of special assessment suggest that four conditions need to be satisfied by a legally defendable special assessment scheme. First, the special assessment zone or district must be well-defined, with limited and well-demarcated boundaries. Second, property situated in the district must receive a special benefit from the improvement. Third, the assessment must be uniform upon the same class of property. Fourth, it may not exceed the special benefit accruing to the property. The benefit is measured by the difference between what a willing buyer would be paying to a willing seller for the property before and after the improvement, taking into account the 'highest and best' use of land. Present use is not a constraint.

Betterment Charges

Betterment is the rise in land value occurring to private individuals on account of community action (Hall 1965, 15). Typically, a betterment levy is a charge or tax on the increase in land value attributable to publicly funded infrastructure, although a betterment can as well arise from land use zoning or planning permission. The levy is collected by a local authority as a surcharge on property tax after development or when a permission to undertake development is granted. Like special assessment, a betterment levy can be compared to a benefit charge to capture land value increments irrespective of their source.

The financing of the Sydney Harbour Bridge in Australia in the 1920s, which involved the imposition of a special levy on increments in land values within a certain distance from the bridge to generate 30 per cent of cost, is a classic example of betterment levy. Latin America has used the levy for long in various forms. The Colombian cities of Bogota, Cali and Medellin have mobilised significant revenues through the instruments of *Contrubucion de Valorisacion* and *Participacion en Plusvalias*—often yielding over 25 per cent of local own-revenue sources (See Borrero et al. 2011). Bogota provides a postcard example of the long-term use of betterment levy to recoup the cost of public works, since 1921.[3] In Argentina, provinces and municipalities have financed public works through betterment levies known as *Contrubuciones de Mejoras*. Over the last decade, the municipality of Cuenca, Ecuador has awarded 1800 public works contracts and collected approximately US$200 per capita as betterment charges. Ninety per cent of households in Cuenca made their contributions in less than four years, with 95 per cent of the works mobilising 60 per cent cost through betterment contribution (Smolka 2013).

Four administrative conditions are found to be important for the effective implementation of a betterment levy: (a) a quantifiable impact on land values, (b) identifiable beneficiaries, (c) a public mechanism to implement the betterment levy and (d) the political will to implement (Bahl and Wallace 2008).

Town Planning Charges

Town planning-related charges, especially layout development and building permit fees are emerging as the most important local government charges in many developing countries. They subscribe to the 'benefit' and 'ability to pay' principles. They also facilitate development according to zoning rules, environmental regulations and public safety norms. However, inordinately high charges adversely impact developers and act against the planned development of urban areas. While charges need to be moderate, 'urbanisation on the cheap' must be avoided at any cost.

Table 6.2

Town Planning-related Charges and Fees: Greater Hyderabad Municipal Corporation, 2013–14

Instrument	Description
Fee for layout development/sub-division of site/construction/reconstruction	Fee for permission to undertake land development/building construction/reconstruction/addition/alteration.
Betterment charges for land development/construction	Charges for on-site installation of internal amenities like water supply, drainage, roads, etc.—₹86 to ₹129 per square metre of site area.
External betterment charges for land development/ construction	Charges for off-site or external amenities like major arterial roads, flyovers, regional parks, etc.—₹86 to ₹176 per square metre of site area.
Development charges	Charges for institution or change of land use—industrial, commercial, residential, agricultural and miscellaneous.
City-level infrastructure impact fee on tall buildings	Fee toward city level infrastructure levied on buildings of height above 15 metres, excluding stilt parking floor—at ₹100 to ₹5,000 per square metre depending on the nature of building, height and location; no impact fee for first 15 metres or five floors (whichever is less) and differential rates for additional floors or part thereof; amount collected to be escrowed—50 per cent for infrastructure development in the same area and balance 50 per cent for city level infrastructure improvements.
Impact fee on commercial buildings on important roads	One-time fee to mitigate the impacts of construction of commercial buildings on major roads that lead to increased traffic requiring decongestion—at ₹2,200 to ₹4,400 per square feet of built-up area depending on the type of road—to be used for on-site and off-site infrastructure under capital improvement and decongestion plan, involving road widening, link roads, junction improvements, flyovers, etc.

Special fees	Development charges on lands/sites/premises abutting or in the vicinity of ring road/other highways/mass rapid transit/light rail transit indicated in the master plan at special rates prescribed by the state government.
Value addition charges	Additional levy per square metre of built-up area in the high-tech city area of Cyberabad where an information technology hub has been developed.
Rain-water harvesting charges	Levy per square metre of built up area for all categories of buildings.
Compounding fee	Fee for compoundable violations of building/layout regulations at a rate 33 per cent higher than normal fee.
Charges for unobjectionable projections into streets	Charges for unobjectionable projections into footpaths or streets by way of balconies, sheds and so on.
Open space contribution	Contribution from proposed developments in layouts that did not provide open space as statutorily required—at 10 per cent of land value for development of parks, compensatory greening programmes, etc.

Source: Greater Hyderabad Municipal Corporation.

Every development ought to contribute its fair share of costs of local and city-wide infrastructure, apart from mitigating the adverse impacts on the community and contributing to social objectives.

In recent years, cities like Hyderabad have made consorted attempt to rationalise the levy of town planning-related charges. Table 6.2 describes the charges currently being levied by the Greater Hyderabad Municipal Corporation (GHMC).

Development charges aim at covering the cost of additional infrastructure needed to service development. They make development pay its way and also compensate for the cost of urban sprawl. An efficient regime of development charges calls for a levy on the developer that approximates the real and full cost of new infrastructure and services in the development area. They include charges for internal or on-site as well as external or off-site facilities. In many developed countries, cities also include a partial subsidy to finance social housing under the ambit of development charges.

In the United States, state legislations require the developers to pay impact fees. These are one-time charges aimed at offsetting the additional costs of public infrastructure and services associated with new development. They are applied when a layout or building permission is issued. They are dedicated toward the costs of water and sewer systems, roads, schools, health centres, recreation facilities, etc. Laws require that impact fees cannot be used for operation, maintenance or repair to existing facilities and also cannot be annexed to city general revenues. They are essentially user fees levied in anticipation of use for expanding the capacity of existing facilities to cope with additional demand. The amount of impact fee cannot be arbitrary but must be clearly linked to the added service costs. Hyderabad is the first city in India to levy impact fees. However, only a handful of ULBs in India have so far adopted an impact fee regime.[4]

Surcharges on Utilities

Utility surcharges are levied on the consumption of utility services such as electricity, landline and mobile telephones, and cable television. Common in developed countries, they constitute an emerging form of benefit charge/tax in developing countries. As surcharges constitute only a small addition to the utility bills, they are widely accepted without much resistance. They also discourage the consumption of services and avoid wastage. There are 11 various taxes and surcharges imposed on cable TV, internet, phone services, etc. in Fairfax County, Virginia in the United States. The charges increase the direct service fee by 11.9 per cent (World Bank 2014, 178). In Rajasthan, a surcharge on the electricity bill has been introduced to meet the increasing cost of street lighting in municipalities.

Frequent road cutting for laying underground utilities is a major problem in Indian cities. A strong case exists for metropolitan cities to lay common duct lines with borrowed funds and levy utility user charges or taxes to service the debt.

'Polluters Pay' Charges

The 'polluters pay' paradigm, a corollary to the benefit principle, states that whoever causes damages to the environment should bear the mitigation or restoration costs. Apart from applying to municipal services such as wastewater and solid waste management, this principle can be used in a variety of situations to raise resources while regulating undesirable activities. The city of Hyderabad has adopted the principle as a part of municipal reforms. Developments not adhering to open space norms prescribed under the layout rules are required to pay 'open space contribution' with a view to creating compensatory open spaces. Similarly, multi-storeyed residential buildings and commercial complexes, which have not adhered to parking norms, are required to pay toward the creation of public parking lots. Establishments discharging sewage into storm water drains without connecting to the city sewerage system are subjected to penal charges that exceed sewerage charges.

'Congesters Pay' Charges

The 'congesters pay' paradigm, another corollary to the benefit principle, suggests that those responsible for creating congestion must pay for decongestion and adverse impacts on public health. Congestion charges based on this principle have been used to regulate traffic, combat air pollution and mobilise revenues to finance infrastructure. Studies show that such charges were effective in reducing congestion—by 14 per cent in Milan in 2008, 15 per cent in London and Singapore during 2002–03 and 22 per cent in Stockholm during January–July 2006 (Beevers and Carslaw 2005, Johansson et al. 2008, Milan Municipality 2009 and Olszewski 2007). In addition, they reduced the emission of air pollutants. Congestion charges curtailed CO_2 emissions up to 19.5 per cent in London (Beevers and Carslaw 2005). Singapore, London and Stockholm provide successful examples of congestion charges that can be adopted by large cities in India.[5]

In Singapore, the proliferation of private vehicles is disincentivised through a vehicle quota system that employs an open bidding process for certificates of entitlement to own a vehicle. This is combined with high initial registration cost (around 150 per cent of the vehicle's market value). There is also an annual road tax that increases with engine capacity and a surcharge for older vehicles. Singapore imposes higher parking fees in areas with a high concentration of vehicles. It introduced cordon pricing by time of day and the vehicle class via manual paper permit system in 1975. This was replaced by a fully automated electronic road pricing from 1998. The funds secured through congestion charges are used for public transportation improvements.

London introduced a congestion charge on vehicles entering a designated congestion charge zone between 0700 and 1830 hours at a flat fee of £5 per day in 2003. This fee was increased to £8 in 2005 and £9 to £12 in 2011. The net revenue from congestion charges is required to be reinvested for public transportation improvements by law. 80 per cent of the same is used for transit and 20 per cent for other transport improvements in the Greater London area. Automated number plate recognition (ANPR) system is used to track payment compliance and to identify violators. Stockholm started levying congestion charge from 2006 through cordon pricing by time of day at SEK10 to SEK20 (about US$1.50 to US$3.0) per crossing of the delineated cordon line into and out of the city centre.

Vehicle Parking Fees

Parking fees have similar effects as congestion charges. Studies reveal that parking fees have resulted in a 12 per cent decrease in vehicle miles of commuters in US cities, a 13 per cent point reduction in car shares in modal splits in British cities, a 20 per cent reduction in single car trips in Ottawa and a 38 per cent increase in car-pooling in Portland, Oregon (Bianco 2000, Dasgupta et al. 1995, Shoup 1997 and Wilson and Shoup 1990). Parking fees are, however, not levied systematically by cities in India. The municipal corporation of Hyderabad, apart from levying street parking charges, collects special parking charges from new developments in areas that have not provided adequate parking facilities as per norms. The amounts are meant for the construction of public parking facilities in the city.

Business Licensing Fees

Business licensing fees/taxes constitute an important source of revenue in many cities of the world, especially Latin America. They are easy to enforce, being linked to legally operating a business. Business licenses also serve other purposes, such as compliance with public health and safety regulations. However, excessive license fees can discourage business development and be eventually transferred to customers. Thus, licensing fees need to be fixed carefully. In India, some cities such as Hyderabad have used the trade licensing fee effectively to generate sizable revenues without burdening business. Reforms by the municipal corporation of Hyderabad with the launching of self-assessment scheme in 1998–99 resulted in a growth of 200 per cent in trade licensing fee collection between 1998–99 and 2001–02.

Advertisement Fees

Advertisement fees or taxes levied on hoardings and on advertisements can be a major source of revenue to municipalities in India. This is a grossly neglected source of local revenues. With cable television advertisements brought into the ambit of advertisement fees/taxes in states, there is a considerable scope to improve the yield from this source. Reforms by the Hyderabad Municipal Corporation led to a growth of 164 per cent in advertisement charges between 1998–99 and 2001–02.

Other Charges and Fees

Other charges and fees levied by municipalities include: property mutation charges, fees for obtaining records, fees for registering developers, builders, architects, structural engineers, assessors and valuers, penalties and fines, etc. In some countries, however, the costs of the collection and enforcement of some of these charges turn out to be greater than the revenue they generate. However, the use of electronic forms and self-declaration procedures can reduce the cost of administering these charges. Experiences of some cities show that penalties and fines can be a major source of revenues in municipalities. They include penal charges for violation of public health laws, town planning and other municipal regulations, charges for late payment of taxes, fines for traffic violations and so on.

Regulation of Municipal Services

The long neglect of cost recovery in municipal services, often linked with the issues of quality of services being delivered, makes out a strong case for their regulation. The HPEC has recommended an urban utility regulator at the state-level for all urban services to address the issues of pricing and delivery of civic services in accordance with set standards (HPEC 2011, 102–03). It has envisaged the following responsibilities of a water regulator: (a) reviewing the roadmaps prepared by ULBs for achieving the proposed service standards; (b) reviewing and recommending the principles to determine tariff structures proposed by the service provider; (c) monitoring the quality of services provided to citizens; (d) collating, analysing and disseminating information on service delivery; (e) overseeing the environmental implications for service delivery; and (f) advising the state government on policies pertaining to the provision of services.

A key question is whether there should be a regulator for each municipal service or a common regulator for all urban services. Our view is that a single regulator for all urban services is desirable as the financing of services is usually done through a mix of user charges, benefit charges, benefit taxes and intergovernmental transfers. Thus, the utility regulator needs to be concerned not only with direct user charges but also with indirect cost recovery through a mix of revenue sources, including benefit charges and taxes. For example, for solid waste management services, the ULBs depend on user charges such as door-to-door collection charges, bulk garbage collection charges and collections under the conservancy tax component of property tax.

Some Directions for Reforms

User charges, benefit charges and service fees are yet to become a major source of city financing in India. This is a concern as they, along with benefit taxes, lie at the core of the 'generalised benefit principle'. This principle, the hallmark of urban public finance, states that those benefitting from local public services must meet their costs (Lindahl 1919 and Musgrave 1938). Thus, 'users pay' and 'beneficiaries pay'. Benefits may be direct through consumption of service or be indirect, say, through increase in property value or upgradation of the environment. As corollaries to the generalised benefit principle, 'polluters pay', 'congesters pay' and 'exacerbaters pay'. The principle guides as to how local public services should be financed, in what quantities they should be produced and who should pay for them. It also assists in the apportionment of costs of local public services and facilities, including operation, maintenance, and capital and other costs, between categories of beneficiaries.

The benefit principle suggests that as a first resort, the services provided by local authorities should be paid for by users of such services, regardless of where they reside. Good international practice reveals that user charges for municipal services should cover the O&M cost and a part of capital and environmental costs, while providing for cross-subsidisation of the poor. The tariff formula must be simple and easily understood by the payers. It should be determined in consultation with stakeholders in a transparent manner. Further, volatility in revision of tariff should be avoided; year-to-year price adjustment needs to be effected instead of resorting to a heavy hike at one go. In general, user charges, benefit charges and benefit taxes should be earmarked for the services for which they are collected and not used to finance unrelated activities. Further, all the instruments to finance civic services should be subjected to independent regulation.

In a city context, the indirect benefits accruing to households and firms due to spatial planning, development of core infrastructure and provision of public services are often more significant than those to direct users. These derive from external economies and 'agglomeration rents' in cities. Land use planning, including zoning, conversion of rural land to urban, institution of land use, change in land use, assignment of development rights, including FSI, TDR and so on confer windfall gains upon landowners. Similarly, the development of trunk infrastructure facilities and transportation-land use integration lead to 'accessibility' and 'serviceability' premiums to properties at vantage locations, resulting in unearned increments in their values. Both direct and externality-induced indirect benefits must be taken into account while designing instruments to mobilise resources for city development and services.

In practice, the application of the generalised benefit principle may pose some difficulties. First, it may not be possible to exclude free-riders from enjoying collective services. Second, when a service is provided by multiple authorities, how much benefit is contributed by whom, needs to be worked out. Third, when the benefits of a public service capitalise into the tax bases of local, state and central governments, what portion of the cost should be met by which level is a complex issue. Fourth, how much of cost recovery should be through user charges, benefit charges, benefit taxes and general taxes is to be determined. Fifth, it may not be politically feasible to recover the full cost of services from the poor. But the extent to which the rich should cross-subsidise the poor through user charge and taxation routes needs to be decided. Thus, a careful structuring of city development projects based on a rigorous cost-benefit analysis is necessary.

In spite of the difficulties in implementation, the generalised benefit principle can be regarded as the guiding star for reforming urban public finance in India. The goal of empowered local self-government, envisaged in the 74th Amendment Act, calls for local public service costs being borne by users and beneficiaries in the first instance. The financing of civic infrastructure and services with user charges, benefit charges and benefit taxes accords legitimacy to the local government system; it also addresses the problem of increasing resistance from tax-payers. The benefit principle also guides the organisation of local government on a sound criterion, namely, internalisation of the costs and benefits of local public services. Further, a close link between taxes and services introduces market principles into the local government budgetary process. While user charges function as prices of local public services, benefit charges and earmarked benefit taxes act as surrogate prices. These instruments promote efficiency in resource allocation and ensure that the services provided by local governments are valued by citizens. Local governments must be equipped with the requisite instruments. Worthwhile programmes that pass the benefit–cost test should generate adequate resources to finance them.

Notes

1. We use the term 'user fee' to include all types of charges and fees levied by municipalities, encompassing 'users pay', 'beneficiaries pay', 'polluters pay', 'exacerbaters pay' and 'congesters pay' instruments.
2. The public finance literature refers to this as the Wicksellian connection. See Wicksell (1896) and Breton (1996).
3. See Chapter 9 for a presentation on the Bogota model of betterment levy.
4. Chapter 8 discusses the design of impact fees in the context of the strategy to finance planned urban development in India.
5. See International Council on Clean Transportation (2010) for international experience in congestion pricing, including that in Singapore, London and Stockholm.

7

Intergovernmental Transfers to Municipalities

Role of Intergovernmental Transfers

Intergovernmental transfers to municipalities play an important role in the financing of city services and infrastructure in both developed and developing countries. They include the sharing of tax base, tax yield and revenues of higher levels of government with local bodies. The key arguments in favour of intergovernmental transfers run in terms of correcting vertical and horizontal imbalances, compensating municipalities for inter-jurisdictional spillovers of benefits and costs of public services, funding national priorities, including merit goods and core infrastructure facilities, and enhancing efficiency in the collection of taxes (Bahl 2000, Bahl and Linn 1992, Boadway and Flatters 1982, Boadway and Shah 2007 and Buchanan 1950).

Vertical imbalance arises when the revenues of a jurisdiction are not adequate to finance its mandated functions. This is rooted in the constitutional scheme of assignment of expenditures and revenues to tiers of government. Horizontal imbalance occurs due to unequal tax bases relative to service burdens between jurisdictions. 'Equalisation' transfers are designed to compensate ULBs for fiscal disabilities owing to poor taxable capacity or disproportionately high spending needs, say, due to a large percentage of residents being poor. They aim at ensuring that different local authorities provide similar public services at similar tax rates. Externalities leading to spillover of costs and benefits between jurisdictions also justify fiscal transfers. Further, higher levels of government provide grants to local bodies to induce them achieve national standards of service. Researchers contend that merit goods like education and health and crucial infrastructure facilities for sustainable urbanisation like public transit will be underprovided if consumption decisions are left to citizens or lower levels of government as they do not recognise the true value of such goods. Intergovernmental transfers are also justified when the collection of major taxes is entrusted to the central or state government for exploiting scale economies in tax administration.

Economists make a strong case for fiscal transfers to local bodies to discharge redistributive functions. Income taxes are ideal instruments to finance poverty alleviation and social assistance programmes. When municipalities do not have access to buoyant taxes like income tax, transfers are necessary to address the problems of poverty, inequality and slums. Central and state governments also set policy priorities in broader public interest, for example, promoting human development, providing basic services to citizens, reducing regional disparities, etc. Thus, programmes are funded by them, but implemented through local governments in view of the latter's proximity to target groups. One example of such a programme is the JNNURM, launched by the GoI in 2005. JNNURM was aimed at a reform-linked provision of city-wide infrastructure and basic services to the urban poor, including land tenure, affordable housing, water, sanitation, education, health and social security. Another example is the RAY, initiated by the GoI in 2011 with the objective of promoting slum-free cities. Recently, the GoI has launched several new initiatives: Smart Cities Mission, AMRUT and Housing for All. They are aimed at promoting competitive, sustainable, equitable and inclusive cities. The central government's support is expected to incentivise cities to leverage resources, adopt smart solutions, undertake reforms and deliver high quality services to citizens.

While the theory and practice of intergovernmental transfers to local bodies underscore the importance of objective principles and criteria for the design of such transfers, the systems practiced in India are largely ad hoc and in a 'highly unsatisfactory state' (Mathur 2013, 23). Even after more than two decades of enactment of the historic Constitution (74th Amendment) Act 1992, municipalities continue to suffer from a serious mismatch between their functions and finances. In many states, they even depend on the state government to disburse staff salaries and discharge basic civic functions. The Constitution of India does provide for two review channels to address the problem of responsibility-revenue mismatch in ULBs—the SFC and CFC. But, the institutions of SFCs and CFC have not been able to make the desired impacts on municipal finances. India is far from an objective, formula-based, efficient and equitable system of fiscal transfers to ULBs.

This chapter reviews the state of intergovernmental transfers to municipalities in India and suggests a road map for reforms. We particularly focus on the issues of design of transfers, because whether a transfer is good or bad depends on its objective and structuring. We draw lessons from principles of public finance and good practices of fiscal transfers to municipalities followed internationally.

State of Transfers to Municipalities in India

Intergovernmental transfers to municipalities in India are artificially divided into plan and non-plan. Plan grants include centrally sponsored schemes, Planning Commission dispensations and state plan programmes. Non-plan grants cover: (a) assigned revenues and compensations from state government, (b) grants from state government based on SFC recommendations and (c) grants from central government based on CFC recommendations. The transfer systems are, however, not in accordance with robust principles of public finance. Importantly, the magnitude of intergovernmental transfers to municipalities in India is very small compared to international benchmark. Transfer revenues constituted only about 0.46 per cent of India's GDP in 2012–13, comprising 0.36 per cent from state sources and 0.10 per cent from central sources. In contrast, transfers to local bodies amounted to 21.3 per cent of GDP in Denmark, 9.9 per cent in United Kingdom, 7.8 per cent in Italy and 6 per cent in Norway.[1] As against the meagre transfers to ULBs from state and central channels, central-state transfers as a ratio of GDP in India stood at 4.62 per cent in 2012-13.

The Constitution (74th Amendment) Act 1992, vide Article 243X, entrusts the determination of assigned revenues, compensations and grants-in-aid to municipalities, in addition to taxes, tolls, charges and fees, to state governments. Article 243Y mandates the SFC to recommend principles of (i) devolution of state revenues to municipalities, (ii) determination of revenue sources to be assigned to or appropriated by municipalities, (iii) provision of grants-in-aid to municipalities and (iv) 'measures' needed to improve municipal finances. Further, amendment to Article 280 of the Constitution mandates the CFC to recommend 'measures' to augment the finances of a state to supplement the resources of municipalities on the basis of recommendations made by the Finance Commission of the state. However, in spite of these constitutional safeguards, municipal finances in India, including intergovernmental transfers remain in a precarious state.

Table 7.1 depicts the major sources of assigned revenues and compensations and Table 7.2, general and specific-purpose transfers to municipal corporations in India. As the tables show, there are significant interstate differences in the patterns of intergovernmental transfers. These have evolved over time in an ad hoc fashion.

A study of 10 cities reveals that per capita non-plan grants varied widely between cities (NIUA 2011). The share of such grants, which are often discretionary, ranged from five per cent of municipal revenues in Ahmedabad in 2006–07 to 42.3 per cent in Chennai, 60.8 per cent in Bhopal and 68.5 per cent in Bhubaneswar in 2007–08. The ratio of non-plan transfers to state own revenue in 2007–08 was 9.3 per cent in Madhya Pradesh, 2.8 per cent in Odisha, 3.7 per cent in Tamil Nadu and 0.7 per cent in Assam. SFC grant-state own revenue ratio in 2007–08 was: 0.7 per cent for Madhya Pradesh, 2.8 per cent for Odisha and 2.6 per cent

Table 7.1

Major Sources of Shared Revenues and Compensations in Municipal Corporations of India

Name of State	Name of Municipal Corporation	Shared Municipal Taxes/Compensations in lieu of Taxes
Gujarat	Ahmedabad	Entertainment tax and octroi compensation
Karnataka	Bengaluru	Entertainment tax, surcharge on stamp duty, octroi compensation and motor vehicle tax compensation
Maharashtra	Greater Mumbai	Non-agricultural assessment tax and entertainment tax
Orissa	Bhubaneswar	Compensation in lieu of octroi, duty on transfer of property and entertainment tax
Punjab	Ludhiana	Excise auction amount and excise tax on alcohol
Tamil Nadu	Chennai	Duty on transfer of property, entertainment tax and assignment from state tax revenues
Telangana	Hyderabad	Surcharge on stamp duty, profession tax, entertainment tax, octroi compensation, property tax compensation and motor vehicles tax compensation
West Bengal	Kolkata	Motor vehicles tax and entertainment tax

Source: Budgets of Municipal Corporations.

Table 7.2

Major Sources of General and Specific Transfers in Municipal Corporations of India

Name of State	Name of Municipal Corporation	General/Specific-purpose Transfers
Gujarat	Ahmedabad	Education grant, family planning grant and small savings grant
Karnataka	Bengaluru	Family planning scheme grant
Maharashtra	Greater Mumbai	Primary education grant and secondary education grant
Orissa	Bhubaneswar	Salary and dearness allowance grant, primary education grant and secondary education grant
Tamil Nadu	Chennai	Health grant, family welfare grant and flood grant
Telangana	Hyderabad	Per capita grant and road grant
Uttar Pradesh	Kanpur	Salary grant, education grant, medical grant and road grant
West Bengal	Kolkata	Grant for increased cost of pay, dearness allowance grant, grant for payment of dues to Kolkata Electricity Supply Corporation and pension relief

Source: Budgets of Municipal Corporations.

for Tamil Nadu. The corresponding ratio for Gujarat was 0.6 per cent in 2006–07. The relative magnitudes of CFC grants to cities have been much smaller (see Table 7.3).

Unlike multi-tier countries, such as Brazil, China, South Africa, Nigeria and Philippines, no major central or state tax is shared with municipalities in India. Compensations to municipalities from states that abolished octroi and took over taxes like toll tax, motor vehicles tax, profession tax and entertainment tax have also remained at abysmally low levels. For example, compensation from the state government to Hyderabad municipal corporation following the abolition of octroi and toll tax has remained below ₹50 lakhs year after year although the annual yield from octroi to the city could have exceeded ₹1,000 crore had the tax not been abolished.[2] The systems of fiscal transfers to ULBs in India are dependency-promoting and against the spirit of decentralisation envisaged in the Constitution (74th Amendment Act). They need to be reformed urgently. International practice and key principles of public finance can provide guidance in the matter.

Table 7.3

Non-plan Transfers, Including Grants-in-aid to Municipalities in Select States

Component	Madhya Pradesh 2007–08	Odisha 2007–08	Tamil Nadu 2007–08	Gujarat 2006–07	Assam 2007–08
Per Capita Non-plan Transfer (₹)					
Assigned revenue	62.0	–	100.3	–	13.1
Compensation in lieu of taxes	420.9	–	5.9	128.7	–
Specific-purpose transfers	151.0	2.1	32.9	124.3	86.7
SFC grants	52.5	340.8	329.1	56.4	–
CFC grants	37.6	63.3	32.7	48.0	1.2
Total non-plan transfers	724.1	406.2	500.9	357.4	100.9
Ratio of Transfers to State Own Revenue (%)					
Non-plan transfers to municipalities as percentage of state own revenue	9.3	2.8	3.7	3.1	0.7
SFC grants to municipalities as percentage of state own revenue	0.7	2.8	2.6	0.6	–

Source: National Institute of Urban Affairs (2011).

International Practice on Transfers

Countries around the globe assign more expenditure functions than revenue sources to sub-national (provincial and local) governments. Vertical imbalance is built into their fiscal federalism. Intergovernmental transfers finance 59.5 per cent of sub-national expenditures in developing countries, 44.1 per cent in transitional countries and 50.3 per cent in developed countries (Alam 2014). They accounted for more than 40 per cent of local government revenues in 13 out of 15 OECD countries in 2010, the figure being more than 50 per cent for Denmark, Hungary, Ireland, Italy and United Kingdom.[3] As regards metropolitan cities, at one end of the spectrum, Addis Ababa, Tokyo, Pune, Seoul, Pretoria, Melbourne, Copenhagen and Busan finance more than 80 per cent of budget with own revenues. At the other end, 81 per cent of revenues of London come from national grants.[4]

Countries adopt three methods to address the mismatch between functions and finances of municipalities: (a) sharing of tax base, (b) sharing of tax yield and (c) sharing of revenue.

Sharing of Tax Base

The sharing of tax base provides municipalities an access to productive and buoyant tax bases of higher levels of government. Typically, taxes are collected by central or state government and ULBs are allowed to 'piggyback' or levy a 'city surcharge' on such taxes. The proceeds are shared between levels of government depending on prior arrangements or agreements. Tax base sharing is common in the United States, Eastern Europe and East Asia, but almost non-existent in developing countries of Africa and Asia. Municipalities in the United States resort to 'piggybacking' on to state income, payroll and sales taxes. Bangkok metropolitan area levies origin-based surcharges on central taxes such as VAT, specific business tax, liquor tax, excise tax and gambling tax on horse races, and liquor and gambling license fees (Shah 2013, 228). Tax-base sharing also occurs in Seoul and Tokyo.

Sharing of Tax Yield

In the case of tax yield sharing, the central or state government collects the shared taxes and assigns a predetermined percentage of the collected amount to municipalities. Tax-by-tax sharing is widely practiced internationally. This promotes collection efficiency, while ensuring transparency and predictability in transfers. However, when the bulk of a shared tax accrues to local bodies, the tax-collecting government has weak incentives to augment tax effort.

Tax sharing is the most significant source of revenue in the metropolitan cities of Europe and East Asia. Bangkok metropolitan area receives a share of five per cent of the national personal income tax. In accordance with the Decentralisation Act, 1999, 18.5 per cent of VAT revenues are made available to local governments in Thailand based on formula; Bangkok metropolitan area received 5.8 per cent of the total pool in 2008. Local governments in Jakarta receive by origin 12 per cent of personal income tax and 64 per cent of other taxes. They also get six per cent of oil and 12 per cent of natural gas revenues (Shah 2013, 231). Chennai gets a share of state entertainment tax and surcharge on stamp duty. Hyderabad receives a share of profession tax, entertainment tax and surcharge on stamp duty collected by the state government.[5]

Sharing of Revenues

Under revenue-sharing arrangements, municipalities have access to a predetermined share of state or central government revenues as a grant. Usually, not all revenue sources of a higher level of government are shared with ULBs. Only some sources are drawn into a distributional pool and a percentage of the same devolves on local bodies. Revenue-sharing mechanisms are divided into general-purpose, or unconditional or non-earmarked and specific-purpose, or conditional or earmarked grants. The advantage of revenue-sharing is that transfers to municipalities automatically increase as the yields from revenue sources go up due to economic growth. In OECD countries, approximately 50 of the grants provided to sub-national governments belong to the non-earmarked category. About 30 per cent of the earmarked grants are with matching requirements; the rest 70 per cent are non-matching transfers (Junghun et al. 2010).

General-purpose Transfers

General-purpose or unconditional transfers to municipalities take the shape of budgetary support, with no strings attached. They aim at protecting the autonomy of local government. They simply augment the recipient's resources and can be spent on any local service or be used to reduce local taxes. General-purpose transfers are typically governed by legal covenants. However, sometimes they are ad hoc or discretionary. Many countries use general purpose transfers as 'equalisation' grants, largely governed by the considerations of horizontal equity, that is, removing fiscal disparities between jurisdictions caused by differences in resource-raising abilities. They aim at enabling cities to achieve reasonably comparable levels of public services at reasonably comparable levels of local taxation.

Specific-purpose Transfers

Specific-purpose or conditional transfers aim at incentivising local governments to undertake predefined programmes or activities. They specify the expenditures eligible for grant financing (input-based conditionality): capital expenditures, operating expenditures or both. Some transfers also require the attainment of specified results in service delivery (output-based conditionality). Conditional transfers are, however, fungible in the sense that there is no guarantee that local bodies will expend the grants in accordance with what the grantor government intended. For example, municipalities earlier spending significant amounts in services brought under grant conditionalities could divert the grants to other purposes and still meet the grantor's requirements.

Conditional grants can be matching or non-matching. Conditional matching grants require municipalities to finance a percentage of expenditures from their own revenues. Conditional non-matching grants provide funds without any matching by the recipient government, so long as amounts are spent for the specified purpose. These grants are suitable for subsidising activities that are considered 'high priority' by the central or state government, but 'low priority' by the local government. Conditional non-matching transfers are called 'block' grants when used to provide broad support in a general area of expenditure (for example, health, education, transport, slum upgradation, etc.) rather than a specific programme. Block grants provide discretions to municipalities in allocating funds to particular uses. Conditional matching transfers aim at promoting ownership of grant-financed expenditures by local bodies. However, matching requirements impose a greater burden on those with limited fiscal capacity. In view of this, countries usually set matching rates in inverse proportion to per capita fiscal capacity of local government in order to enable poorer jurisdictions to participate in the grant-financed programmes.

Matching grants can be open-ended or closed-ended. In open-ended grants, the grantor government matches whatever resources a municipality provides. In closed-ended grants, the grantor matches recipient funds only up to a pre-specified limit. Conditional closed-ended matching transfers ensure that the grantor has some control over the costs of the transfer programme. Conditional open-ended matching transfers are the most suitable vehicles to motivate local bodies to increase expenditures on the grant-assisted functions.

Transfers versus Own Revenues

Table 7.4 presents the composition of municipal revenues, including intergovernmental transfers in select metropolitan cities of the world. As the table shows, transfer regimes in countries vary widely. About 38 per cent of Mexico City's revenues come from general purpose transfers from higher level of government. The figure for Beijing is 17 per cent, while it is seven per cent for Bangkok. London receives 53 per cent of its revenues as specific-purpose transfers. The corresponding figure for Mexico City is 32 per cent; that for Bangkok, 20 per cent. The figure is just 5.2 per cent in the case of Beijing.

Metropolitan regions around the world act as locomotives of growth. They also generate the bulk of central and state government finances. However, in nine out of 28 metropolitan cities for which data are presented in Table 7.4, the ratio of transfer revenues to total municipal revenues exceeds 50 per cent. Only in eight metros is the transfer-dependency less than 20 per cent. Some economists argue that control over fiscal transfers and direct spending in metropolitan areas are tools that higher levels of government use to prompt 'good behaviour' on the part of local authorities and their alignment to broader national priorities. By keeping metropolitan local governments more dependent on transfers vis-à-vis taxes, the competition for metropolitan tax base is also minimised. Thus, the central and state governments are in a position to extract revenues from metropolitan cities to finance 'equalisation' transfers needed by smaller entities. Moreover, elected local government representatives are often averse to imposing politically unpopular taxes (Bahl and Linn 2014, 39–40).

Design of Intergovernmental Transfers

Researchers in public finance have identified key criteria to guide the design of intergovernmental transfers to local bodies (see Box 7.1). However, as some criteria are likely to conflict with others, rarely does any grant programme, in practice, subscribe to all the principles recommended by theory. In particular, a trade-off exists between the autonomy of municipalities and the accountability requirements placed on them by higher levels of government for the utilisation of transfer funds.

In practice, the key factors shaping intergovernmental transfers to municipalities include: (a) legal-institutional framework for determining and implementing transfers, (b) size of distributional pool, (c) formula

Table 7.4

*Transfer versus Own-source Revenues in Select Metropolitan Areas**

	As % of Total Municipal Revenues				
Metro Area	*Shared Taxes**	*General-purpose Transfers*	*Specific-purpose Transfers*	*Total Transfers*	*Own-source Revenues*
Addis Ababa	–	–	–	3.1	96.9
Bangkok	24.0	7.0	20.0	51.0	49.0
Berlin	39.1	18.3	21.9	79.3	20.7
Brussels	36.1	3.0	–	39.0	61.0
Beijing	29.2	16.6	5.2	51.0	49.0
Busan	3.0	2.0	13.0	18.0	82.0
Cape Town	–	20.0	–	20.0	80.0
Canberra	–	27.8	14.6	42.4	57.6
Copenhagen	–	7.0	10.0	17.0	83.0
Istanbul	65.0	–	5.0	69.0	31.0
Jakarta	46.3	–	–	46.3	53.7
London	–	25.6	53.0	80.6	19.4
Melbourne	–	0	0	14.2	85.8
Mexico City	–	38.0	32.0	70.0	30.0
Montreal	–	–	–	24.0	76.0
Prague	40.4	–	–	59.7	40.3
Pretoria	–	–	–	9.9	90.1
Seoul	0.8	–	–	9.1	90.9
Shanghai	32.9	24.7	1.5	59.1	40.9
Tokyo	–	–	–	5.7	94.3
Toronto	–	–	24.0	24.0	76.0
Washington, DC	–	12.0	14.0	26.0	74.0
Chennai	24.0	–	–	34.0	66.0
Delhi	17.9	–	–	26.9	73.1
Hyderabad	25.0	–	–	40.0	60.0
Kolkata	–	–	–	58.4	41.6
Mumbai	–	–	–	20.0	80.0
Pune	–	–	–	9.0	91.0

Source: Shah (2013, 226 and 230).

Notes: * Data pertain to the period 2001–10.
** May include tax-base sharing.

Box 7.1

Principles of Design of Intergovernmental Transfers to Local Bodies

The theory of public finance refers to the following key principles for the design of intergovernmental transfer programmes for local bodies:

Clarity in Objectives: Grant objectives should be clearly and precisely spelt out to guide the design of grant programme.

Autonomy: Local governments should have complete independence and flexibility in setting their priorities and should not be constrained by the categorical structure of grant programmes.

Revenue Adequacy: Local governments should have adequate revenues, including intergovernmental transfers to discharge their assigned responsibilities.

Efficiency: The grant design should be neutral with regard to the choices by local governments for the allocation of resources to different sectors or types of activities.

Equity: Allocated funds should vary directly with fiscal needs and inversely with fiscal capacity of each jurisdiction.

Predictability: The grant programme should ensure predictability and stability in the revenues of local governments so that they can budget and plan for future expenditures.

Simplicity: The grant allocation should be based on objective factors over which individual units have little control. The formula should be easily understood by all stakeholders.

Incentive: The grant design should incentivise sound fiscal management and resource mobilisation effort. There should be no specific transfers to finance local government deficits or bailout non-performing entities.

Accountability: The grantor must be accountable for the design and operation of the grant. The grant-recipient must be accountable to the grantor and citizens for financial integrity, service performance, achievement of grant objectives and adherence to grant conditionalities.

Sources: Bird and Smart (2002) and Shah (2007).

for distribution of transfers, (d) conditionalities for utilisation of grants and (e) mechanisms for monitoring and compliance. In some countries, the legal-institutional framework is prescribed under the constitution or law. In others, transfers are handled through the annual budgetary process. The distributional pool is determined based on one of the following methods: (a) as a share of the grantor government's total revenues or pre-identified taxes, (b) on ad hoc basis or (c) based on cost reimbursement. The distribution of transfers to eligible entities takes places on the basis of one of the following methods: (a) on derivation basis, that is, retention of a share of taxes collected within the recipient's jurisdiction, (b) formula-based sharing, (c) based on cost reimbursement, (d) subject to specific design of transfer programme or (e) on ad hoc method.

Formula for Determining Transfers

Most countries allocate some portion of intergovernmental transfers to municipalities on the basis of a formula to ensure objectivity, transparency and predictability of funds being made available to recipients. Fiscal capacity, fiscal needs and fiscal effort are the key ingredients of such a formula (Bird and Smart 2002 and Yilmaz et al. 2006):

Fiscal Capacity: This aims at measuring the grant recipient's revenue capacity relative to expenditure needs, that is, cost of providing a standardised basket of public goods and services. Revenue capacity is the potential revenue the jurisdiction can mobilise on its own by exploiting taxes, user charges and other revenue sources (Yilmaz et al. 2006). In the United States, the concept of a representative tax system (RTS) was advanced by the Advisory Commission on Intergovernmental Relations (ACIR) in 1962 to estimate the fiscal capacity of state and local governments. Under the RTS, the fiscal capacity of a local jurisdiction is determined based on the per capita tax amount it could raise if statewide average tax rates are applied on all tax bases, irrespective of whether tax rates are actually imposed or not (ACIR 1962). The concept was broadened to a representative revenue system (RRS) in 1986, to include non-tax revenues such as user charges, rents, lottery revenues and so on (ACIR 1993).

Fiscal Needs: These are defined by the funding necessary to discharge the expenditure responsibilities assigned to a local government, adopting some standard levels of service or service level benchmarks. In the United States, the concept of a representative expenditure system (RES) has been applied to estimate the fiscal needs of jurisdictions. This is the expenditure analogue of RRS; it measures the relative public service need of each local government in terms of the per capita expenditure it would have to incur to provide a standard bundle of local public goods and services. In some countries, fiscal needs are represented by proxy variables such as population, geographical area, illiteracy or poverty, infrastructure deficiency, etc. For example, the Central Finance Commissions of India have included population, geographical area and distance from highest per capita income in the formula for centre–state fiscal transfers to capture fiscal needs.

Fiscal Effort: Often used interchangeably with 'revenue effort', this is the extent to which a local government utilises the revenue sources assigned to it. Represented by the ratio of actual revenue mobilised to some measure of revenue capacity, it is meant to capture the intensity of effort by a local government to raise revenue relative to other comparable local governments. Revenue effort reflects the extent to which a local government is exploiting its revenue-raising potential in relation to revenue base. In India, the 10th, 11th and 12th CFCs adopted tax effort as one of the criteria for distributing the divisible pool of central taxes between states.

In addition to fiscal capacity, need and effort-related parameters, transfer distribution formulae sometimes include variables representing fiscal management, performance accountability and social objectives (OECD 2008 and Steytler 2005). In Kenya, the receipt of a percentage of formula-based allocation is contingent on the local government's adoption of new accounting and financial management reforms (Schroeder and Smoke 2003). In India, fiscal discipline is one of the factors taken into account by the 11th, 12th and 13th Finance Commissions while recommending transfers from the centre to states (see Table 7.5).

Table 7.5

Criteria and Weights (Percentage) for Centre–State Fiscal Transfers: 10th, 11th, 12th, 13th and 14th Finance Commissions of India

	10th (1995–2000)	11th (2000–05)	12th (2005–10)	13th (2010–15)	14th (2015–20)
Population	20	10	25	25	17.5
Demographic change	–	–	–	–	10
Geographical area	5	7.5	10	10	15
Income distance/ Fiscal capacity distance	60	62.5	50	47.5	50
Tax effort	10	5.0	7.5	–	–
Infrastructure deficiency index	5	7.5	–	–	–
Fiscal discipline	–	7.5	7.5	17.5	–
Forest cover	–	–	–	–	7.5

Source: Reports of 10th, 11th, 12th, 13th and 14th Finance Commissions of India.

Local governments in Bangkok metropolitan area get a share of national VAT based on a formula that takes into account population, geographical area, revenue and budgetary needs factors. Under the Local Government Code 1991, Philippines allocated 40 per cent of the national internal revenue taxes actually realised during the third fiscal year preceding the current fiscal year to various local government units (LGUs): provinces (23 per cent), cities (23 per cent), municipalities (34 per cent) and *barangays* or village units (20 per cent). The share of each province, city, municipality or *barangay* is determined on the basis of a formula incorporating weights: population (50 per cent), land area (25 per cent) and equal sharing (25 per cent; Llanto 2009). In South Africa, the national government resorts to direct and unconditional transfers to municipalities based on a formula that takes into account fiscal needs, fiscal capacity, fiscal effort, extent of poverty and backlogs in municipalities (see Box 7.2; Chitiga-Mabugu and Monkam 2013, National Treasury, Republic of South Africa 2012).

The Constitution of Nigeria prescribes that the revenues from oil, VAT, customs and corporation income tax be divided between federal, state and local governments in accordance with the formula developed by the Revenue Mobilisation Allocation and Fiscal Commission and approved by the National Assembly. In addition, a small share of revenue to the federation (about 4.2 per cent) goes to four special funds. As per the current devolution formula, 13 per cent of oil revenues are assigned to oil-producing states on 'derivation' principle. The remaining amount is divided between the federal government (53 per cent), state governments (27 per cent) and local governments (20 per cent). Revenues from customs, excise and corporation income taxes are split between the three tiers using the same formula without the derivation principle. Revenues from VAT are divided as follows: federal government (15 per cent), state governments (50 per cent) and local governments (35 per cent). The formula for distribution of divisible oil revenue pool, customs, excise and corporation income tax between states is as follows: 40 per cent on equal sharing; 30 per cent proportionately to population, 10 per cent proportionately to land mass and terrain; 10 per cent for social development factors (education, health and water); and 10 per cent as reward for tax effort. VAT revenues are distributed to states as follows: 50 per cent on equal sharing; 30 per cent proportionately to population; and 20 per cent on derivation principle. The central transfers to municipalities take place through joint accounts of state and local governments based on formulae (World Bank 2013b).

Box 7.2

Unconditional Transfers from National Government to Municipalities in South Africa

The national government in South Africa implements two types of transfers to municipalities: direct and indirect. Direct transfers are divided into conditional and unconditional transfers. Direct conditional transfers include infrastructure support and capacity building grants. Direct unconditional transfers aim at assisting municipalities in operational expenditures. They are allocated through local government equitable share (LES) of national government revenues. Indirect transfers are spent by the national government on infrastructure development and capacity building activities in municipalities.

The LES is defined by the following formula:

$$LES = BS + D + I \pm C$$

where:

BS = a component for the provision of basic services such as water, garbage removal, sanitation, electricity and environmental health care, and free basic services to poor households;

D = a component to capture the development needs of municipalities;

I = an institutional support component aimed at assisting poor municipalities without revenue-raising capacity to fund administration;

RRC = revenue-raising capacity correction component meant to account for varying fiscal capacity of municipalities to mobilise own revenues from taxes, surcharges and user fees; and

C = a general correction and stabilisation factor.

The distribution of nationally raised revenues between national, provincial and local governments in South Africa over the period 2008–09 to 2010–11 was as follows: national 48.1–50.0 per cent; provincial 42.5–43.7 per cent and local 7.5–8.2 per cent.

Local governments in South Africa, apart from receiving formula-based shares in national revenues, are provided with significant capital grants from the national government.

Source: National Government, South Africa. *Budget Review 2012:* Pretoria.

Design of Grants for Capital Projects

In most countries, central and state governments provide conditional capital grants to local governments to undertake the development of critical infrastructure facilities such as public transit. Research on good international practice identifies the following guiding principles for the design of capital grants to cities:

1. Preparation of city development strategy and perspective plan;
2. Formulation of medium-term investment and capital maintenance programmes and projects;
3. Independent technical and financial appraisal of projects to be supported by grant revenues;
4. Leveraging of grant revenues and internal resources of municipalities by accessing borrowed/external funds—equity and debt; and
5. Linkage to the levy of appropriate user charges and benefit taxes to recover full costs and repay debt.

The United States has used federal block grants and revolving funds to promote investment in water and wastewater systems adhering to national laws such as the Clean Water Act 1971. Conditional grants have been used in Brazil to promote investment in major capital projects in cities such as Sao Paulo. South Africa follows a formal system of infrastructure grants to cities. Mexico dedicates a share of intergovernmental transfers to debt repayments in capital projects. In India, programme-based conditional grants from the centre have been extended to states and cities for the development of urban infrastructure, slum upgradation and poverty alleviation, including livelihood promotion. Central grants under JNNURM were subject to cities preparing city development plans (CDP), states and local bodies meeting matching fund requirements and implementing an agenda of 23 reforms, including those relating to levy of user charges and property tax reforms. Table 7.6 provides the financing pattern of the Urban Infrastructure and Governance sub-mission of JNNURM.

Under the newly launched Smart City Mission applicable to 100 cities, a central financial grant will be provided at an average of ₹100 crore per city per year for five years. An equal amount, on a matching basis, will have to be contributed by the State/ULB.

Some Lessons from Practice

Practice on intergovernmental transfers to municipalities suggests that the most effective programmes have simple objectives and transparent criteria, while conditionalities are imposed on outputs or attainment of standards rather than on inputs and processes. Clarity of purpose, adequacy of revenue and incentives for own revenue mobilisation are the key factors behind the success of fiscal transfers to sub-national governments, including local bodies. In Indonesia, a matching grant scheme

Table 7.6

Financing Pattern for Infrastructure Projects under JNNURM

Category of Cities/Towns/Urban Agglomerations (UAs)	Grant		ULB or Parastatal Share/Loan from Financial Institutions
	Centre	State	
Cities/UAs with four million plus population as per 2001 census	35%	15%	50%
Cities/UAs with million plus but less than four million population as per 2001 census	50%	20%	30%
Cities/towns /UAs in North Eastern States and Jammu & Kashmir	90%	10%	–
Cities/UAs other than those mentioned above	80%	10%	10%

Source: Ministry of Urban Development, GoI.

focused on achieving minimum standards in education was critical in modernising the country's education system. Canada implemented a successful conditional transfer scheme to promote universal access to health care. Brazil has both education and health conditional transfer programmes that have generally performed well. The United Kingdom has used conditional grants to promote affordable housing for long. Australia has successfully implemented similar programmes for road development and maintenance. China has used the sharing of national taxes to finance a spectcular process of urban transformation.

Clarity in objective is a fundamental requirement for the effective design of intergovernmental transfers (Bahl and Linn 1992). If the objective is to enhance the welfare of local residents, general-purpose non-matching transfers are appropriate, because they guarantee autonomy of local government. To ensure accountability for results, conditional, non-matching, output-based transfers are preferable to other types of transfers. Output-based transfers aim at according autonomy and budgetary flexibility to local government while promoting incentive and accountability in service delivery. They are appropriate for financing operating expenditures in education, health, public transit and infrastructure. Conditional capital grants are good tools to address infrastructure deficiencies; they promote national standards in service quality and access of citizens and businesses to critical infrastructure facilities.

The following are some lessons from international practice to guide the design of intergovernmental transfers to municipalities in India:

1. A robust municipal finance system is a fundamental requirement for a well-functioning, intergovernmental transfer regime. The system should be viewed as an integrated whole rather than a bundle of disjointed elements.
2. One size does not fit all; a range of transfer programmes is needed, depending upon the context of fiscal federalism and the objective of grantor government.
3. Predominant emphasis in grant financing is on closing the vertical gap, a product of the constitutional framework of fiscal federalism. Grants to compensate for benefit spillovers, result-based transfers and tournament-type approaches to promote competition between municipalities are not widespread.
4. Specifying too many objectives in a single programme of inter-governmental fiscal transfers is not desirable. One category of grant is appropriate for attaining one type of objective.
5. The design of grant is a critical factor for its success. An objectively determined grant formula with weights to fiscal needs, fiscal capacity and fiscal effort ensures predictability—a key factor necessary for any transfer programme to be effective.
6. Specific-purpose transfers are often ad hoc or project-based with input-based conditionality. However, such conditionality tends to be intrusive and unproductive. Similarly, process-based conditionality is seen to be inefficient and incapable of achieving the grant objectives.
7. When the grantor's objective is to promote performance and accountability in local government while preserving autonomy, output-based conditionality is most appropriate. If designed well, output-based transfers can lead to excellence in service delivery and attainment of desired outcomes.
8. General purpose transfers, though formula-based, transparent and predictable, adopt 'one size fits all' formula for all types of local governments. Thus, they fail to cater to the special needs of cities, for example, mass rapid transit in the case of metropolitan cities and discriminate against them.
9. A mix of formula-based, unconditional revenue grants and conditional capital grants is desirable to address vertical and horizontal imbalances and the much-needed investments in regional and urban infrastructure simultaneously.
10. Gap-filling approach needs to be avoided at any cost. Municipalities should be made to face a hard budget constraint.

A key lesson from the implementation of JNNURM in India is that weak capacity to implement transfer programmes can even be more critical than the design of transfer. This is testified by the fact that while the mission envisaged funding support from the GoI to states/cities to the tune of ₹1,00,000 crore over the seven-year mission period of 2005–12, only ₹40,584 crore could be released based on the progress in project preparation and completion, and the implementation of reforms. As regards the two sub-missions pertaining to urban infrastructure under JNNURM, namely, Urban Infrastructure and Governance (UIG) and Urban Infrastructure Development Scheme for Small and Medium Towns (UIDSSMT), only 46 per cent of the projects sanctioned could be completed by 30 September 2013 (Lok Sabha Secretariat 2015).

State Finance Commission Reports

There have been considerable delays by states to appoint SFCs. These institutions have also not adopted comparable approaches to analyse municipal finances to make recommendations. Based on a study of reports of the first, second, third, fourth and fifth generation SFCs, the SFC recommendations can be divided into three broad groups: (a) global sharing, that is, sharing a percentage of state revenues with local bodies, (b) assignment or sharing of a percentage of specific taxes and (c) ad hoc or lump sum transfers. SFCs of states like Tamil Nadu, Karnataka, Andhra Pradesh and Madhya Pradesh have recommended global sharing. In Maharashtra and Punjab, SFCs have recommended the sharing of specific taxes. SFCs of Gujarat, Odisha and most other states have recommended ad hoc transfers, adopting a gap-filling approach. Most SFCs have not provided attention to reforms in the municipal finance system, including intergovernmental transfers. As they have not relied on a normative analysis, the transfers recommended by them turn out to be highly unpredictable as a source of municipal finance. This contrasts with the fact that transfers from the Centre to states based on the recommendations of CFCs have always been determined by objective formulae.

The reports of the 10th, 11th, 12th, 13th and 14th Finance Commissions of India and research studies point to the following shortcomings in the functioning of SFCs and their reports.[6]

1. Most SFCs have failed to emphasise the link between revenue–raising and expenditure responsibilities—the Wicksellian connection that is needed to induce fiscal responsibility.
2. No SFC seems to have devoted attention to fiscal management aspects and the need to impose a hard budget constraint on local governments. The accounting and budgetary practices of local bodies leave many things to be desired.
3. No suggestion has been made by SFCs to reduce the multiple channels of devolution to local bodies that exist, namely, line departments, the Planning Commission, State Planning Board, district agencies, Member of Parliament/Member of Legislative Assembly, centrally-sponsored and state plan schemes, SFC, CFC, etc. There is a need to place state–local fiscal relations on a more rational and predictable footing.
4. While prior to the 74th Amendment, state–local grant system was unsystematic, ad hoc and dependency-promoting, most SFCs have failed to address these shortcomings. Transfers from SFCs are inadequate, apart from being poorly designed and targeted, leading to large unfunded mandates with municipalities (Rao and Bird 2014).

While states demand more devolution from the centre, very few states have embraced the principle of 'subsidiarity'. Several recommendations of SFCs have been summarily rejected by state governments. Actions taken on the accepted recommendations have generally been slow. In this regard, the 12th Finance Commission has made the following observations:

1. Several states did not initiate follow-up action on the SFC recommendations.
2. Recommendations under examination eventually met with a 'natural death'.
3. Very few states have honoured their commitment for the release of additional resources.
4. Budgetary provisions regarding the recommendations have fallen short. The initial enthusiasm shown by state governments in constituting SFCs was lost at the time of implementing their recommendations as it would have put pressure on the finances of state governments.
5. There is a lack of synchronisation between the periods of CFC and SFC reports.

The Constitution (74th Amendment) Act does not provide guidelines for the composition of SFC. In some states, parts of state government machinery were inducted into SFC. This rendered the recommendations for devolution of state resources to local governments biased and often meaningless. Unlike the CFCs, which included eminent experts with subject specialisation as members, the selection of SFC members in most states is done routinely—without regard to the expertise needed in areas such as state and local government finance, fiscal federalism, etc. To address the problem, the 13th Finance Commission, under the conditionalities for states to access performance grants, stipulated that the qualifications of SFC member be prescribed by legislation.

Central Finance Commission Reports

The 10th Finance Commission was the first CFC to have the additional responsibility in its terms of reference to consider the recommendations of SFCs regarding local bodies. However, a major problem the Commission faced was the mismatch in the timing of its constitution and the first generation SFC reports. The 10th CFC could not consider the recommendations of the reports of SFCs as the same were not available. It arbitrarily recommended a grant of ₹1,000 crore for municipalities as grant-in-aid to be distributed among states over 1995–2000. The ULBs were required to raise 'suitable' matching contribution and no amount was to be used for expenditure on salaries and wages.

The terms of reference for the 11th Finance Commission required it to make its own assessment about the manner and the extent of augmentation of state-consolidated funds to supplement the resources of municipalities. However, the Commission arrived at arbitrary conclusions as the relevant SFC reports were not available. It recommended an ad hoc grant of ₹2,000 crore for municipalities for the period 2000–05. The 11th CFC stipulated that activities such as maintenance of accounts, development of database and audit be the first charges on the CFC grant.

Again, the 12th Finance Commission could not make a realistic assessment of the resource gaps of municipalities in the absence of the required SFC reports and details of action taken thereon from state governments. It recommended a sum of ₹5,000 crore as grant-in-aid to states for ULBs covering the period 2005–10. The Commission suggested that 50 per cent of the grants should be earmarked for solid waste management. It also made the following additional recommendations:

1. The SFCs should follow a normative approach in the assessment of revenues and expenditure in order to arrive at the gap that may be considered by the CFC.
2. Principal recommendations of the SFCs may be accepted without modification as in the case of CFC.
3. The states should constitute SFCs with people of eminence and competence.
4. They should compile disaggregated time series data on finances of local bodies.
5. There is a need for synchronisation of the time period of SFCs with that of CFC.

The 13th Finance Commission broke new ground by recommending a percentage of the divisible pool of taxes (over and above the share of states) to be transferred to urban and rural local bodies as grant-in-aid through state governments, observing that the local bodies

[B]e allowed to benefit from the buoyancy of central taxes and the Constitutional design of supplementing the resources of panchayats and municipalities through grant-in-aid. (Finance Commission of India 2009, 174)

With this, the 'third tier' was recognised as a distinct entity in the scheme of intergovernmental fiscal transfers in India to have access to the buoyant revenues of the centre. Also, for the first time, the CFC introduced performance grants to local bodies subject to certain conditionalities aimed at improving their functioning. The grant-in-aid recommended for municipalities for 2010–15 amounted to ₹23,111 crore (₹87,519 for rural and urban local bodies together). The main recommendations of the 13th Finance Commission include the following:

1. 2.5 per cent of the divisible pool of taxes (over and above the share of state) to be transferred to urban and rural local bodies as grant-in-aid through state governments under Article 275 of the Constitution of India.
2. 1.5 per cent of the previous year's divisible pool to be given to states as a general basic grant and special areas grant every year from 2010–11 to 2014–15; 0.5 per cent be transferred as general performance grants for 2011–12 and one per cent per year thereafter from 2012–13 to 2014–15.
3. All states to have access to basic grant as per criteria; the formulae for allocation of basic grant to ULBs is be based on the parameters

and weights as follows: population, 50 per cent; geographical area, 10 per cent; distance from highest per capita sectoral income, 20 per cent; index of devolution, 15 per cent; and Finance Commission's local body grant utilisation index, five per cent.

4. Only those states which meet the stipulations specified by the Commission to be eligible for performance grant. Important conditions for accessing such grant include: putting in place a robust system of audit; an independent local bodies ombudsman to look into complaints of corruption and maladministration against elected members and officials of local bodies; electronic transfer of Finance Commission grants to local bodies within five days of receipt (10 days where not possible); providing for qualifications of members of the SFC by legislation; fully enabling ULBs to levy property tax; establishing a state-level Property Tax Board for independent and transparent assessment of property tax; fixing standards for delivery of all essential civic services; and fire hazards response and mitigation plan for all cities with more than one million population as per the 2001 census.

5. State governments to incentivise revenue collection by local bodies through methods such as mandating some or all local taxes as obligatory at non-zero rates of levy, by deducting deemed own revenue collection from transfer entitlements of local bodies or through a system of matching grants.

6. Local bodies to be associated with city planning function wherever entities like urban development authorities are mandated this function. These authorities should also share their revenues with local bodies.

7. The GoI and the state governments to pay service charges to local bodies in respect of properties owned by them.

8. State governments to share a portion of their income from mining royalties with those local bodies from whose jurisdiction such income originates.

Like its predecessors, the 13th Finance Commission could not recommend the sharing of the divisible pool of central taxes with municipalities in view of limitations placed by the Constitution of India. Considering the constitutional requirement of the CFC to recommend measures to improve finances of municipalities of a state on the basis of the recommendations of the SFC of the state as impractical, it reiterated the recommendations of the 12th Finance Commission that Article 280 be amended to replace the words 'on the basis of' with 'taking into account'.

The 14th Finance Commission chose to base its recommendations on a study of the common concerns raised by SFCs instead of 'principles' in the absence of an amendment to Article 280 of the Constitution and the relevant SFC reports being available. It noted that only two states constituted the fifth SFC; 11, the fourth; six, the third; six, the second and one was yet to do so. The Commission also noted that in per capita terms, the grants recommended by four SFCs, whose recommendation period is co-terminus with that of the 14th CFC, ranged from ₹195 to ₹1, 211 a year. While recommending a quantum jump in the share of states in the divisible pool of central taxes from 32 per cent to 42 per cent, the Commission recommended ₹2,87,436 crore as grant-in-aid for local bodies, including ₹87,144 crore for municipalities. The key recommendations of the 14th Finance Commission regarding grants to ULBs are as follows:

1. The grant-in-aid includes a basic grant and a performance grant for duly constituted local bodies. The division between basic and performance grants to municipalities will be on an 80:20 basis. The grants should be spent only on basic services within the functions assigned to municipalities under the relevant legislations.

2. The basic grant for ULBs shall be distributed between municipal corporations, municipalities and nagar panchayats using the formula given by the respective SFCs, whose recommendations have been accepted. In case the SFC formula is not available, the share of each tier will be determined on the basis of population of 2011 with a weight of 90 per cent and area with a weight of 10 per cent. The amount for each tier will also be distributed among the entities in such tier using the same weights.

3. The performance grants, to be available to municipalities from 2016–17 onwards, require addressing the following issues: (a) making available reliable data on local bodies' receipt and expenditure through audited accounts relating to a year not earlier than two years preceding the year in which the performance grant is claimed, (b) increase in own revenues, excluding the proceeds from octroi and entry tax, over the preceding year, as reflected in the audited statements and (c) measurement and publication of service level benchmarks for basic services while making the same publicly available.

4. The state governments should strengthen SFCs. This would involve timely constitution, proper administrative support and adequate resources for smooth functioning, and the timely placement of the SFC report before state legislature, with action taken note.

5. The states should undertake property tax reforms. In addition to enabling municipalities to levy vacant land tax, a part of land use conversion charges should be shared with local bodies. Further, a clear framework of rules for the levy of betterment tax should be put in place by the states.

6. The local bodies should be empowered to mobilise resources through advertisement tax, entertainment tax and profession tax. While all tiers of municipalities should be empowered to levy advertisement tax, the base of entertainment tax needs to be expanded to include newer forms of entertainment such as boat rides, cable television and internet cafes.

7. The ceiling on profession tax should be raised from ₹2,500 to ₹12,000 per annum. Further, Article 272(2) of the Constitution may be amended to vest the power to increase the limits on profession tax on Parliament, based on the CFC recommendation.

8. ULBs should rationalise their service charges in a way that they are able to at least recover the operation and maintenance costs from beneficiaries.

9. As mining puts a burden on the local environment and infrastructure, to assist local bodies in ameliorating the effects of mining on the local population, a part of the income from mining royalties should be shared with local bodies.

10. The central and state governments examine in depth the issues of properly compensating local bodies for the civic services provided by them to government properties and take necessary action, including enacting suitable legislation.

11. Local bodies and state governments should explore the issuance of municipal bonds as a source of finance with suitable support from the GoI. While the states may allow larger municipal corporations to directly approach the market, an intermediary could be set up to assist medium and small municipalities who may not have the capacity to access the market directly.

As regards the distribution of CFC grants for ULBs between states, different CFCs have adopted different criteria and weights. These are presented in Table 7.7.

A study of the CFC reports indicate that, due to limitations placed by the Constitution of India, they could not recommend a formula-based share for local bodies in the divisible pool of central taxes. They did recommend a few measures to augment the finances of municipalities. However, none of the commissions has dwelt upon a suitable architecture for the municipal

Table 7.7

Distribution of Grants to States for Urban Local Bodies: Criteria and Weights (Percentage) Adopted by Finance Commissions of India

	11th	*12th*	*13th*	*14th*
Population	40	40	50	90
Geographical area	10	10	10	10
Distance from highest per capita income	20	20	20	–
Index of decentralisation	20	–	–	–
Index of devolution	–	–	15	–
Index of deprivation	–	10	–	–
Revenue effort	10	20	–	–
Finance Commission ULB grant utilisation index	–	–	5	–

Source: 11th, 12th, 13th and 14th Finance Commission Reports.

finance system in India with a rightful place for central and state transfers therein. The words 'principles' in Article 243X and 'measures' in Article 280 can be interpreted as providing adequate scope at the SFC and CFC levels for recommending a principle-based design of fiscal architecture for the 'third tier' for consideration by the appropriate government.

Reforming Intergovernmental Transfers

In spite of constitutional provisions and reports of several SFCs and CFCs since 1992, intergovernmental transfers to local bodies in India continue to be ad hoc and haphazard. Multiple channels prevail to address the function–finance mismatch in municipalities: assigned revenues, compensation for loss of revenues, non-plan grants, plan grants and SFC transfers from state government, schemes of ministries, Planning Commission dispensations and CFC transfers from central government, schemes of Members of Parliament and Members of Legislative Assembly/Council, etc. The system of intergovernmental transfers to ULBs in India is complex. The only way to reform it is to ask the basic questions: why transfers are needed and whether the design of a transfer is capable of addressing the objective to be served. In this regard the models adopted by multi-tier countries such as Brazil, South Africa, Nigeria, China and Philippines can be of immense relevance to India.

The Constitution of India requires the CFC to recommend 'measures' to augment the consolidated fund of a state to supplement the resources of municipalities 'on the basis of' recommendations made by the Finance Commission of the state. This is restrictive, and not only impractical but also undesirable. It calls for a study of municipal finances, including intergovernmental transfers in every state by the CFC. As NIUA (2011) clarifies, the patterns of municipal finances drastically differ from state to state, requiring intense state-specific studies. Moreover, confining the CFC to study SFC recommendations alone acts against the very foundation of intergovernmental transfers in a federal country, that is, correcting for vertical imbalance. When the most buoyant taxes are assigned to the centre, the bulk of central revenues originate from cities and national interest calls for supporting cities as engines of growth and generators of public finance for development, the observation of the 13th Finance Commission that local bodies be allowed to benefit from the buoyancy of central taxes needs to be given due weight.

Data constraints have reportedly prevented SFCs and CFCs from meaningfully analysing municipal finances in states and recommending measures to strengthen them. Thus, the approaches of SFCs and CFCs are mostly ad hoc; they do not relate to sound principles or norms of a robust system of municipal finance or intergovernmental transfers. Unlike central transfers to states, there has been little attempt to design transfers for ULBs as a percentage of a divisible pool of the relevant taxes or the revenues of central and state governments. While the 13th Finance Commission took a bold initiative to recommend fiscal transfers for local bodies as a percentage of the pool of central taxes (over and above the share of states), the 14th Finance Commission chose not to adopt the practice. This is a setback to the process of fiscal empowerment of local bodies in the spirit of the 74th Amendment. There is a need to enable the ULBs have access to the divisible pool of buoyant central taxes, which are rooted in agglomeration economies of cities. Similarly, the ULBs must have access to buoyant state taxes like VAT or GST, the bulk of which originate in cities. When cities with agglomeration economies are assisted to exploit the power of their externalities, taxes of higher levels of government are bound to experience a quantum jump.

As regards the design of fiscal transfers, none of the past CFCs have examined 'fiscal needs', 'fiscal capacity' and 'fiscal effort' factors together while recommending a transfer regime for local bodies. The Fourteenth CFC has confined to fiscal needs only. No CFC has dwelt on the issue of fiscal capacity. While the Eleventh and Twelfth CFCs assigned weights to tax effort, the Thirteenth and Fourteenth CFCs have not considered the same.[7] Whatever be the methods chosen by the 10th, 11th, 12th, 13th and 14th Finance Commissions to arrive at the quantum of transfers to municipalities in the post-74th Amendment Act era, the recommended transfers have been small. They bear no relation to the backlog, current and growth needs of cities in India.

The 14th Finance Commission's report is the first CFC report after the publication of the two seminal studies on India's urban infrastructure financing needs: McKinsey (2010) and HPEC (2011). However, the 14th CFC report does not address the questions: how can the colossal investment and O&M requirements of cities be financed to enable them perform as engines of growth and what role can central transfers play in this financing. Laudably, the Fourteenth CFC increased the quantum of grant-in-aid for municipalities from ₹23,111 crore for 2010–15 to ₹87,144 crore for 2015–2020. However, this is not linked to the divisible pool of central taxes by a robust formula. The figure also stands nowhere against the amount of ₹5.92 million crore needed for urban infrastructure and services in India over the period 2012–2031 (HPEC 2011).

The quantum of transfers to municipalities through all central channels, including the CFC, Planning Commission and GoI ministries, translates to 0.10 per cent of GDP in 2012—13.[8] When transfers from state governments are added, the ratio turns out to be about 0.46 per cent. This compares poorly with the ratio of total central-to-state transfers to GDP at 4.78 per cent for 2011–12 and 4.62 per cent for 2012–13. The ratio of transfers to local governments to GDP amounted to 10 per cent in the United Kingdom in 2010. India may perhaps set a road map to achieve a three per cent 'transfers to municipalities-GDP' ratio by the time the country reaches the 50 per cent urban mark—one per cent through central channels and two per cent through state routes, including city GST rate within state GST rate or a formula-based share in state GST.

A key learning from public finance theory and practice is that municipal finance needs to be viewed as an integrated system rather than a bundle of disjointed parts. The system has a distinct place for components such as user charges, benefit charges, benefit taxes, general taxes, transfers and borrowings. That is perhaps the reason why Article 243Y of the Constitution mandates the SFC to review and recommend 'principles' of (a) devolution of state revenues to municipalities, (b) determination of revenue sources to be assigned to or appropriated by municipalities, (c) provision of grants-in-aid to municipalities and (d) 'measures' needed to improve their finances. Also, the amendment to Article 280 of the Constitution mandates the CFC to recommend 'measures' needed to augment the finances of a state to supplement the resources of municipalities on the basis of recommendations made by the Finance Commission of the state. These provisions make it imperative for the CFC to delve into the 'principles' recommended by SFCs. However, no CFC has gone into aspects such as the 'golden principles' of local public finance. Unfortunately, research in local public finance in India, which the SFCs and CFCs could make use of is in a dismal state.

The 'generalised benefit principle' of public finance suggests that municipal services, wherever possible, should be paid for in accordance with the benefits received. Thus, user charges, benefit charges and benefit taxes are suitable instruments to meet the cost of local public services. Further, long gestation infrastructure projects, which generate services for generations, ought to be financed by borrowing. Within the benefit model, intergovernmental fiscal transfers have a role to play in the correction of vertical and horizontal imbalances and inter-jurisdictional spillovers, provision of merit goods, development of core infrastructure like public transit, alleviation of poverty and exploitation of scale economies in tax administration. When vertical imbalance is built into the constitutional scheme of fiscal federalism, there is no way the ULBs can cater to their operational and investment needs without a significant devolution forthcoming from higher levels of government, including the central government.

Principles and practices of public finance point to the following directions for designing reforms in intergovernmental transfers to municipalities in India:

1. Municipalities must have clearly-defined functions and revenue sources to match the mandated expenditure responsibilities; they should have well-defined expenditure assignment, revenue assignment, performance management and accountability systems.
2. Municipalities must be made an integral part of the strategy of resource mobilisation in as much as they have shared responsibilities.
3. Objectivity, transparency and predictability need to be built into municipal budgeting within a medium-term expenditure management and revenue mobilisation framework.
4. Intergovernmental transfers should not perform a 'gap filling' function. Any transfer from a higher to a lower level of government will help to close the fiscal gap. The objective to be served, therefore, assumes significance.

5. Needs, rights, capacities and incentives are key criteria for the design of intergovernmental transfers. A simple distributive formula which gives weights to fiscal needs, rights to minimum basic services, fiscal capacity and incentives for performance is desirable.

6. Efficiency needs to be combined with inter-jurisdictional equity. Efficiency requires that those responsible for service should have adequate resources (assuming the best own revenue effort) and sufficient flexibility to make decisions, while being held accountable for results. Unless increased transfers are matched by a local contribution—however small that may be in the poorest communities—the full benefits of decentralisation are unlikely to be realised.

7. Transfers should not bail out the incompetent and the irresponsible entities. Hard budget constraint should be the rule and soft financing options must be avoided.

8. Infrastructure facilities are critical for growth. In the urban context, capital grants can even be more critical than revenue grants. As long as municipalities are constrained by 'own' revenues, intergovernmental transfers will have a key role in financing urban and regional infrastructure. Capital grants could be used as seed money to leverage borrowings from the market through municipal bonds. A clear framework needs to be put in place to determine what role central and state transfers to ULBs should play in the financing of urban infrastructure and services costing ₹5.92 million crore over the period 2012–2031.

9. Fiscal autonomy cannot be built in a culture of grants. Thus, municipalities need to be enabled to progressively rely on taxes and user charges. They must have an alternative to octroi and adopt land value tax, beneficiaries pay, polluters pay, congesters pay, growth pays and value-capture instruments. If a suitable tax alternative to octroi or a city GST rate is not possible, a formula-based share in state GST will be appropriate in the present context of India's fiscal federalism.

10. A broad framework of municipal finances, including sharing of tax base or tax yield at state level, sharing of the divisible pool of taxes at central level and a partnership-based approach to financing urban infrastructure need to be put in place so that the CFC and SFCs can consider the same as a reference. The CFC and SFCs may also contribute to the development of such a framework based on known 'principles' of public finance and good international practices.

Notes

1. Based on OECD (2012).
2. Compensation for loss of octroi and toll tax to Hyderabad city from state government was ₹42 lakhs in 1999–2000: it was ₹50 lakhs in 2013–14.
3. Based on OECD (2012).
4. See Shah (2013) for a discussion on the theory and international practice of intergovernmental transfers; Table 9.1 and Table 9.2 provide data on the patterns of fiscal transfers in metropolitan cities around the world.
5. Author's own study of municipal finances of Hyderabad city.
6. See reports of the 10th, 11th, 12th, 13th and 14th Finance Commissions of India.
7. The 12th Finance Commission assigned a weightage of 20 per cent to revenue effort— 10 per cent with respect to own revenues of states and 10 per cent with respect to GSDP while recommending transfers for municipalities.
8. With implementation of the recommendations of the 14th Finance Commission for municipalities, the central transfers-GDP ratio may go up to 0.15 per cent per annum.

8

Development Financing Instruments

Land Development Financing

Developed countries around the world have adopted a variety of instruments to finance land development, including infrastructure during their urban transition.[1] These include: (a) 'own revenue' surpluses of municipalities on a 'pay-as-you-go' system, (b) budget appropriations or capital grants from consolidated funds of central and state governments, (c) local user charges, benefit charges and dedicated benefit taxes, (d) borrowings from financial institutions and capital market through municipal bonds and other instruments, (e) private sector participation and public–private partnerships, (f) special purpose vehicles or off-budget agencies to develop and operate infrastructure, adopting a mix of financing—user charges, government grants, equity and debt, (g) development financing and (h) value capture instruments. Developing countries like India, however, have not paid much attention to these sources of financing development.[2] Pay-as-you-go financing of urban infrastructure, currently followed by most ULBs in India is grossly inadequate to meet the 'backlog', 'current' and 'growth' needs of urbanisation. While the system needs to be strengthened to generate surplus revenue to 'leverage' debt for financing urban infrastructure, there is also a need to adopt innovative mechanisms of development financing and value capture financing.

This chapter deals with key instruments of development financing adopted internationally. These are based on 'growth pays' and 'exacerbaters pay' principles. The tools require developers to undertake the construction of public infrastructure facilities needed by new growth or make one-time in-lieu payments to the local authority for the same. They include 'developer exactions' and 'development impact fees' in the United States, 'planning obligations' and 'community infrastructure levy' in the United Kingdom, 'development contributions' in Australia and 'internal and external development charges' in several countries, including India. Development financing tools also encompass innovative 'in-kind' mechanisms such as 'land readjustment', 'land consolidation' and 'land pooling'. These instruments promote planned urban expansion and renewal exploiting land as a resource, without burdening the exchequer of local, state and central governments. They are used in concert with other instruments like zoning, development control, land taxation, debt financing, equity financing, general fund revenue, dedicated fund and land value capture.

Developer Exactions

Developer exactions represent a form of land use regulation that requires a land developer or builder to contribute towards on- and off-site infrastructure facilities needed to serve new development. They are levied under the 'police powers' of local government aimed at protecting public health, safety and welfare of residents and mitigating against the negative impacts of growth. They assist in protecting the community from increased cost of infrastructure through cost-sharing with new residents. Exactions allow local authorities to pass on a portion of the cost of public facilities to the developer when development begins, rather than waiting until taxes or service charges are imposed and collected from new residents.

Between World War I and World War II, as a condition of receiving development permission, developers in the United States were required to provide and dedicate for public use facilities such as streets, sidewalks, water lines, sewers and parks that were within or adjacent to new development. Local governments also established special districts that made new development directly responsible for the infrastructure needs it generated. The Standard Planning Enabling Act of 1928 issued by the US Department of Commerce required developers to cater to infrastructure and services for managing growth and urban sprawl. It stipulated that as a condition of sub-division approval, developers construct all streets, water mains, sewer lines and other utility infrastructure. This Act was soon copied by most states. Thus, since the 1920s, private developers in the United States have been required to install and dedicate civic infrastructure facilities to local authorities.

After World War II, the developers' responsibility for infrastructure expanded to off-site public facilities that benefited the community as a whole. In the 1950s and 1960s, the authority of the local government to collect 'voluntary' contributions or 'developer exactions' on a case-by-case basis as a negotiating tool of development approval was established. Exactions took several forms: dedication—donation of land and/or infrastructure facilities like water and sewer systems and roads for public use; tap fees—toward connecting new development to existing infrastructure networks, for example, highways, trunk water and sewerage lines; fee-in-lieu—monetary levy in lieu of installation of certain public facilities like roads, parks and utilities that could be shared; and linkage fee—towards mitigation of secondary effects of development such as affordable housing, jobs, schools, health care facilities, etc. During the 1970s and 1980s, the use of development exactions was broadened to cover both on-site and off-site infrastructure. This resulted in the emergence of 'development impact fees' through state legislation as a part of the conditions of permission to developers to undertake land development.

Globally, there are many examples of the successful use of developer exactions by other countries. For example, in Bangkok, commercial centres desiring connectivity to metro rail stations were required to pay connection charges and contribute to the cost of connecting bridges (ITDP 2007). In Shanghai, developers met the costs of construction, maintenance and security arrangements for a pedestrian link between metro station and their shopping centre (Zhang 2007a).

Development Impact Fees

Development impact fees 'are scheduled charges applied to new development to generate revenue for the construction or expansion of capital facilities located outside the boundaries of the new development (off-site) that benefit the contributing development' (Snyder and Stegman 1987). Most states in the United States levy impact fees to finance new development. These are 'one-time' charges levied by local governments to make the developer pay a 'fair share' of the cost of public facilities and services necessitated by new development. Impact fees are meant to fund or recoup the cost of capital works or extensions of current infrastructure systems. They aim at offsetting the impact of additional development and residents on existing municipal facilities and services. They shift a part of the burden of providing public infrastructure to serve new development from municipal general revenues to the developers. The principal use of impact fees, which distinguishes them from traditional developer exactions, is the financing of 'off-site' capital facilities to support new development.

Impact fee legislations in the United States cover a vast range of new public facilities, intrinsic and extrinsic to the development upon which the fee is levied. These include: roadways, streets, sidewalks, bridges and traffic control devices; water source, treatment and distribution facilities; wastewater collection and treatment facilities; reclaimed water treatment and distribution facilities; storm water drainage; solid-waste collection equipment and disposal; hazardous toxic waste disposal; underground utilities; electricity generation and distribution facilities; street lighting; roadside tree plantation and median landscaping; regional and local parks; recreational facilities; city hall, civic centres and public libraries; day-care centres; schools; public art, museum and cultural facilities; preservation of heritage precincts; protection of environmental resources including endangered species; law enforcement facilities and equipment; fire protection facilities and equipment; harbour, port and airport improvements; mass transit facilities and equipment; emergency medical services; low- and moderate-income housing; training of civic personnel, etc.

Impact fees are imposed as a condition of approval to proceed with development. Like other forms of developer exactions, they are assessed under the broad 'police' powers of local authority as distinct from 'tax' powers to regulate the use and development of land. These powers owe to the legal 'nuisance' doctrine dealing with elimination of potential negative impacts of new development on the community. Impact fees thus differ from land taxes. They also differ from user charges in that they are not based on 'pay according to share of use'. They are rather levied on the principle that 'polluter or exacerbater pays'. Those who create the cost impact must be fully responsible for mitigating the same. Impact fee legislations prescribe for the preparation of capital improvement plan (CIP) for new areas following statutory planning norms and earmarking impact fees for financing the same. The CIP must take into account the comprehensive city development plan, zoning regulations and master plans for facilities. Impact fees are less administratively cumbersome, more predictable, more equitable and less prone to political and bureaucratic discretions than 'negotiated' exactions. They are considered the most rational step in the evolution of local government financing of infrastructure.

The arguments advanced in support of impact fees are summarised as follows:

1. New developments pay their 'fair share' of infrastructure costs through impact fees, without burdening the community.
2. Impact fees ease pressure on other financial resources of local authorities as 'growth pays its way'.
3. Impact fees are revenues exclusively earmarked for the creation of infrastructure facilities, thereby facilitating fiscal responsibility in local government.
4. The requirement of a CIP to justify impact fees leads to improvements in regional and urban planning and capital budgeting.
5. Impact fee legislation requires a rational nexus between fee payment and infrastructure expenditure; thus impact fees cannot be unduly excessive.
6. Correctly calculated impact fees assess the developer only for the cost of providing infrastructure for new development.
7. The use of impact fees can provide a politically acceptable alternative to increase in land and property taxes on existing residents, which is increasingly being resisted.
8. Impact fees reduce the price of undeveloped land and act against speculation in the urban land market.

The arguments levelled against impact fees are as follows:

1. Infrastructure provision is the responsibility of local government and the community as a whole, not of new development alone.
2. Impact fees tend to be regressive; they penalise new development while the older areas gain due to agglomeration economies and reduced congestion.
3. Impact fees increase the market price of new housing; they may reduce the supply of housing.
4. By earmarking impact fees for spending on infrastructure to serve new development, local governments lose flexibility in financing capital and other expenditures.
5. Impact fees have the potential for abuse and misuse by government functionaries through discretion unless limited by carefully drafted legislation.
6. Administrative costs incurred in connection with impact assessment study and calculation, levy, collection and refund of impact fees may be considerable.

The US Supreme Court has ruled that impact fee assessment is within the legal powers of the local government to finance all types of public facilities as long as state statutes permit such levy and the state and federal constitutional standards are met. These standards pertain to 'due process', 'equal protection' and 'taking of private property for public use without just compensation'. The Court has used three tests to determine the validity of exactions and impact fees: the 'reasonably related', 'essential nexus' and 'proportionality'. First, a legally defensible exaction must demonstrate a reasonable relationship between a fee or exaction and the demand for infrastructure created by new development. Secondly, a 'rational nexus' between the conditions of development permission and 'legitimate state interests' must be established.[3] Thirdly, there should be 'rough proportionality' between a development's projected impact and the fee or exaction.[4] Accordingly, state legislations in the United States prescribe that the local government imposing impact fee must establish the essential link among the new development's need for public facilities (needs test), the benefits to the development (benefits test) and the proportionality of the fee (proportionality test). Proportionality refers to the portion of the cost of public facility improvements that reasonably relates to the needs of and benefits accruing to new development.

In order to ensure equity, fairness, uniformity and non-discrimination, impact fees need to be designed taking into account the full consequences of their imposition. The latter extend to long range infrastructure planning, affordability of housing, municipal budgeting, capacity of revenue administration, etc. Fee calculation, payment, administration and use must be clearly defined by law to limit the potential for misuse. Accordingly, state legislations in the United States delineate broad principles and requirements to eliminate arbitrariness in the levy of impact fees. For example, impact fee legislation in Indiana makes the following stipulations:

(a) An impact fee ordinance must include (1) a schedule prescribing for each impact the amount of the impact fee that is to be imposed on each infrastructure type covered by the ordinance; or (2) a formula for each impact zone by which the amount of the impact fee that is to be imposed for each infrastructure type covered by the ordinance may be devised;

(b) A schedule or formula included in an impact fee ordinance must provide an objective and uniform standard for calculating impact fees that allows fee payments to accurately predict the impact fees that will be imposed on new development. (United States Department of Housing and Urban Development 1993)

The Indiana legislation further requires that the impact fee schedule complies with the 'rational nexus' test. The fee may not exceed the development's proportionate share of the costs of providing community level services, exclusive of the costs needed to raise the current level of service and exclusive of any non-local revenue available to pay for infrastructure of the applicable type and any taxes, charges and fees which will be paid during the 10-year period following the assessment of the impact fee for use within the relevant geographic area.

Impact fee legislation in California requires that the agency imposing impact fee must (a) specify the purpose of the fee, (b) identify the use of the fee, including the public facilities to be financed, (c) show an essential nexus between the fee's use and the development proposed, (d) demonstrate a reasonable relationship between the public facility to be constructed and the type of development and (e) account for and spend the fee collected only for the purpose and projects specifically used in its calculation.

Impact fees have demonstrated a significant potential for raising local revenues to support new development. A study covering 206 representative local governments in the United States in 1991 estimated the average level of impact fee assessment on a 2,000 square feet single-family home at US$9,425 (United States Department of Housing and Urban Development 1993). A 2002 survey of 190 US local governments revealed that the national average impact fee for a single family home was $14,273, while that for a multi-family dwelling was $9,912. The figures for industrial, office and retail development were $4,030, $5,845 and $7,758 respectively (Nicholas 2002).

Local authorities in the United States increasingly prefer impact fees to finance new development due to the mounting opposition from old residents to pay higher property taxes to finance projects that do not benefit them directly. Impact fees are also becoming popular in developing countries. For example, Guatemala has devised an innovative instrument called *Impacto Vial*. When a private development project requests for approval, the municipal authority undertakes a study of its likely impact on the community. An infrastructure plan is then developed to mitigate any negative impact, along with a share of the developer in the estimated cost. The work is then executed by the developer under the supervision of the municipality. If the cost of the work is higher than the developer's estimated share, the value of the license (about 4.5 per cent of the building costs) is also used to make up for the difference. Between 2006 and 2013 this instrument has financed nearly all the road construction works in Guatemala, totalling US$ 20 million (Smolka 2013).

Impact fees remain an unexploited resource for planned urban development in India. However, Hyderabad has been a pioneer in levying impact fees, having implemented the same for over 10 years (see Box 8.1). Recently, Gujarat has mandated the levy of impact fee for providing facilities like parking, sanitation, fire safety and so on while implementing the Gujarat Regularisation of Unauthorised Development Act, 2011. It is estimated that a 10 per cent development impact fee on the cost of new construction in Mumbai could finance as much as 40–50 per cent of all regional infrastructure investments required over the next two decades (Peterson 2009).

An impact fee system calls for expertise in local government in preparing long-term infrastructure investment plan and designing fee. This plan must be able to correctly differentiate the impact that a new development would generate on infrastructure costs by location, land use and property characteristics. A schedule of impact fees presented in this manner can channel urban growth to areas where it can be accommodated most efficiently. The local government must, therefore, be in a position to tie together spatial planning, capital improvement planning, financial planning and capital budgeting. Further, a robust legislative framework for the levy of impact fee is essential. Box 8.2 presents salient guidelines for drafting an impact fee legislation in India based on a study of state legislations in the United States.

Box 8.1

Collection of Impact Fee by Greater Hyderabad Municipal Corporation

Andhra Pradesh was the first state in the country to levy impact fee in cities. From 2001–02, the GHMC has been collecting impact fee from landowners/developers converting land on designated commercial roads from 'other' uses to 'commercial'. The impact fee is required to be spent on the implementation of city capital improvement and decongestion plan, including road-widening, link roads, slip roads, parallel roads, junction improvements including traffic signals, flyovers, road over-bridges, road under-bridges, modern lighting on major roads, development of major drains, parks, etc.

GHMC also collects city-level infrastructure impact fee in respect of built-up area above 15 metres height in multi-storied buildings. This amount has to be credited to and maintained in a separate escrow account. 50 per cent of the fee shall be utilised for development of infrastructure in the area from which it is collected and the other 50 per cent is required to be utilised for improvement of city-level infrastructure.

The total amount collected by GHMC under impact fees has increased from ₹2.04 crore in 2001–02 to ₹135.93 crore in 2012–13.

Source: Greater Hyderabad Municipal Corporation: Budget Documents.

Box 8.2

Guidelines for Drafting Impact Fee Legislation

---

1. Clearly state the jurisdictions authorised to levy impact fees.
2. Identify the specific types of residential, commercial, industrial and other developments and/or buildings brought under the net of impact fee and clearly specify the basis for assessment (for example, square footage, per unit and so on).
3. Single out all types of facilities and expenditures benefiting new development that are eligible for funding through impact fee.
4. Define the service area of facility improvement in terms of population and/or geographical area to ensure that impact fees are calculated, assessed, collected and spent only in the area served by the improvement.
5. Prescribe the application of 'rational nexus' test among the new development's needs for facilities, the amount of fee charged and the benefits accruing to new development from these facilities.
6. Stipulate that impact fees finance only the eligible facilities projected for development in the CIP.
7. Specify the time of fee payment. Timing has unique consequences for the land seller, builder and home buyers. The fees may be assessed early in the development process and collected late.
8. Require the establishment of separate interest-bearing accounts for the deposit of impact fees so that they are not commingled with the funds for other purposes.
9. Specify criteria to be taken into account while devising a formula to determine impact fee assessment.
10. Include statutory provision to guide intergovernmental agreements, citizen advisory committee requirements, public hearings, procedures for fee fixation, appeal and so on.

Source: United States Department of Housing and Urban Development (1993).

Planning Obligations

Under section 106 of the United Kingdom Town and Country Planning Act 1990, local authorities are empowered to negotiate with developers while according development permission to make commitments, known as 'planning obligations'. Section 55 (1) of the Act defines 'development' as, 'carrying out of building, engineering, mining or other operations in, on, over or under land, or the making of any material change in the use of any buildings or other land.' Planning obligations may cover executing capital works, making financial or in-kind contributions, or providing affordable housing. They are formalised by legal agreements, known as Section 106 agreements (see Box 8.3).

Box 8.3

Planning Obligations in the United Kingdom

Section 106 of the UK Town and Country Planning Act 1990 stipulates that any person interested in land in the area of a local planning authority may, by agreement or otherwise, enter into a 'planning obligation', enforceable by the authority:

1. restricting the development or use of the land in any specified way;
2. requiring specified operations or activities to be carried out in, on, under or over the land;
3. requiring the land to be used in any specified way; or
4. requiring a sum or sums to be paid to the authority.

A planning obligation may (a) be unconditional or subject to conditions; (b) impose any restriction or requirement either indefinitely or for such period or periods as may be specified; and (c) if it requires a sum or sums to be paid, require the payment of a specified amount or an amount determined in accordance with the instrument by which the obligation is entered into and, if it requires the payment of periodical sums, require them to be paid indefinitely or for a specified period.

If there is a breach of a requirement in a planning obligation to carry out any operations in, on, under or over the land to which the obligation relates, the authority by whom the obligation is enforceable may (a) enter the land and carry out the operations and (b) recover from the person or persons against whom the obligation is enforceable any expenses reasonably incurred by them in doing so.

A planning obligation shall be a local land charge enforceable under law by the local planning authority.

Source: The United Kingdom Town and Country Planning Act 1990.

Development Contributions

Apart from levying land-related taxes on a number of tax bases such as site value, improved values and rental values of land and building, Australian states have been using 'development contributions' extensively to fund urban infrastructure. Since the 1980s, the range of facilities that can be funded through these contributions has expanded considerably to include major headwork infrastructure such as arterial roads, sewerage treatment plants and social infrastructure facilities like parks, libraries and affordable housing. Development contributions are akin to up-front user charges for future infrastructure services when a nexus is established between the type of development, its infrastructure needs and the contributions mandated. When such a nexus is not envisaged, they are comparable to taxes.

State laws in Australia permit negotiations by local authorities with developers to make contribution by way of land, public works or money (see Box 8.4). Development contributions are legally enforceable instruments and usually assume three forms: (a) contribution in kind—land gifted to the government by developer for roads, drainage and public facilities like open spaces, gardens, schools, health centres and so on; (b) work-in-kind—public infrastructure works and facilities constructed by a developer and handed over to public authorities on completion and (c) monetary charges—financial contributions toward acquisition of land for public use or provision of infrastructure and affordable housing. Where development contributions are in-kind or insufficient to meet the whole of infrastructure costs, the gap is financed from other sources, including borrowing.

Box 8.4

Developer Contributions in New South Wales, Australia

Under the Environmental Planning and Assessment Act 1979 of New South Wales (NSW), local authorities collect development contributions from developers toward shared local infrastructure, facilities or services and certain types of regional infrastructure as condition of granting development consent. The five main types of development contributions in NSW are:

Section 94 contributions: payable to local authority as (a) dedication of land free of cost or (b) monetary contribution, or both, toward the cost of infrastructure and services necessitated by new development. A developer, who has submitted a development or re-zoning application, can be required to provide or bear the capital and recurrent cost of public amenities and services, affordable housing, transport, recreation, other infrastructure and environmental conservation. There is no limit to the value of contributions that can be negotiated.

Section 94A levies: levy paid to local authority as a percentage of the cost of carrying out development.

Planning agreements: negotiated between the developer and planning authority outlining the agreed developer contribution. These constitute alternative or adjunct to Section 94 contribution and section 94A levies.

Affordable housing levy: collected by local council in designated areas due to the development creating a need for affordable housing or reducing availability of the same.

Special infrastructure contribution: paid into an infrastructure fund constituted by the NSW government for development of identified growth centres.

Section 94EA of the Act requires the preparation of contribution plan by local authority indicating the purpose and contents, formulae used to determine section 94 contribution or section 94A levy percentage, etc.

Source: Environmental Planning and Assessment Act 1979, New South Wales, Australia.

In New Zealand, local authorities resort to development contributions from developers under the Local Government Act 2002 toward infrastructure costs; financial contributions under the Resource Management Act 1991 toward recovery of environmental costs, for example, those associated with mitigating, avoiding or remedying negative impacts on environment; and targeted rates under the Local Government (Rating) Act 2002 for tapping funds from identified groups who benefit directly from or are impacted upon by projects.

External Development Charges

State legislations in India provide for the levy of development charges to meet the costs of infrastructure to service land. They cover both internal (on-site) and external (off-site) costs. Haryana Urban Development Authority (HUDA) levies external development charges (EDC) on colonisers. Under the Haryana Development and Regulation of Urban Areas Act, 1975, external development works are defined to include water supply, sewers, drains, necessary provisions for disposal of sewage, sullage and storm water, roads, electrical works, solid waste management and disposal, slaughter houses, colleges, hospitals, stadiums/sports complex, fire stations, grid sub-stations, etc. and any other work which the Director of Town and Country Planning may specify for being executed in the periphery of or outside colony/area for the benefit of the colony/area. The Act mandates the developer to pay 'proportionate development charges' in the external development works to be carried out by the government or local authority. The proportion in which, and the time within which such payment is to be made, are determined by the Director of Town & Country Planning. In 2006, external development charges per acre amounted up to about ₹95 lakh in Faridabad.

Hyderabad collects external betterment charges, in addition to development charges and betterment charges toward recoupment of costs of public facilities such as trunk water and sewer lines, freeways, regional parks, etc. When layouts and buildings are approved, these charges are collected as per the norms adopted.

Land Readjustment/Consolidation

South Korea has used 'land readjustment' and Taiwan, 'land consolidation' successfully for undertaking planned development of cities while capturing a part of the resultant land value increases to finance the same.

Under these techniques, once an area is selected for development, the municipality declares it as a special area under law as the unit for physical planning. A proper site plan is prepared and about one-third of the area is set aside for streets, parks, schools and other public uses. The cost of installation of civic infrastructure and services, such as water supply, drainage, sewerage, roads, electricity and other facilities, needed for residential and non-residential development is then estimated. The next step is to project the likely market value of improved sites and estimate the ratio of capital costs needed for the installation of all infrastructure to such market value. This calculates the percentage of area meant for residential and commercial development that has to be sold to meet the infrastructure costs. The extent of the area so determined is called the 'cost equivalent area'. In most cases this turns out to be about 10 per cent of total area.

About 43 per cent of the area under a land readjustment scheme is required to support a self-financed land development project. If private landowners in the designated area own 10,000 square metres of raw land before readjustment, they would get back about 5,700 square metres of improved sites. Generally, municipalities provide improved sites to landowners as near as possible to their original holdings. The experience of South Korea and Taiwan shows that even if landowners lost up to 50 per cent of the land area they held, the value of improved sites exceeded that of original holdings by many times. Municipalities gained from new development and property as well as other taxes, without any spending from general revenues. In South Korea, the 'cost equivalent area' sites are auctioned by municipalities through a competitive bidding process.

Town Planning Scheme: Gujarat

The town planning scheme (TPS) has been the predominant mechanism for undertaking integrated urban development in Gujarat for decades. It offers an effective alternative to compulsory acquisition of land, being more beneficial to landowners as well as equitable. Based on the concept of land pooling enabled by law, the TPS promotes planned urban expansion without strains on the public exchequer.

Urban planning in Gujarat is a two-step process outlined in the Gujarat Town Planning and Urban Development Act, 1976 and rules thereunder. The first step is to prepare a 'development plan' (DP) for a designated area. The second step is to prepare TPSs. The DP is a broad-brush development vision for the city—a dynamic document that is detailed gradually. The new areas to be opened up for development are clearly marked and divided into smaller areas of about 100 to 200 hectares, typically involving 100 to 250 landowners. Each such area is called a TPS.

The TPS provides for laying or relaying out land, either vacant or already built upon, allocating land for roads, water supply, drainage, sewerage, street lighting, open spaces, gardens, green belts, recreation grounds, schools, markets, and so on and undertaking development. It also caters to the preservation of objects of historical or national interest, or natural beauty. Every TPS is legally required to reserve land to the extent of nearly 10 per cent of total area for socially and economically weaker sections (SEWs). The allotment of land from the scheme area other than for SEWs is made as per the following standards: 15 per cent for roads; five per cent for parks, playgrounds, gardens and open spaces; five per cent for social infrastructure such as schools, dispensaries, fire brigades and public utilities; and 15 per cent for sale by the appropriate authority to meet the cost of infrastructure in the scheme area.

The steps involved in TPS include: topographical survey of area, establishing ownership details of each land parcel, reconciling survey and land-ownership records to prepare a base map, defining the boundary of the area, marking original plots on the base map, tabulating owner-ship details and plot size, laying out roads, carving out plots for ameni-ties, tabulating deduction and plot size, delineating final plot, working out infrastructure costs and betterment charges, conducting landowners' meeting, modifying draft TPS and obtaining approval from the state gov-ernment. Each landowner gets back proportionately reduced developed land, contributing for reservations for public use and sale component to meet the infrastructure costs.

The TPS offers the following advantages: (a) the planning process has all freedom that a new town offers without burdening it with cum-bersome land acquisition, associated costs and court litigations; (b) the reduction in land area, costs and returns of the scheme are spread across all landowners; (c) inclusive development occurs with a reasonable extent of land allocated for weaker sections through the planning system itself; and (d) the local authority is enabled to levy betterment charges on land-owners in proportion to land value increment due to spatial planning and infrastructure improvement.

The TPS as followed in Gujarat provides an excellent example of inclusive and self-financed planned urban development. However, the process is very time-consuming and needs to be simplified. A model of TPS driven by the private sector is also desirable. The TPS is worth rep-lication throughout the country without reservation. With compulsory acquisition of land being increasingly difficult, a partnership between government, farmers and developers appears to be a pragmatic way of addressing the challenges of urbanisation in India.

Magarpatta Township Model: Pune

Magarpatta in Pune, Maharashtra presents a shining example of how rural farmers can be made partners in the process of planned urban development, creating a world-class, self-contained township based on a 'walk to work, walk to school' principle. This township, spread over 430 acres, is located in the outskirts of Pune. The land has been part of Pune Municipal Corporation since 1960, initially falling under the agricultural zone. The township has been developed over a period of 10 years by the original inhabitant-farmers. Today, with environment-friendly development, high quality urban services, excellent modern facilities for education and health and state-of-the-art workplaces, Magarpatta is home to over 35,000 residents and a working population of 65,000. It has attracted multi-national corporations and other corporate entities, particularly IT companies, to set up their offices.

A community of 120 farmers took the crucial decision of organising themselves to form the Magarpatta Township Development and Construction Company, which prepared the Magarpatta city plan. The landowners, through the company, approached the Government of Maharashtra with a proposal for integrated township under the Maharashtra Regional and Town Planning Act, 1966. After receiving approval for the project and change of land use, the township was started in 1994, with farmers as partners in growth. Money from the land was used only for asset creation, thereby providing a safety net for the next generation. All farmers agreed to use a part of the value of their land to buy flats and shops in the township, thereby securing lease rentals. Funding for new business ventures came from banks. In the process, over 250 entrepreneurs in non-agricultural ventures emerged from the farmer community. These first generation entrepreneurs account for a gross annual turnover of ₹150–200 crore. The business strategy of the company has ensured that a farmer with one acre of land at the time of its formation earns a dividend of about ₹15 to 16 lakh per year.

Social integration of the farming community with residents of Magarpatta was carefully planned. Allocation of flats to the farmers was done in such a way that they were located in different parts of the township. Today, it is difficult to differentiate the farmer community from other residents.

The innovative features of the Magarpatta model are: (a) landowners are shareholders in township development and entitled to profit-sharing; (b) they receive a percentage of sale-proceeds in proportion to their land-holdings, thereby benefitting from escalating land prices; (c) no landowner is displaced from his ancestral land, instead land is used to empower him; and (d) landowners have the opportunity to turn into entrepreneurs, thereby creating employment for themselves and others.

Magarpatta provides an excellent example of a township development by the private sector facilitated by the government, with no land acquisition and no cost to public authorities. On the contrary, the city is generating sizable public financial resources for central, state and local governments. The model is being replicated in Nanded in Maharashtra. A community of 235 farmer families have pooled 700 acres of agricultural land for developing a new township. This will have a residential district, a commercial complex, a hospital, a school and 230 acres of green spaces, including over 5.2 km of riverside development, the first of its kind in India.

Road Widening Scheme: Hyderabad

The Municipal Corporation of Hyderabad has been implementing an innovative 'road widening scheme' since the 1980s with a remarkable success (see Box 8.5). By March 2014, it had widened 307 roads with 260 kilometres of length by securing land estimated at ₹1,200 crore from landowners free of cost. The scheme has become popular with landowners as they perceive that the benefits to them would be much more than the foregone cost of land surrendered for road widening.

Market-based Financing Instruments

Key market-based instruments for urban infrastructure include equity and debt financing. Equity financing mechanisms cover self-raised funds, and domestic and foreign capital, including infrastructure equity funds. Debt financing mechanisms cover loans, bonds, credit-enhancement instruments and refinancing mechanisms. Equity and debt are combined with public finance tools to fund capital-intensive urban and regional infrastructure projects. However, a common principle in all of them is that investments have to be paid for directly or indirectly, and by present and future generations.

Box 8.5

Road Widening Scheme in Greater Hyderabad Municipal Corporation

The 'road widening scheme' being implemented by Hyderabad since the 1980s is a unique initiative to secure land free of cost by using development right as a resource. The Government of Andhra Pradesh empowered the Hyderabad municipal corporation with instruments such as relaxation of zoning/development regulations and grant of concessional Floor Area Ration (FAR) to secure land for widening major roads. Vide orders issued in 1998, the government delegated its powers to the corporation to relax FAR up to an extent of 1.0, grant concessions in setbacks and ground coverage and accord permission for conversion to commercial use in respect of remaining land available after road widening, if land for road widening was surrendered free of cost. In particular, the government delegated the authority to grant relaxations in zoning regulations and building rules to the municipal commissioner.

Learning from experience, the state government has incorporated the following concessions for road widening by urban local bodies/development authorities under the Common Building Rules of 2006 and Comprehensive Building Rules of 2012:

1. Upon surrendering area affected in the Statutory Plan/Master Plan road or circulation network or road required to be widened as per road development plan (RDP) free of cost to the sanctioning authority, the site owner shall be entitled to a TDR to be utilised in the remaining land or anywhere within the municipal jurisdiction, or be allowed to construct an extra floor with an equivalent built area for the area surrendered subject to mandatory public safety requirements or be permitted to avail concessions in setbacks, including front setback subject to ensuring a building line of six metres (m) in respect of roads with width of 30 m and above, three m in respect of roads 18–30 m wide and two m in respect of roads of less than 18 m width, and subject to ensuring minimum side and rear setback of two m for buildings of height up to 12 m, 2.5 m for buildings of 12–15 m height and three m for buildings of 15–8 m height.

2. The extent of concessions shall be such that the total built up area after concession shall not exceed the sum of built up area allowed (as proposed) on total area without road widening and built up area equivalent to surrendered area.

3. In the case of plots less than 750 sq. m, in addition to concessions in setbacks and height, cellar floor may be allowed keeping in view its feasibility on ground.

4. In the case of high-rise buildings, concessions in setbacks, other than front setback would be considered subject to maintaining minimum clear setback of seven m on the sides and rear side, and such minimum setback area shall be clear without any obstructions to facilitate movement of fire-fighting vehicles and effective fire-fighting operations.

5. The above concessions shall be considered at the level of sanctioning/ competent authority without referring to the state government. The authority may consider any other concession as deemed fit with the prior approval of government.

Source: Greater Hyderabad Municipal Corporation.

Equity Financing of Infrastructure

Equity financing of infrastructure includes: infrastructure equity, thematic funds and equity-funded direct investments in projects such as special purpose vehicles (SPVs) and joint ventures (JVs). In the case of urban infrastructure, SPVs are formed to plan, finance, build, develop and operate large projects. Joint ventures involve equity participation by multiple partners and are usually not project-specific. SPVs aim at ring-fencing project cash-flows, which are leveraged to raise debt from the market. China has successfully experimented with Urban Development and Investment Companies/Corporations (UDICs), established in most cities by the 1990s. These specialised local enterprises receive land transfer fees as equity to borrow from banks and other sources, manage assets and liabilities, and recover costs. They also raise bonds, when permitted, and enter into joint ventures with private companies to build infrastructure. Usually bank loans are guaranteed by local government resources, including land-based revenues. As urban infrastructure projects require a relatively long period to recover costs, the debts are often rolled over. UIDCs have been the vehicles of the spectacular urban transformation in China.

Debt Financing of Infrastructure

Generally urban infrastructure projects like water supply, sewerage and public transit are lumpy and capital-intensive. Characterised by long gestation periods and stable cash flows only over an extended period, they are suitable for financing through long-tenor debt. Borrowing has a distinct advantage in the case of large utilities wherein the benefits accrue over a long period of time and are reaped by more than one generation of taxpayers. The financing of such projects through short-term debt places the repayment burden entirely on one generation of beneficiaries, while the subsequent generations would essentially be free-riders. Also, short-term borrowings distort investment priorities, particularly in local bodies needing a large investment programme to clear the backlog infrastructure deficits. Financing of projects leading to long-term gains by long-term borrowings, in part or whole, is warranted on both equity and efficiency considerations. In any case, borrowing is the only practical way to finance capital-intensive infrastructure projects. Pay-as-you-go and other financing instruments supplement borrowing.

Borrowing enables local governments and SPVs to mobilise a large amount of capital in a short span of time, while spreading repayment over a long period. Forms of debt financing adopted by local authorities in the United States include municipal tax-free bonds (general obligation and revenue), taxable bonds, lease-purchase contracts, revolving loan funds, bond banks, small issue industrial development bonds, qualified redevelopment bonds, qualified mortgage bonds, green bonds, etc. General obligation bonds are the most secure form of debt a local authority can issue and do not require a debt service reserve. They are limited by set debt ceilings. Unlimited-tax varieties of general obligation bonds pledge future tax collections to repay principal and interest. Limited-tax general obligation bonds are pledged against a fixed tax rate on taxable property. General obligation bonds are usually exempt from federal income taxes. Revenue bonds, generally tax-exempt, finance revenue-generating facilities backed by a stream of revenues pledged from user charges for services. In most cases, interest rates on revenue bonds are higher than those on general obligation bonds. This is because revenue bonds are backed by variable revenues rather than by stable taxes. Taxable bonds are similar to commercial bonds and allow more leeway in the types of projects funded. To attract investors, a higher rate of interest is required on taxable bonds compared to tax-exempt bonds.

Often specialised investment tools are adopted to provide direct funding to private sector investors to catalyse investment in urban infrastructure. In this context, programmes such as tax credits or incentives, seed and venture capital, economic development funds, loan guarantees and underwriting are adopted in the United States. Tax credits cover historic preservation incentive, brownfield tax credit, low income housing tax credit, etc. Other instruments include mezzanine finance and federal funding programmes. Community development block grant (CDBG), community development loan fund (CDLF) and state revolving loan fund (SRLF) programmes have assisted local authorities and business entities in the United States to undertake infrastructure programmes by leveraging own-revenues, market funds and community resources. They have supported, among other things, the acquisition of real property, rehabilitation of public facilities and construction of utility infrastructure.

India introduced tax-free and taxable municipal bonds since the late 1990s, following the US model. Table 8.1 presents the list of bonds issued by municipal corporations and parastatal entities in the country as of 2010.[5]

Table 8.1

Municipal Bonds Issued in India as of 2010

Bond Issuing Authority	Projects	Amount (₹Million)
Bangalore Municipal Corporation (1997)*	City road/drainage projects	1,250
Ahmedabad Municipal Corporation (1998)*	Water supply and sanitation projects	1,000
Ludhiana Municipal Corporation (1999)*	Water supply and sanitation projects	100
Nagpur Municipal Corporation (2001)*	Water supply and sanitation projects	500
Nashik Municipal Corporation (1999)*	Water supply and sanitation projects	1,000
Indore Municipal Corporation (2000)*	City road projects	100
Madurai Municipal Corporation (2001)*	City road projects	300
Ahmedabad Municipal Corporation (2002)	Water supply and sewerage projects	1,000
Nashik Municipal Corporation (2002)	Underground sewerage scheme and storm-water drainage projects	500
Hyderabad Municipal Corporation (2003)	Road construction and widening projects	825
Hyderabad Metropolitan Water Supply & Sewerage Board (2003)	Water supply projects	500
Chennai Metropolitan Water Supply & Sewerage Board (2003)	Water supply projects	420
Visakhapatnam Municipal Corporation (2004)*	Water supply projects	200
Visakhapatnam Municipal Corporation (2004)	Water supply projects	500
Ahmedabad Municipal Corporation (2004)	Water supply, storm-water drainage, roads and bridges and flyover projects	580

(Continued)

(Table 8.1 Continued)

Bond Issuing Authority	Projects	Amount (₹Million)
Chennai Metropolitan Water Supply & Sewerage Board (2005)	Water supply projects	500
Chennai Municipal Corporation (2005)	Road projects	458
Ahmedabad Municipal Corporation (2005)	Road and water supply projects	1,000
Nagpur Municipal Corporation (2007)	Water supply and sewerage projects	212
Tamil Nadu Urban Development Fund (TNUDF): Pooled Issue (2003)	Water and sanitation projects	304
Karnataka Water and Sanitation Pooled Fund (2005)	Greater Bengaluru water supply and sewerage projects	1,000
TNUDF: Pooled Issue (2008)	Tamil Nadu towns' water supply and sewerage projects	450
TNUDF: Pooled Issue (2010)	Tamil Nadu towns' water supply and sewerage projects	832
Total		13,531

Source: Vaidya and Vaidya (2010).

Note: * Taxable Issues.

The municipal bonds programme in India has not met a significant success due to the persisting problem of poor credit-worthiness of municipalities. However, the experience of the United States reveals that, if properly structured, municipal bonds can become a key instrument to finance the ever-growing needs of urban infrastructure in India. A robust regulatory framework for municipal bonds and enabling institutional mechanisms are essential. Recently, the Security Exchange Board of India (SEBI) has issued guidelines for the issue of municipal bonds in India to finance smart cities. Four different structures are envisaged: (a) issuance directly by the municipality, (b) issuance through a corporate municipal entity created by the municipality, (c) creation of a statutory body or intermediary which can borrow from market through bonds for onward lending to municipalities and (d) issuance of securitised debt instruments under a pool finance development fund structure by a special purpose distinct entity (trust) created by one or more municipalities by securitising the receivables. It is hoped that bonds issued by municipalities having good financial track record would offer an alternative investment opportunity to the conservative Indian investor who mainly invests in fixed deposits, small savings or gold.

Financial Intermediation

The access of ULBs in India, especially smaller municipalities to long-term debt is constrained by (a) underdeveloped capital market, (b) lack of access to long tenor funds like insurance, pension and provident funds, (c) cumbersome procedures prescribed by state governments to permit local bodies to borrow and (d) poor track record of municipalities as credit-worthy borrowers. State governments restrict the power of local governments to borrow because they are often required to guarantee the debt. There is, however, a need to promote borrowing by municipalities to enable them access the vast pool of private capital market resources. Further, the internal capacity of local authorities to design and implement investments programmes needs to be strengthened. In this regard, the institutional and funding arrangements adopted internationally vary widely. But, certain fundamental principles underlie the strategy to access market funds. When capital markets are shallow, the smaller local bodies cannot gain access to such resources easily. Larger and more viable institutions, which are in a position to pool risks and borrow with ease, can approach the capital market, national and state-level financial intermediaries, and bilateral and multi-lateral lending institutions on behalf of smaller municipalities for financing their infrastructure projects. Intermediation strategy has been practiced in many countries to finance urban and regional infrastructure.

Internationally, institutional arrangements for financial intermediation have taken forms such as specialised banks, co-operatives, limited companies and rediscount facilities. Municipal credit institutions have a long record of success as financial intermediaries in Western Europe.[6] Bond banks and revolving loan funds are popular in the United States; they leverage central and state grants to secure market funds. Bond banks are created under state statutes to purchase small bond issues of participating local governments and in turn issue bonds large enough to float on the national market. Interest rates on bond bank issues are typically lower compared to what local governments could obtain on their own.

Revolving loan funds are set up with a specific amount of federal and/ or state funds for clearly defined activities. They function as permanent lines of credit for local governments, which are often too small and not able to access the bond market. Municipal finance corporations at the provincial level in Canada play a similar role. Some countries have also experimented with municipal development funds as specialised entities to raise long-term funds from the market for on-lending to local authorities for infrastructure projects.[7] The Housing and Urban Development Corporation (HUDCO), a national financial intermediary in India, aims at supporting city and state entities and private developers to undertake urban sector projects with loans. However, high cost of funds and low credit-worthiness of borrowers for such projects have affected HUDCO's operations adversely.

Two noted examples of state-level financial intermediaries in India to mobilise urban infrastructure finance are the Tamil Nadu Urban Development Fund (TNUDF) and the Karnataka Urban Infrastructure Development and Finance Corporation (KUIDFC). TNUDF is a trust registered in 1996 under the Indian Trust Act 1882 as a public–private partnership between the Government of Tamil Nadu and three all India financial institutions: Industrial Credit and Investment Corporation of India (ICICI) Bank Ltd, Housing Development Finance Corporation (HDFC) Ltd and Infrastructure Leasing and Financial Services (IL&FS) Ltd. It is managed by Tamil Nadu Urban Infrastructure Financial Services Ltd (TNUIFSL), a public limited company incorporated in 1996 under the Companies Act 1956. TNUDF provides long-term debt to municipalities in Tamil Nadu for urban infrastructure on a non-guarantee mode. KUIDFC is a public limited company, incorporated in 1993. It operates as a state-level financial intermediary in Karnataka to assess the infrastructure needs of cities and towns, formulate projects, act as nodal agency for project implementation and raise finances for urban infrastructure.

Both TNUDF and KUIDFC have been successful in assisting smaller municipalities in accessing credit from the market for water and sanitation projects through Water and Sanitation Pooled Fund (WSPF) bonds. Tamil Nadu has issued two WSPF bonds—raising (a) ₹30.4 crore through unsecured, non-convertible, redeemable, 9.2 per cent coupon, 15-year taxable bonds to refinance high cost, fixed rate, 16 per cent interest, 30-year tenor loans for water and sanitation projects of 13 Municipalities in 2002 and (b) ₹89.89 crore by way of 10-year tax-free bonds in two tranches—₹6.70 crore at 7.25 per cent coupon rate in 2008 and ₹83.19 crore at 7.50 per cent coupon rate in 2010 to finance sewerage projects in six municipalities and water supply project in one municipal corporation. TNUIFSL manages the WSPF bond funds. Apart from issuing WSPF bonds, TNUIFSL has assisted Madurai Municipal Corporation in mobilising ₹29 crore through taxable bonds in 2001, Chennai Metropolitan Water Supply and Sewerage Board in raising ₹42 crore in 2001 and ₹50 crore in 2005 in two tax-free bond issues and Chennai Municipal Corporation in mobilising ₹44.80 crore through tax-free bonds in 2005. The Government of Karnataka has raised ₹100 crore by way of tax-free, 5.95 per cent coupon, 15-year municipal bonds in 2005 through the Karnataka Water and Sanitation Pooled Fund, a trust set up by the Government. KUIDFC assisted in bond issue on behalf of eight ULBs in the Bengaluru region for the water supply component of the Greater Bengaluru Water and Sanitation Project.

Lease Purchase Financing

Lease purchase financing is a method increasingly being used by local governments in the United States to acquire real property, including buildings, vehicles and equipment, without resorting to the conventional forms of debt such as general obligation and revenue bonds. It involves the payment of an annually renewable contract for the use and acquisition of property or equipment. The contact usually takes the shape of lease, instalment sale agreement or lease purchase agreement. The local authority often leases facilities while purchasing them. This method allows the purchase of facilities on instalment basis while using the same. Financing is arranged typically through a financial institution, manufacturer, public agency, non-profit organisation or a private leasing company. It usually carries a higher rate of interest compared to outright purchase. The key advantages of lease purchase financing are that the local authority obtains facilities without a large upfront investment and that the cost of facilities is spread over a long period of time without burdening the authority. Sometimes the local authority resorts to lease-sale-back agreement in which it sells a facility to a lessor and then leases it back. This method enables the authority to obtain quick cash for facility.

The success of lease purchase financing depends on finding someone who is willing to invest in the facility to be leased to local authority on the strength of lease rentals. This entity may be a single investor or a group of investors who have acquired undivided shares of the lease obligations. These shares are called Certificates of Participation (CoP). California, by law, allows public entities to issue lease revenue bonds to finance facilities that are leased to local authorities. The bonds' debt service liabilities are met by lease payments received from the lessee authorities.

Dedicated Funds for Infrastructure

Several countries have set up dedicated funds with revenues from general and special taxes, fees and other sources to finance critical investment programmes. Often these funds are backed by statute; they ensure that adequate revenues are mobilised to finance the planned development of core urban infrastructure. For example, in the United States, gasoline and diesel fuel taxes are largely dedicated to financing highways under the National Highway Act 1956 and Highway Revenue Act 1956 through the Highway Trust Fund (HTF). A Mass Transit Account (MTA) under this fund was created by the Highway Revenue Act of 1982. About 85 per cent of the HTF revenues go to the Highway Account and the remaining, to the Mass Transit Account.[8]

California started dedicating gasoline tax for transportation since 1923. Fuel excise tax on gasoline and diesel, truck weight fee—a fee on commercial vehicles based on weight, representing compensation for wear and tear in roadways—and fuel tax swap (additional excise tax on gasoline in lieu of sales tax) accounted for the bulk of the state spending on public transportation in 2011. About two-thirds of the state fuel excise tax goes to state highways under a statutory formula. The remainder goes to counties and cities for roads and streets. These local authorities can also levy a local option sales tax at a rate up to 1.5 per cent under California's Transportation Development Act of 1971. Further, they receive a share from state excise tax on gasoline and diesel fuel, and state as well as federal transportation grants (Caltrans 2011).

In France, since 1971, all establishments located in an urban transport area and employing more than nine persons are required to pay a percentage of their wage bill as *versement transport* or transport tax for funding public transport. This is a hypothecated payroll tax credited to *autorite organisatrice de transport urbain*, the urban regional transport authority responsible for organising regional and urban public transport. In 2000, this tax accounted for about 40 per cent of the total transportation expenditure in France. Initially applicable to urban transport areas with more than 3,00,000 people, the tax was extended to communities with more than 10,000 people by 2000. Tax rate varies from 1.4 per cent to 2.6 per cent in the Ile de France (Paris metropolitan region). It is limited to

0.9 per cent for urban transport areas with fewer than 1,00,000 inhabitants. The transport tax has provided a stable source of funding for the development or extension of 10 light rail transit systems in France since 1985 (Scheurer et al. 2000).

Earmarked Revenues for Projects: Bengaluru

From the nineties, Karnataka has adopted earmarked taxes to mobilise resources for the Mass Rapid Transit System (MRTS), Cauvery Water Supply Project and Bengaluru Ring Road Project. The following sources were earmarked for financing MRTS: (a) 'MRTS Cess' on development permission fee with separate rates for: (i) buildings with ground floor and ground plus first floor, (ii) buildings with ground floor plus two or more than two floors, (iii) industrial and public or semi-public buildings, (iv) private layouts/group housing and (v) civic amenity sites; (b) cess at varying rates on sales tax on petrol, diesel and goods other than declared goods; (c) five per cent cess on luxury tax on lodging charges above ₹750 per day, profession tax, betting tax and motor vehicles tax; (d) five per cent additional stamp duty; and (e) 15 per cent additional licensing fee on liquor manufacturing and selling. For mobilising resources to finance water supply project to bring Cauvery water to Bengaluru, the government of Karnataka levied Cauvery Water Cess on land in urban agglomerations for which development permission or change of land use was sought, with different 'per acre' rates for conversion to residential, commercial, industrial, public and other uses and real estate development. In order to develop the ring road around Bengaluru, Ring Road Surcharge was levied on the conversion of land in Bengaluru metropolitan area to various uses.

Bengaluru has implemented MRTS phase one for a length of 42.3 km. For phase two of the project, covering a length of 72.1 km and costing ₹26,405 crore, the following financing pattern is envisaged: GoI, 20 per cent (equity 15 per cent and subordinate debt five per cent); Government of Karnataka, 34 per cent (equity 15 per cent, subordinate debt 13 per cent and grant six per cent); and senior term debt from external and domestic financial institutions, 46 per cent. The government of Karnataka has embarked on innovative instruments to part finance the state share for the metro through dedicated instruments such as development cess on new layouts/developments in the transit service areas, cess on additional FAR and TDR in lieu of compensation for land.

Beneficiary Capital Contribution: Bengaluru

The Government of Karnataka has introduced BCC to part-finance water supply under the Greater Bengaluru Water and Sanitation Project. A pooled finance framework was adopted for eight ULBs which are recently merged with the Greater Bengaluru Municipal Corporation. Tax-free municipal bonds on behalf of the ULBs were floated in 2005 to raise ₹100 crore through Karnataka Water and Sanitation Pooled Fund, a trust set up by the Karnataka government. The total project cost of ₹447.06 crore is met as follows: BCC–₹119.45 crore, Municipal Bonds–₹100.00 crore, Mega City Loan Scheme–₹153.33 crore and Karnataka government grant–₹74.28 crore. The rates of BCC are as per the scales presented in Table 8.2.

Development Financing Tools in India

Development financing tools form a key component of a toolbox of city financing instruments that include: (a) local taxes; (b) local user fees, utility charges and congestion tolls; (c) central and state government grants, tax abatements and credit assistance, including revolving loan funds, tax credit, seed capital, venture capital, mezzanine funds and loan guarantees; (d) equity, including public–private partnerships; (e) debt, including institutional credit, municipal bond, pooled finance bond, green bond, bond bank and financial intermediation; (f) planning and

Table 8.2

Greater Bengaluru Water and Sanitation Project: Scales of Beneficiary Capital Contribution (in ₹)

Description of Property Seeking Water Connection	Up to 600 sq. ft.	600–1200 sq. ft.	1200–2400 sq. ft.	> 2400 sq. ft.
Residential sites/apartments	Nil	5,000	10,000	15,000
Non-residential/educational institutions/hospitals and so on.	5,000	10,000	15,000	8 per sq. ft.
Commercial establishments/ shops	5,000	10,000	20,000	8 per sq. ft.
Software/hardware companies	7,500	15,000	25,000	5 per sq. ft.
Hostels/restaurants	7,500	15,000	30,000	15 per sq. ft.

Source: Karnataka Urban Infrastructure Development and Finance Corporation (KUIDFC).

development-related instruments such as developer exactions, impact fees, development charges, planning obligations, land readjustment, town planning scheme and dedicated funds; (g) land value capture tools, including special assessment districts, business improvement districts, betterment levies, joint development mechanisms and tax increment financing and (h) emerging financial market instruments such as structured bonds, infrastructure investment funds, risk pooling mechanisms, etc. The importance of development financing tools lies in that they rely on the 'growth pays' principle and are bankable. They rely on the strength of city development strategy, spatial planning, project designing and implementation of mechanisms to make developments pay for themselves. The power of development financing instruments to promote planned urban development needs to be harnessed by India during its urban transformation through proactive policies.

The effective structuring of city development projects and designing of development financing tools call for recognising the role of geography in development. As is often stated, city development is all about 'location, location and location'. Projects in locations with the potential to promote surplus-generating, self-financed or market-worthy investments are primary candidates for the application of development financing tools. Cities grow through vertical expansion, in-fill development, renewal of dilapidated areas and expansion to include new areas, offering multiple alternatives to sequence development. FAR, zoning regulation and investment in 'leading' infrastructure affect the nature, mix and timing of development. They capitalise into land values depending on the 'accessibility' and 'serviceability' of locations. Thus, when development projects are structured to combine the strength of geographic and economic factors, a self-financing process of urban development could be promoted. The synergy between spatial planning, including transportation-land use integration, economic development planning, project designing and structuring of financing instruments need to be harnessed. Master planning in the past neglected this interconnectedness. It tried to confine inherently dynamic economic activities to rigidly defined spatial frames.

Development financing tools address city financing issues at project and area levels. They link to the versatility of development projects and the strength of agglomeration economies in locations. Their efficacy can be enhanced by suitable changes in zoning and development regulations, such as those promoting transport-land use integration and transit-oriented development (TOD). A strategy of spatial development on the principle of 'highest and best use' of land in urban expansion and renewal areas, with adequate attention paid to planning and equity issues can be a driver to unlock inclusive growth in cities. A vibrant city may be regarded as a bundle of enterprises that propel growth, create benefits to various stakeholders and mobilise resources. When the proceeds from development financing, land taxation and benefit capture tools are invested to promote such enterprises, they lead to further benefits, making urban development self-sustaining. A worthwhile city development project that passes the cost-benefit test must be able to generate sufficient resources to finance it.

The issues of equity and protection of the urban environment are aspects which no development financing strategy can ignore. Along with resource mobilisation, considerations of inclusion and carrying capacity-based planning must be integrated into this strategy. In this regard, the town planning scheme in Gujarat, the Magarpatta model in Pune and models of impact fees, development contributions, planning obligations and inclusionary zoning implemented by developed countries need to be seriously considered for replication in India. As the model of master planning adopted by the country in the past weeded the poor out of formal land markets in cities, the location of high density tenements for low income groups around proposed transit nodes, when public transit projects are planned, must be explored. The restructuring of cities with TOD offers opportunities to gain from 'new economic geography', while crafting inclusion into the present model of exclusionary urbanisation in India.

Notes

1. In this chapter, we use the term development financing and land development financing interchangeably.
2. 'Development' in the urban context, with all its grammatical variations, is defined as 'the carrying out of building, engineering, mining or other operations in, on, over or under land or the making of any material change in any building or land and includes redevelopment': The Delhi Development Act, 1957 Section 2 (d).
3. Nollan *vs.* California Coastal Commission 1987.
4. Dolan *vs.* City of Tigard, Oregon 1994.
5. Taxable bonds, ₹4,450 million; tax-free bonds, ₹6,495 million; and pooled finance bonds, ₹2,586 million—totalling ₹13,531 million.
6. Examples include: Credit Communal de Belgique, Belgium; Banco de Credito Local, Spain; Norway Kommunal Bank; Sweden Kommunivest Corporation; Holland Bank Nederlandse Gemeenteen; Credit Local de France, etc.
7. Examples include: Banobras in Mexico, Findeter in Columbia and Tamil Nadu Urban Development Fund in India.
8. See http://www.fhwa.dot.gov./policy/olsp/financingfederalaid/ (accessed on 15 January 2016).

9

Value Creation, Capture and Recycling

Cities and Value Creation

Cities create the wealth of nations through value creation, rooted in their agglomeration economies. These externalities owe to market forces and government policies for economic growth, city planning, infrastructure development, urban renewal, service delivery, traffic decongestion, pollution control, environmental conservation, good governance and the like. They benefit many actors in the urban economy in many ways. If a part of the unearned benefits or 'agglomeration rents' are captured to meet the debt-service needs of regional and urban infrastructure, a self-financed process of planned urban development could be set in motion. Market borrowings through municipal bonds or other instruments can finance leading investments, facilitating agglomeration economies, augmenting land and other tax bases, and repaying debt. VCF offers a significant opportunity to mobilise public finance to develop cities in India during its structural transformation.

Value capture instruments differ from land taxation and development financing tools in that they focus on unlocking unused and under-used assets, primarily land. Land taxation instruments such as land value tax and property tax are generic. Development financing mechanisms such as developer exactions, impact fees and development contributions are specific tools that approach urban development from the cost side. They are one-time, upfront charges to meet the costs of infrastructure. Exactions require developers to install at their own expense internal infrastructure facilities needed by growth or to pay for publicly provided facilities. Impact fees aim at meeting the external costs of new development that generates demand for a system-wide expansion in infrastructure capacity. Developer contributions intend to extract land, infrastructure or money from developers as conditions of development consent or re-zoning permission. Value capture tools, on the contrary, target at appropriating and recycling the values generated by public sector actions and private sector investments. Risks and costs as well as rewards of development are shared between public and private sectors to create a win-win situation for both.

This chapter presents the key instruments of value capture financing adopted internationally. They complement land taxation and development financing, and constitute part of a 'toolbox' of instruments needed to finance planned urban development in India.

The Accessibility Premium

Fred Harrison (2006) argues that many large scale infrastructure projects can be made self-financing and hence completed without a large direct involvement of the public sector. Infrastructure adds enormous value to land at prime locations by enhancing 'accessibility' and leads to 'location rents'. Accessibility reduces inconvenience and time to reach valued destinations such as workplaces, schools, shops, recreation centres, railway stations and airports. It also facilitates human interactions, information flows and knowledge transfers, leading to agglomeration economies. Accessibility translates into price premium for properties at vantage locations. Value capture is a fair and efficient method to capture this premium and finance-worthwhile infrastructure projects by requiring the beneficiaries to contribute toward cost. It also promotes density and prevents sprawl. If an infrastructure project passes the cost-benefit test, the rise in land values in the project-served areas is expected to exceed its cost. Therefore, the project cost can be covered by reclaiming a part of the uplift in land values, leaving the rest to landowners as net windfall gains.

Table 9.1 provides some estimates on the impacts of accessibility to public transit on property prices in select Asian countries.

Closely connected with the concept of accessibility is the notion of serviceability. Access to public services also leads to increases in the land values. To cite an example, in metropolitan Recife, Brazil, investment in wastewater removal led to an increase in land value 3.03 times the investment cost, paving roads to increase 2.58 times the cost and providing piped water supply to increase 1.02 times the cost (Smolka 2007).

Table 9.1

Value from Accessibility: Evidence from Asian Countries

Research Study	City	Type of Public Transit	Impact on Housing Price
Wang (2010), Wang and Wang (2008)	Sanghai	Metro Line 8	A property within 0.5 km from metro has a three per cent price premium as against a property at more than four km. A property between 0.5–1 km has a 1.3 per cent premium.
Sue and Wong (2010)	Singapore	Metro, Bus	Bus interchanges within 0.3 km increase price by 4–9 per cent.
Cervero and Murakami (2009)	Hong Kong	Metro	A property within walking distance of metro stations has 4.7–15.7 per cent price premium.
Jim and Chen (2009)	Hong Kong	Metro	A property within 0.5 km of a metro station has 4.5 per cent price premium.
Choy et al. (2007)	Hong Kong	Metro	A property within 10 minute-walk to a metro station has HK $100,000 price premium.
Zheng and Kahn (2008)	Beijing	Metro, Bus	A 10 per cent increase in distance from urban subways reduces home prices by 0.8–1.6 per cent and from bus stations by 0.3–0.8 per cent.
Pan and Zheng (2008)	Shanghai	Metro	Increase of one km from metro results in a 10 per cent decrease in price.
Chalermpong (2007)	Bangkok	Metro	A 10 per cent increase in distance from metro results in a 0.9 per cent decrease in price.
Wang (2005)	Taipei	Metro	Increase of one km from metro results in 2–3 per cent decrease in price.
Kim and Zhang (2005)	Seoul	Metro	Price rises by $7.54–5.88 per meter closer to public transit station in urban area.
Bae et al. (2003)	Seoul	Metro Line 5	Increase of one km to metro results in a three per cent decrease in price.

Source: Salon and Shewmake (2011).

In addition to accessibility and serviceability due to infrastructure, spatial planning, including zoning, also lead to increased land values and an enormous scope for value capture. The huge opportunity for resource mobilisation through land value capture (LVC) from the combined forces of urban planning and infrastructure development can be seen from the example of Rio de Janeiro, Brazil. Barra da Tijuca, an extended area of Rio's high income zone spanning over 82 sq. km was planned for development in 1967. Master planning and construction of expensive public transit, including elevated expressway and direct access to city through tunnels, led to a nearly 1,900 per cent increase in land prices in the area between 1972 and 1975. During the same period, land prices in most other high-value areas increased by 435 per cent. However, the absence of plans to capture land value increments led to the control of 30 per cent of land in Barra da Tijuca by only three landowners, resulting in a significant loss to the city (Smolka 2013, 5).

Land Value Capture Tools

LVC tools aim at capturing and recycling the public-funded and community-created windfalls accruing to landowners. Unlike impact fees, the rationale for LVC has nothing to do with the charges for beneficial infrastructure. It primarily relates to the paradigm that unearned increments in land values owe to community action and not to landowner's effort. Such gains are appropriate for capture to recover the cost of public infrastructure or undertake new capital works. Spatial planning and infrastructure investments in cities capitalise into land and housing prices due to improved accessibility, better serviceability and greater scope and intensity of development associated with re-zoning. These benefits may be captured indirectly through their conversion into public revenues in the form of taxes and charges, or directly through on-site and off-site infrastructure improvements benefitting the community.

LVC presents a toolbox of funding methods that enable public authorities to trade anticipated future revenues for a present infrastructure programme. It includes fiscal and non-fiscal instruments: 'recurrent' and 'one-time'. Recurrent methods include leasing of space benefiting from infrastructure, special assessment, betterment tax and tax increment financing, encompassing LVT, LVIT, property tax, business taxes, local benefit taxes such as water or sewerage benefit tax, and so on. One-time instruments include developer exactions, impact fees, betterment charges, sale of land and development rights, joint development mechanism and land pooling or readjustment. They require a single lump sum payment in cash or kind by landowners, property developers and commercial interests in the vicinity of infrastructure projects.

Generally, LVC aims at capturing unearned gains from an infrastructure facility over its life cycle so that a single generation is not over-burdened with total cost. At the macro level, local government bonds finance infrastructure, leading to unearned increments in land values for nearby landowners. Yearly valuation of land and property quantifies these gains. Land-based taxes and other instruments recoup a part of the increase in land and property values. Over a period of time, say 20–25 years, higher local government revenues repay bonds. At the micro level, fixed costs are covered by LVC; marginal costs are met by marginal revenues, say water charges in water supply projects or entry fees for parks.

The case for land-based and property taxes, especially LVT and LVIT as value capture instruments is well-argued. These taxes are, however, politically challenging, being highly visible and laden with vested interests. People may be 'asset-rich but cash-poor'. Further, these taxes impact on land or property owners in generic terms. Thus, alternative value capture mechanisms are advocated to target at those directly benefitting from government action. These include: sale of developer land, lease/ sale of project-related land, lease/sale of development rights, monetisation of land assets, joint development mechanisms, special assessments, betterment levies, tax increment financing, etc.

Sale of Developer Land

Developed countries have witnessed considerable investments in urban housing and infrastructure by requiring real estate developers to provide internal and external infrastructure while recovering costs through sale of land or housing. These investments followed the development plans prepared and the planning permissions accorded by local authorities. Developing countries are also adopting this method as part of conditions to develop layouts or undertake construction. Developers are required to provide basic facilities as per planning norms and/or pay internal and external development charges to urban development authorities or municipalities. External development charges extend to water source development and transmission lines, sewerage networks and treatment plants, freeways, regional parks and even maintenance of various facilities for a number of years.

New township development projects attempt to internalise land development and infrastructure connectivity. The cost of trunk infrastructure facilities like rails, roads, storm water drains, water and sewer mains, and so on is a major issue for these townships. However, countries like Denmark and South Korea have successfully developed new towns linked to mother cities with high speed rail transit, mobilising resources through sale of land and housing.

The new town of Orestad in Denmark is connected to Copenhagen City Centre by a 22-kilometre automated metro, opened up in 2003. New town infrastructure and metro line are financed by land sales primarily. A similar approach is being implemented in Egypt on a much larger scale for township development outside Cairo. The New Urban Communities Authority (NUCA) auctioned off substantial parcels of desert land equipped with basic infrastructure facilities, more than recovering the cost of investment. Part of the proceeds is being used to build a major highway connecting the new city to the Cairo Ring Road (Peterson 2009). South Korea has successfully decongested Seoul by creating five new towns—Bundang, Ilsan, Pyungchon, Joondong and Sanbon, using land and housing sale as instruments. These towns are strategically positioned within 20–25 km radius from the central business district of Seoul and connected to the city by expressways and rail transit. Started in the mid-1990s, the towns were developed within five years, accommodating 2.7 million new residents (Lee and Ahn 2005).

Lease/Sale of Project-related Land

A key instrument of LVC is the lease or sale of land in the vicinity of public infrastructure facilities like highways and mass transit after development—often with re-zoning and enhanced development rights. This is possible where the government owns land or can buy land at pre-development prices and zoning laws are not rigid. Often the public authority acquires land in and adjacent to an infrastructure facility before development. After installation of infrastructure, it sells land or enters into long-term lease with developers for the use of sub-surface, ground or air rights, recouping outlays. In case the lease period is very long, substantial payment is received upfront.

A premier example of land lease as a method of capturing value created by public investment is the Hong Kong metro. Urban land there is state-owned and is leased to property developers for long periods, generally 50–99 years, depending on use. Station areas are developed with high density on TOD principle. Lease revenues include: initial upfront amount secured through public auction, payment for modification or renewal of lease and land rents.

When Baron Haussmann rebuilt Paris during the Second French Empire, he used government authority to acquire land for grand avenues along with extra parcels on both sides of the path of reconstruction. The excess land was used as collateral for debt secured to finance new roadways, water and sewer lines, and natural gas grids. Land-value gains on the extra property acquired were used to repay debt. In Australia, for major urban highway projects, public land within a distance from transportation alignment is transferred to a public–private development corporation. This corporation borrows against the land as collateral and finances highway construction. The loan is repaid through sale of adjoining land after its value has gone up due to enhanced accessibility. Where land is owned privately, the public authority acquires more land than required for the highway and this excess land is sold after its price has increased due to the development of infrastructure. This method is known as 'excess condemnation'.

For lease/sale of project-related land to succeed, the local or infrastructure authority must either own the appropriate parcels of land or have the authority to acquire and assemble land adjoining the facility being developed at pre-development prices. It must also be in a position to use zoning and other instruments to enhance land value.

Lease/Sale of Development Rights

The theory of urban planning suggests that urban growth needs to be regulated in public interest. In particular, higher value land uses should not occur in a laissez faire way, but in a rationed manner so as to maximise the overall efficiency of urban development. In a way, this rationing of 'development rights' by authorities is akin to the rationing of water extraction, fishing and forestry right, where unrestricted operation by private players results in a net social dis-benefit due to market failure. Higher value land uses—urban versus rural, industrial, commercial, retail and hospitality use versus residential, high density versus low density use, and so on—also lead to windfall gains to a fortunate group of landowners from the urban planning process. Further, constraints on land uses lead to monopoly rents. Keeping these considerations in view, cities resort to sale or lease of development rights in areas served by public infrastructure to secure contribution toward its development or debt servicing.

From the seventies, Curitiba city in Brazil has implemented a linear growth strategy along a series of structural axes. Each axis comprises a 'trinary' road system with three parallel roadways, located a block apart. The central lane of the central road is exclusively dedicated to high capacity express busway. Two lateral roads cater to through traffic while providing access to adjacent development. In the land parcels situated within one block from a structural axis, the FAR[1] was increased to six, permitting buildings to reach a volume of construction six times the plot area. The FAR permitted along other routes served by public transport was fixed at four. The city master plan provided for decreasing FAR as distance from public transport network increased. Owners of properties which could not be developed because of zoning restrictions were allowed to sell a standard FAR as TDRs to developers who could use the same for high density construction along the structural axes.

Brazil is implementing a scheme of building rights known as *Outorga Onerosa do Direito de Construir* (OODC). This is based on a basic FAR cap on the landowner's building rights beyond which a fee is levied. Between 2002 and 2004, Sao Paulo has reduced FAR in most parts of the city to one as a right to landowner. It permits additional FAR up to five through a system of incentive zoning and TDR, taking into account access to public transport (Lainton 2011). In 2012, Sao Paulo generated US$175 million through OODC payments. These are deposited in a special urban development fund (FUNDURB) earmarked for capital projects, including transportation, parks and green areas, historic preservation, drainage and slum regularisation (Smolka 2013).

Sao Paulo has also adopted a scheme of *Certificados de Potencial Adicional de Construcao* or Certificate of Potential Additional Construction (CEPAC) from 1995, involving the auctioning of building rights. The idea is that new development potential due to re-zoning, permission for additional construction and public investment in infrastructure in designated areas should not be free, but auctioned amongst those intending to take advantage of the future economic benefits. The city issues CEPAC bonds corresponding to additional building rights for purchase by competing developers in public electronic auctions regulated by *Comisao de Valores Mobiliarios,* the Brazilian Securities and Exchange

Commission. Between 2004 and 2010, Sao Paulo auctioned 638,074 CEPACs valued at around US$ 722.9 million (Smolka 2013).

Under land administration law in China, the government owns all urban land and the farmers collectively own all rural land. *Zhengdi* or compulsory acquisition of land plays a key role in supplying land for urbanisation. The acquired land is leased to private individuals, firms and organisations on leasehold tenure. Based on agreements, these parties take part in auction and tender to acquire land use rights which are separated from land-ownership (Chen 2008). Land use characteristics such as FAR are regulated on a parcel-by-parcel basis, through direct negotiations between developer and local government (Gu and Zheng 2008). A national registration system operates in China under which the government issues certificates for land use rights. Leasing of public land and sale of land use rights have emerged as major revenue sources to finance urban development in China from the early 1990s. Hangzhou, which is among the top five Chinese cities in per capita income, generated more than 20 per cent of its total revenues from land use conveyance fees, representing up-front payment of lump sum land rent for leased land (Ding 2005).

Monetisation of Land Assets

Many government authorities in developing countries, including India, own vast extents of unused or underused land in cities. Paradoxically, these cities suffer from serious shortages in infrastructure. It makes good sense to sell or lease some publicly-owned land with re-zoning to generate funds for critical infrastructure facilities needed to augment economic growth. Effective monetisation of land can lead to 'unlocking' of land values and productive use of unproductive assets. The sale of publicly owned land has the additional advantage of channelling private investments to areas where is it productive. Land asset management calls for an inventory of public land holdings and periodic comparison of trends in value of land in public use and in the open market. It also warrants efforts to put public land to 'highest and best' uses, duly exploiting the benefits of spatial planning, including zoning.

Peterson (2009) provides evidence on the potential of converting land assets to infrastructure assets in cities. Revenues mobilised from these source are large relative both to capital investment needed and other potential sources of financing (see Table 9.2; Peterson 2009).

Table 9.2

Land Monetisation: Select Projects in Developing Countries

Location and Activity	Land Financing Amount and Use of Proceeds	Comparative Magnitude
Cairo, Republic of Egypt: auction of desert land for new towns—2100 hectares (May 2007)	US $3.12 billion used to reimburse costs of internal infrastructure and to build connecting highway to Cairo Ring Road	117 times total urban property tax collection in the country—equal to about 10 per cent of total national government revenue.
Cairo, Republic of Egypt: private installation of 'public' infrastructure in return for free transfer of developable desert land (2005–present)	US$1.45 billion of private investment in internal and external infrastructure plus seven per cent of serviced land provided to government for moderate-income housing	A range of urban infrastructure services for more than 3,300 hectare of newly developed land, without financial cost to government.
Mumbai, India: auction of 13 hectares by Mumbai Metropolitan Regional Development Authority (MMRDA) in Bandra Kurla Complex (January 2006, November 2007)	US$1.2 billion to be used primarily to finance projects as per metropolitan regional transportation plan	10 times MMRDA's total capital spending in fiscal 2005; 3.5 times total value of municipal bonds issued by all urban local bodies and local utilities in India in past decade.
Istanbul, Turkey: sale of old municipal bus station and former administrative site (March–April 2007)	US$1.5 billion in auction proceeds to be dedicated to capital investment budgets	In fiscal 2005, total municipal capital spending was US$994 million and municipal borrowing for infrastructure investment, US$97 million.
Cape Town, South Africa: sale of Victoria and Albert Waterfront property by Transnet, the parastatal transportation agency (November 2006)	US$1.0 billion, to be used to recapitalise Transnet and support its investment in core transportation infrastructure	Sale proceeds exceeded Transnet's total capital spending in fiscal 2006—equal to 17 per cent of five-year capital investment plan prepared in 2006.

Source: Peterson (2009).

Joint Development Mechanism

Joint development mechanism (JDM) is a partnership between a public authority and a private developer to build a real estate project on land owned or controlled by the public sector. It is a public–private collaboration for financing, construction, operation and maintenance of facilities. Partnerships under JDM fall into three categories: (a) donation of public land and grant of development right to private developers in return for private investment in public infrastructure, (b) sale of publicly-owned land and development rights to private developers with the proceeds used to finance public infrastructure investment and (c) sharing of land value gains created by public infrastructure through taxes that capture a part of the land-value gains accruing to private landowners, or by voluntary gain-sharing agreements negotiated prior to public investment.

JDM acts as a value capture instrument in that the government attempts to reclaim some of the real estate-related values resulting from public investments. For example, in the case of a public rail transit project, JDM may target railway property above, below or adjacent to rail stations for high density commercial and/or residential development. The developer benefits from superior accessibility and a minimum volume of potential customers frequenting the site. The transit authority gains from captive ridership.

Relying on a contractual framework, JDM avoids undue discretion by public officials. It also does not involve the cumbersome process of assessing the direct and indirect impacts of infrastructure investment, including revenue generation as in impact fee, betterment levy, special assessment or tax increment financing. Further, by avoiding taxation issues JDM does not raise the concerns of efficiency and equity. A PPP project, if designed well, can lead to a win-win situation for both public and private sector partners. The public sector benefits from sharing of project cost and access to broader technical expertise. The private sector gains from reduced risks and an assured potential customer base. The success of JDM, however, depends on the correct forecasting of demand for infrastructure services, stability of real estate market, efficacy of spatial planning and robustness of policy framework for private sector participation in urban development and renewal.

Tokyo has long used JDM along with privatisation of transport services as a value capture strategy. The city has a long history of privately built, owned and operated railways. There are 12 different railway corporations in Tokyo out of which only one is publicly owned (Cervero and Murakami 2008). These corporations which declare rail as their 'core' activity earn more of their profits from associated real estate business and other ventures such as departmental stores and construction enterprises (Tang et al. 2004). The government provides direct subsidies and low interest loans to meet upfront capital costs. It promotes public transport ridership through measures such as road pricing, direct control on car ownership, vehicle and fuel taxes, and tax breaks for public transport users.

Special Assessment District

Special assessment districts are widely used in the United States as value capture mechanisms. Local authorities set boundaries within which differential taxes are assessed on properties expected to increase in value because of proximity to new infrastructure. The origin of special assessment districts can be traced back to the 1691 levy by New York City for the construction of streets and drains. Los Angeles, Oakland, Portland and Kansas City raised 20 per cent of their budget from special assessments in 1913. By 1972, US cities with more than 1,00,000 population and having special assessment districts met a total of 12 per cent of their budgets through this mechanism (Hagman and Misczynski 1978).

Business improvement districts, originally started in Ontario, are widely used in Canada, the United States and Europe since the 1960s. They aim at financing capital improvements in designated areas through agreement with owners and/or tenants of a majority of businesses to pay an additional levy. Once an improvement district is established, it resorts to long-term debt for infrastructure based on a dedicated debt-servicing arrangement linked to the levy. In the case of New York Avenue metro station in Washington DC, approximately one-fourth of the financing of construction in 2004 was voluntarily contributed by local business through a self-imposed special assessment on all commercial properties within 2000 feet of the station's entrances (United States Environment Protection Agency 2013).

Betterment Taxes and Charges

Betterment taxes and charges constitute a key instrument to capture increases in land value due to public policies and investments. The 1909 Housing and Town Planning Act in the United Kingdom recognised that the betterment principle applied to spatial planning apart from infrastructure development.

Most countries in the world have experimented with betterment levy at some point of time, typically aiming to capture 30 to 80 per cent of the imputed gain in land value. Instruments adopted include: (a) tax or charge on land value increment in the benefit area; (b) uniform land tax paid annually without differentiation or discrimination; (c) tax on transaction of land or buildings in designated area, (d) recoupment from purchase of land adjoining projects and re-sale after development of infrastructure; (e) rent from long-term lease of publicly owned or acquired land; (f) sale of land use and development rights along infrastructure alignments, with re-zoning; and (g) set-off or reduction in compensation payable for land acquired for public purpose.

In Australia, the New South Wales Local Government (Town and Country Planning) Amendment Act 1945 permitted taxing up to 80 per cent of the increase in land values arising from town planning schemes. From 1970 to 1973, under the Land Development Contribution Act 1970 and Land Development Contribution Management Act 1970, a betterment levy was imposed on specified rural lands within the Sydney metropolitan region. This was a 30 per cent tax on the gain from re-zoning of rural land, that is, difference between the capital value of unimproved land on the date of rezoning and that on 1 August 1969. The tax proceeds were earmarked for city improvement. The levy was payable by a landowner when land was sold or planning permission to undertake development was accorded (Fensham and Gleeson 2003). Johannesburg levies 'development contribution' to recover one-third of the increase in land values due to grant of higher zoning rights. This goes to a dedicated 'town planning fund' to finance capital projects, including road widening, water supply and sewerage, and purchase of land for parking.

Bogota, Colombia has successfully used betterment levy to capture unearned increments in land values due to public investments in infrastructure and planning and regulatory tools like zoning (see Box 9.1).

Practical difficulties in implementing betterment levy relate to: (a) demarcation of benefit areas, (b) disaggregation of sources of increase in land values such as master planning, development permission, owner's initiatives, economic growth and other factors, and (c) determination of the base of levy, given that land prices increase much before public investment occurs. A levy rate up to 80 per cent attempted by some countries is also regarded as too high by landowners as well as courts. Further, a view is expressed that there is no need for betterment levy on account of public works and spatial planning as they increase rateable values and property tax. However, as experience shows, land value gains due to infrastructure development and zoning tend to be huge—not amenable

Box 9.1

Betterment Levy: Bogota, Colombia

Bogota has used *Contribucion de Valorizacion* to finance public infrastructure projects since 1921. National legislation permitted the imposition of betterment levy in 1887. *Instituto de Desarrollo Urbano* (IDU), the agency responsible for execution of public works in Bogota, calculates the levy by multiplying certain benefit factors relating to size of property, its use, proximity to investment and so on. IDU defines the investment to be made, estimates construction cost, identifies properties that would benefit from investment, determines methodology to impose betterment levy on individual properties, collects parcel information, imposes and collects levy, and enforces penalty for non-compliance. Over 50 per cent of Bogota's main road grid was paid for by betterment levy. Reliance on this instrument, however, declined in the 1980s and 1990s due to several hurdles, including difficulties in attributing land value gains to public works and court litigation. However, during the last several years, Bogota has simplified its betterment levy and adopted a city-wide valorisation fee, differentiated by benefit areas.

The new LVC mechanism in Bogota, introduced in 1997, is *Participacion en Plusvalias*. It aims at capturing increases in land values resulting directly from public investments in infrastructure as well as indirectly through planning and regulatory tools like zoning. Municipalities are authorised to capture 30–50 per cent of the land value increments. The responsibility of valuation was entrusted to a neutral, independent body—*Agustin Codazzi Geographic Institute* (Jaramillo 2001). The proceeds from levy are required to be spent on development works: social housing, infrastructure, open space, mass transit, urban renewal and historic preservation. The new approach has enabled Bogota to revive valorisation as an effective instrument to finance urban infrastructure, mobilising US$1.0 billion during 1997–2007. The levy raised US$900 million from 1.5 million urban lots in 2007. It is being replicated throughout Colombia, yielding about 25 per cent of local own revenues. Other Latin American countries are also resorting to similar levies (Peterson 2009).

Sources: Jaramillo (2001) and Peterson (2009).

for capture through a generic tax scheme. Specific benefits call for specific instruments to exploit them. Moreover, general taxes fail to capture the broader market trends associated with agglomeration externalities, leading to increased land values. International experience suggests that a levy rate of 25–30 per cent of betterment could be reasonable.

Tax Increment Financing

TIF is a tool that relies on using future increases in tax revenues to finance current infrastructure programmes. It aims at promoting development through public authorities earmarking whole or part of the revenue increments arising from it to service the debt needed. TIF has the potential to support a sizable part of the public and private costs associated with development or rejuvenation of designated areas by capturing future increases in revenues. Originally started by California in 1951 as an innovative way to raise local matching funds for federal grants, TIF is extensively used in the United States (see Box 9.2). As many as 49 out of 50 states in USA have some form of TIF enabling legislation. In Australia, the instrument is known as value increment financing. TIF is flexible; the incremental revenues can be used to secure a loan, encourage an up-front investment venture or undertake development on a pay-as-you-go financing principle.

Tax increment financing is based on the rule that growth pays. While the concepts and modalities of TIF differ between cities, it essentially allows a local government to ring-fence 'tax increment' within a designated development area to finance an urban infrastructure or renewal project that contributes to this increment. A TIF essentially represents the reallocation of a part of the growth in revenues from the local authority to the TIF authority, usually a special purpose vehicle of local government or of local and state governments together. Sometimes, tax increments under a TIF scheme are supplemented by special assessment, impact fee or betterment levy.

Box 9.2

Tax Increment Financing (TIF) in Chicago

Chicago has used TIF to a greater extent than any other large city in the United States. In the past three decades, TIF has been the primary source of funding in the city to promote local economic development. The use of TIF funds has been for rejuvenating blight areas, preventing areas from deteriorating into blighted conditions and fostering industrial development. Since inception in the 1980s, the number of TIF districts in Chicago has gone up to 162 in 2010. Nearly \$4.6 billion has been collected from all TIF districts throughout the city. The annual collection from TIF revenues from 2005 to 2010 has been more than \$500 million.

TIF has been instrumental in promoting public and private investments across Chicago. Funds are used to build and repair roads, clean polluted land and put underused or unused properties into productive uses, usually in conjunction with private sector developers. Funds are mobilised through growth in the Equalised Assessed Valuation (EAV) within a designated TIF district over a period of 23 years. The increase in revenue over and above the base is used to pay back bonds or spent on a pay-as-you-go principle.

Source: Bruno and Quesada (2011).

Under the TIF mechanism, a public authority or a private sector business proposes the establishment of a TIF district. At this stage, a general estimation of the land and property values in the designated area and the current tax revenues therein is undertaken. The entity assesses the suitability of the area for TIF. It conducts a detailed study to demonstrate that the proposal conforms to TIF legislation. The concerned local or state government sets up a TIF authority to undertake development or renewal. This authority delineates the TIF district and prepares a development plan with cost estimates in consultation with local and state governments, private developers, community and other stakeholders. The plan follows the local and state planning laws and norms. The TIF authority then raises debt by issuing bonds or adopting other instruments to meet upfront costs. TIF bonds often take the shape of 'infrastructure revenue bonds'. Rating of these bonds to meet the capital market standards ensures that TIF projects are subjected to rigorous scrutiny. Over a period of time, TIF results in property development, higher land and property values, and rise in tax bases in the district. The tax increments generated over and above the pre-TIF tax revenues are ring-fenced to service the debt. The total tax revenues for the TIF district revert to the original taxing authority at the end of the TIF term, which may be five to 25 years, depending on the type and scale of development.

The advantages of TIF are: (a) development pays for itself; (b) value-creating and resource-generating investments fructify; (c) lacunae in collecting upfront contributions from developers through development charges or impact fees, which discourage development, is avoided; (d) a market test for infrastructure funding through debt contributes to rigorous project selection; (e) long-term spatial planning and funding are facilitated; (f) authorities avoid time- and cost-overruns in project implementation as debt-payment is linked to revenue generation; (g) an equitable approach is promoted by spreading cost over generations and making beneficiaries pay; and (h) current fiscal problems of local bodies do not act as a stumbling block to the financing of new projects.

TIF should not be considered as the sole source of financing urban infrastructure. Also, it may not suit all situations in all cities. However, the TIF principle is robust in that it endogenises resource generation into the model of urban development and renewal. It combines land management, spatial planning, infrastructure development and value creation, capture and recycling to catalyse a self-financed process of urban development.

Spatial planning and infrastructure development, including transportation–land use integration and transit-oriented development lead to windfall benefits to firms and households. Infrastructure creates access, access increases value and increased value can finance investments that create further value. A strong case, therefore, exists for financing infrastructure through TIF which converts low-value real estate to high-value enterprises. The success of TIF, however, depends on a flexible spatial planning framework. If a TIF project requires certain relaxations in the master plan, such relaxations in the form of 'incentive zoning' are justified on the ground of planned urban development at no cost to public authorities.

The broad principle of TIF can be extended to private sector projects as well as PPPs. One PPP option is that the private developer securitises loans on the basis of expected public monies and undertakes development based on an annuity model. A second option is that the public authority develops connectivity infrastructure and the private sector undertakes development on a revenue-sharing formula. A third option is that the public authority proactively facilitates spatial planning or zoning and the private partner takes up development at its cost. A shining example of value-creation in this regard is Magarpatta, developed in 430 acres of land at the outskirts of Pune over a period of just 10 years. 120 farmers pooled their land and formed the Magarpatta Town Development and Construction Company as shareholders. This company acted like a TIF entity and developed a world-class township with borrowed funds. In this case, there was no need for escrowing tax increments accruing to the local body to repay debt. Facilitation by the Pune municipal corporation and the government of Maharashtra permitting the development of an integrated township under the Maharashtra Regional Town Planning Act, 1996 was adequate to create sufficient values. In fact, the municipal corporation is now benefitting through a sizable increase in property tax from Magarpatta. The state and central governments are also reaping tax increments through growth in VAT and income tax respectively.

A key message from TIF is that when ULBs are unable to generate current revenue surplus, they can still rely upon future increments in value, based on a planned urban development strategy aimed at creating, capturing and recycling land values.

Examples of Value Capture

Value increments are associated with all types of planned infrastructure development projects, ranging from irrigation to water supply, sewerage, parks, highways, mass rapid transit and so on. Some oft-cited examples of the potential of value capture to finance infrastructure investments are presented as follows:

Don Pedro Dam, California

Don Pedro dam on Tuolumne River, located in California, United States, was completed in 1923. At one time, the tallest gravity dam in the world with a height of 86 m, the entire project was conceived and funded by the two irrigation districts of Modesto and Turlock. The upfront cost was met by selling bonds which were repaid over time by property taxes imposed only within the districts. Farmer-landowners supported the project as they understood that the increase in profitability of their farms would surpass the hike in their tax bills. Adequacy of land value capture for funding infrastructure was guaranteed because the taxes were assessed on market value of land. The Wright Act dating from 1887, amended in 1909, provided for an enabling legislation to limit assessments in all new districts to land value only. It left old districts to adopt land value taxes by local option. Modesto did it in 1911; Turlock in 1915. In 1917, the California legislature made it mandatory for all districts to exempt improvements from taxes.

By 1927, the districts in California grew to include over four million acres, elevating it to the top farm state in the United States, using desert land and creating the most spectacularly successful story of farm economic development. Legislator Albert Henley, who crafted the modified district, observed:

> The discovery of the legal formula of the organizations was of infinitely greater value to California than the discovery of gold a generation before. They are extraordinary potent engine of the creation of wealth. (Gaffney et al. 1994)

Central Park, New York

Central Park, located in the centre of Manhattan in New York City, is a National Historic Landmark in the United States, declared as such in 1963. It covers 843 acres, or six per cent, of Manhattan's total acreage, including 150 acres in seven water bodies, 250 acres in lawns and 136 acres in woodlands. The park, which does not levy any entry cost, is the most visited public park in the United States. As many as 35 million visitors visit the Central Park every year. The park was initially opened on 770 acres of city-owned land and was later expanded to 843 acres. In 1858, American landscape architect Frederick Law Olmsted and English architect Calvert Vaux won a design competition to improve and expand the park. Construction began the same year and was completed in 1873.

Olmstead had argued that land and property values in the vicinity of the park would rise—more than sufficient to pay for development of the park and its future maintenance. His subsequent analysis revealed that prior to the establishment of the park, the three wards adjacent to the park had contributed 7.5 per cent of the New York City's budget and after its development the same properties contributed 33 per cent even though acquiring the land for Central Park removed 10,000 lots from the city's property tax roll. Olmstead tracked the value of property immediately adjacent to Central Park from 1856 to 1873, in order to justify the expenditure of $13 million incurred on its creation. He found that over the 17-year period there was a $209 million increase in the value of the property impacted by the park. The annual excess of increase in tax was $4 million more than the increase in annual debt payments for the land and improvement. As a result of building Central Park, New York City made a profit. In addition, tax revenues from increased retail and tourism-related activities further enhanced the municipal revenues (Crompton 2001a, 2001b and 2004). The premium for views of the park ranged from $10,000 to $7,00,000 in 1989, depending on the size of apartment and type of view (New York Times 1989).

Centennial Olympic Park, Atlanta

Less than two decades ago, Centennial Olympic Park's neighbourhood in Atlanta, Georgia, in the United States, was a run-down part of the city. The chief executive officer of the Atlanta Committee for the Olympic Games, Billy Payne, floated the idea of transforming a multi-block eyesore into a magnificent congregation spot for visitors and residents during the 1996 Centennial Olympic Games. The estimated $75 million in development costs for the 21 acre park came entirely from private-sector contributions: commemorative bricks for pathways, funds raised by the Atlanta Chamber of Commerce and grants secured from local philanthropic foundations. This community support, coupled with the willingness of the Georgia state to lead the park's development and to assume ownership after the Games, culminated in the famed Centennial Olympic Park. Following the Olympic Games, a large portion of the park was redesigned for daily public use. The landscaped park and its expanded amenities were opened to the public in March 1998. Located near the Georgia World Congress Centre, Georgia Dome and hotel district, the park includes a signature plaza, a 'fountain of rings', 1,200-seat amphitheatre and six acres of lawns. After the Centennial Olympic Park was built, adjacent condominium prices rose by more than 117 per cent a square foot—from $115 to $250 (American Planning Association 2002).

Hyde Park: London

Hyde Park is one of the eight Royal Parks of London. The park, with abundant trees and magnificent landscaping, is home to a large variety of birds and animals. It is responsible for enhancing the aesthetic and economic value of the entire surroundings. Residents, tourists and visitors are attracted to the park and the events organised therein. The largest bird-watching event in the world was once organised in Hyde Park. The authority managing Hyde Park earns huge revenues from media events and film shooting there; it is the most-filmed park in the United Kingdom. Monmoth House, located at the gate of Hyde Park, with just 5,300 square feet of built-up space, was sold for £2,25,000 in 1975. It was placed in the market for sale at an astronomical figure of £6.5 million pounds in 2002, an increase of 2,790 per cent (Economist 2002).

Jubilee Line Extension, London

Jubilee Line Extension (JLE) to London Underground from Green Park to Stratford—linking Central London and East London—was opened in 1999. A well-known study by property developer, Don Riley estimated that the £3.5 billion invested in the JLE by taxpayers resulted in an increase in land value of £13.5 billion across a 1,000 yards radius along the track one year after creation (Riley 2001). He calculated the average increase in site values per unit area within 400 yards of each of five sample stations, between 400 and 800 yards and between 800 and 1,000 yards. The averages were converted to totals and extended to other stations. Riley found that if 27 per cent of the uplift in site values had been captured through the tax system, leaving the other 73 per cent for lucky property owners, the JLE could have paid for itself without burdening the taxpayers. A more sophisticated and rigorous study estimated the increase in land values at £9.75 billion (Mitchell and Vickers 2003). Even if assuming that property price inflation was 100 per cent, still, the landowners had access to £7 billion of additional value through a 'free rider' effect. Riley observed:

> I landed up at Dover after a choppy crossing the Channel in 1962, and for the next 40 years, I paid my taxes to Her Majesty's Treasury.... I did not dodge my obligations to the public purse. After all I was married, raising two children and using the public services; so I was happy to pay my share of the costs of the schools and hospitals that my family needed.
>
> Then as the millennium was dawning, a miracle happened...Taxpayers generously funded the extension of the Jubilee Line, one of London's Underground lines. Two of the stations were located to office properties that I own. These two stations raised the value of my properties by more than all the taxes that I had paid into the public coffers over the previous 40 years.
>
> A nice windfall for this colonial boy. (Harrison 2006)

Hong Kong Mass Transit

The Hong Kong government derives a major portion of its revenues from land, including premium on new land and modification of existing leases, property taxes, stamp duty, rents, etc. In 1993–94 such revenues, net of land production costs, amounted to 35 per cent of total government revenues (Hong Kong Democratic Foundation 1996). This did not include profit tax on property transactions. Between 1996 and 2000, annual revenues from public land leasing were more than enough to cover the costs of all infrastructure works. On average, lease revenues accounted for about 17 per cent of total revenues.

The Hong Kong Mass Transit Railway Corporation (MTRC) earns profit for its shareholders, including the government. The metro caters to 20 per cent of the transit trips in Hong Kong, a city with 90 per cent of all trips by transit mode (Zhang 2007a and 2007b). The MTRC develops rail and properties around transit stations concurrently. It secures land from government at pre-development rates and leases the same after metro rail development at substantially higher prices. It adopts various forms of land value capture, including land sale, long-term leasing of development rights, joint development and leasing of commercial space in and around metro stations. The MTRC has consistently paid dividends, disproving the myth that public transit can never be profitable. Over the period 2000–12, property development produced 38 per cent of MTRC's corporate income, commercial and property management businesses such as advertising and sales 15 per cent, land and air rights lease 13 per cent, and transport operations 34 per cent (Tang and Lo 2010 and World Bank 2015).

TransMilenio, Bogota

Bogota's TransMilenio is one of the world's most successful examples of bus rapid transit (BRT). It is characterised by dedicated main trunk routes for high speed buses, physically separated from the rest of traffic. The bus stations are well-connected with systematic feeder services. The first phase of Bogota's TransMilenio was launched in 2000 along two corridors. The second phase, which started operating in 2003, gradually added three more corridors. As of November 2007, the system had 114 stations, ran more than 1,000 buses and carried 1.4 million one-way trips per day at a speed of 27 km per hour.

Monthly property rental prices were found to decrease by 6.8 to 9.3 per cent for every additional five minutes of walking time from a BRT station, after controlling for structural characteristics, neighbourhood attributes, etc (Rodriguez and Targa 2004). Property price premium for being within 0.5 kilometre of a TransMilenio station was estimated at 5–17 per cent (Perdomo-Calvo et al. 2007). An increase of one kilometre from the transit resulted in a seven–eight per cent decrease in property value (Mendieta and Perdomo-Calvo 2007). Data gathered on property asking prices for 2001–06 revealed that the BRT extensions resulted in asking price premium for properties served by BRT to the extent of 15 to 20 per cent (Rodriguez and Mojica 2008).

Copenhagen Metro-Orestad Township

In 1992, the Danish Parliament passed the Orestad Act for integrated development of a strategically located undeveloped chunk of land in Orestad and a metro rail line of 22 kilometres linking it to

Copenhagen City Centre, international airport (Kastrup) and other parts of the city. Orestad covers an area of 3.1 million square metres with length of five kilometres and width of 600 metres. The Orestad Development Corporation (ODC) was formed with joint ownership of the City of Copenhagen (55 per cent) and the Danish State (45 per cent). It was mandated to undertake planning of Orestad area, sell land and plan, build and operate the new transport system. The new township aims at transit-oriented development with mixed land use: 60 per cent space for office, 20 per cent for housing and 20 per cent for services. Since 1992, the development of Orestad and the metro have proceeded in parallel. The first three phases of the metro have been completed and the fourth stage is scheduled for completion by 2018 (Peterson 2019).

The Copenhagen metro-Orestad township scheme was estimated to cost €1.6 billion. The design and construction of the metro envisaged the creation of land value through planned development. Increased accessibility raised the demand for land adjacent to the metro among developers and investors. 52 per cent of the whole site was sold or under construction by 2006, with the overall sale values amounting to €623 million. Furthermore, value was captured from direct payments (10 per cent), real estate taxes (10 per cent) and operating profits from metro (30 per cent). The captured value paid for the construction of the metro by repaying €2.3 billion of debt incurred during construction.[2]

Singapore: Urban Strategy

Singapore has used long-term urban strategy to create, capture and recycle increments in land values. It channels development toward transportation nodes and corridors and subsidises public transport ridership. The Urban Redevelopment Authority (URA) in Singapore stipulates the type of development that the government prefers in a particular area as well as the guidelines for urban design. It charges private developments with a development charge while granting permission for development exceeding prescribed densities. It also levies charges on developments that require a modification to zoning prescribed in the master plan. Increasing land use density and intensity has facilitated land being used on the principle of 'highest and best use'. Public leasing of urban land raises more revenues in Singapore than any tax, accounting for two-fifths of government budget (See earthrights.net/course/?q=node/99, accessed 15 January 2016).

Value Capture Financing in India

Land values in many of India's large cities are exorbitantly high. These cities have experienced huge increases in land value due to periodic real estate booms. However, land-based instruments are yet to be adopted by cities in India in a major way. While some states have experimented with innovative methods of land-based financing, value capture instruments have not been adopted widely. This has resulted in cities not being able to tap the phenomenal increases in land values they experienced in the past to build critical infrastructure facilities for growth. The lack of urban land policy, non-availability of suitable instruments with ULBs and absence of political commitment to exploit land as a resource are responsible for the present state of affairs.

Some examples of the use of land value capture in India include: land monetisation in Bandra Kurla Complex by Mumbai Metropolitan Regional Development Authority (MMRDA), value capture financing by Bengaluru metro rail and town planning charges in Hyderabad.

Bandra Kurla Complex, Mumbai

With the objective of creating a secondary sub-urban commercial and office node to relieve congestion in central Mumbai, the MMRDA has undertaken since the 1980s the development of a 553-acre site from marshland and industrial slums. It has used long-term lease of land (for 80 years) to private developers with permission for high density development to generate resources. The price per square meter of land sold was ₹30,000 in 1993, ₹42,500 in 1995 (Diamond Bourse), ₹86,000 in 2000 (Citibank), ₹1,53,000 in January 2006 (Convention Centre) and ₹5,04,000 in November 2007 (Commercial Complex and Car Park). In just two land auctions of 2006 and 2007 involving 13 hectares, MMRDA generated about ₹51 billion. The developers in Bandra Kurla Complex are responsible for all on-site and approach infrastructure at their own expense. MMRDA has planned to use the proceeds of the land sale for major regional infrastructure projects, including Mumbai urban transit.

Bengaluru: Mass Rapid Transit Cess

Recently, in connection with the construction of Bengaluru MRTS, the government of Karnataka has introduced a number of innovative measures to create a dedicated resource pool, including special cess to capture land value increments due to transit (see Box 9.3).

Town Planning Charges: Hyderabad

The GHMC levies vacant land tax at 0.5% on prevailing registration value of land. Betterment and external betterment charges are collected at the time of according approval for layouts and construction of buildings. Betterment charges connected to on-site installation of internal amenities like water supply, drainage, roads and so on. range from ₹86 to ₹129 per square metre of site area. External betterment charges connected to off-site or external amenities such as major arterial roads, flyovers, regional parks and so on are levied at ₹86 to ₹176 per square metre of site

Box 9.3

Bengaluru Mass Rapid Transit System: Value Capture Tools

The government of Karnataka has embarked on innovative value capture instruments to finance Bengaluru mass rapid transit system as follows:

Development Cess on new layouts/developments: A cess at five per cent of market value of land or/and building in future property developments and new layouts. This cess will be credited to Metro Infrastructure Fund and shared between Bengaluru Metropolitan Rail Corporation Ltd (BMRCL), Bengaluru Water Supply & Sewerage Board (BWSSB) and Bengaluru Development Authority (BDA), in the ratio of 65 per cent, 20 per cent and 15 per cent respectively, to finance the metro directly by BMRCL and to augment other civic infrastructure to complement the metro system by other agencies.

Cess on Additional Floor Area Ratio: FAR up to 4.0 is to be allowed for all properties lying within an influence area of 500 meters on either side of the alignment of both phase one and phase two. A part of the benefit accruing to property owners due to the higher FAR will be collected through a cess of 10 per cent in respect of residential buildings and 20 per cent in respect of commercial buildings. The cess proceeds from both phase one and phase two influence areas will be shared between BMRCL, Bruhat Bengaluru Mahanagar Palike (BBMP), BWSSB and BDA, in the ratio of 60 per cent, 20 per cent, 10 per cent and 10 per cent respectively, for servicing the senior term debt raised by BMRCL and for financing the augmentation of civic infrastructure by other agencies in view of more dense urban growth due to higher FAR.

TDR in lieu of compensation for land: BMRCL to issue TDR in lieu of compensation for acquisition of land for metro rail. Systemic improvements will be made for making the TDR scheme more market-friendly and beneficial to all stakeholders.

Source: Government of Karnataka Urban Development Secretariat.

area. Apart from development charges for institution or change of land use, city-level infrastructure impact fee on high rise buildings and impact fee on commercial buildings abutting designated roads, GHMC collects special development charges on lands/sites/premises abutting or in the vicinity of Ring Road/other Highways/Mass Rapid Transit indicated in the city master plan at special rates. Value addition charges are also levied as additional levy per square metre of built-up area in the high-tech city area of Cyberabad where an information technology hub has been established. For widening major roads, grant of additional FSI, zoning concessions and TDRs are provided to landowners surrendering land free of cost. Further, open space contribution at 10 per cent of land value is collected from proposed developments in layouts that did not provide open space as statutorily required for parks and conservation areas.

The collection under town planning-related charges and fees in GHMC has increased from ₹173.2 crore in 2007–08 to ₹733.5 crore in 2012–13—representing an average annual growth of 64 per cent. The largest contributors to town planning-related revenues in order in 2012–13 were building permit fee, layout regularisation scheme, impact fee, betterment charges, building penalisation scheme, development charges and open space contribution. Almost 70 per cent of the town planning-related revenues are related to planning permission for new construction.

Designing Value Capture Instruments

Value increment financing instruments are yet to be adopted in India in a systematic way to finance urban and regional infrastructure. Often authorities operating at city level such as municipality, urban planning authority, highway department, transit authority and other infrastructure development agencies do not follow an integrated and mutually-agreed strategy for value creation, capture and recycling. They are also not equipped with appropriate instruments to mobilise value increments. Further, many of them do not regard landowners and developers as effective partners in city development. Due to these factors, cities fail to exploit their agglomeration potential to raise resources for planned urban development.[3]

When vibrant external economies of agglomeration are present in cities, the benefits from planned urban development are likely to exceed costs. City externalities lead to substantial 'agglomeration rents' to land for capture and recycling. Thus, if beneficiaries of agglomeration

externalities, facilitated by spatial planning and infrastructure development are made effective partners in the value creation processes in a city,
a self-sustained method of planned urban development and renewal can
be set in motion. The design of land value capture instruments, however,
is critical for its success. In this regard, international experience points to
certain guidelines (see Box 9.4).

There are three conditions for LVC to succeed as a mechanism to
finance public investments. First, actions by public authorities, say, spatial
planning and infrastructure development, generate sufficient land and

Box 9.4

Guidelines for Designing Land Value Capture Instruments

1. The context of the city is important. How land and property rights are defined,
   how such rights are publicly recorded, recognised and defended, the ease of
   operation of land and property markets and the capacity of local authorities are
   key considerations in the design of LVC.
2. Effective implementation of LVC requires a robust legislative framework for
   land and property taxation, decentralised authority, political championship
   and administrative expertise. Political will to implement LVC is necessary in
   view of pervasive vested interests.
3. The yield from LVC can be greatly enhanced if accompanied by effective regional
   and urban planning, including zoning, transportation-land use integration and
   investments in 'leading' infrastructure facilities.
4. LVC instruments must aim at harnessing windfall gains from both spatial planning and infrastructure development, taking into account the cycle through
   which land value increases and identifying the gainers at different stages.
5. Efficient, timely, accurate and easy-to-implement land valuation system is a
   must. The use of GIS and CAMA techniques to quantify land value increases
   is desirable. There is also a need for building institutional and human resource
   capacity to implement LVC.
6. LVC instruments must be rooted in the model of planned development and
   renewal of cities and their peripheral areas, leading to land value creation,
   capture and recycling. They must be combined with land and property taxation
   and land development financing instruments.
7. The capacity to implement LVC instruments at the local level in developing
   countries is limited. Concerted efforts are necessary to build capacity to design
   and administer value creation, capture and recycling mechanisms.
8. There is a need to increase knowledge about theory and practice of land value
   capture; greater public understanding and participation of landowners and
   developers in city planning and development need to be promoted.

Source: Walters (2011) and Mohanty (2014).

property values to be captured. Second, there are appropriate institutions and instruments, including valuation systems to track increases in land and property values. The local authorities must also be in a position to adopt appropriate tax and non-tax instruments such as land value tax, betterment levy and land pooling at vantage locations. In the case of public–private partnership projects, the local government must be in a position to act as an effective business partner with the private sector. Third, the landowners and developers are assured that the contributions they make are used to create further values for them and the community.

In the Indian context, the authorities taking up planned development projects may not be able to capture the land value increments generated by such projects due to the lack of suitable fiscal instruments with them. For example, land use conversion charges and non-agricultural assessments accrue to state governments under law. Charges for institution and change of land use, development impact fees and external development charges are often levied by parastatals such as urban development authorities, who may not share the same with municipalities. Similarly, water supply and sewerage boards are not authorised to collect water and sewerage betterment levies and municipalities may not share such levies with the boards. These anomalous situations need to be addressed by institutional reforms. One way is to structure partnerships between authorities through the formation of SPVs for projects while ring-fencing taxes, charges and project revenues on the benefit principle. The efficacy of a value capture strategy requires that the authority creating benefits must be in a position to capture and recycle some of them to create further benefits to the community.

The successful use of land value capture calls for making landowners integral partners in the city development process. However, researchers in the past have been somewhat biased against landowners, arguing that they appropriate unearned increments in land values without risking or economising. But, transactions in urban land and property in the face of volatile market fluctuations, dubious land records, court litigations and compulsion to protect property from encroachment do involve considerable risk-taking by landowners and developers. Thus, an inordinately high rate of tax on land value increment or property needs to be avoided as it would dampen development and strike at the very root of value creation. Further, efforts should be made to ensure that land value capture instruments and their links to city development programmes are understood well by all stakeholders, including landowners, developers, policymakers, planners, administrators and the urban community.

Notes

1. Defined as permissible built-up area divided by plot area—alternatively called Floor Space Index (FSI).
2. See www.trm.dk (accessed on 18 December 2015) and www.orestad.dk (accessed on 18 December 2015).
3. Delhi provides an example of non-application of value capture financing principles due to the lack of a common strategy by Delhi Development Authority, National Capital Region Planning Board, Municipal Corporations, New Delhi Municipal Committee, Delhi Metro Rail Corporation, Indian Railways, Government of National Capital Territory of Delhi and authorities of neighbouring states. Lack of transit-oriented development in the past has led to non-exploitation of the potential of ring railway and mass rapid transit system in shaping urban form and raising resources.

10

Conclusion:
An Agenda for Reforms

India's Urban Fiscal Problem

Indian municipalities are amongst the weakest globally in terms of access to resources, revenue-raising capacity and fiscal autonomy. They suffer from a gross mismatch between their functions and finances. According to McKinsey (2010), India needs to spend ₹9.74 million crore on its cities by 2030, including capital expenditure of ₹5.31 million crore. The largest demand for capital funding is from affordable housing (33.4 per cent), followed by mass transit (33.2 per cent) and urban roads (16.8 per cent).[1] If we exclude affordable housing, the capital expenditure required till 2030 would be ₹3.54 million crore (McKinsey 2010). HPEC (2011) projects the investment needed by India's core urban infrastructure sectors over the period 2012–31 at ₹3.92 million crore. If O&M costs are added, the figure would increase to ₹5.92 million crore (HPEC 2011). The O&M norms adopted by HPEC suggest that Indian municipalities spend about 20 per cent of what is needed for the efficient delivery of public services (Mathur 2013).

Per capita municipal revenue in India in 2012–13 is estimated at ₹3,123. The estimated per capita municipal expenditure for the same year is ₹3,116, comprising per capita revenue expenditure of ₹1,986 and per capita capital expenditure of ₹1,130 (ASCI 2014).[2] McKinsey (2010) reveals that India's annual per capita spending on cities of $50 is 14 per cent of China's $362, less than 10 per cent of South Africa's $508 and less than three per cent of the United Kingdom's $1,772. In terms of capital expenditure, India's annual per capita urban spending is $17 as against $116 in China, $127 in South Africa and $391 in the United Kingdom. The study argues that India needs to increase its per capita capital spending on cities eightfold, to $134, raising it from 0.5 per cent of GDP to two per cent of GDP a year. Municipalities in India will have to meet a large part of this spending either directly or in partnership with other entities, including the private sector. However, they are ill-equipped to face the challenge in view of their precarious finance and deficient management systems. Many municipalities even depend on state governments for staff salaries, pensions and provision of elementary services.

While cities in India face huge demands on expenditure, their revenue base is narrow, inflexible and non-buoyant. The share of municipal revenues in combined central and state revenues in the country declined from 3.92 per cent in 2007–08 to 3.62 per cent in 2012–13.[3] This is disturbing as the contribution of urban areas to GDP is phenomenal and rising. In 2007, cities and towns, with 30 per cent of population, contributed 62–63 per cent of India's GDP; this contribution is expected to increase to about 75 per cent by 2021 (Planning Commission 2008). The role of cities as engines of growth cannot be sustained unless the ULBs are enabled to meet the backlog, current and growth needs of firms and households for infrastructure and services.

The size of the municipal sector in India is very small compared to international benchmark. The ratio of municipal revenues to GDP at factor cost is estimated at about one per cent for 2007–08 and 2012–13,[4] compared to South Africa (6.0 per cent) and Brazil (7.4 per cent; see Afonso and Araujo (2006) for Brazil, Buckley (2005) for South Africa. Table 10.1 shows how poorly the state of municipal finance in India compares with that of local government finance in OECD countries.[5]

India's municipalities are not only financially weak, but they are also subjected to a progressive erosion in fiscal autonomy. In 2002–03, 'own revenues' accounted for 63 per cent of municipal revenues in India. This share has decreased to 55.7 per cent in 2007–08 and 51.6 per cent in 2012–13. The ratio of municipal taxes to central taxes declined from 4.49 per cent in 2007–08 to 2.98 per cent in 2012–13. The ratio of municipal taxes to state taxes decreased from 6.63 per cent to 3.10 per cent between the two years. Municipal taxes as a percentage of GDP at market price also dwindled from 0.37 per cent in 2007–08 to 0.31 per cent in 2012–13. This ratio is very small compared to the combined (centre + state) tax–GDP ratio of more 17 per cent in both 2007–08 and 2012–13 (see Table 10.2).

Table 10.1

State of Municipal Finance in India vis-à-vis OECD Countries[6]

India	OECD Countries
Municipal expenditures as % of GDP 2012–13 (1.00)	Local government expenditures as % of GDP 2010: Denmark (37.3), Sweden (25.1), Finland (22.6), Netherlands (17.2), Italy (15.9), Norway (15.2), Poland (15.0), United Kingdom (14.0), Korea (13.0), France (11.8), Austria (8.2), Germany (7.9), Switzerland (7.5), Spain (7.3) and Belgium (7.0)
Municipal revenues as % of GDP 2012–13 (1.03)	Local government revenues as % of GDP 2010: Denmark (37.1), Finland (22.4), Italy (15.3), Norway (14.2), United Kingdom (13.9), Czech Republic (11.6), Hungary (11.5), Austria (7.8), Germany (7.3) and Spain (6.4)
Municipal tax revenues as % of GDP 2012–13 (0.33)	Local government tax revenues as % of GDP 2010: Denmark (12.7), Finland (10.3), Italy (6.1), Norway (5.8), Austria (4.8), Czech Republic (4.7), Germany (2.9), Spain (2.9), Hungary (2.4) and United Kingdom (1.8)
Municipal property tax revenues as % of GDP 2012–13 (0.16)	Property taxes as % of GDP 2012: United Kingdom (3.9), France (3.8), Belgium (3.3), Canada (3.3), United States (2.9), Italy (2.7), Japan (2.7), Korea (2.6), Australia (2.4), New Zealand (2.1), Spain (2.0), Denmark (1.8), Switzerland (1.8), Finland (1.2), Norway (1.2), Poland (1.2), Netherlands (1.1) and Sweden (1.0)
Municipal non-tax revenues as % of GDP 2012–13 (0.20)	Local government user fee revenues as % of GDP 2010: Finland (4.8), Czech Republic (1.9), Denmark (1.8), Norway (1.8), United Kingdom (1.8), Hungary (1.2), Germany (1.1), Italy (1.1), Austria (0.8) and Spain (0.6)
Municipal transfer revenues as % of GDP (0.46)	Local government transfer revenues as % of GDP 2010: Denmark (21.3), United Kingdom (10.0), Italy (7.8), Hungary (7.7), Finland (6.6), Norway (6.0), Czech Republic (4.8), Germany (3.0), Spain (2.8) and Austria (1.5)
Municipal expenditures as % of total expenditures (centre + state + municipal) 2012–13 (3.32)	Local expenditures as % of country total expenditure (all tiers together) 2010: Denmark (64.4), Sweden (47.9), Korea (43.2), Finland (40.7), Netherlands (33.6), Norway (33.5), Poland (33.2), Italy (31.6), Austria (30.0), United Kingdom (27.8), Switzerland (22.1), France (20.9), Germany (16.6), Spain (15.8) and Belgium (13.3)
Municipal taxes as % of total taxes (centre + state + municipal) 2012–13 (1.79)	Local taxes as % of country total (all tiers together) taxes 2010: Sweden (35.4), Denmark (26.7), Japan (25.9), Finland (24.4), Korea (16.7), United States (16.1), Switzerland (15.6), Italy (15.4), Norway (13.6), Poland (12.7), France (10.8), Canada (10.2), Spain (9.5), New Zealand (7.2), Germany (7.0), Hungary (6.4), Belgium (5.1), United Kingdom (5.1), Australia (3.5) and Netherlands (3.8)

Sources: ASCI (2014) and Indian Public Finance Statistics 2013–14; OCED (2011): OECD National Accounts Statistics (database); OECD (2012): Revenue Statistics 1965–2011; Bird and Slack (2013).

Table 10.2

Trends in Municipal Finances in India: Key Ratios, 2007–08 and 2012–13

	As Percentage of			
	GDP at Factor Cost (Current Prices)		GDP at Market Price (Current Prices)	
Ratio	2007–08	2012–13	2007–08	2012–13
Municipal Revenues	1.08	1.03	0.99	0.96
Municipal Own Revenues	0.60	0.53	0.55	0.49
Municipal Taxes	0.40	0.33	0.37	0.31
Municipal Property Tax	0.18	0.16	0.16	0.15
Central Transfers for Municipalities	0.10	0.10	0.10	0.10
State Transfers to Municipalities	0.33	0.36	0.32	0.33
Total Transfers to Municipalities	0.43	0.46	0.42	0.43
State Taxes			5.60	6.80
Central Taxes			11.90	10.30
Combined (Central + State) Taxes			17.50	17.10

Source: ASCI (2014), Indian Public Finance Statistics 2013–14, 14th Finance Commission (2015).

Genesis of Urban Fiscal Problem

A key factor behind the growing function–finance mismatch in Indian cities is the progressive decline in the share of municipal 'own revenues', especially taxes in total municipal revenues. India is peculiar in the sense that in spite of increasing urbanisation and rising contribution of cities to GDP, the tax powers of municipalities have dwindled over the years.

In the 1919 GoI Act, octroi, terminal tax and tax on trade, professions and callings were reserved for municipalities, in addition to land and property taxes including LVT. The Local Finance Enquiry Committee 1951 recommended some more local taxes, namely tax on consumption or sale of electricity, tax on advertisements other than those published in newspapers, tax on vehicles, capitation tax and tax on entertainment exclusively for municipalities. The Taxation Enquiry Commission (1953–54) added duty on transfer of property to the list. However, with octroi abolished and states appropriating 'local taxes' such as profession tax, motor vehicles tax, entertainment tax, duty on transfer of property and tax on consumption or sale of electricity, municipalities in India have reached a state where they cannot even meet the cost of their most basic functions with 'own' resources.

Excepting in Maharashtra, which permits Mumbai to levy octroi, property tax is the only major municipal tax in India. Thus, cities are deprived of the buoyancy they create in the economy through their externalities. Unlike many countries, municipalities in India do not have access to income, sales, value added, goods and services, excise and business tax bases that keep pace with growth (see Table 10.3).

Not only do the ULBs in India have a narrow tax base, but they also have no access to a formula-based sharing in major national and state taxes as in multi-tier countries like Brazil, China, South Africa, Nigeria and Philippines (see Box 10.1). Even compensations to ULBs from states, which abolished octroi and took over 'local taxes', have remained at precariously low levels. For example, the compensation from the erstwhile state government to municipal corporation of Hyderabad for the loss of

Table 10.3

Distribution of Tax Revenue Sources of Select Metropolitan Cities*

Name of City	Year of Data	Composition of Municipal Tax Revenues (% of Total)
Barcelona	2009	Property tax (64.7), VAT share (12.0), sales tax (11.8), vehicle tax (8.6) and construction tax (2.9)
Beijing	2009	Sales tax (39.3), corporation income tax (22.5), VAT share (9.4), individual income tax (9.3), property tax (8.1), deed tax (5.4), construction tax (3.7), stamp tax (1.7) and vehicle tax (0.6)
Buenos Aires	2007	VAT share (78.5), property tax (9.0), vehicle tax (8.7) and stamp tax (3.8)
Cape Town	2009	Utilities tax (68.2) and property tax (31.8)
Chicago	2009	Property tax (39.3), state sales tax share (9.6), sales tax (8.5), utilities tax (8.3), state income tax share (8.2), gasoline tax (6.7), telecommunications tax (6.0), transportation tax (4.0), amusement tax (3.3), excise tax (2.7), hotel tax (2.0) and other taxes (1.0)
Lima	2010	Property tax (58.8), vehicle tax (22.6), excise tax (8.3), gambling tax (7.9) and other taxes (2.5)
Sao Paulo	2010	Sales tax (53.9), property tax (38.2), individual income tax (6.6) and other taxes (1.4)
Tokyo	2008	Individual income tax (42.4), corporation income tax (23.9), excise tax (5.6), vehicle tax (2.0) and other taxes (7.2)
Delhi	2010	Property tax (88.8) and utilities tax (11.2)

Source: Martinez-Vazquez (2013, 204).

Note: * Includes both own and assigned tax revenues.

Box 10.1

Tax-sharing with Municipalities: Brazil, China, Nigeria, South Africa and Philippines

Brazil: Brazilian municipalities received the following shares in federal and state taxes in 2005: federal income tax (22.5 per cent), federal value added tax on manufactured goods (22.5 per cent), federal financial operations tax on gold (70 per cent), federal rural land and property tax (50 per cent), state tax on motor vehicles (50 per cent) and state value added tax on goods and interstate and intercity transportation and communication services (25 per cent; Afonso and Araujo 2006).

China: Sub-provincial governments in China were provided with the following shares from national and provincial taxes in 2003: value added tax (19 per cent), business taxes (70 per cent), enterprise income tax (21 per cent), individual income tax (24 per cent), urban maintenance and construction tax (90 per cent) and agriculture taxes (96 per cent; Qiao and Shah 2006). China allows its cities to retain 25 per of value added tax (equivalent to $4.5 billion per year in Shanghai; McKinsey 2010).

Nigeria: In Nigeria, 13 per cent of oil revenues are assigned to oil-producing states on 'derivation' principle. The remaining amount is divided between the federal government (53 per cent), state governments (27 per cent) and local governments (20 per cent). Revenues from customs, excise and corporation income taxes are split between the three tiers using the same formula without the derivation principle. Revenues from VAT are divided as follows: federal government (15 per cent), state governments (50 per cent) and local governments (35 per cent).

South Africa: In South Africa, the distribution of nationally raised revenues between national, provincial and local governments over the period 2008–09 to 2010–11 were as follows: national 48.1–50.0 per cent, provincial 42.5–43.7 per cent and local 7.5–8.2 per cent. The central government funds 40–50 per cent of infrastructure investments in large cities and 60–70 in small cities through grants and loans (McKinsey 2010).

Philippines: Under the Local Government Code 1991, Philippines allocates 40 per cent of the national internal revenue taxes actually realised during the third fiscal year preceding the current fiscal year to various LGUs: provinces (23 per cent), cities (23 per cent), municipalities (34 per cent) and *barangays* or village units (20 per cent).

Sources: Afonso and Araujo (2006) for Brazil, Chitiga-Mabugu and Monkam (2013) for South Africa, Llanto (2009) for Philippines, Qiao and Shah (2006) for China, World Bank (2013b) for Nigeria.

octroi and toll tax has remained below ₹50 lakhs year after year, although the yield from octroi alone could have been ₹1,000 crore annually had the tax not been abolished.[7] No doubt, octroi is an 'inefficient' and 'distortionary' tax. But the inefficiencies and distortions that have overwhelmed India's cities due to underinvestment in infrastructure for decades might have surpassed those due to octroi by many times.

Internationally, country municipal finance regimes can be divided into two groups. Municipalities in a large number of federal and unitary countries have access to high-yielding taxes like income tax, and goods and services tax. In a small group of unitary countries, where property tax is the dominant local tax, municipalities receive substantial formulae-based grants from the central government. For example, grants from the national government accounted for 70–80 per cent of local body expenditures in the United Kingdom (McKinsey 2010, 21). In London, central grants amounted to 78.6 per cent of municipal revenues, with specific-purpose transfers accounting for 25.6 per cent and general-purpose transfers, 53.0 per cent (Shah 2013, 226). Unfortunately, municipalities in India have access neither to a broad-based basket of own taxes nor to a sizable pool of fiscal transfers from central and state governments.

Fundamental Issues at Stake

The neglect of urban public finance in India for long is perhaps rooted in the inadequate understanding of the role of cities and their agglomeration externalities in economic growth. While pondering why developing countries have lagged in 'action front' to reform their outdated system of city finances in spite of the broad clarity provided by researchers in the early nineties (see Bahl and Linn 1992), Douglas Keare, in his foreword to Bahl, Linn and Wetzel (2013), *Financing Metropolitan Governments in Developing Countries*, observes:

> [T]he central importance of cities, of urban agglomerations, remains far too imperfectly understood by most people, including many extremely well-meaning people: advocates of alleviating rural poverty; many environmentalists; and above all, most of the influential policy makers who might be able to get the ball rolling. (2013, xii)

The earlier-mentioned statement may apply to India to a great extent.

Cities are hubs of economic activity, employment, education and entertainment. They catalyse agglomeration, knowledge and infrastructure externalities that drive economic transformation. They generate growth and public finance for development. Yet cities have not received the attention they deserve from policymakers, planners and academicians in India. The euphoria in the 1950s to set up expert committees to enhance the tax powers of municipalities beyond what was stipulated in the 1919 GoI Act soon got lost and was never revived. Sporadic attempts to find a tax alternative to octroi in the absence of substantive research on the subject met with no success. Urban economics in general and urban public finance in particular remain grossly neglected disciplines of study in the country. While reputed Indian universities do not even teach these subjects, serious research on the economics of cities and their financing, combining theory and practice, is missing.

If growth is the most critical concern of India, 'where growth occurs' ought to be a key area of attention. Jane Jacobs, a profound thinker on cities, observes that it is principally cities, and not countries, that are engines of economic development. She questions the frame of analysis adopted by Adam Smith in his celebrated book of 1776, *An Enquiry into the Nature and Causes of the Wealth of Nations* (Smith 1776). She argues that nations are political and military entities and not the basic units for probe into the mysteries of economic structure. They are grab bags of different regional economies, some rich and others poor. The real generators of national wealth are cities that nurture the fundamental processes leading to economic expansion. The wealth of nations is the wealth of cities (Jacobs 1969, 1984).

Urban economics, NGT and NEG suggest that economic growth does not occur everywhere. Growth localises in city regions due to their externalities, leading to increasing returns—at firm, industry, local, urban and regional scales. Economic activities that drive growth are heavily concentrated in urban areas. For these activities both scale and location matter. Cities form and grow to reap external economies of agglomeration. They lead to scale, scope, localisation and urbanisation economies, facilitating production and trade. Cities offer benefits of market size, backward and forward linkages, knowledge spillovers, learning, matching and sharing. Metropolitan city regions represent a mass of interconnected activities, typically characterised by high productivity due to 'jointly-generated' and 'mutually-reinforcing' agglomeration and networking economies. Metcalfe's law suggests that the value of a network increases with the square of the number of connected users in the system.[8]

Apart from agglomeration externalities, cities are homes to knowledge and human capital externalities. In a city setting, the production of new knowledge by one firm generates a positive externality to other firms as knowledge spills over and cannot be kept secret (Romer 1986). The effects of 'external human capital' are rooted in the ways people interact, exchange and learn in cities (Lucas 1988). Shaped by market forces and growth-promoting policies, agglomeration and knowledge externalities reinforce each other through 'circular and cumulative causation'. Growth leads to agglomeration that fosters growth by facilitating creation, transmission and diffusion of knowledge and nurturing specialisation, diversity, competition and innovation. Agglomeration and knowledge externalities establish the unique importance of cities in the structural transformation of nations. The experiences of Asian countries also reveal:

> [U]rban agglomerative effects are the most important driving forces causing cities to grow, especially large cities. Due to difficulties in measuring these effects, it is hard to establish strong empirical evidence, which make agglomerative effects poorly understood among policy and planning decision makers. Nevertheless, limited empirical studies have concluded that agglomerative effects become more important when a city's economy upgrades from manufacturing towards knowledge-based sectors. (Ding and Zhao 2012)

Empirical studies find a strong positive correlation between economic growth and agglomeration (Mohanty 2014). A study based on panel data set covering up to 70 countries over 1960–90 shows that urban primacy, measured by the share in population of a country's largest city, is advantageous to growth in low-income countries. Urbanisation per se, however, has no significant growth-promoting effect (Henderson 2003b). Another study examining the effects of spatial concentration of economic activity within European regions over 1980–2000 lends evidence to the growth-inducing effects of agglomeration (Crozet and Koenig 2005). A recent research using cross-country data set for 105 countries for 1960–2000 finds 'consistent evidence' in favour of the hypothesis that agglomeration boosts GDP growth up to a level of development. The critical threshold is some US$10,000 per capita in 2006 PPP prices, corresponding roughly to the current level of development of Brazil (Brulhart and Sbergami 2009). India is way below this threshold. Thus, at the present stage of India's evolution, as the country moves to a knowledge-based economy, it has a historic opportunity to accelerate economic growth and reduce poverty by developing cities and harnessing the untapped power of their external economies.

Apart from the importance of cities as catalysts of growth, their role as generators of public finance is also not well-understood. McKinsey (2010) reports that 80–85 per cent of India's tax revenues would come from its cities in the next two decades. A key reason for this is that externalities of cities capitalise into tax bases of all levels of government and manifest in 'agglomeration rents'. Cities around the world thus act as instruments to mobilise income tax, corporation tax, service tax, value added tax, goods and services tax, business tax, excise tax, stamp duty, motor vehicles tax, land value tax, property tax, profession tax, advertisement tax, entertainment tax, etc. However, researchers, policymakers and planners in India in the past hardly recognised the role of spatial externalities in growth and public finance. In the process, they neglected the fundamental issue of how economic development could be financed without vibrant cities to generate resources.

While democratic decentralisation and fiscal empowerment of cities in a large country like India, with 814 million people projected to live in cities by 2050, have their own intrinsic merit, economic growth and public finance are fundamental issues at stake in the neglect of urban public finance. No doubt, rural development and poverty alleviation are India's pressing concerns. But addressing them requires resources and the same can only be mobilised by cities. Jane Jacobs (1984) emphasises the role of cities as 'the greatest yielders of revenues in a nation or empire'. She informs that when the United States income tax was first adopted in 1913, a third of the nation's entire tax yield came from New York State alone, most of it from New York City. Jacobs cautions that until a nation has well-developed and productive cities, it cannot afford programmes for basic necessities or transfer payments, including those to the rural poor (Jacobs 1984, 186).

The importance of cities in economic growth and public finance suggests that at this stage of India's evolution, a strategy to develop agglomeration-augmenting, congestion-mitigating and resource-generating cities offers a cost-effective way to address the country's economic development concerns. This strategy will harness the powers of externalities and spillover effects generated by cities to augment growth, mobilise public finance and drive structural transformation.

Approach to Designing Reforms

Both rural areas and cities cannot be subsidised simultaneously. It is cities that have to generate resources for rural as well as urban development. Thus, a key objective of reforms in urban public finance in India is to not only meet the needs of city infrastructure and services, but also mobilise finance for rural development and poverty alleviation. Urban economics, NGT and NEG suggest that when agglomeration economies are vibrant in cities, benefit taxation and value capture financing instruments provide opportunities for a self-financed or even a surplus-generating process of urban development. In particular, externalities in cities lead to many benefits to many actors in the urban economy in many ways; they manifest in 'agglomeration rents' that can be captured and recycled. A recent body of research in NEG also suggests that agglomeration rents occur not only to immobile factors, but also to mobile factors of production. These can be taxed without losing the tax base to finance local public goods and generate further agglomerative effects. A two-pronged approach to reforms is called for: (a) enabling growth pay its way and (b) making beneficiaries of windfall gains pay for planned urban development, benefitting them and the society at large.

The fiscal federalism literature does not consider the type spatial externalities due to agglomeration, human capital accumulation and infrastructure development that urban economics, NGT and NEG consider to be of paramount importance for growth. However, it highlights a fundamental principle of organising local government, namely local public services should be provided by the jurisdiction nearest to the people that is capable of internalising the benefits and costs of such services. This principle, known as 'subsidiarity' calls for designing local revenue instruments based on the 'benefit' criterion. Municipalities must make the beneficiaries of civic infrastructure and services pay for costs. As a corollary, those creating dis-benefits or negative externalities to the society must pay for their mitigation. Thus, 'users pay', 'beneficiaries pay', 'polluters play', 'exacerbaters pay', 'congesters pay' and 'growth pays'. We embrace these paradigms under the caption of 'generalised benefit principle' and regard the same as the cornerstone of urban public finance reforms in a developing country like India.

Whereas public economics recommends linking local taxes to local benefits to raise sufficient resources while promoting accountability in public service delivery, urban economics, NGT and NEG suggest that the definition of benefits be expanded beyond those accruing to direct users of services. In fact, the indirect benefits to some agents in the economy due to externalities and 'circular and cumulative causation' processes may be far more than what direct users of services obtain. These are facilitated by public policies to induce economic growth, undertake spatial planning, develop core infrastructure and promote good urban governance. For example, land use planning, 'leading' regional and urban infrastructure development, and public service provision generate unearned increments in land values to owners of land at vantage locations. Zoning, conversion of rural land to urban, institution of land use, change of land use, assignment of development rights, including FSI, TDR, urban renewal incentives and so on create huge windfall gains to a lucky group of landowners. Similarly, the development of trunk infrastructure facilities confers 'serviceability' and 'accessibility' premiums on properties located in their zones of influence.

While adopting the generalised benefit principle to design instruments to finance city development and services in India, it is also important to ensure that they yield adequate revenues to meet the backlog, current and growth needs. In this context, keeping international practice in view, a minimal consideration in reforms is that the 'local taxes' that municipalities had prior to independence and those recommended by expert committees in the fifties must be restored back or assigned to them. Thus, the empowerment of ULBs with an alternative as productive and buoyant as octroi and other local taxes should be non-negotiable.

Centrality of Generalised Benefit Principle

The generalised benefit principle is central to reforms in urban public finance in a developing country like India for a number of reasons. First, by establishing a close link between municipal expenditures and revenues, it promotes accountability in service delivery. Second, it acts against the resistance of taxpayers, increasingly becoming common, as they care about whether and how their 'own' money translates into benefits for them and the city. Third, it emphasises that while as a first resort the services provided by local governments should be paid for by users, beneficiaries gaining through agglomeration externalities must also contribute towards planned urban development. Thus, in a way, the principle guarantees the availability of adequate resources for city public goods and services.

The generalised benefit principle constitutes the bedrock of the golden rules of urban public finance that guide the choice of revenue sources appropriate to financing particular types of local public expenditures. These rules are stated as follows (Bahl and Linn 1992):

1. Where the benefits of public services are measurable and accrue to readily identified individuals in a jurisdiction, user charges are the most appropriate financing instruments;
2. Local public services such as administration, traffic control, street lighting and security, which are services to the general public in the sense that identification of beneficiaries and measurement of benefits and costs to individuals are difficult, are most appropriately financed by taxes on local residents;
3. The cost of services for which significant spillovers to neighbouring jurisdictions occur (for example, health, education and

welfare), should be financed substantially by state or national intergovernmental transfers; and

4. Borrowing is an appropriate source to finance capital outlays on infrastructure projects, particularly public utilities and roads, where investment requirements are large and benefits accrue to generations.

The golden rules of urban public finance suggest that user charges are the most appropriate instruments to finance local public services. Where charging is not feasible, benefit charges and benefit taxes on local residents are desirable. General taxes and intergovernmental transfers are necessary to finance such services when user charges, benefit charges and benefit taxes are not adequate. Borrowing is appropriate for long gestation infrastructure projects whose benefits accrue to more than one generation. Thus, a portfolio of revenue instruments needs to be authorised to municipalities. Table 10.4 presents a range of revenue instruments that are suitable to finance particular types of expenditures in cities based on the generalised benefit principle.

The Imperative of Earmarking

In the urban context, where the benefit principle is central to resource mobilisation, earmarking is a desirable principle. Expenditures, benefits and revenues must be linked to ensure accountability in public service delivery and a steady flow of funds for priority activities. The case for earmarking of particular revenues to particular expenditures in cities rests not only on theoretical arguments, but also on practical considerations. Faced with endemic financial constraints, cities have been subjected to massive under-spending in core infrastructure facilities for long. With no revenue-expenditure linking, planned urban development has been left to haphazard and residuary methods of financing. For example, while transport makes or mars a city, practically all cities in India have neglected public transit investments. Thus, they have foregone the benefits of 'transportation-land use integration' and 'wider economic benefits' that could have been engineered through agglomeration externalities.

A key problem in urban planning in India has been the lack of realistic estimates of sectoral requirements of funds in cities. For almost five decades, till McKinsey (2010) and HPEC (2011) reports were published, planners and policymakers relied on the civic service norms developed

Table 10.4

Instruments of Financing Urban Public Services and Infrastructure: User Charges to General Taxes

Instrument	Characteristic Features	Examples
User charges	Analogous to market prices for private goods and services, benefits are measurable and accrue to readily identified individuals and payment depends on consumption.	Water supply charges, park entrance fees, road tolls and charges for public transportation services
Benefit charges	Charges linked to consumption of collective services through a surrogate method due to benefits arising from joint effects of many services or being subject to measurement problems and payment depends on parameters of access to services and cannot be excessive.	Sewerage and storm drainage charges hooked onto water charges; access or connectivity charges to water, sewerage, drainage and road networks; charges for roads, street lighting, solid waste management, fire and other services linked to property characteristics such as plinth area or unit area value, road frontage, road width, etc.; surcharge on electricity consumption to meet street lighting costs; development charges; impact fees and betterment charges.
Special assessments	Compulsory levies on real property in a well-defined or demarcated development area, for example, special assessment district or business improvement district to recoup costs of specific investments in infrastructure.	Taxes levied on residents of designated areas to finance costs of internal and external infrastructure and services, covering facilities such as roads, public transit, street lighting, water supply, sewerage, drainage, fire protection and affordable housing and betterment taxes, etc.
Administrative and regulatory charges or fees for services	Payments towards cost of administrative and regulatory services, akin to prices or benefit charges.	Trade licensing fee, including enforcement charges; building permit fee, including administrative charges; layout and sub-division approval charges; advertising fee; polluters pay, exacerbates pay and congesters pay charges.
General benefit taxes	Taxes on activities or purchases which are generally, but often indirectly related to the use of public facilities.	General property tax, land value tax, vacant land tax, utility user taxes, profession tax, payroll tax, entertainment tax; advertisement tax, etc.

(continued)

(continued)

Instrument	Characteristic Features	Examples
General taxes	Compulsory levies towards financing government and tax payments are not linked, directly or indirectly to public service consumption.	Local option (piggyback) taxes, revenue-shared income tax, business tax, excise tax, sales tax, value added tax, goods and services tax, etc.[9]

Source: Author.

by the Zakaria Committee (Zakaria 1963). However, as no realistic assessments of sectoral demands were available, no meaningful planning of investments in critical areas could be possible. This might have led to the neglect of earmarked revenue instruments in financing critical expenditures in cities.

Table 10.5 presents estimates of funds needed in core urban sectors based on HPEC (2011). The sectoral requirements vary widely, calling for varying strategies to meet them. For example, the amount needed for roads, transport and traffic infrastructure is disproportionately large. Ironically, earmarking is a preferred strategy internationally to develop these important sectors. For example, interstate highways and public transit in the United States and other countries have been financed through earmarked fuel and vehicles taxes. In France, establishments located in urban transport areas and employing more than nine persons have been required to pay a percentage of their wage bill as *versement transport* or transport tax. This has provided stable funding for the development or extension of 10 light rail transit systems in France since 1985 (Scheurer et al. 2000).

Apart from public transport, earmarking is regarded suitable for financing utility services such as water supply, sewerage and drainage. User charges, benefit charges, benefit taxes, beneficiary capital contributions and debt financing tools are combined to meet the costs of these services. Tariffs are linked to the consumption of water, which is measured. Benefit charges and taxes are related to property characteristics. As public facilities enhance the 'serviceability' of locations and properties, they create scope for mobilising revenues based on benefit criteria. In India, water and sewer benefit taxes are imposed in Mumbai; beneficiary capital contribution is levied in Bengaluru to raise resources for water supply and sewerage projects. Recently, the government of Rajasthan has introduced a cess on electricity to meet the increasing costs of street lighting in municipalities.

Table 10.5

Expenditure Estimates for Core Urban Sectors 2012–13 (at 2009–10 Prices)

Sector	Total Capital Expenditure (₹ Crore)	Total O&M Expenditure (₹ Crore)	Average Per Capita Investment Cost (₹)	Average Per Capita O&M Cost (Annual in ₹)
Water Supply	3,20,908	5,46,095	5,099	501
Sewerage	2,42,688	2,36,964	4,704	286
Solid Waste Management	48,582	2,73,906	391	155
Urban Roads	17,28,941	3,75,267	22,974	397
Storm Water Drains	1,91,031	34,612	3,526	53
Urban Transport	4,49,426	3,04,386	5,380	371
Traffic Support Infrastructure	97,985	36,690	945	34
Street Lighting	18,580	4,717	366	8
Total (Core Sectors)	30,98,141	18,12,637	43,385	1,806

Source: High Powered Expert Committee on Urban Infrastructure Report (2011, 69–84).

An Urban Finance Framework

The generalised benefit principle, including golden rules of local public finance and the principle of earmarked benefit taxes, guide how local public services should be financed and who should pay for them. They aim at matching benefit areas with financing areas, expenditure responsibilities with revenue sources and revenue instruments with services provided. Adopting these paradigms, we present an urban finance framework to guide the design of city financing instruments in India as follows:

1. Wherever possible, user charges should be levied for public services as the first resort to recover O&M costs, an element of cross-subsidisation for the poor and a proportionate amount towards capital costs.
2. For achieving efficiency in resource allocation, user charges should be imposed on the direct recipients of benefits in all cases where services can be measured and beneficiaries can be identified.
3. Where user charging is not feasible, benefit charges may be levied on properties benefitted from public infrastructure facilities and services on considerations of 'accessibility' and 'serviceability'. Special assessments, betterment levies and specific benefit taxes such as water, sewer, drainage and fire benefit taxes on local residents can also be adopted.

4. Earmarking of specific benefit taxes is appropriate for financing infrastructure and services when clear, specific and tight linkages between revenues raised and facilities provided are established.

5. General benefit taxes such as land value tax, land value increment tax and general property tax are appropriate to finance the costs of 'collective' services and city-wide or regional infrastructure facilities.

6. For administrative and regulatory services, full costs may be recovered from those receiving benefits and those imposing costs on the society through appropriate fees.

7. For licenses and permissions, a general principle is that when a public authority grants a right to some and not to others, those benefiting from such right must pay to the authority for expenditures. This may correspond to the value of the rights, measured by what the non-beneficiaries would be willing to pay to secure them.

8. The cost of services availed by non-residents may be recovered through non-residence-based taxes such as profession tax, payroll tax, toll tax, hotel tax or value added tax so as to capture a part of the benefits accruing to them and to achieve full cost recovery.

9. When user charges, benefit charges and benefit taxes are not adequate to finance public infrastructure services and facilities, municipalities may be provided with access to other taxes, including revenue-shared taxes.

10. The poor may be subsidised directly rather than by reducing prices to all users and creating distortions in the entire market for public services. However, some cross-subsidisation for water could be designed with a lifeline tariff within an increasing block tariff framework, forming part of a two-part tariff. The fixed charge part may be a contribution towards capital costs and the volumetric charge for recovering O&M and other variable costs.

11. Facilities and services, which spillover to other jurisdictions and which cannot be fully met by residence and non-residence-based benefit taxes, may be financed substantially by intergovernmental transfers; such transfers are also necessary for financing merit goods and crucial regional and urban infrastructure such as public transit and wastewater disposal facilities, and correcting vertical and horizontal imbalances.

12. Debt financing constitutes an appropriate instrument to finance projects requiring large capital investments and whose benefits spread over generations. Debt-servicing may be linked to earmarked benefit charges, including development charges, special assessments and impact fees, benefit taxes, value increment financing instruments, general taxes and dedicated intergovernmental revenues.

The urban finance framework suggests that the basket of revenue instruments to be assigned to municipalities following the generalised benefit principle must be broad-based. This conclusion is also overwhelmingly supported by the international practice in local public finance.

Portfolio of Local Revenue Instruments

Table 10.6 presents a summary of major sources of municipal revenues internationally. A comparison of the revenue instruments of ULBs in India and in other countries suggests that the tax base of Indian municipalities is non-buoyant and needs to be broadened considerably.

As Table 10.6 shows, municipalities in other countries have access to a range of non-property tax instruments unlike India. While there is considerable scope to enhance the yield from property tax in the country, raising it to one per cent of GDP over a decade or so, confining municipalities to property tax as the only major tax deprives them of the buoyant tax bases they create through agglomeration economies. Property tax will also not be adequate to meet the huge demands of urban infrastructure and services as India urbanises. In fact, property tax constituted only five per cent of total revenues in OECD countries in 2012; taxes on income and profit accounted for 34 per cent, consumption taxes, 31 per cent and social security contributions, 26 per cent. The share of property tax in total revenues of these countries also declined from eight per cent in 1965 to five per cent in 2012. Property tax–GDP ratio fell from 1.9 per cent to 1.8 per cent over the same period. On the contrary, income tax-GDP ratio increased from 8.7 per cent to 11.4 per cent and goods and services tax-GDP ratio from 9.4 per cent to 10.8 per cent (see OECD 2014).[10] These trends in OECD countries indicate that if Indian cities are to discharge their fundamental role as engines of economic growth, they must have recourse to income tax and goods and services tax bases or appropriate transfers from central and state governments linked to these taxes.

While Indian municipalities need to be enabled to have statutory access to 'local taxes' like land value tax, land use conversion tax, transfer of property tax, profession tax, business licensing tax, advertisement tax, entertainment tax, utility user taxes, motor vehicles tax and so on, the new GST regime should also fully compensate them for the loss of octroi and other local taxes abolished or appropriated by state governments in the past, or being subsumed under the GST. Given the present limitations

Table 10.6

Revenue Instruments of Municipalities: International Practice

Category of Instrument	Description of Instrument and Countries/Provinces/Cities where Practiced
Land-based Taxes	Property tax (most countries), vacant land tax (Brazil, Andhra Pradesh, Telangana), land value tax and land value increment tax (Taiwan), site value tax (Australia), comprehensive real estate holding tax (Korea), land gains tax (United States and Canada), windfall tax (Ireland), real property gains tax (Malaysia), urban land tax (Tamil Nadu) and real estate transfer tax (United States, Andhra Pradesh, Tamil Nadu, Telangana).
Non-land based Taxes	Local income tax, local sales tax, local excise tax, local payroll tax and local motor vehicles tax (United States, Europe); profession tax (Andhra Pradesh, Kerala); entertainment Tax (Andhra Pradesh, Telangana); advertisement Tax (Andhra Pradesh, Karnataka, Telangana, West Bengal); business licensing tax (Latin America); water benefit tax and sewer benefit tax (Mumbai) and utility user taxes (Chicago, Cape Town, Delhi).
User Charges	Water charges (Most cities); PAYT charges and tipping fees (United States) and bulk garbage collection charges (Hyderabad).
Benefit Charges	Sewerage and storm drainage charges hooked onto water charges (Most countries), special assessment districts (United States), business improvement districts (Canada, United States), betterment charges (*Contribucion de Valorizacion; Participacion en Plusvalias* and *Contrubuciones de Mejoras* in Latin America).
Shared Taxes	Income tax (Brazil, China, Japan), value added tax (Argentina, Brazil, China, Spain), excise tax (Japan, Peru, Punjab), vehicle tax (Argentina, Brazil, Peru, Spain), motor fuel tax (United States, dedicated to highways and transit) and business taxes (China, Latin America).
Shared General Revenues/ Transfers	Practically all countries, including Brazil, China, Nigeria, Philippines and South Africa.
Development Financing Tools	Developer exactions (United States), impact fees (United States, Hyderabad, Ahmedabad), developer contribution (Australia), planning obligations (United Kingdom), community infrastructure levy (United Kingdom) and incentive zoning (United States).
Value Capture Financing Tools	Sale of developer land (most countries); lease/sale of project-related land (Australia, France, China); lease/sale of development rights (FSI charges, *Outorga Onerosa do Direito de Construir* (OODC) in Brazil, auctionable development rights, *Certificados de Potencial Adicional de Construcao* (CEPAC) in Brazil); monetisation of land assets (Mumbai Metropolitan Regional Development Authority, Bandra Kurla Complex); joint development mechanism (Japan, China); betterment taxes (Latin America) and tax increment financing (United States).

Source: Bahl and Linn (1992), Bahl et al. (2013) and Mohanty (2014).

of India's fiscal federalism, a separate statutory city GST rate within state GST rate or a formula-based city share in state GST seems to be the most appropriate alternative.

Value Increment Financing of Cities

Cities create value by catalysing growth and transformation of low-value assets to high-value enterprises. The value creation process is rooted in their externalities, facilitated by market forces and public policies. These externalities translate into tax bases of not only local but also state and central governments. Thus, the financing of planned development of cities should be linked to such tax bases based on the benefit principle.

Experience suggests that the market value of rural land adjacent to a metropolitan city can go up 10–20 times when such land is included in the city master plan. Similarly, transportation-land use integration, regional infrastructure connectivities and strategic densification of growth nodes lead to huge location-based rents. The unearned increments in land values increase substantially, if accompanied by favourable changes in zoning following a flexible spatial planning framework that responds to the dynamics of cities. Thus, market borrowing can lead to a self-financed process of planned urban development, facilitating agglomeration economies, mitigating congestion diseconomies and creating revenues to repay debt. The importance of value increment financing lies in that when cities are unable to generate a current revenue surplus, they can still bank upon future value increments to implement their current development strategy with fiscal discipline.

The land pooling and land readjustment schemes in Korea, Japan, Taiwan, Latin America and Gujarat state present successful models of value increment financing with no burden on government finances. These can be implemented by public authorities, private developers and PPP. A possible PPP option is that public authorities facilitate value-creating land use planning and the private sector takes up urban development or renewal at its cost. A good example of this is Magarpatta in Pune, developed by the Magarpatta Town Development and Construction Company with 120 farmers as shareholders. Facilitated by Pune Municipal Corporation and Government of Maharashtra under the Maharashtra Regional Town Planning Act, 1996, sufficient value increments were generated through meticulous spatial planning and debt-financed development, creating a world-class township and contributing to local, state and central revenues.

TIF is a key tool of value increment financing. It aims at using anticipated increases in tax revenues to finance a current infrastructure programme executed by public authorities or private sector partners or both. Based on the rule that growth pays, TIF facilitates planned urban development and renewal, with public authorities earmarking a part or whole of the incremental revenues, including taxes and charges resulting from such development for debt-servicing. The instrument is flexible. Tax increments can be used to secure a loan, leverage an up-front investment or undertake 'pay-as-you-go' development. A TIF mechanism essentially allows a local authority to ring-fence future tax increments within a designated development area or the 'TIF district', to finance development that contributes to this increment. The TIF authority is usually a special purpose vehicle of local and state governments, sometimes involving private partners. Tax increments are supplemented by other land-related instruments such as special assessment, impact fee, betterment levy and dedicated fund.

There is considerable scope for value increment financing of Indian cities adopting the TIF framework during India's structural transformation process. Most ULBs do not have a current surplus. However, a well-designed programme for their development could be possible, with favourable changes in zoning and density norms, by earmarking a portion of the future collections from land-based and other benefit taxes of different tiers of government for debt-servicing. A special purpose vehicle, representing the local body, private sector partner, state and central governments can act as a TIF authority. It may raise resources upfront through tax-free municipal bonds or other forms of debt with a long maturity period of, say, 20–25 years, to meet the infrastructure costs. Long-term funds like provident funds, pension funds and insurance funds may subscribe to these bonds. As in the United States, the financing options for a TIF may also include debt service coverage provided by higher levels of government for the first few years when TIF is most risky. Once TIF revenues stabilise, the programme could be refinanced through bonds. This arrangement would enhance the rating of TIF bonds and lower their coupon rate. The central and state governments could also provide seed money and other support to improve the bankability of TIF ventures.

Build India Bonds for City Development

HPEC (2011) projects that India would need to invest ₹3.92 million crore in core urban infrastructure over the period 2012–31. The only practical way to mobilise this huge sum is by borrowing. Moreover, as the golden rules of local public finance suggest, borrowing is an appropriate instrument for long gestation projects whose benefits spread over generations. In the United States, municipal bonds have been the principal instruments to finance lumpy capital improvement projects in cities. They have been amongst the safest long-term investments in the country. The US municipal securities market has grown from $20 billion in 1945 to $361 billion in 1981 and $3.7 trillion of debt outstanding at present.[11]

Following the US model, India introduced tax-free and taxable municipal bonds in the late nineties. The Ministry of Urban Development, GoI issued guidelines for tax-free bonds. By 2010, 23 municipal bonds were issued in the country, raising revenues to the tune of about ₹13,531 crore, mostly on private placement basis. However, with the launch of JNNURM in 2005, the municipal bonds programme received a setback as ULBs and utilities accessed central grant fund and matching state share to undertake projects. Considering the massive requirement of infrastructure investment in urban India, there is a need to renew emphasis on municipal bonds adopting a value increment financing framework. The SEBI has recently established regulations for the issuance of revenue bonds by municipalities to raise resources from public and institutional investors, including sovereign wealth funds and pension funds.

The US experience with revenue bonds and general obligation bonds suggests that the creation of a vibrant municipal bonds market in India would require long-term action on several fronts: (a) substantially enhancing the size of the municipal sector, (b) implementing a comprehensive programme of municipal finance reforms, including assignment of a basket of municipal taxes and formula-based transfers from central and state government to municipalities, (c) easing restrictions on borrowing by ULBs and regional authorities, (d) improving budgeting, accounting and financial reporting, (e) enhancing transparency and disclosure, (f) establishing a culture credit rating, (g) instituting mechanisms of investor protection, including bond assurance programmes and development of a secondary market, (h) visibly linking bonds to development projects that generate tax increments and (i) creating awareness amongst investors and the general public. The past guidelines of the GoI, making only bonds carrying interest rate up to a maximum of eight per cent interest per annum eligible for tax-free status are restrictive. There is need for flexibility in setting interest cap by linking it to a benchmark market rate.

The access of smaller municipalities to bonds may not be possible due to their poor finances. Thus, larger and more viable entities, that can pool risks and raise funds at lower costs, may be positioned to access the capital market on their behalf. Financial intermediaries, if structured well, can assist the smaller municipalities in: (a) value increment financing, (b) benefitting from long tenor funds and scale economies, (c) accessing credit enhancement mechanisms, (d) scientific costing of services, (e) adopting functional budgeting, fund-based accounting and good financial disclosure practices, (f) preparing capital budgets, (g) undertaking credit rating, (h) developing commercially viable projects, (i) entering into PPPs, (j) increasing capacity to plan, finance and manage projects and (k) participating in pooled financing bond issues.[12] Two noted examples of urban financial intermediaries in India are the TNUDF and the KUIDFC. Both TNUDF and KUIDFC have been successful in assisting small municipalities in accessing credit from the market through WSPF bonds.

The most critical reform for developing a vibrant municipal bonds market in India is to systematically promote credit-worthy cities with track record. The SEBI guidelines stipulate that the issuer's contribution for each project should be at least be 20 per cent of the project costs. This calls for municipalities substantially enhancing their revenue effort. It is apparent that in view of precarious cost recovery, most ULBs in the country may not be able to issue pure revenue bonds. Inelasticities in urban project-based revenues also suggest that the marketing of pure revenue bonds on a project-specific basis alone may also not be feasible. Thus, efforts are necessary to structure revenue bonds with general obligation covenants. The revenue-generation potential of projects financed and general revenues of the borrowing authority may supplement each other to improve the marketability of bonds. Further, credit enhancement and risk-mitigating mechanisms, including bond assurance programmes, would need to be instituted to satisfy investors regarding the application of their funds. All bond proceeds must be earmarked for projects that lead to visible improvements in local conditions and generate a steady stream of revenues. These measures can facilitate the structuring of bonds on a revenue-specific basis over time.

The fact that India could raise a meagre ₹13,531 crore through 23 municipal bonds over a period of 15 years suggests that the apprehension that such bonds would lead to fiscal deficit is not warranted. On the contrary, an all-out effort is needed to enable ULBs and regional authorities to enhance fiscal discipline, improve credit rating and issue Build India municipal bonds to accelerate growth and catalyse a self-financed process of planned urban development. Predictable long-term seed capital support from the centre, formula-based intergovernmental transfers for capital projects and dedicated investment funds can speed up the development of a vibrant municipal bonds market in India.

Importance of Good Governance

Good governance is perhaps the single most important factor for sustained financing of cities during India's structural transformation.[13] For good governance, both outcomes and processes matter. Without providing public services effectively and securing the goodwill of citizens, no strategy of urban public finance reforms will succeed. The fact that as against 1,345 urban infrastructure projects sanctioned under JNNURM over the seven-year mission period 2005–12, only 701 projects could be completed by August 2014 is a reflection on the deficient governance capacity of Indian cities.[14]

Key attributes of good governance include: rule of law, strategic vision, consensus orientation, efficiency, effectiveness, equity, transparency, accountability, responsibility, responsiveness and community participation. Outcomes and processes both matter. The good governance paradigm calls for strengthening governance institutions and organisations, and their human resource management systems. The effectiveness of an organisation in implementing the institutional mandate calls for the alignment of seven key elements: shared values, strategy, structure, system, style, staff and skills. Shared values represent long-term vision and guiding principles of an organisation. Strategy is the plan to allocate financial and non-financial resources, over time, to attain the organisational goals. Structure is the way organisational units connect to each other. System refers to routines, processes and procedures that the members in an organisation follow to get jobs done. Style is the culture of leadership adopted to pursue organisational goals. Staff represents employees and their general capabilities. Skill refers to acquired competencies of employees within the organisation as a whole. All these elements must be addressed holistically with an organisation development (OD) approach to make municipal organisations effective.

The lack of professional management is a critical factor plaguing service delivery in Indian cities. In addition to being politically empowered, the ULBs need to be equipped with professional cadres to manage portfolios such as general administration, legal, finance, accounts, public works, public health, urban planning, including transportation planning, parks and plantations, environmental conservation, sports, information technology and urban community development, including slum upgradation and poverty alleviation. Cadre development in ULBs needs to be accompanied by modernisation of municipal, town planning and urban development laws. In addition, service delivery systems in cities have to be simplified and made citizen-friendly. Corporatisation of utility services where beneficial, re-engineering of processes, rationalisation of budgeting, accounting, internal control and auditing systems, proactive disclosure of information under Section 4(1) of the Right to Information Act 2005 and institution of social accountability mechanisms, including social auditing of service delivery need to be pursued by municipalities. The use of e-governance and m-governance tools, including human resource, financial and public works management information systems, GIS, GPS, CAMA, e-procurement, online payment of taxes and utility bills, across-the-counter delivery of licenses, permits, certificates and other services can enhance municipal efficiency and reduce corruption.[15]

Good governance is critical for value increment financing of cities. For example, without improving project management, financial management and disclosure practices in municipalities, the issue of Build India municipal bonds with a TIF framework cannot be sustained. Capacity-building activities need to be pursued with consistency to address the endemic institutional, organisational and human resource constraints in ULBs. Political empowerment of municipalities and professionalisation of municipal management must go hand in hand. About 70,000 elected representatives are currently in position in cities. In several states, more than 50 per cent of them are women. The energy and enthusiasm of these representatives for their people must be harnessed.

Agenda for Urban Public Finance Reforms

The size of the municipal sector in India is not only small but also declining. International benchmarking suggests that the ratio of municipal expenditures to GDP should be enhanced from the present abysmal level of one per cent to five per cent by the time India reaches 50 per cent urban mark, about two per cent for capital expenditure and three per cent for O&M and debt-servicing.[16] This goal, which may be broken into five-year targets, calls for a conscious joint effort by central, state and local governments. The basic approach to reforming urban public finance in India should be to enhance the fiscal autonomy of municipalities and to enable them function as an effective 'third tier' of government. In this context, endowing them with 'local taxes', including a versatile alternative to octroi remains a critical unfinished task.

Both the Central and State Finance Commissions are mandated by the Constitution (74th Amendment) Act to recommend 'measures', including 'principles' to strengthen municipal finances. However, none has considered a suitable substitute for octroi so far. It is time that the central government takes a lead to work out a national consensus on the substitute for octroi. This tax was abolished by states in response to a national call to remove impediments to interstate trade and commerce. If a tax alternative to octroi cannot be agreed upon, the second-best choice is to enable ULBs to have a city GST rate within state GST rate or a statutory, formula-based share in state GST. This may be kept in view while deciding the central and state GST rates. In addition, the ULBs may be enabled to have access to the divisible pool of central taxes, including central GST to address vertical and horizontal imbalances and finance the ₹5.92 million crore expenditure needed for urban infrastructure and services by 2031.[17] The 15th Finance Commission may be explicitly assigned the task of recommending a formula-based share in the divisible pool of central taxes and grants-in-aid for municipalities and a new fiscal architecture for the third tier.

Considering the critical stakes involved, we suggest that a long-term national programme of urban public finance reforms be designed and pursued following certain broad principles: subsidiarity; internalisation of externalities; generalised benefit principle; golden rules of local public finance; revenue-expenditure linking; earmarked benefit taxes; formula-based intergovernmental transfers; creation, capture and recycling of urban values; and Build India tax-free municipal bonds rooted in a value increment financing framework. Our suggestions for the key elements of such a programme are as follows:[18]

Expenditure Assignment

1. The municipal functions listed in the 12th Schedule of the Constitution may be categorised into three broad groups as follows:
   (i) 'Essentially municipal' functions: urban planning including town planning; public health, sanitation, conservancy and solid waste management; provision of urban amenities and facilities such as parks, gardens and playgrounds; public amenities including street lighting, parking lots, bus stops and public conveniences; regulation of land use and construction of buildings; burials and burial grounds, cremations, cremation ghats/grounds and electric crematoria; cattle pounds, prevention of cruelty to animals; vital statistics including registration of births and deaths; regulation of slaughter houses and tanneries.

(ii) 'Agency' functions: safeguarding the interests of weaker sections of society, including the handicapped and mentally retarded; slum improvement and upgradation; urban poverty alleviation.

(iii) 'Shared' or 'concurrent' functions: planning for economic and social development; roads and bridges; water supply for domestic, industrial and commercial purposes; fire services; promotion of cultural, educational and aesthetic aspects; urban forestry, protection of the environment and promotion of ecological aspects.

Revenue Assignment

1. The following general rules may be followed in designing revenue assignment to municipalities relative to expenditure assignment:
   (i) the 'essentially municipal' functions be financed by user charges, service fees and other 'own' revenues, including benefit charges and benefit taxes;
   (ii) the 'agency' functions, by intergovernmental transfers, primarily based on centre–state partnerships with a small contribution by the municipality to induce 'ownership'; and
   (iii) the 'shared' functions, through a mix of user charges, benefit taxes and 'revenue-shared' taxes.
2. The size of the municipal sector in India is extremely small. It needs to be increased from one per cent of GDP to five per cent over a period of three to four decades based on a road map. Broadening the tax powers of municipalities, enabling them to have a predictable share in the benefit taxes levied by other tiers of government, enhancing municipal effort to levy user charges and benefit charges, and adopting borrowing as a key instrument to finance infrastructure are broad directions for reforms.

User Charges and Benefit Charges

1. As a rule, user charges should be directly levied on the recipients of 'measurable' services as first resort. Water supply being measurable and beneficiaries of water being identifiable, user charges should finance its O&M costs, with an element of cross-subsidisation

for the poor and an amount for recouping capital costs. A two-part tariff, with a fixed charge and a volumetric charge in an IBT framework may be appropriate.

2. In view of the close linkage between water use and sewage generation, sewerage charges may be hooked onto water charges. Similarly, storm water drainage charges may be levied as a percentage of water charges. Sewerage and drainage charges must cover O&M costs, a cross-subsidisation element and a part of capital costs.

3. While water tax, sewer tax and drainage tax components of property tax may be replaced by user charges, specific benefit taxes such as water benefit tax and sewerage benefit tax, practiced in Mumbai, may be adopted and earmarked towards servicing of debt to finance the capital costs of water, sewer and drainage projects.

4. Solid waste management may be financed on PAYT principle, with households paying door-to-door collection charges and bulk garbage generators like hotels, functions halls, markets, hospitals and so on paying bulk garbage collection charges. Tipping fees may also be imposed for recovering the cost of waste disposal through sanitary landfill sites and other acceptable mechanisms. As collections may not be sufficient in view of the free-rider problems, a conservancy tax may be levied on property as a specific benefit tax.

5. The O&M costs of municipal roads may be met through a street tax on property as a specific benefit tax. A part of state motor vehicles and fuel taxes may be shared with municipalities and dedicated towards public transportation improvement projects, including mass rapid transit or bus rapid transit.

6. The O&M and capital costs of street lighting may be met through a cess on the consumption of electricity as in Rajasthan or a specific street lighting benefit tax on property. Delhi and Cape Town offer examples of a tax on the consumption or sale of electricity.

7. The O&M and capital costs of fire services may be met by a fire tax levied on property as a specific benefit tax.

8. Users pay, beneficiaries pay, polluters pay, exacerbaters pay, congesters pay and growth pays may be adopted as key principles of city financing. Special assessments, planning and infrastructure betterment levies, development charges, impact fees, floor space index charges, auctionable development rights and so on can be pooled into a dedicated fund to repay debt incurred to finance urban and regional infrastructure.

Land and Property Taxes

1. Land-based taxes were exploited by developed countries to develop cities during their urban transition; India may adopt the same practice. LVT and LVIT offer a significant opportunity to raise resources for financing city infrastructure during India's structural transformation.

2. Property tax may be levied separately on land and built-up property, adopting a split- rate approach: one rate for land and another rate for building. The land tax will enable cities to gain access to their increasing land values, arising due to agglomeration economies and growth. The building tax may be linked to the consumption of collective local services.

3. As the built-up area of property, taking into account building and use characteristics, is a good proxy for consumption of non-measurable services, specific benefit taxes may be levied as a composite city services tax on building based on UAM. The tax may be levied on owner of property, who could be legally empowered to recover it from tenants.

4. The UAM is particularly suitable for residential properties that are easily divided into homogeneous groups. For highly heterogeneous non-residential properties, the principle of 'averaging' inherent in the UAM makes the unit area tax regressive, apart from foregoing taxes legitimately due from high value properties. Thus, utmost care should be taken to classify non-residential properties.

5. The land or general tax component of property tax may be levied as a graduated land value tax, based on the capital value of land.

6. Vacant land may be taxed at a higher rate compared to built-up property to promote land development, including housing. VLT may be a progressive land value tax, with tax rate increasing with the time period land is held idle, as in Brazil. A VLT rate of 0.2 to 0.5 per cent may be adopted, to start with, following the practice in Andhra Pradesh and Telangana. For calculating VLT, the ready reckoner value of land may be adopted.

7. Efforts may be initiated by larger cities to shift the base of property tax to capital value of land and buildings to benefit from the ongoing increases in real estate values due to urbanisation, agglomeration externalities and economic growth. The UAV method, followed by Bengaluru Municipal Corporation with GIS-mapping of properties is worth emulating.

8. A city real estate transfer tax may be considered for being levied on the seller subject to appropriate deductions under the capital gains component of income tax. This will require an amendment to the Income Tax Act.

9. The land tax component of property tax, vacant land tax and real estate transfer tax may be escrowed to 'leverage' debt for infrastructure projects like public transit, leading to increased land values to owners and making way for further resource mobilisation on the benefit principle.

Taxation of Government Properties

1. Central government properties may pay, by law, service charges following the GoI circulars of 1954, 1967, 1976 and 1985 in view of the Supreme Court judgment in Rajkot Municipal Corporation case.[19] Properties that avail all municipal services may pay 75 per cent of the tax payable by similar private properties. As there may not be any central government property which does not avail a municipal service, such as access to city airport, railway station, parks, water supply, sewerage and storm drainage systems, the minimum service charges payable by a central government property may be fixed at 50 per cent.

2. Properties of state governments and central and state government undertakings do not enjoy the immunity granted by Article 285 of the Constitution in view of the Supreme Court judgment in Dum Dum Municipality case.[20] Thus, they should be made to pay property taxes as applicable to similar private properties with pre-identified entries in their budgets.

Access to Other Benefit Taxes

1. Apart from land and property taxes, municipalities may be endowed with other local benefit taxes that include entertainment tax, advertisement tax, business licensing tax, utility user taxes and profession tax. State motor vehicles and motor fuel taxes may be shared with ULBs, based on a pre-determined formula. The

shared revenues may be earmarked for city and regional transport, including rail-based transit and ring roads.

2. Taxes like income tax, service tax, excise tax, value added tax and goods and services tax are general benefit taxes on the living, working and shopping in the city. Thus, the principle of 'piggy-back' local option taxes ought to be recognised by policymakers and planners. However, as 'piggybacking' may not be feasible in the present context of India's fiscal federalism, a statutory city GST rate within state GST rate or a formula-based statutory share in state GST is desirable. This aspect may be kept in mind while determining central and state GST rates.

Compensating for Octroi and Other Taxes

1. The revenues that could have accrued to ULBs had octroi not been abolished or 'local' taxes not taken over by state governments over the years or subsumed under GST should be the baseline to arrive at city GST rate. International practice in multi-tier countries (for example, Brazil, China and Nigeria) suggests that a city GST rate equal to 25 per cent of state GST rate may be appropriate.[21] Alternatively, the ULBs may have a statutory share in state GST, at 25 per cent to start with. Further, they may be enabled to have a share in the divisible pool of central taxes, including central GST through the Central Finance Commission route.

Municipal Finance List

1. The Constitution of India may be amended to include a 'municipal finance list' corresponding to the 12th Schedule. This may include: property tax, land value tax, land use conversion tax, profession tax, payroll tax, business licensing tax, advertisement tax, entertainment tax, utility user taxes, carbon tax, a statutory share in motor vehicles tax, motor fuel tax, transfer of property tax/stamp duty and mining royalties, city GST or a statutory share of municipalities in state GST, user charges, benefit charges including FSI charges, betterment charges, development charges and impact fees.

Design of Inter-governmental Transfers

1. Fiscal transfers to ULBs need to be designed to correct vertical and horizontal imbalances and inter-jurisdictional spillovers, provide merit goods, discharge redistributive functions and facilitate investment in core urban and regional infrastructure. The criteria of fiscal needs, fiscal capacity and fiscal effort should be integrated into the transfer design, while promoting a hard budget constraint for ULBs.

2. Both SFCs and CFC may be required to consider a formula-based devolution of revenues from the relevant taxes or divisible pools to ensure adequacy, objectivity and predictability of transfers to ULBs.

3. Income tax being an ideal tax to support redistributive functions, urban poverty alleviation, slum development and provision of basic services to the urban poor may be financed by the centre through long-term centre–state–local partnerships and implemented by municipalities.

4. National motor vehicle and fuel taxes, apart from being available for highways, may also be dedicated to public transit through a special account as in the United States. Suitable schemes with matching support from state and city governments may be designed to execute public transit projects that have a long gestation period.

5. Fiscal autonomy cannot be built in a culture of grants. Thus, municipalities must to be incentivised to rely progressively on 'own' taxes and charges. They may be enabled to adopt land value taxation, users pay, beneficiaries pay, polluters pay, congesters pay, growth pays, value-capture financing and bond instruments.

6. The requirement of funds for urban infrastructure being colossal, there is need for a system of reform-linked capital grants to ULBs to 'leverage' the vast pool of long tenor funds for their investment programmes. These grants may be linked to Build India municipal bonds rooted in a value increment financing framework.

7. India may aim at a transfer-GDP ratio of three per cent for municipalities by the time the country reaches the 50 per cent urban mark—one per cent through central channels and two per cent through state channels, including city GST rate within state GST rate or a formula-based share in state GST.

Financing of Urban Infrastructure

1. Development financing mechanisms, being bankable and often self-paying, must be fully explored. Land assembly models such as town planning scheme in Gujarat and land-pooling with farmers as shareholders in Magarpatta need to be applied throughout India. A robust legal framework is necessary to replicate these models. Other development financing instruments include developer exactions and impact fees (United States), developer contributions (Australia) and planning obligations (United Kingdom).

2. Value capture financing instruments, including TIF must be promoted in a big way. These include land value tax and land value increment tax (Taiwan), site value tax (Australia), windfall tax (Ireland), comprehensive land holding tax (Korea), betterment levy (*Participacion en Plusvalias*: Colombia and *Contrubuciones de Mejoras*, Argentina), floor space index charges (*Outorga Onerosa do Direito de Construir*, Sao Paulo), auctioning of development rights (*Certificados de Potencial Adicional de Construcao*, Sao Paulo) and land monetisation (Mumbai Metropolitan Regional Development Authority, Bandra Kurla Complex).

3. Borrowing is the only practical way to meet the colossal needs of urban and regional infrastructure in India. Taxation, development financing and value capture tools need to be combined with debt and equity funding mechanisms, including revolving loan, seed capital, venture capital and mezzanine funds, tax credits, loan guarantees, municipal bonds, pooled finance bonds, green bonds, bond banks, financial intermediation, infrastructure investment funds, etc.

4. Well-structured special purpose vehicles involving the local body, other tiers of government and private sector partners to effectively plan, design, borrow, implement and repay debt for infrastructure projects with ring-fenced revenues need to be promoted.[22]

5. There is need for all-out effort to promote municipal bonds in India as in the United States. These may be linked to project revenues supplemented by land value taxation, development financing and value increment financing, and dedicated funds. The structuring of these bonds with escrowing mechanism, credit enhancement, underwriting facility and so on is important. While the recent guidelines by SEBI refer to 'revenue bonds', municipalities would also need to be enabled to issue 'general obligation bonds'. However, the baseline is to put in place a robust

system of urban public finance that facilitates the emergence of credit-worthy municipalities. Smart cities require smart ways to finance, built on the right fundamentals.

Data, Research and Capacity Building

1. Data problems relating municipal services and finances, which have prevented five successive CFCs and many SFCs from recommending concrete measures to strengthen municipal finances, must be addressed.
2. The state of research on urban issues, including urban public finance, is dismal. There is need to invest in research in urban economics, land economics, urban public finance, including benefit taxation and value increment financing, urban management and inclusive city development strategy.
3. Governance cuts across all reforms in financing cities. The issues of political empowerment, professionalisation of cadres, and institutional and human resource capacity-building in municipalities need to be addressed through a comprehensive, long-range strategy rather than scheme-linked programmes as at present.

A Case for Cooperative Federalism

Experience with TIF suggests that the benefits of planned urban development do not confine to value increments for local government alone. Facilitated by externalities, they manifest in higher income tax, goods and services tax, business tax, property transfer tax, motor vehicles tax and other revenues in cities. Thus, both central and state governments gain from a TIF regime through increased revenues, apart from growth, employment, socio-economic regeneration of derelict areas, public safety improvement, etc. In a 'status quo' or 'no TIF' scenario, no authority stands to gain. On the contrary, when a TIF is implemented well, all the tiers of government reap substantial fiscal and non-fiscal benefits. Thus, a revenue-sharing partnership between them to repay TIF debt is justified based on the generalised benefit principle. The case for partnering with and supporting cities lies in the vast spillover effects they create.

Due to the limitations of fiscal federalism, local and regional authorities engaged in value-creating ventures in an urban area, such as a ring road, a mass rapid transit system, a knowledge hub, an international financial district or a city-wide slum development programme, may not be able to internalise the benefits generated by their efforts. This is because they may not have the necessary fiscal instruments authorised to them under the Constitution or law. Thus, inter-jurisdictional partnerships beyond the traditional inter se distribution of functions and finances between tiers of government are inevitable. When central, state and local governments cooperate in value increment financing of cities, a self-financed process of planned urban development can be engineered with debt secured through bonds and other instruments. The private sector can play a key role in this scheme, contributing expertise and resources. The country needs a model of city financing that integrates regional and urban planning, local economic development, land management, infrastructure creation, service delivery, municipal taxation including land value taxation, development financing, value capture and recycling, revenue sharing, and intergovernmental and public–private partnerships.

As India faces a resource crunch to meet the concerns of development, there is a need to search for investments that cost less but bring more dividends through multiplier effects. At this stage of the country's transformation, cities present opportunities for such investments. They create growth and public finance by catalysing agglomeration, knowledge and infrastructure externalities, and promoting circular and cumulative causation processes. However, these externalities spill over the constitutional boundaries of revenue assignment. Thus, a cooperative federalism framework is warranted. This will also enable India to compete for an increasing share of global growth. It will power the country to address the concerns of development, including rural development. The bottom line is to catalyse agglomeration-augmenting, congestion-mitigating, resource-generating, credit-worthy and bankable cities, which subscribe to the 'generalised benefit principle', embrace the 'golden rules' of urban public finance and adopt 'users pay', 'beneficiaries pay', 'polluter pay', 'exacerbaters pay', 'congesters pay' and 'growth pays' instruments. These cities and special purpose vehicles representing partnerships between various levels of governments and the private sector need to be prepared to issue Build India municipal bonds grounded in value increment financing. Good urban governance lies at the heart of this paradigm.

Notes

1. Affordable housing has been in the agenda of central and state governments in India. The GoI, after implementing BSUP and IHSDP under the JNNURM, has recently launched a new programme of affordable housing for all by 2022 through Pradhan Mantri Awas Yojana (PMAY). This book does not specifically address the financing of affordable housing.
2. Municipalities in India are required by law to balance their budgets.
3. The figures are based on author's estimates using data submitted by state governments to the 14th Finance Commission, ASCI (2014) and *Indian Public Finance Statistics 2013–14*.
4. Based on data furnished by state governments to the 14th Finance Commission of India, ASCI (2014).
5. Figures for India pertain to finances of municipalities. Those for OECD countries, which are predominantly urban, are for local bodies.
6. Includes both three-tier (federal) and two-tier (unitary) countries.
7. The Municipal Corporation of Greater Mumbai has set an octroi collection target of ₹7,900 crore for 2015–16.
8. Attributed to Robert Metcalfe, the co-inventor of Ethernet.
9. In theory, local option taxes on income, business, excise, sales, value added and goods and services are regarded as general benefit taxes levied on the living, working and shopping in the city.
10. Overall tax-GDP ratio in OECD countries increased from 24.8 per cent in 1965 to 33.7 per cent in 2012.
11. US Securities and Exchange Commission: *The State the Municipal Securities Market*. See https://www.sec.gov/spotlight/muniicpal securities.shtml (accessed on 30 March 2015).
12. The larger municipal corporations and utilities can themselves access the market for funds directly based on their own credit rating. They could also assist smaller municipalities by making them partners in bond issues to finance regional infrastructure projects such as rapid transit, water supply and sewerage.
13. See Mohanty (2014) for a discussion on the key issues of urban governance.
14. Figures are based on Lok Sabha Secretariat (2015). This report informs that as against the central grant of ₹100,000 crore initially envisaged and ₹66,085 crore subsequently committed, only ₹40,484 crore could be released by the end of the mission period 2015–12.
15. Electronic governance and mobile governance are successfully used by municipal corporations such as Hyderabad and Bengaluru to deliver services.
16. May comprise of one per cent devolution through central channel, two per cent devolution through state channel (including statutory city GST rate within state GST rate or formula-based share in state GST) and two per cent urban local bodies own revenues.
17. Projected by HPEC (2011).
18. The reader may refer to the earlier chapters for justification behind these suggestions.

19. Supreme Court judgment dated 19 November 2009 in *Civil Appeal No.9458-63/2003:Rajkot Municipal Corporation and Others Vs. Union of India and Others.*

20. Supreme Court judgment in *Municipal Commissioner of Dum Dum Municipality and Others Vs. India Tourism Development Corporation and Others (1995) 5 SCC 251.*

21. In Brazil, local authorities receive 22.5 per cent share in federal income tax and are provided with an equal share in federal value added tax on manufactured goods. In Nigeria, 35 per cent revenue from VAT is assigned to local governments. In China, cities are allowed to retain 25 per cent of VAT.

22. UDICs have been the central pillars to build core urban infrastructure projects in China.

Bibliography

Advisory Commission on Intergovernmental Relations (ACIR). 1962. *Measures of State and Local Fiscal Capacity and Tax Effort*. Report No. M-16. Washington, D.C.: GPO.

——. 1993. *State Laws Governing Local Government Structure and Administration*. Washington, D.C.: US ACIR.

Afonso, J. R. and E. A. Araujo. 2006. 'Local Government Organisation and Finance: Brazil'. In *Local Governance in Developing Countries*, edited by Anwar Shah. Washington, D.C.: The World Bank.

Agrawal, O. P. 2006. 'Urban Transport'. In *Indian Infrastructure Report 2006, 3i Network*, New Delhi: Oxford University Press.

Ahluwalia, Isher, R. Kanbur and P. K. Mohanty. 2014. *Challenges of Urbanisation in India*. New Delhi: SAGE Publications.

Alam, Munawwar. ed. 2014. *Intergovernmental Fiscal Transfers in Developing Countries: Case Studies from the Commonwealth*. London: Commonwealth Secretariat.

American Planning Association. 2002. *How Cities Use Parks for Economic Development*. City Parks Forum Briefing Papers. Chicago.

Andelson, Robert V., ed. 2000. *Land-value Taxation Around the World*. Malden, MA: Blackwell.

Anderson, John E. 2009. 'A Review of the Evidence on Land Value Taxation'. In *Land Value Taxation: Theory, Evidence, and Practice*, edited by Richard F. Dye and Richard W. England. Cambridge, MA: Lincoln Institute of Land Policy.

Andersson, Fredrik and Rikard Forslid. 2003. 'Tax Competition and Economic Geography'. *Journal of Public Economic Theory*, 5 (2): 279–303.

Annez, P. and G. Peterson. 2007. *Financing Cities: Fiscal Responsibility and Urban Infrastructure in Brazil, China, India, Poland and South Africa*. Thousand Oaks, CA: SAGE Publications.

Aschauer, David Alan. 1989. 'Is Public Expenditure Productive?' *Journal of Monetary Economics*, 23: 177–200.

ASCI, Administrative Staff College of India. 2014. *Municipal Finances and Service Delivery in India: A Study Sponsored by the Fourteenth Finance Commission*, Government of India, ASCI, Hyderabad.

Au, Chun-Chung and J. Vernon Henderson. 2006a. 'Are Chinese Cities Too Small?' *Review of Economic Studies*, 73 (3): 549–76.

——. 2006b. 'How Migration Restrictions Limit Agglomeration and Productivity in China'. *Journal of Development Economics*, 80 (2): 350–88.

Bahl, Roy. 2000. *Inter-governmental Transfers in Developing and Transition Countries: Principles and Practice*. Washington, D.C.: The World Bank.

——. 2001. 'Fiscal Decentralization, Revenue Assignment, and the Case for the Property Tax in South Africa'. International Studies Program Working Paper Series, GSU Paper No. 0107, Andrew Young School of Policy Studies, Georgia State University.

Bahl, Roy. 2008. 'Opportunities and Risks of Fiscal Decentralization: A Developing Country Perspective'. In *Achieving Decentralization Objectives*, edited by Gregory Ingram. Cambridge, MA: Lincoln Institute of Land Policy.

———. Financing Metropolitan Areas. In: United Cities and Local Governments (UCLG) ed. *Local Government Finance: The Challenges of the 21ˢᵗ Century*. Cheltenham, U.K.: Edward Elgar.

———. 2013. 'The Decentralization of Governance in Metropolitan Areas'. In *Financing Metropolitan Governments in Developing Countries*, edited by Roy W. Bahl, Johannes F. Linn and Deborah L. Wetzel. Cambridge, MA: Lincoln Institute of Land Policy.

Bahl, Roy and Johannes Linn. 1992. *Urban Public Finance in Developing Countries*. New York: Oxford University Press.

———. 2014. *Governing and Financing Cities in the Developing World*. Cambridge, MA: Lincoln Institute of Land Policy.

Bahl, Roy W., Johannes F. Linn, and Deborah L. Wetzel. 2013. 'Governing and Financing Metropolitan Areas in the Developing World'. In *Financing Metropolitan Governments in Developing Countries*. Cambridge, MA: Lincoln Institute of Land Policy.

Bahl, Roy and Jorge Martinez-Vazquez. 2008. 'The Property Tax in Developing Countries: Current Practice and Prospects'. In: Roy Bahl, Jorge Martinex-Vazquez and Joan Youngman eds. *Making the Property Tax Work: Experiences in Developing and Transitional Countries*, Cambridge, MA: Lincoln Institute of Land Policy.

Bahl, Roy, Jorge Martinez-Vazquez and Joan Youngman (eds). 2008. *Making the Property Tax Work: Experiences in Developing and Transitional Countries*. Cambridge, MA: Lincoln Institute of Land Policy.

Bahl, Roy and Richard Bird. (Winter) 2008. 'Subnational Taxes in Developing Countries: The Way Forward', *Public Budgeting and Finance*, 28 (4): 1–25.

Bahl, Roy and Sally Wallace. 2005. 'Public Financing in Developing and Transition Countries'. *Public Budgeting & Finance*, Silver Anniversary Issue: 83–98.

Bailey, Stephen. 1999. *Local Government Economics: Theory, Policy and Practice*. Basingstoke, U K.: McMillan.

Baldwin, Richard E., Rikard Forslid, Philippe Martin, Gianmarco Ottaviano and Frederic Robert-Nicoud. 2003. *Economic Geography and Public Policy*. Princeton: University Press.

Baldwin, Richard, and Paul Krugman. 2004. 'Agglomeration, Integration and Tax Harmonization'. *European Economic Review*, 48 (1): 1–23.

Ballaney, Shirley. 2008. *The Town Planning Mechanism in Gujarat, India*. Washington, D.C.: World Bank Institute.

Barker, Kate. 2004. *Review of Housing Supply*. London: Her Majesty's Treasury.

———. 2006. *Review of Land Use Planning*. London: Her Majesty's Treasury.

Barter, Paul. 2010. 'Parking Policy in Asian Cities'. Paper No. Lkyssp, 10–15. Singapore: Lee Kuan Yew School of Public Policy, National University of Singapore.

Becken, Susanne, Nicole Garofano, Char-Lee McLennan, Stewart Moore, Raj Rajan, and Melinda Watt. 2014. *From Challenges to Solutions: 2nd White Paper on Tourism and Water: Providing the Business Case*. Griffith Institute of Tourism Research Report Series, Report No.1, Griffith University. Available at: griiﬁth.edu.au/grifﬁth-institute-tourism (accessed on 18 December 2015).

Beckhard, R. 1969. *Organization Development: Strategies and Models*. Reading, MA: Addison–Wesley.

Beckman, M. J. 1976. 'Spatial Equilibrium in the Dispersed City'. In *Mathematical Land Use Theory*, edited by Y. Y. Papageorgiou, 117–125. Lexington, MA: Lexington Books.

Beevers, Sean D. and David C. Carslaw. 2005. 'The Impact of Congestion Charging on Vehicle Emissions in London'. *Atmospheric Environment*, 39: 1–5, Elsevier.

Bell, Michael. 2011. *Implementing Local Property Tax when there is no Market: The Case of Commonly Owned Land in Rural South Africa*, George Washington Institute of Public Policy, January 2011: reported in Norregaard, John. 2013. 'Taxing Immovable Property: Revenue Potential and Implementation Challenges'. IMF Working Paper No. WP/13/129. Washington, D.C.: International Monetary Fund.

Bianco, M. 2000. 'Effective Transportation Demand Management: Combining Parking Pricing, Transit Incentives, and Transportation Management in a Commercial District of Portland, Oregon'. *Journal of the Transportation Research Board*, 1711: 46–54. Transportation Research Board, Washington, D.C.

Bird, Richard M. 1992. *Tax Policy and Economic Development*. Baltimore: Johns Hopkins University Press.

———. 1994. 'Financing Local Services: Patterns, Problems and Possibilities'. Paper prepared for Global Report on Human Settlements, UN-HABITAT.

———. 2000. 'Rethinking Subnational Taxes: A New Look at Tax Assignment'. *Tax Notes International* 20, May 8: 2069–96.

———. 2003. A New Look at Local Business Taxes. *Tax Notes International* 30 (7): 695–711.

———. 2005. 'Getting it Right: Financing Urban Development in China'. *Asia-Pacific Tax Bulletin*, 11 (2): 107–17.

———. 2006. 'Fiscal Flows, Fiscal Balance and Fiscal Sustainability'. In *Perspectives on Fiscal Federalism*, edited by R. M. Bird and F. Vaillancourt, 81–97.Washington, D.C.: The World Bank.

———. 2008. 'Tax Assignment Revisited'. International Studies Program Working Paper No. 08-05, Andrew Young School of Policy Studies, Georgia State University, December 2008.

———. 2010a. 'Subnational Taxation in Emerging Countries: Lessons from the Literature'. Policy Research Working Paper No. WPS5450, The World Bank.

———. 2010b. *Local Government Finance: Trends and Questions*, Institute for Municipal Finance and Governance, University of Toronto.

———. 2012. Fiscal Decentralisation in Columbia: A Work (Still) in Progress. Andrew Young School of Policy Studies, International Center for Public Policy, Working Paper 12–13, Georgia State University: Atlanta.

Bird, Richard M. and Enid Slack. 1991. 'Financing Local Government in OECD Countries: The Role of Taxes and User Charges'. In *Local Government: An International Perspective*, edited by Jeffrey Owens and Giorgio Panella. Amsterdam: North–Holland.

———. 2004. *International Handbook of Land and Property Taxation*. Cheltenham, UK: Edward Elgar Publication.

———. 'Metropolitan Public Finance: An Overview'. In *Financing Metropolitan Governments in Developing Countries* edited by Roy W. Bahl, Johannes F. Linn and Deborah L. Wetzel. Cambridge, MA: Lincoln Institute of Land Policy.

Bird, Richard M. and Michael Smart. 2002. 'Intergovernmental Fiscal Transfers: International Lessons for Developing Countries'. World Development, 30 (6): 899–912.

———. 2010. 'Assigning State Taxes in a Federal Country: The Case of Australia'. In *Australia's Future Tax and Transfer Policy Conference*. Melbourne: Melbourne Institute of Applied Economic and Social Research, 72–94.

Bird R. and P. P. Gendron. 2001. 'VATs in Federal Countries: International Experience and Emerging Possibilities', *Bulletin for International Fiscal Documentation*, 293–309.

Bird, Richard M. and O. Oldman. 1990. *Taxation in Developing Countries*, 4th ed. Baltimore: Johns Hopkins University Press.

Bird, M. Richard and Thomas Tsiopoulos. 1997. 'User Charges for Public Services: Potentials and Problems'. *Canadian Tax Journal*, Volume 45 (1): 25–86.

Boadway, Robin and Anwar Shah, eds. 2007. *Intergovernmental Fiscal Transfers: Principles and Practice*. Public Sector Governance and Accountability Series. Washington, D.C.: The World Bank.

Boadway, Robin and Frank Flatters. 1982. 'Efficiency and Equalisation Payments in a Federal System of Government: A Synthesis and Extension of Recent Results'. *The Canadian Journal of Economics*, 15 (4): 613–33.

Boadway, Robin, Sandra Roberts, and Anwar Shah. 2000. 'Fiscal Federalism: Dimensions of Tax Reform in Developing Countries'. Policy Research Working Paper Series No. 1385. Washington, D.C.: The World Bank.

Borck, Rainald, and Michaei Pfluger. 2006. 'Agglomeration and Tax Competition'. *European Economic Review*, 50 (3): 647–68.

Borrero, O., E. Duran, J. Hernandez and M. Montana. 2011. 'Evaluating the Practice of Betterment Levies in Colombia: The Experience of Bogota and Manizales'. Working Paper. Cambridge, MA: Lincoln Institute of Land Policy.

Bourassa, Steven C. 2009. 'United States Experience with Land Value Taxation'. In *Land Value Taxation: Theory, Evidence, and Practice*, edited by Richard F. Dye and Richard W. England. Cambridge, MA: Lincoln Institute of Land Policy.

Breton, A. 1996. *Competitive Governments*. Cambridge: Cambridge University Press

Brulhart, Marius and Federca Sbergami. 2009. 'Agglomeration and Growth: Cross-Country Evidence'. *Journal of Urban Economics*, 65 (1): 48–63.

Bruno, Robert and Alison Dickson Quesada. 2011. 'Tax Increment Financing and Chicago Public Schools: A New Approach to Comprehending a Complex Relationship'. Labor Education Program White Paper, University of Illinois at Urbana-Champaign. Available at: www.illinoislabored@illinois.edu (accessed on 19 April 2015).

Buchanan, J.M. 1950. 'Federalism and Fiscal Equity'. *American Economic Review*, 40 (4) (September): 421–32.

———. 1963. 'The Economics of Earmarked Taxes'. *Journal of Political Economy*, 71: 457–69.

———. 1965. 'An Economic Theory of Clubs'. *Economica*, 32: 1–14.

———. 1967. *Public Finance in Democratic Process*. Chapel Hill: University of North Carolina Press.

Buckley, Robert. 2005. *Macro Linkages with Municipal Finance: An Overview*. Available at: http://www.world Bank.org/uicconference (accessed on 5 October 2014).

Caltrans, California Department of Transportation. 2011. *2010–11 Caltrans Annual Report*.

Census of India 1991, 2001, 2011, Office of the Registrar General. New Delhi: Government of India.

Cervero, Robert and Jin Murakami. 2008. 'Rail + Property Development: A Model of Sustainable Transport Finance and Urbanism'. Working Paper No. UCB-ITS-VWP-2008-5, UC Berkeley Center for Future Urban Transport.

———. 2009. 'Rail and Property Development in Hong Kong: Experiences and Extensions'. *Urban Studies*, 46 (10): 2019–43.

Cervero, R. and M. Duncan. 2002. *Land Value Impacts of Rail Transit Services in Los Angeles County*. Report Prepared for the National Association of Realtors, Urban Land Institute. Available at: https://drcog.org/documents/todvaluelosangeles.pdf (accessed on 15 January 2016).

Chen, Yang. 2008. 'Urban Agglomeration Policy in China'. Background Note for the World Development Report 2009, Washington DC: World Bank.

Chitiga-Mabugu, Margaret and Nara Monkam. 2013. 'Assessing Fiscal Capacity at the Local Government Level in South Africa'. Working Paper No. 2013-76, University of Pretoria, Department of Economics.

Citizens Budget Commission. 2015. *A Better Way to Pay for Solid Waste Management.* New York.

Council of Europe. 15 October 1985. 'European Charter of Local Self-Government'. European Treaty Series 122: Local Self-Government, Strasbourg.

———. 2010. *European Charter of Local Self-Government.* Strasbourg: Council of Europe Publishing.

Central Pollution Control Board (CPCB). 2009. 'Status of Water Supply, Wastewater Generation and Treatment in Class-I Cities and Class-II Towns of India'. Control of Urban Pollution Series: CUP/70/2009-10. Delhi: CPCB

Crompton, J. L. 2001a. 'The Impact of Parks on Property Values: A Review of the Empirical Evidence'. *Journal of Leisure Research,* 33 (1): 1-31.

———. 2001b. 'Perceptions of How the Presence of Greenway Trails Affects the Value of Proximate Properties'. *Journal of Park and Recreation Administration,* 19 (3): 33-51.

———. 2004. *The Proximate Principle: The Impact of Parks, Open Space and Water Features on Residential Property Values and the Property Tax Base.* Ashburn, VA: National Recreation and Park Association.

Crozet, M., and P. Koenig. 2007. 'The Cohesion vs Growth Tradeoff: Evidence from EU Regions'. Working Paper, University of Paris (ERSA Conference Paper No. ersa05p716, European Regional Science Association).

Danish Ministry of the Environment. 2007. *Spatial Planning in Denmark.* Copenhagen: Agency for Spatial and Environmental Planning. Available at: www.blst.dk (accessed on 11 December 2015).

Dasgupta, M., R. Oldfield, K. Sharman and V. Webster. 1994. 'Impact of Transport Policies in Five Cities'. Project Report No.107, Transport Research Laboratory, Crowthome, Berkshire.

Davis, Kingsley. 1962. 'Urbanisation in India—Past and Future'. In *India's Urban Future,* edited by R. Turner. Berkley: University of California Press.

———. 1965. 'The Urbanization of the Human Population'. *Scientific American,* 213 (3): 41-53

Dekle, Robert, and Jonathan Eaton. 1999. 'Agglomeration and Land Rents: Evidence from the Prefectures'. *Journal of Urban Economics,* 46 (2): 200-14.

Ding, Changri and Xingshuo Zhao. 2012. 'Urbanisation in Japan, South Korea and China'. In Nancy Brooks, Kieran Donaghy and Gerrit-Jan Knapp (eds), *The Oxford Handbook of Urban Economics and Planning,* Oxford: Oxford University Press.

Ding, Chengri. 2005. 'Property Tax Development in China'. *Land Lines,* 17 (3): 8-11.

Dolan vs. City of Tigard, Oregon 1994. Supreme Court of the United States No. 93-518 (June 24, 1994).

Duranton, Gilles and Diego Puga. 2004. 'Micro-Foundations of Urban Agglomeration Economies'. In *Handbook of Urban and Regional Economies, Vol. 4,* edited by J. Vernon Henderson and Jacque Thisse. Amsterdam: North-Holland.

Duranton, Gilles and Mathew A. Turner. 2012. 'Urban Growth and Transportation'. *Review of Economic Studies* 79 (4): 1407-40.

Dye, Richard F. and Richard W. England. 2010. *Assessing the Theory and Practice of Land Value Taxation.* Cambridge, MA: Lincoln Institute of Land Policy.

Easterly, W. and S. Rebelo. 1993. 'Fiscal Policy and Economic Growth'. *Journal of Monetary Economics*, 32 (3): 417–58.

———. 2002. 'House prices Going through the Roof'. *The Economist*, 354 (8157):

Epple, D., B. Gordon, and Holder Sieg. 2010. 'A New Approach to Estimating the Production Function for Housing'. *American Economic Review*, 100 (June): 905–24.

Farvacque-Vitkovic, Catherine, and Mihaly Kopanyi, eds. 2014. *Municipal Finances: A Handbook for Local Governments*, The World Bank.

Fensham, P. and B. Gleeson. 2003. 'Capturing Value for Urban Management: A New Agenda for Betterment'. *Urban Policy and Research*, 21 (1): 93–112.

Finance Commission of India, Government of India. 1995. *Report of the Tenth Finance Commission*, Government of India, New Delhi.

———. 2000. *Report of the Eleventh Finance Commission*, Government of India, New Delhi.

———. 2005. *Report of the Twelfth Finance Commission*, Government of India, New Delhi.

———. 2009. *Report of the Thirteenth Finance Commission*, Government of India, New Delhi.

———. 2015. *Report of the Fourteenth Finance Commission*, Government of India, New Delhi.

Fox, William F. and Enid Slack. 2010. 'Local Public Finance in North America'. In *Local Government Finance: The Challenge of the 21st Century*, edited by United Cities and Local Governments. Cheltenham, UK: Edward Elgar.

Franzsen, Riel, and William J. McCluskey. 2008. 'The Feasibility of Site Value Taxation'. In *Making the Property Tax Work: Experiences in Developing and Transitional Countries*, edited by Roy W. Bahl, Jorge Martinez-Vazquez and Joan Youngman, 268–306. Cambridge, MA: Lincoln Institute of Land Policy.

Freire, Maria E. 1913. 'Slum Upgrading'. In *Financing Metropolitan Governments in Developing Countries*, edited by Roy W. Bahl, Johannes F. Linn and Deborah L. Wetzel. Cambridge, MA: Lincoln Institute of Land Policy.

Freire, Maria Emilia and Hernando Garzon. 2014. Managing Local Revenues. In *Municipal Finances: A Handbook for Local Governments*, edited by Farvacque-Vitkovic and Mihaly Kopanyi. Washington, D.C: The World Bank.

Fujita, Masahisa and Jacques-Francois Thisse. 2002. *Economics of Agglomeration: Cities, Industrial Location, and Regional Growth*. Cambridge: Cambridge University Press.

Fujita, Masahisa, Paul Krugman, and Anthony J. Venables. 1999. *The Spatial Economy: Cities, Regions, and International Economy*. Cambridge, MA: MIT Press.

Gaffney, M. 1994. Land as a Distinctive Factor of Production. In Land and Taxation, edited by N. Tideman. London: Shepherd-Welwyn.

George, Henry. 1897. *The Science of Political Economy*. New York: Doubleday & McClure Co.

George, Henry. 1962. *Progress and Poverty*. (Original ed. 1879, Centenary ed. 1979). New York: Robert Schalkenbach Foundation.

Gill, Indermit, and Homi Kharas. 2007. *An East Asia Renaissance: Ideas for Economic Growth*. Washington, D.C.: World Bank.

Glaeser, Edward L. and Joshua D. Gottlieb. 2009. 'The Wealth of Cities: Agglomeration Economies and Spatial Equilibrium in the United States'. *Journal of Economic Literature*, 47 (4, December): 983–1028.

Glaeser, Edward L, Jose A. Scheinkman and, Andrei Schleifer. 1995. 'Economic Growth in a Cross Section of Cities'. *Journal of Monetary Economics*, 36 (1): 177–43.

Glaeser, Edward L. 2008. *Cities, Agglomeration and Spatial Equilibrium*. Oxford: Oxford University Press.

———. 2011. *Triumph of the City: How Our Greatest Invention Makes Us Richer, Smarter, Greener, Healthier, and Happier*. New York: Penguin Books.

Glaeser, Edward. L., Heidi D. Kallal, Jose A. Scheinkman, and Andrei Shleifer. 1992. 'Growth in Cities'. *Journal of Political Economy*, 100 (6): 1126–52.

Government of India, 1998. *Guidelines for Property Tax Reforms*, Ministry of Urban Development, New Delhi, October 1998.

Gu, Yizhen and Siqi Zheng. 2008. 'The Impacts of Rail Transit on Housing Prices and Land Development Intensity: The Case of No.13 Line of Beijing'. Beijing Municipal Institute of City Planning and Design and Tsinghua University-Institute of Real Estate Studies. Also available at SSRN: http://ssrn.com/abstract=1150058 (accessed 15 January 2016).

Hagman, Donald G. and Dean J. Misczynski (eds). 1978. *Windfalls for Wipeouts: Land Value Capture and Compensation*. Chicago: American Society of Planning Officials.

Harrison, Fred. 2006. *Wheels of Fortune: Self-funding Infrastructure and the Free Market Case for a Land Tax*, The Institute of Economic Affairs (IEA), London.

Henderson, J. Vernon. 2000. 'How Urban Concentration affects Economic Growth'. World Bank Policy Research Working Paper No. 2326. Washington DC: World Bank.

———. 2003a. 'Marshall's Scale Economies'. *Journal of Urban Economics*, 53 (1): 1–28.

———. 2003b. 'The Urbanization Process and Economic Growth: The So-What Question'. *Journal of Economic Growth*, 8 (1): 47–71.

———. 2005a. 'Development and Growth'. In *Handbook of Economic Growth, Vol. 1, Part B*, edited by Philippe Aghion and Steven N. Durlauf. Amsterdam: North-Holland.

———. 2005b. 'Urbanization and Growth'. In *Handbook of Economic Growth*, edited by Philippe Aghion and Steven N. Durlauf. Amsterdam: North-Holland.

Hirsch, Werner Z. 1970. *The Economics of State and Local Governments*. New York: McGraw Hill Book Company.

Hirschman, A. 1958. *The Strategy of Economic Development*. New Haven, CT: Yale University Press.

Hohenberg, Paul M. and Lynn Hollen Lee. 1985. *The Making of Urban Europe, 1000–1950*. Cambridge MA: Harvard University Press.

Hong Kong Democratic Foundation. 1996. '"Land Tax" and High Land Prices in Hong Kong'. HKDF Policy Paper dt. 1/1/1996. Hong Kong.

Hong, Y. 1998. 'Transaction Costs of Allocating Increased Land Value Under Public Leasehold Systems: Hong Kong'. *Urban Studies*, 35 (9 August).

Hong, Yu-Hung. 2007. 'Assembling Land for Urban Development: Issues and Opportunities'. In *Analyzing Land Readjustment: Economics, Law, and Collective Action*, edited by Yu Hung Hong and Barry Needham, 3–34. Cambridge, MA: Lincoln Institute for Land Policy.

High Powered Expert Committee (HPEC). 2011. *Report on Indian Urban Infrastructure and Services*, The High Powered Expert Committee (HPEC) for Estimating the Investment Requirements for Urban Infrastructure Services. New Delhi.

Huayapa, Margarita Gamarra. 2001. 'Experience with the Betterment Levy in Peru'. Working Paper. Lincoln Institute of Land Policy.

International Council on Clean Transportation (ICCT). 2010. *Congestion Charging: Challenges and Opportunities*. Washington, D.C.: ICCT.

The Institute of Economic Affairs (IEA). 2006. *Wheels of Fortune: Self-funding Infrastructure and the Free Market Case of Land Tax*. London: IEA.

Ingram K. Gregory, Zhi Liu, and Karin L. Brandt. 2013. 'Metropolitan Infrastructure and Capital Finance'. In *Financing Metropolitan Governments in Developing Countries*, edited by Roy W. Bahl, Johannes Linn, and Deborah L. Wetzel. Cambridge, MA: Lincoln Institute of Land Policy.

Institute for Transportation and Development Policy (ITDP). 2007. *Bus Rapid Transit Planning Guide*. New York: ITDP.

Jacobs, Jane. 1969. *The Economy of Cities*. New York: Vintage.
———. 1984. *Cities and the Wealth of Nations*. New York: Vintage.
Jaramillo, Samuel. 2001. *The Betterment Levy and Participation in Land Value Increments: The Colombian Experience*. Cambridge, MA: Lincoln Institute for Land Policy.
Johansson, C., L. Burman and B. Forsberg. 2008. 'The Effect of Congestions Tax on Air Quality and Health'. *Atmospheric Environment*, 42: 1–12.
Junghun, K., L. Jorgen and J. M. Niels. 2010. *General Grants vs. Earmarked Grants: Theory and Practice: The Copenhagen Workshop 2009*, Korea Institute of Public Finance and Danish Ministry of Interior and Health, Seoul and Copenhagen.
Kelly, Roy. 1995. 'Property Tax Reform in Southeast Asia: A Comparative Analysis of Indonesia, the Philippines and Thailand'. *Journal of Property Tax Assessment and Administration*, 2 (1): 60–81.
Kenworthy, J., and Peter Newmann. 1994. 'Toronto: Paradigm Regained'. *Australian Planner*, 31 (3): 137–147.
Kilkenny, Maureen. 1998. *Economies of Scale. Lecture for Economics 376: Rural, Urban and Regional Economics*, Iowa State University. Ames, IA.
Krugman, Paul R. 1979. 'Increasing Returns, Monopolistic Competition, and International Trade'. *Journal of International Economics*, 9: 469–80.
———. 1993. 'First Nature, Second Nature, and Metropolitan Location'. *Journal of Regional Science*, 33 (2): 129–44.
———. 1991a. *Geography and Trade*. Cambridge, MA: MIT Press.
———. 1991b. 'Increasing Returns and Economic Geography'. *Journal of Political Economy*, 99 (3): 483–99.
———. 1995. 'Innovation and Agglomeration: Two Parables Suggested by City-Size Distributions'. *Japan and the World Economy*, 7 (4): 371–90.
———. 2007. 'The "New" Economic Geography: Where Are We?' In *Regional Integration in East Asia*, edited by Masahisa Fujita. New York: Palgrave Macmillan.
Krugman, Paul R. and A.J. Venables. 1995. 'Globalization and the Inequality of Income'. *Quarterly Journal of Economics*, 110 (4): 857–80.
Kundu, Amitabh, and L. Saraswati. 30 June 2012. 'Migration and Exclusionary Urbanisation in India'. *Economic and Political Weekly*, XLVII (26–27): 212–27.
Lainton, Andrew. 2011. *Decisions, Decisions, Decisions*. Available at: htttp://andrewlainton.wordpress.com /author/andrewlainton (accessed on 28 December 2015): reported in World Bank 2012b.
Lall, Somik V., Hyoung Gun Wang, and Uwe Deichmann. 2008. 'Infrastructure and City Competitiveness in India'. Policy Research Working Paper, Washington, D.C.: World Bank.
Lam, A. H. S. 2000. 'Republic of China (Taiwan)'. *The American Journal of Economics and Sociology*, 59(5), 327–37. Also in Andelson, R.V., ed. 2000. *Land-Value Taxation around the World*. Malden, MA: Blackwell.
League of California Cities. 2005. *A Primer on California City Finance*. Sacramento, California.
Lee, Annabel. 2008. 'A History of Korea's Spatial Transformation and Economic Growth', reported in World Development Report 2009: Reshaping Economic Geography, Washington, D.C.: World Bank.
Lee, Chang-Moo, and Kun-Hyuck Ahn. 2005. 'Five New Towns in the Seoul Metropolitan Area and their Attractions in Non-working Trips: Implications on Self-containment of New Towns'. *Habitat International*, 29 (4): 647–66.
Lee, Tai-Il. 2000. 'Republic of Korea (South Korea)'. In: Andelson, Robert V. ed. *Land Value Taxation around the World*. Malden, MA: Blackwell.

Lefmann, O. and K. K. Larsen. 2000. 'Denmark'. *The American Journal of Economics and Sociology*, 59 (5): 185–205. Also in Andelson R.V., ed. 2000. *Land-Value Taxation Around the World*. Malden, MA: Blackwell.

Lin, J., and C. Hwang. 2004. 'Analysis of Property Prices Before and After the Opening of the Taipei Subway System'. *The Annals of Regional Science*, 38 (4): 687–704.

Lindahl, Erik R.1919. The Justness of Taxation. Lund, Sweden: University of Lund.

Litvack, J., Ahmad, J., and Bird, R. 1998. *Rethinking Decentralization in Developing Countries. Sector Studies Series, Poverty Reduction and Economic Management.* Washington, D.C.: The World Bank.

Llanto, Gilberto, M, 2009. 'Fiscal Decentralisation and Local Finance Reforms in the Philippines'. Philippine Institute for Development Studies. Discussion Paper Series No. 2009–10. Makati City, Philippines.

Lo, H. K., S. Tang, and D. Z. W. Wang. 2008. 'Managing Accessibility on Mass Public Transit: The Case of Hong Kong'. *Journal of Transport and Land Use*, 1 (2): 23–49.

Lok Sabha Secretariat, 2015. *Public Accounts Committee Eighteenth Report: Jawaharlal Nehru National Urban Renewal Mission*. New Delhi.

Lucas, Robert E. Jr. 1988. 'On the Mechanics of Economic Development'. *Journal of Monetary Economics*, 22 (1): 3–42.

———. 2004. 'Life Earnings and Rural-Urban Migration'. *Journal of Political Economy*, 112 (1): 29–59.

Ludema, Rodney, and Ian Wooton. 2000. 'Economic Geography and the Fiscal Effects of Integration'. *Journal of International Economics*, 52: 331–357.

Mankiw, N. Gregory. 2004. *Principles of Economics*. Mason, OH: Thomson/South-Western.

Marshall, Alfred. 1920 [1890]. *Principles of Economics*, 8th edition. London: Macmillan.

Martin, Philippe and Gianmarco Ottaviano. 1999. Growing Locations: Industry Location in a Model of Endogenous Growth'. *European Economic Review*, 43 (2): 281–302.

Martinez-Vazquez Jorge. 2013. 'Local Non-property Revenues.' In *Financing Metropolitan Governments in Developing Countries*, edited by Roy W. Bahl, Johannes Linn, and Deborah L. Wetzel. Cambridge, MA: Lincoln Institute of Land Policy.

Martinez-Vazquez, Jorge, Charles McLure, and Francois Vaillancourt. 2006. 'Revenues and Expenditures in an Intergovernmental Framework'. In *Perspectives on Fiscal Federalism*, edited by Richard Bird and Francois Vaillancourt. WBI Learning Resources Series. Washington, D.C.: The World Bank.

Mathur, Om Prakash, D. Thakur, and N. Rajadhyaksha. 2009. *Urban Property Tax Potential in India*. New Delhi: National Institute of Public Finance and Policy.

Mathur, Om Prakash. 1 June 2013. 'Finances of Municipalities: Issues before the Fourteenth Finance Commission'. *Economic and Political Weekly*, XLVIII (22): 23–27.

McCluskey J. William and Riel C. D. Franzsen. 2013. 'Property Taxes in Metropolitan Cities'. In *Financing Metropolitan Governments in Developing Countries*, edited by Roy W. Bahl, Johannes Linn and Deborah L. Wetzel. Cambridge, MA: Lincoln Institute of Land Policy.

McKinsey Global Institute. 2010. *India's Urban Awakening: Building Inclusive Cities, Sustaining Economic Growth*. McKinsey and Company.

Mehrotra, S., A. Gandhi, B. K. Sahoo and P. Saha. 12 May 2012. 'Creating Employment in the Twelfth Five Year Plan'. *Economic and Political Weekly*, XLVII (19): 63–73.

Melo, P.C., D.J. Graham, and R. B. Noland. 2009. 'A Meta-Analysis of Estimates of Urban Agglomeration Economies'. *Regional Science and Urban Economics*, 39 (3): 332–42.

Mendieta, J. and Perdomo-Calvo, J. (2007). Especificatióny estimación de un modelo de precios hedónico espacial para evaluar el impacto de Transmilenio sobre el valor de la propiedad en Bogotá, documento CEDE, Working Papers in Economics No. 07–22, Universided de LosAndes, Bogotá.

Milan Municipality. 2009. *Monitoraggio Ecopas, Gennaio: Dicembre 2008*, Agenzia Milanee Mobilita Ambiente: reported in OECD. 2009a. *OECD Territorial Reviews Toronto 2009*, Canada OECD, Paris.

Ministry of Health. Government of India. 1965. *Report of the Committee on Urban Land Policy*. Government of India, New Delhi.

Ministry of Housing & Urban Poverty Alleviation, Government of India. 2013. *Report of the Technical Group on Estimation of Housing Shortage in India*, New Delhi: National Buildings Organisation.

———. 2013. *South Korea: A Guide to Korean Taxation*.

Ministry of Urban Development, Government of India. 1985. *The Report of the Committee on Octroi*. New Delhi: Government of India.

———. 1993. *The Constitution (Seventy-fourth) Amendment Act, 1992 on Municipalities*. New Delhi: Ministry of Urban Development, Government of India.

———. 2012. *Report of the Working Group on Urban Transport for the 12th Five Year Plan*. New Delhi: Government of India.

Mitchell, Stephen R. and A. J. M. Vickers. 2003. 'The Impact of Jubilee Line Extension of the London Underground Rail Network on Land Values'. Working Paper No. 035M1, Cambridge, MA: Lincoln Institute of Land Policy.

Mohan, Rakesh. 1996. *Urbanisation in India: Patterns and Emerging Policy Issues*. Mimeo

———. 2006. 'Asia's Urban Century: Emerging Trends'. Key note address delivered at the Conference of Land and Policies and Urban Development, Lincoln Institute of Land Policy, Cambridge, MA, 5 June.

Mohanty, P. K. 1991. Rural-Urban Migration and the Urban Public Economy in a Developing Country. Ph.D. Dissertation: Department of Economics, Boston University.

———. 1995. 'Reforming Municipal Finances: Some suggestions in the Context of India's Decentralisation Initiative'. *Urban India*, (January–June) 1995. New Delhi: National Institute of Urban Affairs.

———. 1996a. 'Defining the Functional Domain of Urban Local Bodies: Some Suggestions in the Context of India's Decentralisation Initiative'. In *Mega City Management in the Asian and Pacific Region*, edited by Jeffrey Stubbs & Giles Clarke. Manila: Asian Development Bank.

———. 1996b. 'Urban Development Planning in India'. In *Mega City Management in the Asian and Pacific Region*, edited by Jeffrey Stubbs & Giles Clarke. Manila: Asian Development Bank.

———. 2014. *Cities and Public Policy: An Urban Agenda for India*. New Delhi: SAGE Publications

Mohanty, P.K., B.M. Mishra, R. Goyal, and P.D. Jeromi. 2007. 'Municipal Finance in India: An Assessment'. Study No. 26, Department of Economic Analysis and Policy, Reserve Bank of India, Mumbai.

Ministry of Health and Family Welfare (MoHFW). 2009. *Health and Living Conditions in 8 Indian Cities*. Government of India, New Delhi.

Ministry of Health. 1969. *Report of the Committee on Urban Land Policy*. Government of India, New Delhi.

Muller, A. 2000. 'Property Taxes and Valuation in Denmark'. Paper presented at OECD Seminar on Property Tax Reforms and Valuation, Vienna, 19–21 September 2000. Available at: http://www.andywightman.com/ docs/muller.pdf (accessed on 19 January 2014).

Mumford, Lewis. 1963. *The Highway and the City*. New York: Harcourt Brace and the World Bank.

Munnell, A. 1990. 'Why has Productivity Growth Declined? Productivity and Public Investment'. *New England Economic Review*, (January/February): 3–22.

Musgrave, R.A. and P.B. Musgrave. 1989. *Public Finance in Theory and Practice*, 4th ed. New York: McGraw-Hill.

Musgrave, Richard A. 1938. 'The Voluntary Exchange Theory of Public Economy'. *Quarterly Journal of Economic*, 53 (2): 213–57.

———. 1983. 'Who Should Tax, Where and What?' In *Tax Assignment in Federal Countries*, edited by Charles McLure. Canberra: Centre for Research on Federal Financial Relations, Australian National University.

———. 1959. *The Theory of Public Finance*. New York: McGraw Hill.

Myrdal, G. 1957. Economic *Theory and Under-developed Regions*. London: Duckworth.

———. 1974. 'What is Development?' *Journal of Economic Issues*, 8 (4): 729–36.

National Commission on Urban Problems, 1969. *Building the American City: Report of the National Commission on Urban Problems to the Congress and to the President of the United States*. 396. Washington, D.C.: National Commission on Urban Problems.

National Institute of Urban Affairs. 2009. 'Pimpri-Chinchwad Bus Rapid Transit System'. In *Urban Transport Initiatives in India: Best Practices in PPP*, 108–21. New Delhi: National Institute of Urban Affairs.

———. 2010. 'Best Practices on Property Tax Reforms in India.' Research Study Series No. 111, National Institute of Urban Affairs, New Delhi.

———. 2011. *Tracking Central Finance Commissions and State Finance Commissions Grants to Selected States and Urban Local Bodies in India*, National Institute of Urban Affairs, New Delhi.

National Treasury, Republic of South Africa. 2012. *Budget Review, 22 February 2012*. Available at: www.treasury.gov.za (accessed on 19 April 2015).

New York Times, 1989. 'Putting a Price on the Priceless in Manhattan'. November 12.

Nicholas, J. 2002. *National Average Impact Fee by Type. Growth Management Studies Program*. Gainsville: University of Florida.

Nollan vs. California Coastal Commission 1987. US Supreme Court, 483 U.S. 825. No. 86–133 Dt. June 26 1987.

Norregaard, John. 2013. 'Taxing Immovable Property: Revenue Potential and Implementation Challenges'. IMF Working Paper No. WP/13/129, Washington, D.C.: International Monetary Fund.

North, Douglass. 1990. *Institutions, Institutional Change and Economic Performance*. Cambridge: Cambridge University Press.

———. 2005. *Understanding the Process of Economic Change*. Princeton: Princeton University Press.

Oates, Wallace E. 1972. *Fiscal Federalism*. New York: Harcourt Brace Jovanovich.

———. 1996. Taxation in a Federal State: The Tax-assignment Problem'. *Public Economics Review: Taiwan*. 1: 55–60.

———. 1998. 'Federalism and Government Finance'. In *The Economics of Fiscal Federalism and Local Finance*, edited by Wallace Oates. Cheltenham, UK: An Elgar Reference Collection.

———. 1999. 'An Essay on Fiscal Federalism'. *Journal of Economic Literature*, American Economic Association, 37 (3, September): 1120–149.

———. 2006. 'On the Theory and Practice of Fiscal Decentralization'. Working Papers 2006–05, University of Kentucky, Institute for Federalism and Intergovernmental Relations.

Oates, Wallace E. 2008. 'On the Devolution of Fiscal Federalism: Theory and Institutions'. *National Tax Journal*, 61 (2): 313–34.

Organisation for Economic Co-operation and Development (OECD). 1999. *Taxing Powers of State and Local Governments*. Paris: OECD.

——. 2006. *Fiscal Autonomy of Sub-Central* Governments. Paris: OECD.

——. 2008. 'Cities for Citizens: Improving Metropolitan Governance'. *Territorial Review*, Cape Town, South Africa: OECD, Paris.

——. 2009a. *OECD Territorial Reviews*, Toronto, Canada: OECD.

——. 2009b. *National Accounts of OECD Countries*. Paris: OECD.

——. 2010a. *Tax Policy Reform and Economic Growth*, OECD Tax Policy Studies, No. 20, Paris: OECD Publishing.

——. 2010b. *Trends in Urbanisation and Urban Policies in OECD Countries: What Lessons for China?* Paris: China Development Research Foundation and OECD.

——. 2011. OECD National Accounts Statistics (database), Paris: OECD.

——. 2012. 'General Government Accounts: Public Finance and Employment: Revenues'. *OECD National Accounts Statistics*. Paris: OECD.

——. 2014. *OECD Revenue Statistics, 1965–2013*. Paris: OECD.

Office of the Registrar General, Government of India 1991, 2001, 2011, *Census of India*, Government of India.

Olson, Mancur. 1969. 'The Principle of "Fiscal Equivalence": The Division of Responsibilities among Different Levels of Government', *American Economic Review*, 59 (2): 479–87.

Olszewski, P. 2007. 'Singapore Motorisation Restraint and its Implications on Travel Behaviour and Urban Sustainability'. *Transportation*, 34 (3): 319–35.

Orestad Corporation. 2005. *Annual Report 2005*. Copenhagen: Orestad Corporation.

——. 2006. *Annual Report 2006*. Copenhagen: Orestad Corporation.

——. 2007. *Annual Report 2007*. Copenhagen: Orestad Corporation.

Pan, Haixiao, and Ming Zhang. 2008. 'Rail Transit Impacts on Land Use: Evidence from Shanghai, China'. *Transportation Research Record: Journal of the Transportation Research Board*. No. 2048: 16–25.

Pascale, R., and A. Athos. 1981. *The Art of Japanese Management*. London: Penguin Books.

Perdomo-Calvo, J.A., C. A. Mendoza-Alvarez, J. C. Mendieta-Lopez, and A. F. Baquero-Ruiz. 2007. 'Study of the Effect of the TransMilenio Mass Transit Projects on the Value of Properties in Bogotá, Colombia'. Working Paper, QP07CA1, Lincoln Institute of Land Policy.

Peters, T., and R. Waterman. 1982. *In Search of Excellence*. New York and London: Harper & Row.

Peterson, George E. 2009. *Unlocking Land Values to Finance Urban Infrastructure*, The World Bank, Washington, D.C.

Pethe Abhay, 2013. 'Metropolitan Public Finances: The Case of Mumbai'. In *Financing Metropolitan Governments in Developing Countries*, edited by Roy W. Bahl, Johannes Linn and Deborah L. Wetzel. Cambridge, MA: Lincoln Institute of Land Policy.

Pigou, A.C. 1927. *A Study in Public Finance*. London: Macmillan.

Planning Commission, Government of India. 2006. *Towards Faster and More Inclusive Growth: An Approach to the Eleventh Five Year Plan 2007–2012*. New Delhi: Government of India.

——. 2008. *Eleventh Five Year Plan 2007–2012*. New Delhi: Government of India.

——. 2013. *Twelfth Five Year Plan 2012–2017*. New Delhi: Government of India.

Porter, Michael E. 1990. *The Competitive Advantage of Nations*. New York: Free Press.

Prest, A. R. 1981. *The Taxation of Urban Land* Manchester: Manchester University Press.

Puga, Diego. 2010. 'The Magnitude and Causes of Agglomeration Economies'. *Journal of Regional Science*, 50 (1): 203–19.

Qiao, Baoyun, and Anwar Shah. 2006. 'Local Government Organization and Finance in China'. In *Local Governance in Developing Countries*, edited by Anwar Shah. Washington, D.C.: World Bank.

Ramnarayan, S. 2003. 'Improving Municipal Organizations'. Working Paper No. 9, Centre for Good Governance, Hyderabad, India.

Ramnarayan, S., and T.V. Rao. 2011. *Organization Development: Accelerating Learning and Transformation*. New Delhi: SAGE Publications.

Rao, Govinda M. 2013. 'Property Tax System in India: Problems and Prospects for Reform. National Institute of Public Finance and Policy'. Working Paper No. 2013–114. New Delhi: NIPFP.

Rao, M. Govinda, and Nirvikar Singh. 2005. *The Political Economy of Federalism in India*. New Delhi: Oxford University Press

Rao, M. Govinda, and Richard M. Bird. 2014. Governance and Fiscal Federalism. In Ahluwalia, Isher, R. Kanbur, and P.K. Mohanty. 2014. Challenges of Urbanisation in India, New Delhi: SAGE Publications.

Report of the National Commission on Urban Problems to the Congress and to the President of the United States. 1969. Available at: https://bulk.resource.org/gao. gov/89-117/00004F44.pdf (accessed on 15 January 2016).

Ricardo, 1817. On the Principles of Political Economy and Taxation.

Riley, D. 2001. *Taken for a Ride: Trains, Taxpayers, and the Treasury*, Centre for Land Policy Studies, London.

Robbins, S. P. 1986. *Organisation Behaviour*. New Jersey: Prentice Hall.

Robbins, S. P., B. Millett, R. Cacioppe and T. Waters-Marsh. 1998. *Organisational Behaviour: Leading and Managing in Australia and New Zealand*, Sydney: Prentice Hall.

Rodriguez, D., and F. Targa. 2004. 'Value of Accessibility to Bogotá's Bus Rapid Transit System'. *Transport Reviews*, 24 (5): 587–610.

Rodríguez, D. A. and C. H. Mojica. 2008. *Land Value Impacts of Bus Rapid Transit: The Case of Bogotá's Bus Rapid Transit*. Land Lines. Cambridge, MA: Lincoln Institute of Land Policy.

———. 2009. 'Capitalization of BRT Network Expansion Effects into Prices of Non-expansion Areas'. *Transportation Research Part A*, 43 (5): 561–75.

Rodrik, Daniel. 2000. 'Institutions for High-quality Growth: What They Are and How to Acquire Them'. Studies in Comparative International Development, 35 (3): 3–31.

Romer, Paul M. 1986. 'Increasing Returns in Long-Run Growth'. *Journal of Political Economy*, 94 (5): 1002–37.

———. 1990. 'Endogenous Technological Change'. *Journal of Political Economy*, 98 (5): 71–102.

———. 1994. 'The Origins of Endogenous Growth'. *Journal of Economic Perspectives*, 8 (1): 3–22.

Rosenthal, Stuart S., and William C. Strange. 2004. 'Evidence on the Nature and Sources of Agglomeration Economies'. In *Handbook of Regional and Urban Economics*, Vol. 4, edited by J. Vernon Henderson and Jacque Thisse, 2119–71. Amsterdam: North-Holland.

Rubin, Marilyn. M. 2010. *A Guide to New York City Taxes: History, Issues and Concerns*. New York: Peter J. Solomon Family Foundation.

Santos, Georgina, and Blake Shaffer. 2004. 'Preliminary Results of the London Congestion Charging Scheme'. *Public Work Management and Policy*, 9 (2): 164–81.

Scheurer Jan, Peter Newman, and Jeff Kenworthy. 2000. *Can Rail Pay? Light Rail Transit and Urban Redevelopment with Value Capture Funding and Joint Development Mechanisms,* Institute for Sustainability and Technology Policy, Murdoch University.

Schroeder, L. and Paul Smoke. 2003. 'Intergovernmental Fiscal Transfers: Concepts, International Practice, and Policy Issues'. In P. Smoke and Y. H. Kim (eds), *Intergovernmental Fiscal Transfers in Asia: Current Practices and Challenges for the Future,* Manila: Asian Development Bank.

Second Administrative Reforms Commission. Government of India. 2007. *Sixth Report: Local Governance: An Inspiring Journey into the Future.* New Delhi: Government of India.

Segal, David. 1976. 'Are There Returns to Scale in City Size?' *Review of Economics and Statistics,* 58 (3): 339–50.

Shah, M. Anwar. 1994. *The Reform of Inter-governmental Fiscal Relations in Developing and Emerging Market Economies.* Washington, D.C.: The World Bank.

———. 2007. 'A Practitioner's Guide to Intergovernmental Fiscal Transfers'. In: Robin Boadway and Anwar Shah eds. *Intergovernmental Fiscal Transfers: Principles and the Practice,* 1–54. Washington, DC: The World Bank.

Shah, M. Anwar. 2013. 'Grant Financing of Metropolitan Areas: A Review of Principles and Worldwide Practices'. In *Financing Metropolitan Governments in Developing Countries,* edited by Roy W. Bahl, Johannes Linn and Deborah L. Wetzel. Cambridge, MA: Lincoln Institute of Land Policy.

Shoup, D. 1997. 'The High Cost of Free Parking'. *Journal of Planning Education and Research,* 17 (1): 3–20. London: SAGE Publications.

Shukla, V. 1984. The Productivity of Indian Cities and Some Implications for Development Policy. Ph.D. Dissertation: Department of Economics, Princeton University.

Sivaramakrishnan, K. C. 2011. *Re-Visioning Indian Cities: The Urban Renewal Mission.* New Delhi: SAGE Publications.

Smith, Adam. [1776] 1976. *An Inquiry into the Nature and Causes of the Wealth of Nations.* Chicago: University of Chicago Press. Cannan's edition of the Wealth of Nations was originally published in 1904 by Methuen & Co. Ltd.

Smith, J. and T. Gihring. 2006. 'Financing Transit Systems through Value Capture: An Annotated Bibliography'. *American Journal of Economics and Sociology,* 65 (3): 751–86.

Smolka, Martim O. 2007. La regulacion de los mer cados de suelo en America Latina: Cuestiones claves: reported in Peterson, George E. 2009. *Unlocking Land Values to Finance Urban Infrastructure.* Washington, D.C.: The World Bank.

———. 2013. *Implementing Land Value Capture in Latin America (Policy Focus Report): Policies and Tools for Urban Development.* Cambridge, MA: Lincoln Institute of Land Policy.

Snyder, Thomas P. and Michael A. Stegman. 1987. *Paying for Growth: Using Development Fees to Finance Infrastructure.* Washington, D.C.: Urban Land Institute.

Song, Yan, and Mark Stevens. 2012. 'The Economics of New Urbanism and Smart Growth: Comparing Price Gains and Costs between New Urbanist and Conventional Developments'. In The Oxford Handbook of Urban Economics and Planning, edited by Nancy Brooks, Kieran Donaghy and Gerrit-Jan Knapp. Oxford: Oxford University Press.

Sridhar, K.S., and O.P. Mathur. 2009. *Costs and Challenges of Local Urban Services.* New Delhi: Oxford University Press.

State Governments in India. 1993. *Amendments to Municipal Acts in pursuance of the Constitution (74th) Amendment Act, 1992.*

Stein, E. 1998. 'Fiscal Decentralization and Government size in Latin America'. In *Democracy, Decentralisation and Deficit in Latin America*, edited by K. Fukasaku and R. Haussmann. Paris: OECD.

Stewart Dona. 1996. 'Cities in the Desert: The Egyptian New-own Program'. *Annals of the Association of American Geographers*, 86 (3, September): 459–80.

Steytler, Nico. 2005. *The Place and Role of Local Government in Federal Systems*. Johannesburg: Konrad-Adenauer Stiftung.

Straub, S. 2008. 'Infrastructure and Growth in Developing Countries: Recent Advances and Research Challenges'. World Bank Policy Research Working Paper No. 4460. Washington, DC.: World Bank.

Steytler, Nico. 2013. Governance and Finance of two South African Metropolitan Areas. In: Enid Slack and Rupak Chattopadhyay eds. *Finance and Governance of Metropolitan Areas in Federal Systems*. Toronto: Oxford University Press.

Suzuki, Hiroaki, Jin Murakami, Yu-Hung Hong and Beth Tamayose. 2015. *Financing Transit Oriented Development with Land Value Capture*. Washington, D.C.: World Bank Group.

Sveikauskas, Leo A. 1975. 'The Productivity of Cities'. *Quarterly Journal of Economics*, 89 (3): 393–413.

Tang, B.S., Y.H. Chiang, A.N. Baldwin, and C.W. Yeung. 2004. *Study of the Integrated Rail Property Development Model in Hong Kong*, The Hong Kong Polytechnic University.

Tang, Siman B., and Hong K. Lo. 2010. 'On the Financial Viability of Mass Transit Development: The Case of Hong Kong'. *Transportation*. 37 (2): 299–316.

Tanzi, Vito. 1996. 'Fiscal Federalism and Decentralization: A Review of Some Macro Economic and Fiscal Aspects'. *Annual World Bank Conference on Development Economics 1995*. Washington, D.C.: World Bank.

Taylor, G. R. 1951. *The Transportation Revolution 1815–1860*. New York: Holt, Rinehart & Winston.

Ter-Minassian, T. 1997. *Fiscal Federalism in Theory and Practice*. Washington, D.C.: International Monetary Fund.

The City Statute of Brazil. 2001. *Federal Law No. 10.257 of July 10, 2001*. Available at: https://www.cbd.int/doc/groups/cities/cities-2008-bz-cite-statute-en.pdf (accessed 15 January 2016).

The Constitution (Seventy-fourth) Amendment Act, 1992 on Municipalities, 1993.

Thomas, M.A. 2010. 'What do the Worldwide Governance Indicators Measure?' *European Journal of Development Research*, 22 (1): 31–54.

Tsui, Steve Waicho. 2006. 'Alternative Value Capture Instruments: The Case of Taiwan, International Studies Program'. Working Paper No. 06–41, Andrew Young School of Policy Studies. Atlanta: Georgia State University.

United Nations Development Programme (UNDP). 1997. *Governance and Sustainable Development*. New York: UNDP. 2–3.

———. 2000. *Strategy Note on Governance for Human Development*. New York: UNDP

———. 2011. *Human Development Report 2011: Sustainability and Equity: A Better Future for All*. New York: UNDP.

UN–HABITAT. 2002. Global Campaign on Urban Governance Concept Paper, Nairobi: UN-HABITAT.

———. 2006. *State of the World's Cities 2006/2007: 30 Years of Shaping the Habitat Agenda*, Earthscan, London, UK and Sterling, VA.

———. 2008. *State of the World's Cities 2008/2009: Harmonious Cities*, Earthscan, London, UK and Sterling, VA.

———. 2010. *State of the World's Cities 2010/2011: Bridging the Urban Divide*, Earthscan, London, UK and Sterling, VA.

UN–HABITAT. 2011. *Innovative Land and Property Taxation, Global Land Tool Network.* Nairobi: UN-HABITAT.

———. 2012. *State of the World's Cities 2012/2013: Prosperity of Cities,* Earthscan, London, UK and Sterling, VA.

UNICEF. 2013. *Water in India: Situation and Prospects.* UNICEF: New Delhi.

United Nations Social Commission for Asia and the Pacific. 2009. 'What is Good Governance?' Available at: http://www.unescap.org/pdd/prs/projectactivities/ongoing/gg/governance.asp (accessed on 2 January 2012).

United Nations. 2012. *World Urbanization Prospects: The 2011 Revision,* United Nations, Department of Economic and Social Affairs, Population Division, New York.

———. 2014. *World Urbanization Prospects: The 2014 Revision,* United Nations, Department of Economic and Social Affairs, Population Division, New York.

United States Census Bureau. 2012. *Census 2010.* Washington, D.C.

United States Department of Housing and Urban Development. 1993. *Impact Fees and the Role of the State: Guidance for Drafting Legislation.* Washington, D.C.: HUD.

United States Environment Protection Agency. 2013. *Infrastructure Financing Options for Transit-Oriented Development,* Washington, D.C. and Arlington, VA.

Vaidya, C. and H. Vaidya. 2010. 'Market-Based Financing of Urban Infrastructure in India'. In *Building from the Bottom,* edited by S. Kochar, and M. Ramachandran, New Delhi, India: Academic Foundation,

Venables, Anthony J. 2007. 'Evaluating Urban Transport Improvements: Cost-benefit Analysis in the Presence of Agglomeration and Income Taxation'. *Journal of Transportation Economics and Policy,* 20 (2): 211–28.

Vickrey, William. 1999. 'Simplifications, Progression, and a Level Playing Field'. In Kenneth C. Wenzer ed. *Land-Value Taxation: The Equitable and Efficient Source of Public Finance,* 17–23. Armonk, NY: M.E. Sharpe.

Wallis, John J. 2000. 'American Government Finance in the Long Run: 1790 to 1990'. *Journal of Economic Perspectives,* 14 (1, Winter): 61–82.

Walters, L.C. 2011. *Land and Property Tax: A Policy Guide.* Nairobi: UN–Habitat and the Global Land Tool Network.

Wang, A.M. 2005. 'Measuring the Benefits of Urban Green Areas: A Spatial Hedonic Approach'. Proceedings in the 10th Asian Real Estate Society (AsRES) International Conference, 18–21 July 2005, Sydney, Australia.

Wang, L. 2010. 'Impact of Urban Rapid Transit on Residential Property Values'. *The Chine Economy,* 43 (2): 33–52.

Waterman, R. Jr., T. Peters, and J. R. Phillips. 1980. 'Structure Is Not Organisation'. *Business Horizons,* 23 (3): 14–26.

'Second-Generation Fiscal Federalism: Implications for Decentralized Democratic Governance and Economic Development,' Hoover Institution Working Paper, Stanford University, June.

———. June 2006. 'Second-Generation Fiscal Federalism: Implications for Decentralized Democratic Governance and Economic Development'. Hoover Institution Working Paper.

Wetzel L. Deborah. 2013. 'Metropolitan Governance and Finance in Sao Paulo'. In *Financing Metropolitan Governments in Developing Countries,* edited by Roy W. Bahl, Johannes F. Linn and Deborah L. Wetzel. Cambridge, MA: Lincoln Institute of Land Policy.

Williamson, Jeffrey. 1965. 'Regional Inequality and the Process of National Development: A Description of the Patterns'. *Economic Development and Cultural Change,* 13 (4): 1–84.

Wilson, John Douglas. 1999. 'Theory of Tax Competition'. *National Tax Journal,* 52 (2): 269–304.

Wilson, R. and D. Shoup. 1990. *The Effects of Employer-Paid Parking in Downtown Los Angeles: A Study of Office Workers and their Employers*, Graduate School of Architecture and Urban Planning, University of California, Los Angeles.

WMO, World Meteorological Organization. 1992. *The Dublin Statement on Water and Sustainable Development, International Conference on Water and the Environment: Development Issues for the 21st Century*, Technical Report. Dublin: WMO.

Wong P. Christine, 2013. 'Paying for Urbanization in China: Challenges of Municipal Finance in the Twenty-First Century'. In *Financing Metropolitan Governments in Developing Countries*, edited by Roy W. Bahl, Johannes F. Linn and Deborah L. Wetzel. Cambridge, MA: Lincoln Institute of Land Policy.

World Bank. 1991. *Urban Policy and Economic Development: An Agenda for the 1990s*, Washington, D.C.: The World Bank.

———. 1994. *World Development Report: Infrastructure for Development*. Washington, D.C.

———. 1997, *World Development Report 1997: The Role of the State in a Changing World*. Washington, D.C.: The World Bank.

———. 2002. *World Development Report: Building Institutions for Markets*. Washington, D.C.: The World Bank.

———. 2009. World *Development Report 2009: Reshaping Economic Geography*. Washington, D.C.: The World Bank.

———. 2013a. *India: Urbanisation Beyond Municipalities*. Washington, D.C.: The World Bank.

———. 2013b. *Nigeria Economic Report*. Washington, D.C.: The World Bank.

———. 2014. *Municipal Finances: A Handbook for Local Governments*, edited by Catherine Farvacque-Vitkovic and Mihaly Kopanyi, Washington, D.C.

———. 2015. *Leveraging Urbanisation in South Asia: Managing Spatial Transformation for Prosperity and Livability*. Conference Edition. Washington, D.C.

Wicksell, K. 1896. 'A New Principle of Just Taxation'. In R. Musgrave and A. Peacock eds. *Classics in the Theory of Public Finance*. London: Macmillan, 72–118.

Yilmaz, Yesis, Sonya Hoo, Mathew Nagowski, Kim Rueben, and Robert Tannenwald. 2006. *Fiscal Disparities Across States, FY 2002*. Washington, D.C.: Urban Institute and the New England Public Policy Centre at the Federal Bank of Boston.

Younghoon Ro. 2001. 'Land Value Taxation in South Korea'. Lincoln Institute of Land Policy Working Paper, Cambridge, MA: Lincoln Institute of Land Policy.

Yusuf Shahid. 2013. 'Metropolitan Cities: Their Rise, Role, and Future'. In *Financing Metropolitan Governments in Developing Countries*, edited by Roy W. Bahl, Johannes F. Linn and Deborah L. Wetzel. Cambridge, MA: Lincoln Institute of Land Policy.

Zakaria, Rafiq. 1963. *Report of the Committee of Ministers Constituted by the All India Council of Local Self Government on Augmentation of Financial Resources for Urban Local Bodies*, New Delhi: Government of India.

Zhang, M. 2007a. 'Value Capture through Integrated Land Use-Transit Development: Experience from Hong Kong, Taipei and Shanghai'. In *Urbanization in China: Critical Issues in an Era of Rapid Growth*, edited by Y. Song and C. Ding, 29–46. Lincoln Institute of Land Policy.

———. 2007b. 'Chinese Edition of Transit-Oriented Development'. *Transportation Research Record: Journal of the Transportation Research Board*, No. 2038: 120–27.

Index

About the Author

Prasanna K. Mohanty is Chair Professor of Economics at the University of Hyderabad and also Honorary Executive Chair at the National Institute of Urban Management and Centre for Good Governance, Hyderabad.

An Indian Administrative Service (IAS) officer, Dr Mohanty retired as Chief Secretary to the Government of Andhra Pradesh in June 2014. He was earlier Mission Director, Jawaharlal Nehru National Urban Renewal Mission, Government of India, and Municipal Commissioner of Visakhapatnam and Hyderabad metropolitan cities.

He has a PhD in Economics from Boston University and was a Postdoctoral Fellow, Economics, in Harvard University. He has authored *Cities and Public Policy: An Urban Agenda for India* (2014) and edited *Urbanisation in India: Challenges, Opportunities and the Way Forward* (2014), both published by SAGE Publications.